Pulitzer's Gold

Pulitzer's Gold

BEHIND THE PRIZE FOR PUBLIC SERVICE JOURNALISM

Roy J. Harris Jr.

UNIVERSITY OF MISSOURI PRESS

COLUMBIA AND LONDON

Copyright © 2007 by
The Curators of the University of Missouri
University of Missouri Press, Columbia, Missouri 65201
Printed and bound in the United States of America
All rights reserved
5   4   3   2   1   11   10   09   08   07

Library of Congress Cataloging-in-Publication Data

Harris, Roy J., 1946–
    Pulitzer's gold : behind the prize for public service journalism /
Roy J. Harris Jr.
        p. cm.
    Summary: "Examines the ninety-year history of the Pulitzer
Prize for Public Service awarded to newspapers. Harris recalls many
stories including the New York Times's Pentagon Papers exclusive, the
Watergate scandal that was uncovered by the Washington Post and
coverage of Hurricane Katrina by the Times-Picayune of New Orleans
and the Sun Herald of Biloxi, Mississippi"—Provided by publisher.
    Includes bibliographical references and index.
    ISBN 978-0-8262-1768-4 (alk. paper)
    1. Journalism—Awards—United States.   2. Pulitzer Prizes—
History.   I. Title.
    PN4798.H37 2007
    071'.3079—dc22

                                                    2007031461

⊗™ This paper meets the requirements of the
American National Standard for Permanence of Paper
for Printed Library Materials, Z39.48, 1984.

Designer: Kristie Lee
Typesetter: The Composing Room of Michigan, Inc.
Printer and binder: The Maple-Vail Book Manufacturing Group
Typefaces: Adobe Garamond and Edwardian Script

To a century of journalists who mined Pulitzer's gold,
and in memory of one in particular: my Dad.

CONTENTS

Part Three
The Golden Seventies

Part Four
Challenges for a New Era

ACKNOWLEDGMENTS

The obstacles to writing this book were far less daunting than those facing the reporters and editors who broke their Pulitzer Prize stories. But I never could have overcome my own barriers without the steadfast encouragement and patience of my wife, Eileen Carol McIntyre. She and my sisters, Ann O'Keefe Brewer and Judy Wolman, also were my first readers, and I thank them for their many suggestions.

The talented Poynter Institute faculty was bedrock for this project, and two directors, Jim Naughton and Karen Brown Dunlap, supported the research from its inception, as did Bill Mitchell and Pam Johnson. How nice that I was able to benefit from this support at Poynter's St. Petersburg campus, especially during the New England winters. When I needed a tough but constructive editor to catch my clichés, Bill Blundell filled that role in spades. (Sorry, Bill.) Thanks go to Beverly Jarrett at the University of Missouri Press, and to my editor there, John Brenner. Bob Woodward provided a helpful and encouraging review of some early chapters.

Pulitzer administrator Sig Gissler and deputy administrator Edward M. "Bud" Kliment at Columbia University provided invaluable access to the Pulitzer Prize files and generously shared their time. My editor at *CFO* magazine, Julia Homer, granted me the breaks I needed, and my associates there never complained about having to fill in while I was gone.

At home, I had the support of my sons, Dave and R. J., and the spirit of their mom that they carry within them. Jesse, my stepson, offered constant hope that great journalism can have appeal for twenty-somethings too.

I am indebted to numerous librarians who guided me to critical documents—especially Deborah Wassertzug and Bernard Crystal at Columbia and Ann Dalton at the Hingham Public Library. Thanks also to Johanna Seltz for her insights and editing help, and to Lauren Wolfe for her research assistance at Columbia.

Finally, my appreciation to the scores of journalists who trusted me with their stories of a lifetime. It is a privilege to be able to tell them.

Pulitzer's Gold

INTRODUCTION

Filling a Black Hole

*D*eclining readership, daunting Internet challenges, and flagging profitability get most of the blame for what ails today's American newspaper business. Some lovers of the print medium, though, see another affliction within the fifteen hundred dailies that survived the last century's industry consolidation. These readers lament the steady rise in numbers of what people commonly call "once-great newspapers."

A sickness of the soul—and a bit of amnesia about the newspaper's societal role—underlies that phenomenon. Pleading poverty, but acting with editorial timidity, some publishers forgo devoting precious resources to public-service projects, confronting serious community plagues, or even pursuing basic reader concerns through daily beat coverage. Such work cannot be done with papers on life-support, managements may argue. When budgets are cut, though, these same publications often target the senior journalists most able to do meaningful and inspirational work, worsening the crisis.

Greatness survives, and even thrives, in hundreds of newspaper oases around the country, of course. That's why competition still heats up early each year for journalism's Pulitzer Prizes, especially the most coveted prize of all: the Public Service Gold Medal.

What kind of work attains the rarefied distinction of Pulitzer Gold Medal winner? Journalism that reveals an unacceptably high number of police shootings of civilians and helps reverse the trend, as a *Washington Post* team did to earn the honor in 1999. Or that blows the whistle on racism infecting a federal agency, as Portland's *Oregonian,* the 2001 winner, did in its investigation of the Immigration and Naturalization Service. Journalists may be honored for opening our eyes to a scan-

dal involving Catholic priests who were sexual predators and the Church's equally shocking cover-up—the *Boston Globe*'s claim to the 2003 prize. Or for employ-
ing every ounce of a battered newspaper's strength to help communities recover
from a hurricane, as was the case with the *Sun Herald* in Gulfport, Mississippi, and
the *Times-Picayune* in New Orleans during the devastating 2005 summer of Katrina. The *New York Times* earned a 2002 prize for creating "A Nation Challenged,"
a daily section that included "Portraits of Grief," which gave New Yorkers tools for
coping with the September 11 attacks and their aftermath.

The dramatic contributions to the public welfare continued with the 2007 Gold
Medal, awarded to the *Wall Street Journal* for disclosing how companies had secretly and improperly backdated the stock-purchase options they had granted to
their executives. The *Journal*'s team of four reporters—one of them a recent Yale
University math major—developed its own algorithm to measure the most egregious cases. In the scandal's wake, at least seventy executives lost their jobs and the
federal government launched investigations at more than 140 companies.

This kind of public service may pay off in higher newsstand sales or additional advertising dollars. Or it may not. Sometimes the business side actually suffers
from outstanding journalism, at least in the short term. The *Fort Worth Star-
Telegram* won its 1985 Gold Medal for investigating a design flaw that led to a slew
of fatal Bell Helicopter crashes—coverage that sparked Bell, the area's largest employer, to boycott the paper. For Little Rock's *Arkansas Gazette,* balanced coverage
of school integration won it the Public Service Pulitzer in 1958, but cost it dearly
in readers. And in the case of Ohio's *Canton Daily News,* honored in 1927, exposure of politically connected local thugs led first to the editor's murder and then
the paper's closure.

If today's reporters and editors don't know much about these important moments in U.S. journalism history, it is perhaps symptomatic of the industry's spir-
itual ailment.

Bill Blundell, who travels from paper to paper as one of the country's top writing coaches, sees the malady as "a black hole that exists at the heart of our business: the nearly universal failure of newspaper staffs to learn from the past, including the past of the very newspapers they may be working for at the moment."
The hole is especially gaping in the case of public service, where so little work has
been done to expose today's journalists to the best projects that have been done in
that field.

Why hasn't a book on Pulitzer Gold Medal winners been written before? After
all, Pulitzer-winning photography, feature writing, editorials, and cartoons all have
their own books. For one thing, newspapers earning the Public Service Prize often

emphasize the team elements involved. That is noble, and may accurately reflect the nature of many projects. But team studies can be complex, and may not be easily understood by readers. Not surprisingly, the inner workings of newspapers—*All the President's Men* notwithstanding—stir less and less interest in this day of glitzier media.

Further, with the Public Service award especially, the event being *covered* gets the attention—not the distinguished journalism associated with that event. While books have been written studying the Catholic priest scandal from all sides, little until now has been written about the reporting that brought it to our attention. Four papers over the past fifteen years won Pulitzer Gold Medals for how they covered storms, yet the storms themselves are what attract the nonfiction writer. That is as it should be, for the most part. But unfortunately, it cheats journalists out of their own history.

The best-known exception also is the best-known Pulitzer Public Service winner: the *Washington Post* Watergate coverage that made celebrities of Carl Bernstein, Bob Woodward, and Ben Bradlee. Bernstein and Woodward's book *All the President's Men*—and, of course, the movie based on the book—served journalism just as powerfully as their reporting served the nation.

My book is intended for journalists and students seeking to learn about great newspaper work of the recent and less-recent past. I hope that American history buffs, curious about the interplay of press and society, find value in it as well.

Where possible, *Pulitzer's Gold* attempts to capture the "Aha!" as reporters and editors discovered that some seemingly routine assignment was becoming the story of a lifetime. For many readers, that will be the most interesting element of these case studies.

Like most obsessions, this project began as a labor of love, and started small. On September 9, 2002, the hundredth anniversary of my father's birth, I presented a program about the Public Service Prizes won by the *St. Louis Post-Dispatch*. My father, a career news reporter, had won a Public Service Prize for the paper in 1950, and had helped it win three others between 1937 and 1948. When the *Post-Dispatch* won yet again in 1952, it became the only paper at that time to own five Gold Medals. Yet the St. Louis journalists at my presentation, from the editor on down, knew nothing of that distinction, of what the paper had done to earn those five great honors, or of the reporters, editors, and publisher responsible.

In doing the research for that presentation, I discovered how little had been written about Public Service award winners as a genre. The deeper I dug, the more I was moved by these often overlooked stories that demonstrated how basic journalism practices, even reporting and newsroom management techniques, remained the same over the years—despite technological evolution and ever-deepening newsroom economic pressures.

Of the ninety-two Gold Medals awarded through 2006, *Pulitzer's Gold* examines the latest dozen in detail. Other cases were chosen because they are not only terrific stories but also fine illustrations of how Pulitzer Prize–winning work has evolved over the years, displaying a variety of topics and reporting styles. The appendix contains briefer chronological accounts of the remaining Public Service winners.

What will become of newspaper journalism through the current period of turmoil? Former *Los Angeles Times* editor John Carroll raises dire warnings. Shortly after his *Times* won the 2005 Public Service Pulitzer for exposing problems at a large public hospital, he left the paper in a dispute with its Tribune Company owners in Chicago.

In April 2006, from his post at Harvard's Jane Shorenstein Center on the Press, Politics and Public Policy, Carroll was asking tough questions of journalists. In a speech to the American Society of Newspaper Editors titled "Last Call at the ASNE Saloon," he challenged editors to imagine a "newspaper-free" America. If the police decide to beat confessions out of suspects in such a country, he asked, "who will sound the alarm, as the *Philadelphia Inquirer* did?" when it won the 1978 Pulitzer Gold Medal. "More routinely, who will make the checks at City Hall? Who, in cities and towns across America, will go down to the courthouse every day, or to the police station? Who will inspect the tens of thousands of politicians who seek to govern?" More broadly, he asks, "How long has it been since an editor was so rash as to cite public service in justifying a budget? You might as well ask to be branded with a scarlet N, for naïve."

But when the Pulitzers are announced in April, journalists across America still will stop a moment, as they do every year, to reflect on what their profession has done—and on what they and their papers might do to join the ranks of Pulitzer winners.

As we search for new models to allow the newspaper business to thrive again, both financially and journalistically, the hope is that the cases presented here will recall the irreplaceable role of the press in American democracy. Whatever models emerge, public service should be at their center.

Roy J. Harris Jr.
Hingham, Massachusetts

Part One

Gold for a New Century

CHAPTER I

The Storm before the Calm

God plays a real part in many of the Public Service awards.

—Michael Gartner, Pulitzer Prize Board member, 1982 to 1991

*A*ugust was fading fast along the Gulf coast, but the 2005 hurricane season was at its peak. *Times-Picayune* editor Jim Amoss had taken to watching storms like Tropical Depression Number 12 with equal parts awe and anticipation. His New Orleans newspaper was prepared for the worst. Or so he thought.

Amoss, who had led the paper to national acclaim during his fifteen years in charge, had put together a staff that was especially adept at pursuing big reporting projects. In 1992, 1996, 1997, and 1999, in fact, *Times-Picayune* entries had been finalists for Pulitzer Prizes, the most sought-after honors in American newspaper journalism. Stories making the Pulitzer short list had explored a range of environmental and social topics. And in one of those years, 1997, the paper had been selected for its first two Pulitzers ever. Cartoonist Walt Handelsman had won, and so had the *Times-Picayune* itself, in the Public Service category. That award had honored a series of articles titled "Oceans of Trouble," which analyzed the problems faced by fisheries across the Gulf of Mexico and around the world.

Building on the prize-winning work, Amoss had turned his staff's attention to another coastal problem: how poorly the below-sea-level city was protected against nature's inevitable onslaughts. The work uncovered evidence of inadequate hurricane preparation in the community. Reporter Mark Schleifstein—working with John McQuaid, his partner from the "Oceans of Trouble" series—helped prepare a five-part series in 2002 that pointed up serious weaknesses in the area's system of levees. It was titled "Washing Away," and its second-day headline read "The Big

One: A Major Hurricane Could Decimate the Region, but Flooding from Even a Moderate Storm Could Kill Thousands. It's Just a Matter of Time."

That time would come during the early hours of Monday, August 29, 2005, with the arrival of Tropical Depression Number 12, renamed Hurricane Katrina by the National Weather Service. The Gulf coast would remember it as Killer Katrina.

The newspaper had designed its building—located south of Lake Pontchartrain and north of the Mississippi River bend that gives the Crescent City its nickname—to be ready for a major hurricane. Beneath its conspicuous tower, the building was outfitted with a windowless "bunker" area operating as a generator-powered emergency newsroom. Still, it was sobering for the 140 staffers, camping overnight there, when the hum of the main, nonemergency power stopped at 4 a.m. that Monday. The sudden quiet within contrasted sharply with the howling wind without. Any who were dozing early that morning awoke abruptly. A large window in an executive office blew in, and then another and another. The storm was at full force: torrents of rain, and increasing structural destruction readily visible in the huge gashes appearing on the Superdome nearby. Much later, Amoss could wax poetic about the moment. "Standing in our building's lobby, you could hear the oddly peaceful melody of the wind whistling past the entrance cavity—three sad, flute-like notes played over and over," he wrote. "At times, the wind would shriek to a high-pitched wail before returning to the three-note dirge."

Then the raging storm crested. It was time for the *Times-Picayune* to step up.

"On Monday morning I told the staff that this was the biggest story of our lives, and that it was absolutely vital that we tell it as only we can tell it," said Amoss. The telling would require resources unique to a newspaper, and especially their newspaper, and it would flow from the staff's accumulated, layered knowledge of the complex New Orleans community.

Reporters and photographers fanned out from the centrally located headquarters by any means possible, including boat and bicycle, to see what Katrina had wrought. With phones out and even cell phones dead, however, there would be none of the typical minute-to-minute reports flowing into headquarters during the day. The reporters' notes would have to be brought back to the newsroom in person.

From what Amoss could see and hear, broadcast reporters and journalists from out of town clearly had too narrow a focus on what was happening across the city. Many were ensconced in French Quarter and Garden District tourist areas along the river. But there was one thing the out-of-towners seemed to be getting right: As the winds finally died down with little apparent flooding, they declared that New Orleans had dodged a bullet. And that meant that so had the 137-year-old *Times-Picayune*. "This is great. We're OK," Amoss remembers thinking.

At 9:30 on Monday night, Amoss gathered his editors under the emergency lights of the bunker to plan the coverage for the next day. As he described it, "When we started the meeting, we were deciding how to best report the apparent duality of the situation: that the city had been saved, but that the Lower Ninth Ward and St. Bernard Parish had been devastated." Then in an instant, that duality vanished.

Breathlessly, features editor James O'Byrne and art critic Doug MacCash dashed into the meeting with a report no one wanted to hear: On a six-hour bike ride, they had witnessed breaks in the levee along the Seventeenth Street Canal that led into the lake. To the north, huge portions of the city were being flooded, and the lake waters were moving inexorably south. From a train bridge over Canal Boulevard they had seen a newly formed rushing river, seven feet deep, heading toward the city's business district.

"Don't worry about spinning it," O'Byrne advised his editors. "We're going under water."

As disbelief turned to horror, thoughts of winning another Pulitzer Prize were far from anyone's mind. Self-preservation was a more real concern. Most staffers already had evacuated their families, but they had no picture of what it would take to cover the destruction around them. Further, they worried about whether anyone would be reading their reports. The decision had been made on Monday not to publish a print version for the next day. The paper would appear instead online, on its affiliated Web site www.nola.com (for New Orleans, Louisiana).

Still, the drive to get the news out had never been more critical. The banner headline they prepared for the online version of page one: "CATASTROPHIC."

"The Camille Standard"

In fact, there had been relatively little direct wind damage to New Orleans, even at the height of Katrina. Seventy-five miles to the east, though, the storm unmercifully hammered the coastal cities of Gulfport and Biloxi, Mississippi, with a level of destruction never before seen on American shores. Right in its path was the *Sun Herald*.

The forty-seven-thousand-circulation Gulfport-based paper, with fifty-five staffers, was only a fifth the size of the *Times-Picayune*. Like most small dailies, the *Sun Herald* had never won a Pulitzer.

For five years executive editor Stan Tiner had led the paper with a supportive, instructive style that won him his nickname, "the coach." Tiner had come from a miserable experience editing the Gaylord family's *Daily Oklahoman*. The buzz in 1999, when he arrived in Oklahoma City, was that the Gaylords hired him to alleviate the ignominy of the *Oklahoman* being named the worst newspaper in

America by the *Columbia Journalism Review.* After rankling the Gaylords and a few staffers as well, however, Tiner was fired only eight months later. Some suggested his tough approach to stories examining local business was to blame. But while he did not talk much in Gulfport about his abrupt dismissal from his former job, it was clear that he was still bitter about it, and perhaps had something to prove. Editing at the *Sun Herald* returned him to a part of the country where he had been happy. For seven years prior to his stint at the *Oklahoman* he had run Alabama's *Mobile Register.* The *Sun Herald* was the right fit for Tiner.

Like the *Times-Picayune,* the Mississippi paper had fortified its building and trained staffers to deal with storms. The 121-year-old *Sun Herald* had not missed a publication date since the hurricane of 1947, and the staff did not want to break that string. The newspaper also had created an emergency plan—one that involved drawing on outside help if necessary. Working through the chain that owned it, Knight Ridder Incorporated, the *Sun Herald* arranged for its sister publication farther inland, Columbus, Georgia's *Ledger-Enquirer,* to publish the Mississippi paper if a coastal catastrophe stopped its own presses. Knight Ridder tradition called for providing financial aid and lending journalistic support from its other papers during emergencies.

"Stan rallied the troops and on the Friday before, he laid out our mission," says features editor Scott Hawkins. The rallying cry: "This is going to transform our coast forever, and will put us to the test as a newspaper."

On Saturday, Tiner's theme became personal safety for his team. He and publisher Ricky Mathews advised staffers to care for themselves and their families first, then get back to the newsroom as soon as possible. As the warnings about Katrina became more dire, a disturbing thought occurred to Tiner: "We had no way of knowing how many of our staff we might have seen for the last time."

In the beginning, southern Mississippi used the "Camille standard" to measure the new storm. People still could see the old water lines, marking how far inland the seas had reached during the area's previous record hurricane, in 1969. That was the worst-case scenario in the minds of long-term residents. Many who were outside the area ravaged by Camille chose not to evacuate. "They had a sense of invulnerability," according to Tiner. "They thought they were immune from death."

As the storm's power built on Monday, though, it was clear that Camille no longer was the worst case. Katrina was sending surges far higher—creating walls of water twenty-eight feet high—and causing destruction much farther inland.

A skeleton crew was able to keep the solid one-story headquarters building open, even as two-thirds of the *Sun Herald*'s reporters, editors, and photographers remained largely scattered. The www.SunHerald.com Web site continued to churn out information. For the many south Mississippians who had evacuated, and those few in the area who had electricity, the site provided a valuable source of eyewitness news as Katrina drove inland west of Gulfport on Monday morning. Everywhere, staffers crossed their fingers that the arrangement with the Georgia paper would allow Tuesday's papers to be published, and to make their way south to the *Sun Herald*'s battered coastal market.

In short, Monday at the *Sun Herald* was not a day for thinking about awards any more than it was at the *Times-Picayune*. Survival came first. Overcoming the many natural obstacles to getting essential information to beleaguered readers was, of necessity, secondary.

"Big Casino"

The stories of how the two publications recovered—not just persevering, but earning the year's top honor for journalistic public service—are unusual. But they are not unique.

Since 1917, the American press has had a system for weighing and rewarding extraordinary newspaper achievement. It is part of the Pulitzer Prizes, established at Columbia University to recognize contributions both to journalism and to the arts.

As detailed in the will of publishing pioneer Joseph Pulitzer, who died in 1911, a "gold medal costing $500" was to be given each year for "the most meritorious and disinterested public service rendered by any American newspaper." First among the three journalism awards he envisioned, the Public Service Prize was also the only one intended to go to a news organization rather than individuals. The other two awards were honors for a reporter and an editorial writer, originally coming with prize money of one thousand dollars and five hundred dollars, respectively.

Today there are fourteen journalism categories in various areas of news and opinion writing, photography, and cartooning. For each, except the Public Service Prize, ten thousand dollars in cash now accompanies the award. With the non-journalism prizes, honoring work in arts and letters, twenty-one Pulitzers in all are awarded in a typical year, subject to more than one prize, or no prize, being given in a category.

The Pulitzer Prize Board picks the winners. Its nineteen members are a diverse assortment of top-ranking newspaper journalists and academics from around the nation. Board members meet for two days in April in the Columbia Graduate School of Journalism's World Room, named for the long-gone New York newspaper once owned by the benefactor of the prizes. There in the Morningside Heights area of Manhattan, the members typically work to choose one of three finalists selected in each category by "nominating juries." The juries also are diverse, and often have past Pulitzer winners in their ranks when they meet for three days, a month before the board's session.

Over the years there has been friction between jurors and the Pulitzer board members, who have the power to move entries between categories and to overrule jury recommendations—and frequently do. In the past, especially, juries that accepted the intense job of reading and ranking entries often resented having their favorites passed over by the final arbiters. But in recent years the relationship between the jury and the board has been smoother. Jurors no longer are asked to present their choices in order of preference, and instead list the top three selections alphabetically. This keeps the board from being in the position of "overruling" a jury favorite. Now, the juror selections tend to become the Pulitzer finalists, and the board generally picks one of those as the winner.

While much has changed in the Pulitzer selection system over nine decades, the Public Service Prize remains relatively the same. It still takes the form of a medal just under three inches in diameter bearing Benjamin Franklin's profile on one side and a shirtless Franklin-era printer working his press on the reverse. Columbia commissioned the original design from Massachusetts sculptor Daniel Chester French, later known for his seated Abraham Lincoln statue in the Lincoln Memorial on the National Mall in Washington, D.C. Though now gold-plated silver instead of solid gold—and valued at about two thousand dollars—the Joseph Pulitzer Medal continues to be awarded each year to one news organization, except in the unusual circumstance of dual winners being voted. The lack of prize money associated with the Public Service award hardly tarnishes the Gold Medal's appeal among newspaper editors.

"That's Big Casino. It's the cream of the cream. It's the one you want to win if you have a choice," says retired *Washington Post* executive editor Ben Bradlee Sr., who is associated with arguably the most famous of all journalism Pulitzer Prizes. That was the Public Service Gold Medal won by the *Post* in 1973, primarily for Bob Woodward and Carl Bernstein's reporting of events after the break-in at Democratic National Headquarters in the Washington office building known as Watergate.

For any paper, winning a Gold Medal is a historic moment. The *Times-Picayune's* 1997 Public Service Prize had been "the strongest reverberating recognition that this newspaper had arrived at a certain level journalistically," Jim Amoss says. "It was not only a Pulitzer, but *the* Pulitzer. It was enormously rewarding and affirming of what we thought we had been doing for some time."

Generally, board members pondering Public Service candidates look for measurable impact in the community, whether that means the paper's immediate locale, its region, or the nation as a whole. Government action in response to coverage—a law passed or a wrongdoer charged, for example—carries special weight.

In the language of today's prizes, the Gold Medal recognizes a paper for meritorious service "through the use of its journalistic resources which, as well as reporting, may include editorials, cartoons, photographs, graphics and online material." Thus, juries and the Pulitzer board also tend to look for interaction among various areas of a newspaper operation. (The paper's Web site has gotten attention in Public Service since 1998; online work was included in consideration of other journalism categories for the first time in 2006.)

The style of journalism represented by winners of the Public Service Prize varies widely. Behind some Gold Medals lies a multi-part team writing project, like that conducted by the *New York Times,* Pulitzer winner in 1972 for publishing and analyzing the top-secret Pentagon Papers. Those government documents confirmed how a series of U.S. administrations often had deceived the public in pursuit of the Vietnam War. The lengthy *Times* series, interrupted by a challenge from President Nixon's administration on national security grounds, resumed only after the paper won a landmark Supreme Court victory. Project-based awards date to the earliest years of the Pulitzers, though. In 1923, a twenty-three-part nationwide examination of the Ku Klux Klan won for the *New York World.*

Many other Gold Medals over the years have recognized newspapers' incremental coverage of events. The *Washington Post*'s Watergate reporting, which Bob Woodward today half-jokingly describes as "boring," is a prime example. It was built on gradual, relatively small-scale discoveries that he and Carl Bernstein made over months of investigating. Only taken together did the stories expose the clear involvement of the Nixon White House in the crime and its cover-up. Similar incremental reporting had led to the 1921 prize honoring the old *Boston Post* for exposing the illicit operations of a firm run by Charles Ponzi—who gave his name to the type of "pyramid" scheme that still suckers investors today.

Often, prize-winning stories have been hybrids of incremental and project-style journalism. Staffers may uncover shocking information through daily reporting, and then develop stories that can be featured. The *Boston Globe* did this to win the 2003 Gold Medal when investigations revealed the extent of criminal sexual misconduct by Catholic priests and the Church's subsequent cover-up. Legal action by the *Globe*'s lawyers unsealed court documents—another example of a newspaper's various departments interacting—and the paper fleshed out the story by aggressively pursuing its own investigations of priests and church officials.

Papers big and little compete against each other for this most prized Pulitzer.

And board members sometimes display a fondness for small-town entries, perhaps because of the sheer gall it takes for a tiny publication to challenge authority. In 1977, the diminutive *Lufkin News* in east Texas won a Gold Medal for discovering the facts behind the death of a local boy who had joined the Marines and been fatally beaten by other trainees during basic training in San Diego. Reporters for the thirteen-thousand-circulation, low-budget *News* never left their home county to get the story, but they told it chillingly and changed training standards across the armed services as a result.

In terms of subject matter, two of every five Gold Medals awarded since the Pulitzers began have involved some exposure of government wrongdoing on the local, state, or national level. One in five has been for exploring human rights abuses or other social ills. And increasingly, the Public Service Prize has acknowledged environmental journalism, which accounts for about one of every ten awards.

Any attempt to classify Public Service Prizes must recognize disaster coverage as a genre all its own. In 1948 the *St. Louis Post-Dispatch* won for an investigation of a fatal coal mine explosion in Centralia, Illinois, which turned up inspection lapses and payoffs to state officials. Two papers won for covering natural disasters in the 1990s: the *Miami Herald* in 1993 for Hurricane Andrew and North Dakota's *Grand Forks Herald* five years later, for its service to the community during a plague of Red River flooding, fire, and blizzard.

The Pulitzer bar is high for such stories. Former Pulitzer board member Michael Gartner, onetime president of NBC News and editor of two Iowa newspapers, the *Des Moines Register* and the Ames *Daily Tribune,* notes that his fellow board members often seemed jaded when faced with disaster-related submissions shooting for the Gold Medal. "You shouldn't automatically win the prize because a plane hits a building in your town," says Gartner. "That's when you're *supposed* to do a good job."

Thus, the *Miami Herald*'s citation for Hurricane Andrew noted a range of incisive stories, like revealing shoddy building-code enforcement that left the area more susceptible to the storm's destruction. When the Pulitzer board awarded the Public Service Prize to the *New York Times* in 2002—one of the paper's record seven Pulitzers that year—the Gold Medal specifically honored the paper's creation of the daily "A Nation Challenged" section and its poignant "Portraits of Grief" component, which helped readers see victims of the 9/11 terrorist attacks as Americans just like themselves.

The Public Service jurors and Pulitzer board in 2006 would also hold the *Sun Herald* and the *Times-Picayune* to a high standard in considering coverage of Hurricane Katrina and its aftermath.

Waiting on the Levee

Times-Picayune staffers, camped out in the newspaper's building as dawn broke on Tuesday, August 30, had only to look on their own doorstep for proof that the observations from James O'Byrne and Doug MacCash's bike trip were accurate.

The sky was cloudless, and Katrina was being downgraded again to a tropical storm. Yet water was at the third stair of the *Times-Picayune* entryway, rising one inch every seven minutes. Cell-phone communications in the city remained out. No signs of federal assistance were evident, and as far as reporters could detect, little effort was going into public safety—barring the SWAT team dispatched to quell disturbances at the Orleans Parish Prison just across the Interstate. (Guards lost track of fourteen prisoners, some of whose orange prison overalls were later found just outside the *Times-Picayune* building.)

It was time to evacuate. "We had planned for wind, water and an extended period without electricity," Amoss wrote later. "But with almost an entire city going under for an indefinite period, with no civil authority functioning, with a communications blackout, with no federal presence and with no sign that order would be restored any time soon, we were facing an unprecedented challenge for an American newspaper."

Loaded in the back of a flotilla of newspaper delivery trucks, the staff took off for higher ground, unsure exactly where the next stop would be. "We left with the queasy fear that, for the first time since the Civil War, we might not produce a newspaper for tomorrow"—even an electronic version, according to the editor. "We already knew that New Orleans had become a dangerous and difficult place to practice journalism. It would get worse."

Only as the trucks rolled toward the city limits did staffers begin to see the big picture emerge. Eighty percent of New Orleans was flooded. Gradually, the staff began to make the first plans for forming teams for the complex dual job ahead: covering the scene, and creating and managing a remote working newsroom that could sustain a full-fledged news operation.

Veteran reporter Mark Schleifstein had continued to follow the levee systems' weaknesses since his "Washing Away" series. (In fact, he had become not only a weather expert but also something of a Cassandra, to the point of advising readers to keep an ax in their attic for emergency escape from floodwaters. For many, it would be life-saving advice.) Schleifstein recalls the tide of emotions as the staff split up during the evacuation that Tuesday. He was among the majority of staffers choosing to relocate to a temporary newsroom to the west and inland, in the town of Houma. There the *Times-Picayune* planned to publish for a time using the presses of the New York Times Company–owned *Houma Courier*. Schleifstein's family had been evacuated, and his home was under twelve feet of water. He was planning to serve in that temporary newsroom, where he could do broader stories that might not need to be written from within the city limits. "More important, I know how to take dictation and I know all the editors. I was the grunt, but I was enjoying it," he says. That is why he did not join the team of a dozen reporters, editors, and photographers who headed back south into the damaged city to set up a bureau and report from the scene.

"Now," he adds, "I wish I'd been with them."

The staffers who made the return trip to New Orleans ran into trouble almost immediately. Witnessing a Wal-Mart being looted on a mass scale and police officers participating in the rampage, reporters dove in until they began to feel threatened by the mob. Finally the editor in charge, David Meeks, pulled his *Times-Picayune* team back. The spot story describing the Wal-Mart melee—headlined "Looters Leave Nothing Behind in Storm's Wake"—was the first of many accounts of post-storm events in areas of the city that other news media had not reached. The *Times-Picayune* stories, for the most part written in a makeshift news bureau at the house of one of the team members, continued to have the feel of reports from the front lines of some strange domestic battlefield.

Meanwhile, the newspaper operation created to get the paper out—electronically only for that first Tuesday, Wednesday, and Thursday—remained in exile. After Houma, it moved north along the Mississippi to Baton Rouge, where for six weeks the staff used facilities of Louisiana State University's Manship School of Journalism. A fleet of thirty rental cars kept the staff mobile.

Work prepared under such conditions, both for the online and the print editions over a period of months, was compiled to become the *Times-Picayune*'s Public Service Pulitzer entry at the start of 2006.

One story, on September 26, carried the provocative headline "Rape. Murder. Gunfights," although the deck line suggested something entirely different. It read: "For three anguished days the world's headlines blared that the Superdome and Convention Center had descended into anarchy. But the truth is that while conditions were squalid for the thousands stuck there, much of the violence NEVER HAPPENED." The debunking grew from *Times-Picayune* reporters' failed efforts to confirm reports of mass criminality from the Superdome and Convention Center. Some false reports circulated widely on the Internet, and ended up in many respected publications around the globe. Some aired on such popular broadcast outlets as Oprah Winfrey's television program. (Police Chief Eddie Compass told Winfrey on September 6 that "some of the little babies [are] getting raped" in the Dome. And Mayor Ray Nagin added more horrors: "They have people standing out there . . . in that frickin' Superdome for five days watching dead bodies, watching hooligans killing people, raping people." *Times-Picayune* reporters, checking out every report, told a different story:

> As the fog of warlike conditions in Hurricane Katrina's aftermath has cleared, the vast majority of reported atrocities committed by evacuees have turned out to be false, or at least unsupported by any evidence, according to key military, law enforcement, medical and civilian officials in positions to know.
> "I think 99 percent of it is bulls—," said Sgt. 1st Class Jason Lachney, who played a key role in security and humanitarian work inside the Dome. "Don't get me wrong, bad things happened, but I didn't see any killing and raping and cutting of throats or anything. . . . Ninety-nine percent of the people in the Dome were very well-behaved." Dr. Louis Cataldie, the state Health and Human Services Department administrator overseeing the body recovery operation, said his teams were inundated with false reports about the Dome and Convention Center.

Michael Perlstein, a criminal justice beat reporter who worked on several debunking stories, recalls helping check out reports that a nine-year-old girl had been raped and had her throat slit at the Convention Center. "Once we heard that, obviously we scrambled to corroborate it," he says. But the closer they looked, the more the stories changed: "She was 13; she was 6; she was 9. There were more than one. There was a freezer full of bodies. That's when we realized, we can't go with this. It was like that grade-school game of telephone: A person who died of natural causes, and was under a blanket, then it's that he got killed, then it's a murder, then it gets multiplied."

Amoss now writes off the worst of the crime stories as racist. "You see it again and again, even today," he says. "The urban legends that arise often have a basis in assumptions of racial primitivism. And there are stories going around New Orleans now about all sorts of incredible anarchy and crime being committed that have some racial basis, and that turn out to be totally untrue."

Managing editor Peter Kovacs quickly came to the conclusion that these news leads were wildly exaggerated. "Most journalists would be skeptical about these kinds of reports coming from their own hometown," he says. "If you looked at who was in the centers, it was families with their kids; it was old people; it was people you see in New Orleans every day. If what people were saying was true, why were people staying there like sitting ducks?" The answer was that the stories were not true. The tales were largely fabricated, as the reporters found out. "It was unfair to the victims of New Orleans, to suggest that people were so lawless, and that the victims put up with it. It disrespected what they really did suffer," Kovacs says, adding, "Now I understand how the Salem witch hunt happened."

The newspaper was drawing more than thirty million daily visits to the www.nola.com site from around the world, but the printed *Times-Picayune* made a special impression when it began reappearing in free deliveries to homeless shelters and areas of the city where people congregated. It proved the city was alive, its life's blood—its news—still circulating.

The *Times-Picayune's* 2006 Public Service entry blended print and online-published material, as the Pulitzer rules allow. It contained breaking-news revelations and analytical pieces, including several intensive looks at why the levees built by the U.S. Army Corps of Engineers failed. (One headline, "Soft Soils under Levee Sank City," ran on October 15. Another, "Corps Never Pursued Design Doubts," ran on December 30.) Some analysis had a global slant: a November 13 article titled "Beating Back the Sea" examined the steps taken in the Netherlands to manage similar flooding threats in the European country's below-sea-level lands. A November 30 front-page editorial, an unusual step for the paper, argued: "The federal government wrapped levees around New Orleans so that the rest of the country could share in our bounty." With the failure of those Army Corps of Engineers–built levees, the editorial argued that "Now it's time for a nation to return the favor."

A Pulitzer Surprise

In addition to the storm's human toll, the price tag for the damage was soaring—and would eventually exceed $80 billion nationally, making it the costliest U.S. storm ever. More than eighteen hundred people would die Katrina-related deaths. And with the hurricane ranking among the top American stories of the year, Jim Amoss and the *Times-Picayune's* coverage quickly became the talk of journalists around the country. Beyond those thirty million Web site hits, dozens of articles focused on the excellence of the paper's coverage.

Not that the paper was cocky. Far from it. The staff knew well that the *Times-Picayune* faced enormous business challenges as 2006 began, with advertising and circulation both a shadow of their former levels. As a business, it had lost much of its market to the storm—readers and advertisers—without any idea when it might return.

Amoss himself is a low-key native New Orleanian who spreads credit around freely and does not much like to brag. "Any good newspaper has to have a staff that can spring into action as a team, and be deployed in a coordinated way and have a maestro, or several levels of maestros, directing it," he says. "But it would be disingenuous to suggest that I imagined this in some fashion. It is so unimaginable what happened to this community and what happened to this newspaper that it really couldn't have been planned for."

Still, when his staff's accomplishments were celebrated in the *Columbia Journalism Review,* or in the article Amoss wrote for *Quill,* the Society of Professional Journalists' magazine, other newspaper editors took note. And in February, *Editor & Publisher* named him editor of the year.

Thus, many journalists were shocked when word began to spread on March 8, the day the Pulitzer jurors ended their deliberations, that the *Times-Picayune* was not among the three finalists in Public Service. Instead, Mississippi's *Sun Herald* was on the list for its Katrina coverage, along with the *Washington Post* and the Toledo *Blade.* The second two choices had been expected. The *Post* had examined the split between national security and individual liberties during the nation's war on terrorism, while the *Blade* had exposed illegal activity—involving Ohio's governor and others—in connection with a state investment fund in rare coins. With the New Orleans paper in the running, the *Sun Herald* had been considered a definite dark horse, if it was mentioned at all.

How the *Times-Picayune* failed to make the jury's cut, yet nonetheless ended up with a Gold Medal, is a study in the circuitous process by which winners sometimes are chosen. The board may start with the nominations presented to it by jurors, but it has full discretion to add, subtract, or to draw from other categories for its final award determinations.

When the jurors congregated on Monday at Columbia, the seven members assigned to Public Service were led by *Tampa Tribune* executive editor Janet Weaver. Having worked just southeast along the Gulf Coast from where the storm hit the hardest, she was quite familiar with the work of the *Tribune's* neighbor papers. She also had been a junior-level editor on the *Miami Herald,* another Knight Ridder paper, fourteen years earlier during its Hurricane Andrew coverage. (Both dailies that won Public Service prizes for storm coverage in the 1990s—the *Grand Forks Herald* being the other—were Knight Ridder–owned.)

It was Weaver's third time as a juror, though her first in Public Service. She mulled what it was that made the Gold Medal different from other Pulitzers, and kept the question active among others on the panel. "We kept going back and reading the description of the award as we went through the daunting stack of entries," she says. "We looked for a paper using the full weight and force of its resources, and we looked for impact."

While there were seventy-eight entries, the number was actually about 15 percent lower than in recent years. Weaver believed the decrease reflected other papers withholding submissions in the category because the *Times-Picayune* seemed a shoo-in. But the jurors were committed to starting from scratch, and not letting prejudgments affect their review.

As she read the entries, she noted the wide variety of story types compared to the narrower range from her past Pulitzer jury duty. It made the job harder, but more interesting. "On other juries you tend to get the same style of writing because it's a particular type of journalism," she says. "When you judge Explanatory, at the end of the first day your eyes are bleeding because of the certain sameness of what you're reading."

Also on Weaver's jury were journalists from Akron, Baltimore, Indianapolis, and Seattle, along with an *International Herald Tribune* editor and one former Pulitzer board member and journalism legend: University of Maryland journalism professor Eugene Roberts. Roberts had turned the *Philadelphia Inquirer* into a virtual Pulitzer-winning machine in the 1970s, and before that he had been a reporter who led the *New York Times's* civil rights coverage in the 1960s.

On the first day of deliberations, individual jurors started reading entries. Rejects were taken off the table, literally, and piled onto the floor. By the end of the first day, half the Public Service submissions remained in contention. On the second day the jury cut the candidates down to twenty, and then winnowed them down to about twelve.

At that point, the job got much tougher, Roberts remembers. "I thought as many as eight or ten of the entries in Public Service were extraordinary," he says. Indeed, in his mind there were five or six that legitimately could have earned the Public Service Pulitzer in another year. But in 2006, the Public Service panel was riveted by the storm and the two papers that had covered it so well. When only six entries remained on the table, they included the *Times-Picayune* and *Sun Herald.* The jury was reluctant to give two of its three finalist selections to coverage of one event, even an event like America's worst hurricane ever. The jurors decided to nominate the *Post* and the *Blade,* for certain. But for their third choice, they split between the *Times-Picayune* and the *Sun Herald.* So a query was sent to Pulitzer administrator Sig Gissler. Could the jury simply make a joint entry, nominating both Gulf Coast papers, along with the Toledo and Washington nominations?

"Basically, he said no, it wasn't possible," according to Roberts. "We should come up with a total of three, and if the board wanted to award two Gold Medals, then that was its prerogative, but not ours."

A vote was taken, and the third pick became the paper whose hurricane coverage was a slight favorite: the *Sun Herald.* Jurors then prepared a note to the board elaborating on their thinking and listing the *Times-Picayune* among its three "alternates" for the Public Service Prize. "We knew there was going to be a buzz about our finalists," recalls Weaver. But by including the New Orleans paper among the alternates she believes the jury sent a signal that both Gulf Coast papers were worthy.

If the jury really wanted both papers to win Gold Medals, however, that nuance escaped "the Cabal," a group of journalists who fuel an informal rumor mill devoted to spreading early word about the Pulitzers and the finalists for the prizes.

Columbia's Pulitzer organization has tried to keep prize nominations a secret before the official announcement of winners, wanting to reveal both winners and finalists at the same time. For that reason jurors sign a pledge not to reveal their choices early. But within a day of the jury session breaking up, the Cabal, as usual, had tapped sources among the jurors in all fourteen journalism categories, trading tidbits about who was in and who was out, and spreading the word by phone, e-mail, and Web sites. *Editor & Publisher* provided an online outlet on its well-read channel, with an uncannily accurate advance list. Within weeks, the *New York Times* had published a comparison of the *Sun Herald*'s and *Times-Picayune*'s hurricane coverage, claiming that the latter's exclusion as a finalist had disappointed editors in New Orleans and created a rivalry between the two. Wrote the *Times,* "The *Sun Herald* likes to emphasize that it did not miss a day of print publication, while the *Times-Picayune* points to the scope of the disaster in New Orleans and its near-impossible reporting conditions."

Overshadowed in Mississippi

Why had the Public Service jurors favored the *Sun Herald*?

Most of those who died storm-related deaths had been southern Louisianans, and much of the damage had been in that state's Delta region. But Katrina killed more than two hundred and displaced hundreds of thousands along the Mississippi coast as well, flattening whole communities that had been the Gulfport paper's market. And while the *Times-Picayune* clearly had distinguished itself, few denied that the Mississippi paper had pulled off a near miracle of publishing.

"This was a smaller paper, with a newsroom that was a victim of the disaster as much as its community had been, and you saw the completeness of their voice," says Weaver. "Its editorial message got stronger and stronger and stronger." The message? "We are a community and we are being forgotten here, and we need help in the face of disaster and the ineptitude of the relief effort. What we saw in the entry was a paper picking up everything it has and throwing it—and not in a helter-skelter way. It was trying to make order out of chaos."

Roberts, who was as high as any juror on the work of the *Times-Picayune*, notes the continuity with which the *Sun Herald* explored the story in every aspect with its spot news, features, and editorial writing. "It seemed to me that they must have had even the janitors writing," he says, "because they were everywhere for a staff that size."

The Web site's public service "was just mind-boggling," adds Roberts. "They were responding to individual requests, putting out constant notice of where people could get relief. If you had been a victim of the storm it would have given you up-to-the-minute ideas about what to do."

And then there was the underdog factor. It was something that Stan Tiner alluded to in his Pulitzer nomination letter: "Much of the country was focused on New Orleans. . . . [M]eanwhile South Mississippi was struggling to survive, having taken the full force of Katrina's killer winds and deadly storm surge head-on," he wrote. "The *Sun Herald* provided hope to its community, giving authentic voice to their struggle, their anger and triumph." He recalled that on Monday, August 29, "thousands of South Mississippians, dazed and disoriented, living in improvised shelters or in the shells of their own homes were handed an eight-page *Sun Herald* detailing the full scope of the disaster and timely information on where to turn for help. Many actually cried in disbelief." Asked one woman, looking through the pages from amid the rubble of East Biloxi's Main Street: "A paper? How did you do this?"

Both the *Times-Picayune* and *Sun Herald* had used their online presence powerfully. While print editions were nearly impossible to distribute to readers—even if the presses *were* rolling—"the greatest service to those communities may have been through the online content, at least for seventy-two hours," says Weaver.

If the jurors *did* factor in the *Sun Herald*'s ability to put out a print edition without missing a day—thanks to its effective prearrangement with its Georgia sister paper—it certainly was no more a factor than the paper that the staff turned out. It was both artful and helpful, filled with hard news and sympathetic editorials geared to its stricken readership. And it contained some of the most remarkable color photography ever taken in a disaster. Stunning shots appeared each day during the storm, sometimes presented sideways on a full page to help capture the scope of the horror and the pathos.

Executive editor Tiner had dispatched a team of five copy editors and designers to Columbus—nearly 10 percent of his staff—and a Monday paper was distributed free at shelters where survivors were congregated. On Tuesday the page one banner, "Our Tsunami: At Least 50 Die in a Storm as Fearsome as Camille," echoed remarks by Biloxi Mayor A. J. Holloway. Inside that eight-pager, headlines included "Damage Report," "Wind's Wrath," "How It Felt," and "After Landfall: What Mississippi—and the Nation—Can Expect as Katrina Moves North."

With two-thirds of the reporters still not heard from on Tuesday, the Wednesday paper was largely written by a handful of staffers in the *Sun Herald* building using the intermittent power from a generator, and pulling together what technology they could to send their material to Columbus for publication. On Monday night, out-of-town reinforcements arrived, causing quite a stir. Working with Bryan Monroe, Knight Ridder's assistant vice president for news in San Jose, California, the *Sun Herald* had arranged for a team of journalists from the *Miami Herald, Charlotte Observer,* and elsewhere to fly in to Atlanta the day before the storm. The team had driven down through Montgomery, Alabama, finding ways to circumvent downed bridges and other obstacles and arriving late on Monday evening. There, Tiner had been in a hallway when hulking shadows began to move forward from the emergency lighting near the side entry.

"Bryan's a large guy, and with the lights so low there was an eerie feel to it when they showed up. We hugged in the hallway, and I said, 'The Marines are here,'" recalls Tiner, himself a former Marine. Along with them, Monroe's team members brought gasoline, water, chain saws—and at least twelve thousand dollars in cash. "There wasn't anything to buy," Tiner notes, "but it was a good feeling knowing you had some money, anyway."

The banner on Wednesday encapsulated the message that Tiner saw developing from the disaster: "Hope Amid Ruin: Hundreds Now Feared Dead, but Survivors Emerge." It ran above a large photo of a mother and son reunited and embracing amid the destruction of their neighborhood, and a smaller photo of three firemen removing a body from similar surroundings.

Both in print and online, the suffering readers saw their plight personalized and understood. Beyond a daily chart headlined "What You Need to Know," the paper ran a bulletin board of messages from family members and others seeking lost loved ones, and trying to match needs with services being offered. The precedent for these two approaches, in fact, had been set at the two other Knight Ridder papers that had won Public Service Prizes for their storm coverage in the recent past. In writing about Hurricane Andrew thirteen years earlier, the *Miami Herald* pioneered the bulletin-board approach. The *Grand Forks Herald* came up with the directory of services when the North Dakota paper covered its Red River flooding disaster. It, too, had served readers with a bulletin board.

The Mississippi paper added many touches of its own, launching the "I'm OK" phone line, for example. The 800 number and e-mail discussion board for readers was part of its extensive Web-based service. The paper registered 1.6 million "page views" online on its peak day Wednesday, compared with an average of about ninety thousand before the storm.

While his staff nearly doubled to around ninety eventually, thanks to the temporary out-of-state Knight Ridder influx, *Sun Herald* bylines still were prominent. Their editor's input was vital, staffers say. Tiner referred to his coverage strategy as "journalistic triage." The paper couldn't tell all the stories that were flowing in, so it took what editors considered the most important—emphasizing where possible that growing theme of hope. "We could have written stories for five years about how many people died and how the government screwed it up," he says. "But part of the plan was to try to organize the storytelling in a way that did not cause our people despair."

He laughs about how he often seemed to have the easiest job at the *Sun Herald:* standing and cheering for the reporters. "The moment a big story like this comes, you can't tell people what they've got to do," says Tiner. "Their instincts as reporters and editors and photographers are to go where the information is and get it back to this nerve center. I learned during all this how good my staff was. We're a small paper in a place that people don't pay much attention to. But I watched how the staff rose to the challenge, willing to work around the clock."

Tiner knew that small papers had a chance at the big prize. He was friends with editor Joe Murray, whose *Lufkin News* had won the 1977 Gold Medal for coverage of the Marine trainee's death. "I've thought for a long time that the prize has value for little guys like us, whether we ever win it or not," says Tiner. "It's probably not going to happen," with the *New York Times, Washington Post,* and other powerhouses on the job. "But if I work hard and do the best journalism that I and my little staff are capable of doing, the gods of journalism just might smile on us."

If the gods didn't smile on the *Sun Herald,* the Pulitzer board certainly did. At the April meeting, it voted the *Sun Herald* a 2006 Joseph Pulitzer Medal, with the *Washington Post* and Toledo *Blade* as finalists. That move, of course, validated the jury's choices.

But in yet another surprise to the journalism community, the board elected to give a second Medal to the *Times-Picayune.* It was the first time since 1990 that two Public Service winners were named in a single year, and only the sixth time in Pulitzer history.

From Janet Weaver and Gene Roberts' perspective, it was absolutely the right decision. Roberts remembers the memo that the jury had sent to the board along with the three official nominations. "The tone was that we were in some dismay because we had been told that we couldn't make a joint recommendation," he says. "We almost extended an invitation to award two Pulitzers"—one to the *Sun Herald* and another to the *Times-Picayune.*

The New Orleans paper would win a second 2006 Pulitzer Prize for Breaking News Reporting, and it was a finalist in Commentary for the columns of Chris Rose. (The *New York Times's* Nicholas Kristof won.) *Sun Herald* staffers were also finalists in Editorial Writing. That prize went to writers for Portland's *Oregonian,* a Newhouse sister paper of the *Times-Picayune.*

There was perhaps special satisfaction in the result for Janet Weaver, who had the job of putting together the jury's nomination note and accompanying memo to the Pulitzer board. "There's nothing more painful for an editor than to be edited by six very talented journalists," she laughs in describing her collaboration with the rest of the jurors. But like Roberts, she believes the board knew that the jury's preference was for both the *Sun Herald* and *Times-Picayune* to be acknowledged. "Every journalist knows from years of reporting and editing," says Weaver, "that it's how you write the nomination that counts."

2006—*Sun Herald,* Biloxi-Gulfport, Mississippi: For its valorous and comprehensive coverage of Hurricane Katrina, providing a lifeline for devastated readers, in print and online, during their time of greatest need.

2006—*Times-Picayune,* New Orleans: For its heroic, multifaceted coverage of Hurricane Katrina and its aftermath, making exceptional use of the newspaper's resources to serve an inundated city even after evacuation of the newspaper plant. (Selected by the board from the Public Service category, where it was entered.)

Times-Picayune employees evacuate their New Orleans building in a newspaper delivery truck as water rises the morning after Hurricane Katrina hit. From left, A. J. Sisco, Kim Chatelain, editor Jim Amoss, page-one editor Terry Baquet, managing editor Dan Shea, Mark Schleifstein, and sports editor David Meeks. *Times-Picayune* staff photo by Kathy Anderson.

Times-Picayune features editor James O'Byrne and art critic Doug MacCash were first to report on the levee breaks, after a bike ride to areas otherwise unreachable. "Don't worry about spinning it," O'Byrne told stunned editors. "We're going under water." *Times-Picayune* staff photos.

Environmental reporter Mark Schleifstein, whose work had helped lead to the *Times-Picayune*'s 1997 Gold Medal, wrote a subsequent series that forecast the kind of damage Hurricane Katrina was to cause. *Times-Picayune* staff photo.

'It's over. They are with the Lord.'

HOPE AMID RUIN

Hundreds now feared dead, but survivors emerge

Dustin Duvall is hugged by his mother Elizabeth Duvall after the two were reunited outside the destroyed remains of their neighborhood in east Biloxi.

Sun Herald front page two days after Hurricane Katrina hit.
Used by permission.

Sun Herald executive editor Stan Tiner leads a celebration as reporter and columnist Gary Holland (back to camera) and assistant city editor Blake Kaplan (with identification badge) exult in the 2006 Pulitzer Prize announcement. *Sun Herald* photo by David Purdy.

CHAPTER 2

The Most Prized Pulitzer

I think I am safe in saying that the members of the Board . . . consider the gold medal for public service as easily the most important prize of the year. I feel certain that they share my belief that my father so regarded it. Journalistic public service was my father's passion.

—Joseph Pulitzer II, Pulitzer board chairman, 1940–1955

The *New York Times*'s Pentagon Papers coverage and the *Washington Post*'s Watergate reporting, honored in 1972 and 1973, respectively, rise like twin peaks above the majestic range of newspaper enterprises that won Public Service Pulitzer Prizes through the last half of the twentieth century. Exactly thirty years later, at the beginning of a new century, two more summits stand out: the *Times*'s response to the terrorist attacks of September 11, and the *Boston Globe*'s revelations, the next year, of the sexual abuse of young parishioners by Catholic priests.

Taken together, though, the nearly one hundred Gold Medals not only mark some of the best U.S. journalism since 1917 but also dramatize the course of national events over that period. Indeed, *Post* publisher Philip Graham's famous 1960s-era definition of the American newspaper as "a first rough draft of a history that will never be completed" could just as well describe the work honored with the Public Service Prize.

Newspapers winning this particular Pulitzer often ventured far beyond recounting events, becoming entwined with their stories. Certainly that was the case with the Pentagon Papers, Watergate, and the disclosures about abusive priests. Yet pick any decade of Pulitzer Prizes, and other examples emerge of journalists exposing major governmental wrongdoing or exploring new social issues and improving the world around them. History was served with the very first Public Service Prize, which was given to the *New York Times* for its coverage of World War I and encouraged more such saturation reporting of international affairs. Later winning stories delved into the economic malaise in the 1920s, the Great Depression and organized crime of the thirties, another world war in the forties, and civil rights in the fifties. The old *Chicago Daily News* won in 1963 for reports on birth control services, while *Newsday's* study of the global heroin trade led to the 1974 prize. The *Anchorage Daily News* won in 1986 for exploring the plight of native Alaskans, and the *Des Moines Register* took on the underreported nature of rape in a project honored in 1991.

Often, the Pulitzer board's selection recognizes a newspaper's courage in blowing the whistle on those with the power to harm the messenger. The 1927 prize acknowledged Ohio's *Canton Daily News,* whose editor, Don R. Mellett, was murdered for his criticism of local politicians who had become too close to a criminal gang. In 1953 the board cited the *Whiteville News Reporter* and *Tabor City Tribune,* two North Carolina weeklies that took both fiscal and physical risks by exposing a local revival of the Ku Klux Klan. Another case involved an even smaller weekly, Marin County, California's *Point Reyes Light,* which took on the locally based Synanon cult. The paper intensified its fight after a lawyer who opposed Synanon was bitten by a rattlesnake that group members had stuffed in his mailbox.

Of course, the year's Gold Medal winner hasn't always glittered so brightly, especially in the early years, as the Pulitzer Prizes struggled to establish an identity. The 1919 Public Service award to the *Milwaukee Journal* hailed the paper's opposition to "German-ism" during the Great War, when the *Journal* argued for schools to stop teaching the German language, for example. Some other early Public Service honorees basically submitted a range of their best stories, without a central theme. (Newspapers also learned slowly what qualities it took to produce a Gold Medal winner. In 1929, the *Cleveland News* submitted the work it had done to simplify its headline styles. It lost.)

Ask winners about the value of awards like the Pulitzers and they will toss in a few caveats. "We don't write for prizes," *New York Times* publisher Arthur O. Sulzberger Jr. says with emphasis. Nonetheless, by 2004 his paper had claimed five Gold Medals. "We are delighted to win them but our journalism is aimed at enhancing society, not winning prizes," he reiterates.

The cult of self-congratulation that some see in the proliferation of press awards, and to some extent the Pulitzers, certainly has its critics. Among those who find flaws in the Pulitzer process itself, few have sterner reservations than Ben Bradlee, who became a celebrity after the *Washington Post's* Watergate Pulitzer and the *All the President's Men* phenomenon. In a 1995 autobiography the then-seventy-five-year-old editor declared that "as a standard of excellence the Pulitzer prizes are overrated and suspect." The opinion, he said, is based on observations from his service on the Pulitzer board from 1969 to 1980:

> It is this board, political and establishmentarian, that clouds the prizes. Mind you, it's better to win them than lose them, but only because reporters and publishers love them. In my experience, the best entries don't win prizes more than half the time.

More recently, however, he has found the Gold Medal to be relatively pure. "The Public Service Prize is what it says it is," according to Bradlee. "The Public Service gene is very strong in all good journalists."

The McClatchy Company prides itself in having that genetic structure. Before its 2006 purchase of Knight Ridder, McClatchy boasted of having five Public Service Prizes among its small group of papers: two each for the *Sacramento Bee* and *Anchorage Daily News* and one for the Raleigh, North Carolina, *News & Observer*. Buying Knight Ridder added significantly to its stable of papers with Pulitzer-winning traditions. As the second-largest American newspaper publisher now, McClatchy has thirty-two dailies that among them possess thirteen Gold Medals, the largest cache for a single chain. Gary Pruitt, McClatchy's chief executive officer, sees an intangible value for publishers from winning the medal. For one thing, he says, "the Pulitzer Prize, particularly the Public Service Prize, resonates in terms of recruiting talent. Those things don't happen by accident; they're a reflection of commitment of resources on a sustained basis."

As various ownership trends have spread in the newspaper industry—from consolidation under publicly traded publishing companies like McClatchy and Tribune Co. (nine Gold Medals) to the spin-off to local ownership interests of papers like the *Philadelphia Inquirer* (two Gold Medals)—the Public Service Prize has remained a relatively simple standard for measuring newspaper excellence.

"The Germ of an Idea"

The wide acceptance of this standard doubtless would please Joseph Pulitzer, who in August 1902 had what he called "the germ of an idea" for a system of awards to honor the best of both American journalism and arts and letters. At Chatwold, his secluded summer retreat on Maine's Mount Desert Isle, he dictated his thoughts: "My idea is to recognize that journalism is, or ought to be, one of the great and intellectual professions; to encourage, elevate, and educate in a practical way the present and, still more, future members of that profession, exactly as if it were the profession of law or medicine."

Two years later, he inserted into his will a $500,000 bequest to Columbia University for the prizes. It was part of a $2 million overall gift that also endowed a journalism school at Columbia. In 1912, the year after Pulitzer died at age sixty-four aboard his yacht *Liberty* in Charleston Harbor, the university got the journalism school running. That established the framework, under terms of the will, for a system to consider entries from 1916 for the new Pulitzer Prizes. The first prizes were awarded at Columbia's commencement in June the next year.

The Pulitzer Prizes in journalism were a revolutionary notion. Not that the thought of a major awards program was so unusual. Sweden's first Nobel Prizes had been awarded in 1901, just before Joseph Pulitzer dreamed up his own system of awards. The Nobels were globally celebrated as a way of honoring scientific and literary achievements, and of furthering the cause of peace. And in 1896, the modern Olympic organization had resurrected the ancient Greek games, bestowing gold, silver, and bronze medals on the world's sports heroes. (Indeed, preparations were heating up for the 1904 Olympics in Pulitzer's old hometown of St. Louis, where the Hungarian immigrant had settled in 1865.)

What was outlandish about the Pulitzer Prizes, rather, was the thought of praising *journalism* at the turn of the century. Newspaper work was a suspect occupation at best as practiced by most of the publications of the day. That had certainly been true of Pulitzer's own *New York World* as recently as the late 1890s, when it was the epicenter of that shameful period of press history known as yellow journalism. That term for rampant sensationalism, in fact, was taken from one of Pulitzer's many *World* innovations, the first comic strip, known as "The Yellow Kid."

Joseph Pulitzer's career had started brilliantly. In 1878 he had merged two small papers into the *St. Louis Post-Dispatch,* which was a hugely successful operation when he left its day-to-day management five years later and moved to New York to take over the *World.* At both papers he promoted investigative reporting and campaigns against government corruption, part of a broad strategy designed to appeal to the masses of average readers. The approach produced handsome profits, and Pulitzer's ability to spur prolific readership gains by combining hard-hitting journalism and public promotions became a model for other publishers.

One such Pulitzer promotion made the *World* the leader in raising money for a pedestal on Bedloes Island in New York Harbor, without which France's gift of a dramatic "Statue of Liberty" would have remained only a dream. Its erection had been unpopular among wealthy New Yorkers, but the *World* taunted the rich for their unwillingness to finance the construction and promised to publish the name of every contributor, no matter how small. Circulation soared as a result.

Then came a darker period for Pulitzer and journalism. When an all-out war

for New Yorkers' pennies broke out among newspaper publishers, Pulitzer reacted desperately in an effort to keep his circulation high. Competing with William
Randolph Hearst at the *New York Journal,* among others, Pulitzer's *World* carried
absurdities and exaggerations in the news pages. It was a nasty, no-holds-barred
conflict, particularly when Charles A. Dana of the *Sun* turned on Pulitzer personally and labeled him "Jewseph Pulitzer" and "Judas Pulitzer [who has] denied his
race and religion." (It was a thinly veiled attempt by Dana to win new audiences
by turning both anti-Semitic readers and Jewish readers against the *World.*) The
proliferation of sensational news accompanied chauvinism of the worst kind, winning the *World, Journal,* and other papers a place in journalism infamy for having
helped foment the Spanish-American War.

Pulitzer was pained by the descent of his papers, even though he clearly had allowed it, sacrificing his principles to hold onto circulation. After the war he quickly restored sanity in the newsrooms. But he was tortured in other ways. His health,
never very good, deteriorated further. He became nearly blind and extremely sensitive to noise, and suffered from debilitating nervousness and depression.

He also had become an absentee publisher, controlling from afar the activities
in the twenty-story, gold-domed *World* building with which he had graced lower
Manhattan. (As the 1880s ended, it was the tallest skyscraper in the city, eclipsing
Dana's humble *Sun* offices across the street.) Pulitzer began spending nearly all his
time at Chatwold—equipped with a stone "tower of silence" where he could concentrate deeply—and his other homes in America and Europe, and eventually
aboard the *Liberty.*

He became a statesman for the press, championing the newspaper's role in pre-
serving democracy by giving readers all the facts. In an article for the *North American Review* the same year as his will, Pulitzer wrote:

> Our Republic and its press will rise or fall together. An able, disinterested, public-
> spirited press, with trained intelligence to know the right and the courage to do
> it, can preserve the public virtue without which popular government is a sham
> and a mockery. A cynical, mercenary, demagogic press will produce in time a peo-
> ple as base as itself.

In those later years, he made sure his own papers—the *Post-Dispatch* and the
World—followed that creed. The "platform" he wrote when he stepped down from
the editor job in St. Louis proclaimed that the paper should "always fight for
progress and reform" and "always oppose privileged classes and public plunderers."

Another Pulitzer comment presaged, in a way, what the *Washington Post* was to
do almost sixty-five years later in winning its 1973 Gold Medal. A 1909 letter he

wrote to *World* editorial page editor Frank Cobb expressed Pulitzer's thoughts on Theodore Roosevelt's support of the Panamanian revolution, which preceded the completion of the Panama Canal by American industry. The *World* had argued that $40 million in improper payments were made along the way:

> [I]f this is to be a government of the people, for the people, by the people, it is a crime to put into the hands of the President such powers as no Monarch, no King, or Emperor has ever possessed. He has too much power already . . . . I would rather have corruption than the power of one man.

Nobels and Pulitzers

A near recluse as his maladies intensified and he entered his mid-fifties, Pulitzer contemplated his mortality. He began envisioning a personal legacy—one that would recognize his lifelong devotion to newspapers and the role he believed they should play in a democratic society.

The spirit of philanthropy was in the air, stirred by vast gifts to benefit the public good from industrialists like Andrew Carnegie, who was very public about the need for the rich to give back to society. But Swedish munitions mogul Alfred Nobel may have seemed a better model to Pulitzer, providing both inspiration and a method for his benefaction.

Some historians have suggested that Pulitzer and Nobel indeed shared a hidden motivation for their desire to take on worthy causes. According to this view, the Nobel Prizes designed by the inventor of dynamite and the blasting cap were sparked by a macabre happenstance in 1888. That year, some French newspapers mistakenly reported Nobel's demise after they confused him with his brother Ludvig. "Le Marchand de la Mort Est Mort," one paper proclaimed: "The Merchant of Death Is Dead." Seeing how he was fated to be remembered, these accounts suggest, a horrified Nobel changed his life overnight—much in the manner of Dickens's Ebenezer Scrooge on that ghostly Christmas Eve. Eventually, by devoting part of his fortune to the commemoration of great world achievements, Nobel saved his reputation for posterity.

Whether Pulitzer acted out of a need for redemption for earlier career sins is likewise open to speculation. But he also designed his prizes to be established after his death and made them part of a grand benefaction, in combination with a bequest designed to create the first university-based school of journalism. (As it turned out, the University of Missouri's journalism school opened in 1908, giving it that distinction by four years.)

Columbia had been Pulitzer's first choice as a home for the journalism school and the awards, largely because of his love of New York and its place as the center of the publishing universe. (He had briefly considered Harvard, until that school responded coolly to the idea.) Pulitzer's will dictated that the awards in journalism and letters would exist "for the encouragement of public service, public morals, American literature, and the advancement of education." In his negotiations with Columbia president Nicholas Murray Butler, Pulitzer was particularly insistent on giving control of the prizes to a special new board that would be dominated by newspaper editors. The group originally had the name Advisory Board of the Columbia School of Journalism, even though its main responsibility was always the prizes. (In 1950 it became the Advisory Board on the Pulitzer Prizes, then in 1979 simply the Pulitzer Prize Board.)

Neither the plan for the school nor the plan for the prizes was popular with Pulitzer's aides. One of them, Don C. Seitz, suggested a better investment for the $2 million: "Endow the *World*. Make it foolproof." There was some prescience in Seitz's recommendation. While the *World* would turn out some great journalism in the two decades after Pulitzer's death, it would finally be run into the ground by sons Ralph and Herbert, who sold it to Scripps-Howard in 1931 and watched it disappear.

But the deal for the bequest was sealed with Columbia's Butler, and the will was signed on April 26, 1904. Columbia was required to prove to the new advisory board that the journalism school had functioned successfully for three years before the money for the prizes would be established.

Including the journalism prizes with related awards to honor American novelists, historians, biographers, and dramatists was a brilliant stroke on Pulitzer's part. The association of lowly newspaper work with achievement in fine arts did indeed help elevate the press. The timing was just right, too, for innovations like prizes and university-based journalism schools. Early in the twentieth century, Pulitzer's own papers in New York and St. Louis were helping create what was called the New Journalism, turning away from the pure sensationalism and political bias of the past and emphasizing fairness and balance instead. At the same time, the papers launched crusades to right various public wrongs on the readers' behalf.

The first advisory board contained a handful of powerful newspaper editors, and was chaired by Pulitzer's son, thirty-five-year-old *World* editor Ralph Pulitzer. Only two of the eleven editors or publishers on the board—one from the *Post-Dispatch* and one from the *Chicago Daily News*—worked outside the Northeast. Besides Columbia's Butler and Ralph Pulitzer, the board included the *World*'s John Langdon Heaton; Edward P. Mitchell of the *Sun;* Charles Ransom Miller of the *New York Times;* St. Clair McKelway of the *Brooklyn Eagle;* Melville E. Stone of the Associated Press; Samuel Calvin Wells of the *Philadelphia Press;* Samuel Bowles of the *Springfield* (Massachusetts) *Republican;* and Charles H. Taylor of the *Boston Globe.* Early on, a rule was established calling for editors to step out of the room whenever their own papers' entries were considered.

The original designations for the annual awards adopted language from the Pulitzer will, including a description of the medal for "the most disinterested and meritorious public service." The Reporting Prize was for "the best example of a reporter's work during the year; the test being strict accuracy, terseness, the accomplishment of some public good commanding public attention and respect." The reference to terseness, long since removed from the reporting description, is worth a chuckle in this day of multipart, multipage entries that sometimes tax even jurors' abilities to get through them.

While the first board was guided by Joseph Pulitzer's terms and seemed intent on honoring his memory by selecting high-quality winners, it had few submissions to work with in the early years. That was true even though Columbia advertised for entries. The infrastructure that had been designed for the prizes was weak, leaving much of the judging in the hands of Columbia professors. They were assigned to look through the entries and pass on their recommendations to the board. In one of his histories on the Pulitzer Prizes, John Hohenberg suggested that Columbia president Butler wanted the *faculty* to make the final selection of winners, with the board doing the nominating. Hohenberg, who was Columbia's administrator of the prizes from 1954 to 1976, noted that the journalists of the advisory board soon took charge of the final designation of prize-winners. They have never relinquished that task. And as the jury system evolved, smaller panels of journalists eventually took the job from professors.

Length of service on the board was not limited during the early years of the Pulitzer Prizes, and a number of members stayed on well over a decade. Several strong factions developed over its early decades, opening the board of those years to charges that it was something of an "old boy network." Ralph Pulitzer's younger brother, Joseph Pulitzer II, editor and publisher of the *Post-Dispatch,* joined the board in 1920 for what was to be a thirty-four-year stay, the last fifteen years as chairman. He was a modest man who generally was happy acting as moderator while the powerful editors around the table expressed their opinions. But his devotion to his father's principles was a beacon for the board. And that grounding in Pulitzer family values continued when his own son, Joseph Pulitzer III, known as Joseph Pulitzer Jr., took over as chairman after J.P. II died in 1955. When J.P. Jr. retired in 1986, he left the board without a Pulitzer in charge for the first time in seven decades.

The "Everyman" Question

Almost from the beginning, the Pulitzer boards were steeped in secrecy, which they believed was necessary to allow for a candid discussion of candidates. Until recent years the board did not identify entries that had been finalists, and said next to nothing about the selection process.

In 1985, *Los Angeles Times* media critic David Shaw, a student of the Pulitzer Prizes and a winner himself, wrote about the power struggles that had played a role in past board choices for the prize, and described some of the board's selections as capricious. But Shaw wrote that in the late 1970s a nine-year-maximum term limitation and other board-instituted reforms had improved the process. Since then, he wrote, "although some prizes are still won (or lost) for reasons other than journalistic merit—sentiment, tradition, geography, luck—no one man (or group of men) dominates the Pulitzer board today. Voting blocs shift constantly, depending on the issues involved in any particular award or procedural question."

Jurors today infuse the Pulitzer process with energy. They view jury duty as an honor—"Pulitzer juror" looks very good on a résumé—and value a networking experience that inspires them to bring their best to the historic World Room. The room is dominated by the ninety-square-foot "Liberty Window," a blue stained-glass representation of Lady Liberty raising her lamp between the globe's two hemispheres. Columbia received the memorial to Joseph Pulitzer's Statue-of-Liberty campaign after the *World* building—its former home—was torn down in the 1950s to improve access to the Brooklyn Bridge.

Although Howard Weaver first served as a Public Service juror in 1988—the first of his three times on that particular panel—he remembers the experience as though it were yesterday. "I was just gaga to be there," says Weaver, then an *Anchorage Daily News* editor whose work had been part of a Gold Medal project about Alaska's Teamsters Union a dozen years earlier, when he was twenty-five. Now there he was, debating the best public service of the prior year with a distinguished panel of reporters and editors from around the country, faced with the job of narrowing about a hundred entries to three.

In the process of selecting finalists—including the eventual winner, the *Charlotte Observer,* for its exposé of the PTL television ministry's misuse of funds—Weaver was involved in a heated discussion about the publication that would be the jury's third pick. His position won out, he says. "It was one of those moments when I realized how important the jury work was," he says. "And I also realized, here's this kid editor from Anchorage, Alaska, who made the difference. If I'd been slightly less passionate, the nomination would have gone the other way."

The journalist-jurors often are moved by the humble origins of stories that mushroom into projects that made a difference in their communities. Some evolve from classic "everyman" puzzles, like the question that occurred to *Boston Globe*'s investigative "Spotlight Team" as it discussed the plethora of court cases against John J. Geoghan: How many Father Geoghans are there? A dozen years earlier, jurors were similarly enthralled by the simple origins of the stories on the American blood industry from *Philadelphia Inquirer* reporter Gilbert Gaul. Participating in a blood drive at his office, like so many others had done, Gaul began ruminating about what happened to the fluid after it flowed from his vein and into a Red Cross bag. Months later, the result was the 1990 Gold Medal for his exploration of the intricacies, peculiarities, and deceptions of the blood industry. Tighter government regulation resulted.

These days, team-based journalism projects normally involve the extensive use of databases and combine computer-assisted reporting with those everyman questions in a powerful linkage. *Washington Post* reporters followed up a simple statistical discovery—that more people in their city than in any other were being shot by police—with computer research and extensive interviews that led them all the way to the 1999 Public Service Prize. Using dramatic examples, their stories explained why so many shootings occurred.

The lack of a formal fact-checking capability within the entry-judging system has hurt the overall journalism Pulitzers over the years. Still, the jurors and board members often have checked out the reporting on their own, quietly rejecting entries when they found problems. In the worst case of an undetected Pulitzer fraud, the *Washington Post* returned the 1981 Feature Writing Prize of reporter Janet Cooke after it learned that she had made up her story about a child hooked on heroin. Since then, skepticism has played a much greater part in the judging process for both jurors and Pulitzer board members.

But former board member Geneva Overholser, for one, maintains that it would be hard to improve on a Pulitzer selection system that puts the task in the hands of the nation's top editors, backed by academics familiar with journalism. "I challenge anyone to think of a better way to recognize extraordinary journalism. The record speaks for itself," says University of Missouri professor Overholser, who cites among her own proudest moments accepting the 1991 Gold Medal for the stories written for the newspaper she edited at the time, the *Des Moines Register.* "It's like that wonderful Churchill statement about democracy being the worst form of government, except for every other form of government."

In 2006, the nineteen-member board was chaired by *Wall Street Journal* managing editor Paul Steiger and contained editors and publishers from large and small media outlets all over the country, including easterners from New York, Philadelphia, Washington, and Concord, New Hampshire, and westerners from Seattle and Denver. Other journalist members were from Chicago, Minneapolis, St. Petersburg, New Orleans, and Austin. There were faculty members from Harvard and Stanford, along with Columbia president Lee C. Bollinger and journalism dean Nicholas Lemann, and Pulitzer administrator Sig Gissler.

When the winners are revealed at exactly 3 p.m. on the first Monday after the April board meeting, it is Gissler who steps to a lectern in front of the Liberty Window to, as he put it one year, "sprinkle fairy dust on people and change their lives forever." An old-fashioned press affair, the session starts with reporters grabbing press kits and running for the phones. Some eager correspondents are from wire services while others represent winning newspapers whose editors want to get the news first, and firsthand. Within fifteen minutes, the whole package of information is on the Pulitzer Web site.

The press conference takes a while. Winners in twenty-one journalism and non-journalism categories are announced, with seven prizes honoring various kinds of reporting: investigative, explanatory, breaking news, beat, national, international, and feature writing. The other journalism awards cite excellence in public service, commentary, criticism, editorial writing, editorial cartooning, breaking news photography, and feature photography. The Pulitzers for arts and letters are awarded for fiction, general nonfiction, history, biography or autobiography, drama, poetry, and music.

Around the nation, cheers go up and champagne corks pop at more than a dozen newspapers—whose editors most often have been told in advance. At others, though, the mood is somber as the official word goes to finalists that there will be no prize for them that year.

As was the case in 2006, surprises sometimes enliven the Pulitzer announcements. In both 2002 and 2003, however, there was little mystery about who would win the Gold Medal. The announcements validated the foregone conclusions of editors around the nation.

The 2006 Pulitzer Prize Board poses in front of the World Room's Liberty Window at the Columbia University Graduate School of Journalism. Seated, left to right: Kathleen Carroll, Associated Press; Henry Louis Gates Jr., Harvard University; Joann Byrd, *Seattle Post-Intelligencer;* Amanda Bennett, Bloomberg News; Sig Gissler, administrator, the Pulitzer Prizes. Standing: Anders Gyllenhaal, *Star-Tribune,* Minneapolis–St. Paul; Thomas L. Friedman Jr., *New York Times;* Gregory L. Moore, *Denver Post;* Nicholas Lemann, Columbia University; Donald Graham, *Washington Post;* Ann Marie Lipinski, *Chicago Tribune;* Paul Steiger, *Wall Street Journal;* Jay T. Harris, University of Southern California; Paul Tash, *St. Petersburg Times;* Lee C. Bollinger, Columbia University; David M. Kennedy, Stanford University; Richard Oppel, *Austin American-Statesman;* Jim Amoss, *Times-Picayune,* New Orleans; and Mike Pride, *Concord* (N.H.) *Monitor.* Photo by Michael Dames, used courtesy of Columbia University.

Pulitzer jurors in the World Room, March 1990. Photo by Joe Pineiro. Used by permission of the University Archives, Columbia University in the City of New York.

Pulitzer Prize administrator Sig Gissler announces the winners from the World Room, 2007. Photo by Andrew Russeth. Used by permission, Columbia University.

CHAPTER 3

Spotlight on the Church

> Newspapers exist so that investigative journalism can take place. It's how we fulfill the responsibility we have because of our privileges under the First Amendment.
>
> —Mike Rezendes, on why he joined the *Boston Globe* Spotlight Team

*E*very new editor likes to make a splash the first day on the job. But Martin Baron's inaugural Monday morning story meeting at the *Boston Globe* on July 30, 2001, would hit with all the force of one of those rare summer hurricanes that sweeps up the Atlantic Coast to hammer New England.

The Florida-born Baron—forty-six at the time, and a twenty-five-year newspaper veteran—had held senior editing posts at the *Los Angeles Times* and *New York Times* before returning to his native state to serve the last eighteen months as executive editor of the *Miami Herald.* There, he had been on a fantastic roll. The *Herald* had won national praise for its aggressive handling of the Florida vote-count debacle, in which the presidential race between George W. Bush and Al Gore teetered on a review of "hanging chads" and other ballot peculiarities. In pursuit of the story, the *Herald* sponsored its own recount and launched legal challenges, running up a bill of $850,000 for its owner, Knight Ridder. Then, in April, the *Herald* had received the 2001 Pulitzer Prize for Breaking News Reporting, for "balanced and gripping on-the-scene coverage" of the Elian Gonzalez affair. Young Elian's story had riveted the nation twelve months before, when federal agents seized the boy from his Miami relatives to reunite him with his Cuban father.

Along with prizes, Baron's management of such high-profile work had won him editor-of-the-year recognition from *Editor & Publisher.* No wonder Baron was atop the list being kept by the *Globe*'s owner of the last nine years, the New York Times

Company, for the plum assignment of running one of the nation's premier papers. The *Globe,* which blanketed New England with a daily circulation of more than four hundred thousand, was also one of America's most honored publications. The *Globe* or its staff members had won an extremely respectable total of sixteen Pulitzer Prizes since its first prize in 1966.

Despite Baron's own impressive press clippings, the new editor tended to make a low-key first impression, asking questions rather than calling shots. At sessions like the morning editorial meeting—which Matthew Storin, his predecessor, had established as the standard day-starter—the main order of business was a critique of the morning's paper and a review of what stories were in the works. And Baron was content to use his first meeting for those purposes.

The *Globe* had been flown down to Baron in Miami for about a month, so he was familiar with some of its running coverage when he first walked through doors of the paper's huge brick Morrissey Boulevard complex south of downtown. One continuing story involved the legal case of a defrocked Catholic priest named John J. Geoghan, accused of sexually abusing children years earlier. A court filing that had managed to escape a judge-ordered confidentiality order—and that had been written about in the *Globe* only after it first appeared in the rival tabloid, the *Boston Herald*—suggested that Cardinal Bernard F. Law had been involved in keeping Geoghan active in the priesthood for years. The document said that Law had transferred Geoghan to another parish in 1984, after the priest had been accused of molesting young people in his care.

While the Geoghan stories were not particularly prominent, two consecutive Sunday pieces by *Globe* columnist Eileen McNamara caught Baron's eye in the week before the meeting. They piqued his curiosity both about his new paper and about the Massachusetts court system. McNamara had noted that a Church-requested seal on the Geoghan case prevented the public from peering "into corners of the Church that the cardinal would prefer to keep forever in shadow." Baron was somewhat surprised by the response of the assembled editors as he ran down a list of possible stories, and got to the Geoghan case. There wasn't any follow-up planned, they said. The paper seemed stumped by the court's confidentiality order.

The editor, however, had just come from a state where so-called Sunshine Laws tended to keep the media from being shut out. "I mentioned that I didn't know what the laws of Massachusetts are, but in Florida there's a more expansive public records law, and an inclination to make everything public. I asked whether there had been any consideration given to challenging the confidentiality order in court," Baron recalls. "There was some silence, and the answer was no."

He could certainly see why his new subordinates might be reluctant to pursue a major Geoghan article that lacked documentary support from court filings or interviews with the parties involved. Such coverage would be nearly devoid of the detail necessary to make the case come alive. "Of course I was looking for interesting stories," says Baron. "But I find people just arguing with each other to be pretty dissatisfying. It's important to get beyond the 'he-said, she-said' quality of news reports, to what actually happened, to what the underlying truth is." To do the Geoghan case that kind of journalistic justice would mean detailing the actions of the abusers, how their crimes had impacted the victims, and how the Church hierarchy had responded, for starters.

That day, a call went out to *Globe* attorney Jonathan M. Albano, asking him to look into the prospects for getting the court seal lifted. By mid-afternoon Baron had summoned to his office the paper's two top investigative editors: Ben Bradlee Jr., deputy managing editor for projects and investigations, and Walter V. Robinson, head of the Spotlight Team of investigative journalists and also its chief reporter. The subject was Geoghan: both the possibility that the paper might try to open up the court files, and that Spotlight might begin looking into the circumstances surrounding the priest's alleged abuse of young parishioners.

Bradlee and Robinson were among the paper's most experienced and respected editors—and were the keys to launching any major investigative project. Affectionately known to the staff as Robby, Robinson was a graduate of the Catholic Boston College High School, just across Morrissey from the *Globe*, and had joined the paper after graduating from Boston's Northeastern University in 1974. He had covered numerous major local, national, and international beats, and had been Middle East bureau chief during the 1991 Gulf War and a White House correspondent under Presidents Reagan and George H. W. Bush.

Bradlee—a seasoned reporter and editor who had spent the last nine of his twenty-three years at the *Globe* managing the paper's special projects—had investigative work in his blood. He was the son of the *Washington Post* editor of Watergate Pulitzer Public Service fame.

The *Globe* owned two Gold Medals among the sixteen Pulitzers on its trophy wall. The 1966 prize had honored its service through a campaign that kept a politically connected jurist from being appointed a federal judge. Then, in 1975, the paper's coverage of Boston school desegregation had been cited.

The "Prospecting" Begins

Baron's idea about trying to get the court records unsealed and investigating Geoghan's life as a sexual predator struck Bradlee and Robinson as particularly courageous because of its potential to embarrass the most powerful institution in their heavily Catholic city. Also, the decisiveness and speed with which the new editor had called such a critical meeting with his investigative leaders was a gust of fresh air blowing from the editor's office. While such snap sessions might seem normal in many newsrooms, in previous *Globe* administrations such a Baron-Bradlee-Robinson session probably would not have taken place without a half-dozen other editors being marshaled as well, and possibly even with publisher Richard Gilman being consulted. It was the *Globe's* culture.

It also crossed Robinson's mind, he later wrote, that actually pursuing such a story would represent "the assignment from hell: A newspaper's investigative team pointed at the city's—any city's—preeminent sacred cow." The Boston archdiocese, in addition to being almost paranoid about what it perceived as "negative press," was known for extreme secretiveness in matters concerning its priests. So, Robinson thought, Spotlight would face a seemingly insurmountable obstacle: "How do you breach an institution that has neither the obligation nor the inclination to make its records public, nor to discuss how it operates?"

Bradlee and Robinson enthusiastically agreed that Spotlight should take a look at whether to pursue a Geoghan project, however. That meant starting with a team process that Robinson calls "prospecting."

The initial session with Bradlee and Robinson was only a discussion, as Baron puts it, about going beyond a document search "and actually embarking on a broader investigation of the whole case, apart and parallel with the legal action." A call on whether to pursue the story would be made later, when the results of Spotlight's prospecting were in.

While the lawyers began to study the chances for a motion challenging the confidentiality order in the Geoghan case, the scene shifted that afternoon to what Robinson calls the "mineshaft that is known as the mezzanine." The tiny suite of offices, which is purposely hard to get to from the newsroom one floor above it, is the space that the Spotlight Team calls home. (Bradlee's office was upstairs, in the newsroom.)

Spotlight itself was one of the oldest standing investigative units among U.S. newspapers. Created in 1970, it was largely modeled on the "Insight" teams of the London *Sunday Times,* although some ideas had come from visits with members of the "Greene Team" at *Newsday.* The Long Island, New York, paper had launched the team concept under veteran investigative reporter Bob Greene.

On the *Globe's* trophy wall, Spotlight was responsible for two of the sixteen Pulitzers, both of them for Investigative Reporting. One, in 1972, for exposing corruption in the suburb of Somerville, also had been a Public Service finalist in the year that the *New York Times* won the Gold Medal for publishing the Pentagon Papers.

If the unit itself had a long history, the 2001 edition was relatively new. Only Matt Carroll, the team's computer-assisted reporting specialist, had been there more than a year. Robinson had taken the team-leader job just after the 2000 elections, partly drawn to it by the prospect of being able to hand-pick two reporters to fill vacancies on a squad of four members, including himself.

Looking for complementary skills and personalities—and steering clear of the "substantial egos" that he had seen infect the investigative ranks at some papers—he had selected statehouse reporter Michael Rezendes and legal affairs writer Sacha Pfeiffer. As it turned out, that meant that the new Spotlight was made up of four native Bostonians, all of whom happened to have Roman Catholic upbringings. (Robinson himself, though still having some Church-related associations, jokes that he is more of a "collapsed Catholic.")

Rezendes remembers that on the afternoon of July 30, Robinson called the team into his office and told members about the discussions upstairs. They agreed to do some more reporting, short of engaging in a project at that point. "The idea," says Rezendes, "was to look at how many others besides Geoghan there might be."

Spotlight typically came up with its own ideas. Says Robinson: "We go to the editors and we say we want to look into 'A.' We don't actually launch a project on 'A' until we've done enough of what I call prospecting to determine that we can get 'A.' Can we get documents? Can we get people to talk to us? Is it worth Spotlight's effort?" Working this way, Spotlight rolled out three or four major projects a year, along with a few shorter-term stories.

A Geoghan investigation hardly would be typical, of course. For one thing, Spotlight had been asked to check things out by the paper's new editor. That gave it special weight. For another, all the team members knew—even without having done any reporting—that the story had the potential to dwarf any previous Spotlight project.

Rezendes never had known anyone personally who claimed to have been abused. Still, he says, "I remember having the thought, long before I got on the Spotlight Team, that clergy sexual abuse was an epidemic." And Pfeiffer had a particular professional interest in the subject. In her coverage of the courts, she had written occasional spot stories about suits that had been filed by lawyer Mitchell Garabedian on behalf of Geoghan's victims. In those stories, though, the detail was extremely thin, leaving to the imagination what awful specifics of child abuse were sealed away in the court filings.

The team members also were aware that stories about Geoghan and a Church cover-up of clergy sexual abuse were hardly new. Indeed, along with the story the *Herald* had broken about Cardinal Law's awareness of Geoghan's history, reporter Kristen Lombardi of Boston's weekly *Phoenix* had focused on the priest and some of his victims earlier in the year. No documentation backed up the suggestion that the Church was coddling Geoghan or other accused priests, however. Mostly, Spotlight was curious about how far Geoghan's sexual abuse had extended, and whether the problem went much beyond the case of one bad apple.

Prospecting involved total immersion in the topic: starting with calls to lawyers, known victims, the relative handful of experts in the field of clergy sexual abuse, and any priests or Church officials who would discuss the situation, off the record or on. In terms of previously reported cases, the team reviewed a scandal that had involved abuse allegations against Father James R. Porter in the early 1990s. The charges and resulting news stories had rocked the Fall River diocese in the southeast corner of Massachusetts. Porter's case, heavily covered by the *Globe* at the time, also stirred up a storm of press controversy within the Church. At one point, in fact, Cardinal Law had called down "the power of God" on the media—and especially the *Globe*—for suggesting in its Porter stories that sexual abuse by priests was a problem wider than *that* one bad apple.

While no one on the Spotlight Team or in the newsroom upstairs could have suspected it at the time, the July 30 meetings set the stage for a crusade that eventually would double Spotlight's size, produce a total of nearly nine hundred articles by the end of 2002, and become the greatest journalistic success ever for the 126-year-old paper.

A Green Light for Spotlight

In a way, the timing was extremely good for the team to take on such a challenge. Without a current project to work on, says Rezendes, "Spotlight was in one of those modes, evaluating tips, chewing on various ideas." The team had just completed a project analyzing shoddy work in the construction industry, which had followed the normal Spotlight-reporting progression: several months of research culminating in a series of several parts. A former reporter for Boston's *Phoenix,* the *San Jose Mercury News,* and the *Washington Post,* Rezendes had been lured to the *Globe* in 1989 by Ben Bradlee Jr. (He figures he's one of a very few reporters to have worked for "both Ben Bradlees.") Over the years Rezendes had also honed an ability to talk with blue-collar Bostonians, having once run a small paper in a lower-middle-class East Boston neighborhood. It was to be a talent of great value to the new project.

"After several days of rummaging around we came upon people who told us that Geoghan was the tip of the iceberg," Robinson says. "I remember at the time saying to my wife, 'What if it was ten or twelve priests? What an extraordinary story that would be.'" The Church's own studies showed that pedophilia was a problem among no more than 0.5 percent of priests, or one of every two hundred, about the same as the population as a whole. But what Spotlight was hearing suggested a problem more insidious among the 650 priests in the Boston archdiocese than the occasional bad apple infecting the clergy's barrel. Perhaps far more insidious.

Robinson reported first to Bradlee, then to Baron. "We hadn't advanced the ball much on Geoghan," he told them, but the team had heard reliably that Geoghan was one of many. And Geoghan was unusual not for the number of his victims, but "because his case had actually gotten to the lawsuit stage in court, whereas a large number of other cases had been quietly settled in chancery court."

Baron immediately gave the green light to Spotlight. Albano, the leader of the *Globe* legal team, provided arguments for and against trying to unseal the documents, calling the chance of success about fifty-fifty. "Those are actually pretty good odds for newspapers," says Baron, "so we decided to go to court." He had called publisher Richard Gilman before the decision to pursue the reporting and the court documents, and gotten the go-ahead. Says Baron, "I doubt he expected his new editor, as his first act—or ever, for that matter—to be confronting the Catholic Church in court." It was the start of many months of encouragement from the top.

Down in the mezzanine office, the names of half a dozen priests had surfaced in the early calling, most the subjects of repeated molestation complaints or lawsuits, and one or two who had been mentioned in articles. Spotlight divvied them up. "It was the first time I was cognizant that the *Globe* was really stepping off a cliff," Robinson says. "Remember, there were four reporters here who really didn't have much experience doing Church stuff."

Indeed, editors had reached a decision not to bring religion reporter Michael Paulson onto the team—at least not yet. Paulson and Robinson had discussed it, but historically beat reporters had been excluded from Spotlight investigations because it might interfere with their daily beat responsibility. Furthermore, says the Spotlight chief, "when the story breaks, we need to have an honest intermediate broker, the beat reporter who has credibility with the people he covers, because sometimes they won't talk to us."

On the Spotlight Team, Rezendes was "the Geoghan guy," which meant getting to know Mitchell Garabedian, who as attorney for eighty-six victims had filed a total of eighty-four separate lawsuits. Rezendes's approach involved a lot of schmoozing with the lawyer, something he considered himself quite good at. "But mostly I got close to his clients," he says. He spent weeks interviewing victims, many of them lower-middle-class young adults who had been abused years before. Rezendes's experience in East Boston was valuable. "Some victim would be telling me his story, but be embarrassed and untrusting, and I'd say, 'Where do you live?'

And he'd say over on Hyde Park Avenue. And I'd say, 'Oh, yeah, over by the Hi-Top Liquor Store.' Because I knew the neighborhoods, I could shoot the breeze."

One other early source—Phil Saviano, himself a former victim who had become involved with a support group called Survivors Network of Those Abused by Priests, or SNAP—left a vivid impression on Rezendes after Saviano was invited in early August to brief the team at the Spotlight office. Rezendes found Saviano's information, even if it was unproved, to be a "good road map." More important, in a four-hour visit Saviano had spoken in a way that helped team members visualize the shock of an unsuspecting adolescent being approached by a priest—perhaps one known to his family for years—for sex. Well-adjusted youngsters with strong family backgrounds might find ways to deal with it. "But if you're a kid from a broken home and you're really in need of an adult's attention, then you might gravitate to someone who will pay that kind of attention to you," says Rezendes. Because so many victims had such backgrounds, their allegations were often dismissed as false even if they spoke up.

The task of building a database of priests fell to Carroll, who had grown up in suburban Dedham and started in journalism on the staff of the rival *Boston Herald.* Joining the *Globe* business department fourteen years before as a copy editor, he had moved up the business-reporting ranks before getting into computer-assisted reporting in the 1990s. He brought that specialty to Spotlight in 1996. That gave him four years' seniority as a Spotlight Team member, even if he tended to see himself as a newcomer compared to veterans like Robinson and Rezendes.

Carroll had trained in CAR, as computer-assisted reporting is known, and had taught its techniques to other *Globe* staffers. Somewhere he had heard in class that CAR had played a critical role in every Pulitzer Prize for Public Service since 1980. In the early days investigating the Geoghan story, the database was kept on a simple, even primitive spreadsheet. "We just started getting names from different people, and we put them in files, before we had any documents at all," Carroll says. But even using that rudimentary collection method, the database swelled, fed by conversations with lawyers, victims, Church officials, and others.

Robinson was not the leader on the computer work. "I had no idea until Matt Carroll told me that this was really computer assisted reporting, on a spreadsheet," he says with a laugh.

It was thanks to Robinson, though, that the database got its first big infusion. "Robby had this bright idea, which was to look at the annual reports issued by the diocese—their Yellow Pages for priests, basically," says Carroll. Stacking two decades of directories in the office and scanning them name by name, team members found some bland-looking yet suspicious notations. For a large number of priests, the directories used terms like "awaiting assignment," "sick leave," "clergy personnel office," or simply "unassigned"—this in a Church with a severe priest shortage. Sometimes, of course, the priest would really be sick, as checks by Spotlight would show. But in many cases the team's investigations turned up a background of sordid abuse allegations that correlated with the bland annotations.

Eventually, the team's file would expand to include nearly two hundred names of suspect priests. Each name was cross-referenced to reporters' unpublished memos or to articles that had appeared about that individual priest. With each new report, another entry would be made. Eventually, the database would be made easily searchable by name or key word.

Carroll, like the rest of the team, found Robinson an inspiring—and untiring—boss. "Nothing fazes him. He's done every job at the paper, and he is a madman for work," says Carroll. As the Geoghan story developed, Robinson's day in the office started at 5:30 in the morning, ninety minutes before his normal start time. He was often the one to close the office, too. His deft editing touch was something else Carroll appreciated, because, he says, "I'm not the most writer-ly person in the world."

The team did not publish any stories based on its database or initial interviews, which sometimes were off the record. Rather, it built a critical mass of material that, the team expected, would help Robinson and Bradlee determine the story theme. Even without writing, though, there was plenty to do in the office. Looking through the Church directories for "red flags"—those sick-leave or awaiting-assignment designations—led to a grueling but productive team ritual, says Sacha Pfeiffer. "One person would be typing, one person would be calling out information, and we would be divvying up this tedious task of typing and reading," she says. "I think a lot of us lost some eyesight looking through all the fine print in those books." But huge numbers of priests were appearing under some categories. "We tracked those categorizations back for about twenty years not knowing at the time whether it would be valuable—and later finding out it was invaluable."

Reporters contacted more attorneys who had filed cases against the Church. And Spotlight studied every lawsuit it could find that named the institution, to see what was alleged and what documents might be available. "Obviously, a lot of cases were slip-and-fall cases," Pfeiffer says, "but there were plenty that weren't."

Reporters as Counselors

When it came to interviewing victims of priests, Pfeiffer's skills were quickly noted by fellow team members in the confines of their small office area. She had a special gift for the delicate task of drawing people out and getting them at least to consider going public about their harrowing long-ago experiences. The early interviews "gave us a sense of the dimension and the scale and the volume of the complaints. It was very depressing and sad," she says. "Sometimes we talked about how we were being put into this counseling role that we were totally not trained to be in." Each interview, of course, expanded the database.

Pfeiffer developed her patient, compassionate interviewing style with people clearly in distress about terrible remembrances of things past. Even talking off-the-record, interviewees could be extremely sensitive. "We often had these victims who were so embarrassed, and in an embarrassed way were trying to explain how this happened—still wrestling with it themselves." Working through it with them, she says, "after a while you begin to understand yourself how it could happen."

Then there was the uncontrollable emotion. During an early interview with Arthur Austin, who had been victimized by Father Paul R. Shanley, "Arthur just cried and cried and cried." Austin and Pfeiffer were in a restaurant as he talked about his encounters with Shanley, who had gained some fame as a "street priest" in the 1970s. "The waitress was trying to figure out how to approach the table because he was in tears the whole time," says Pfeiffer. But the reporter found that the interview helped her develop the ability to manage sensitively the many phone interviews that were to lie ahead. "I think I'm pretty genuine when I talk to people, because I really do care," she says.

For one thing, she attuned herself to the earlier eras in which much of the abuse had occurred. Beyond the sense of being betrayed by someone in a position of trust, she says, "people were afraid of being labeled as gay, with all the terrible consequences that came with that." Sometimes, Pfeiffer got dramatic results when she was able to get an interviewee to move past that fear. "This wall broke down, and people just told their stories. Before, there had been this stigma, and people were embarrassed and afraid and ashamed, with all the self-blame that comes with sexual abuse—multiplied, because it was priests who were doing it," she says. "Then all of a sudden the stigma was gone, and they had this waterfall of stories." Occasionally victims decided to tell her their stories of abuse before communicating with their own families. Pfeiffer wouldn't let them. "In some ways, we ended up protecting the victims from themselves," she says.

While Rezendes had been assigned to Geoghan, Pfeiffer drew Paul Shanley, Joseph Birmingham, and Ronald Paquin, three men who had been the subject of repeated abuse allegations from the 1960s to the 1980s. Their crimes had managed to stay out of the public eye for the most part. Shanley's work on the street had been largely with gays and disaffected minorities, such as drug addicts. Secretly, though, he had been a sexual predator. Birmingham had died in 1989, but left behind scores of victims whose complaints had been ignored by the Church for decades. She learned that Paquin had been the driver during a 1981 New Hampshire auto accident in which one of four altar boys was killed. The five were returning to Massachusetts from a weekend of drinking together. The crash had resulted in no criminal charges, and Paquin had not been removed from his parish until nine years later.

As they compared notes, discussing among themselves the terrors that young Catholics were being put through by Geoghan and others, the four reporters related to each other on a personal level—something unfamiliar to them from previous Spotlight work. It was then that they realized for the first time that each had been raised Catholic, although none was personally acquainted with victims of accused priests, at least as far as they knew. Each had a visceral reaction to the idea of priests violating the trust of families by preying on their children, though. That Church officials would protect the priests, rather than their young victims, seemed almost inconceivable.

With the unsealing of the Geoghan court documents uncertain, Pfeiffer wondered how the story would develop for the *Globe*. If it was the typical Spotlight story, a series of several days would run and the team would move on. "So this was a story that we thought would be a three-day story," she says. "We'd get picketed, probably, by people angry with us for taking on the Church. But we never ever thought this was a story that would consume two years of our time, and would continue to this day."

The image of what constituted a Spotlight story was about to change at the paper. In fact, a dramatic shift had already occurred in what other reporters thought of the team. "When I first went down there, someone said to me, 'Enjoy your early retirement,'" Pfeiffer laughs. Because only a few Spotlight projects saw print each year, the team had also offered what Robinson called "the lure of never having to write a lead that contains the word 'yesterday.'" And the work schedule? "Spotlight was a job you could do and still get home for dinner." These were luxuries that would not last.

As the team labored on, religion writer Paulson followed closely from his desk upstairs. He accepted the arguments of his editors about keeping him off the team. He was the only religion reporter, and would have had to abandon the beat indefinitely if he joined Spotlight. Further, the paper did not consider priests' sexual abuse of children as a religious story. Rather, Paulson says, it was viewed as a legal story, and "we were better off handling these cases through our cops and courts reporters."

The decision to keep him on the religion beat did allow Paulson to pursue a personal mission he had committed himself to when he took it over after moving to Boston from the *Seattle Post-Intelligencer* in January 2000. The mission—soon to be severely tested—involved improving long-ailing relations with the archdiocese. In Paulson's mind, problems between the paper and the Church stretched back way before the Father Porter coverage that had angered Cardinal Law. The *Globe* editorial page also had supported positions on issues such as birth control, abortion, and gay rights that were anathema to the Church hierarchy. In the reporter's studied opinion, the *Globe* had first disaffected many rank-and-file Catholics in the mid-1970s. They had turned against the paper, he reasoned, over what they perceived to be its support of school busing in all-white neighborhoods as a means of achieving racial integration.

Reporting on school busing had won the *Globe* its second Pulitzer Public Service Gold Medal, in 1975. Back then, the Pulitzer board had cited the *Globe*'s "massive and balanced coverage of the Boston school desegregation crisis." Robinson, who had been among the staffers covering the busing crisis, shared Paulson's view that many blue-collar, conservative Catholics had soured on the paper during the controversy. For a quarter-century, the *Globe* had lived with it. Neither Robinson nor Paulson had any idea how this new challenge to the Church might affect the way these disaffected Catholics viewed the *Globe*. They did know, though, that if the Church story developed into a huge project, bringing Paulson onto Spotlight was an option that would help the *Globe* explain some of these deeper issues.

Robinson describes the early progress on the team's research as "chipping away at a thick wall with the dull edge of a knife." As August wound down, though, prospects for a good story, and maybe several, seemed better each day. Not only was progress being made on the Geoghan case, but the number of priests in the database was swelling.

The *Globe* was nearing a decision about whether to move forward with legally challenging the confidentiality order in the Geoghan case. It was a sensitive internal issue in the Boston newsroom because the New York Times Company policy calls for corporate lawyers in New York to review all legal actions by its news enterprises, including the *Globe*.

Was there any danger that the existence of a full-fledged *Globe* investigative project about the Church might reach the ears of a *Times* reporter? "Of course I was worried that *New York Times* lawyers would tell *New York Times* journalists," Baron says. But he had to trust that the editorial "wall" between that publication and its sister paper would not be breached. (In retrospect, he says of the Times Company lawyers: "They were helpful—and entirely honorable.") In writing its motion seeking to unseal the documents, the *Globe* and Times Company attorneys focused on the public-interest aspect—not prurient details or the names of victims. "What we were interested in was the Church, and whether it and the cardinal had fulfilled their responsibilities to protect children who were in their care," says Baron.

On September 6, with Rezendes the only reporter present, Albano argued the *Globe*'s case in the Springfield courtroom of Massachusetts Superior Court Judge Constance M. Sweeney, a graduate of Springfield's Cathedral High School, and of Newton College of the Sacred Heart, now a part of Boston College. The parties prepared for a ruling that might take two months or so.

The next day, Robinson had a reporting breakthrough. He met in downtown Boston with two sources. They provided a list of priests who had been accused of sexual abuse, but whose accusers had been paid so that they would not sue. There were about thirty-five names on the list—three times the number that Robinson had considered worthy of a major story just a month earlier.

How to proceed now seemed clear: With the Geoghan angle becoming more competitive—if court documents *were* unsealed, they would go to the *Herald* and the *Phoenix,* too, of course—Spotlight would attack the story on two major Church-related fronts. One front would explore the Geoghan case in depth, no matter what the decision was on court-imposed confidentiality. The other would capitalize on the team's exclusive information about the shockingly high number of priests accused of being child molesters. Their reporting had also turned up information about the actions of Cardinal Law and others in allowing accused priests to keep working with children in parishes.

There was every reason to believe that a story along the second front, at least, could be readied before year-end, and perhaps before a decision was made on whether to unseal the court records.

While it may not have crossed the minds of the *Globe* editors or reporters, that timing—with a group of stories appearing before December 31, 2001—would also qualify the work to be entered for the 2002 Pulitzer Prizes. Especially if the *Globe* attorneys somehow managed to get the Geoghan case unsealed, a public service in itself, Eileen McNamara's columns might be packaged with a year-end series of articles. It could be a potent entry for the Pulitzer Public Service category.

But then, quite literally, a bolt from the blue struck. It instantly transformed life at the *Globe,* American journalism—and the world as we know it.

Wait 'til Next Year

After departing from Boston's Logan Airport on a warm, sunny Tuesday morning, two Boeing 767 jetliners operated by American and United, loaded with fuel for their transcontinental flights, were hijacked by terrorists. Three hundred miles down the coast, they were flown into the upper stories of New York's World Trade Center. A third 767, on a flight originating from Washington, D.C., smashed into the outer E- and D-Rings of the five-ringed Pentagon. A fourth jetliner crashed in a field in western Pennsylvania without hitting a target, likely after passengers over-powered the terrorists.

In the heart-stopping shock of September 11, only one thing was clear in the *Globe* newsroom as editors and reporters watched the Twin Towers collapse: the paper's best people needed to be thrown immediately into a story with such glob-al, national, regional, and local impact. Work on the Church stories stopped.

"The whole paper was mobilized to work on the 9/11 attacks," says Marty Baron. "If that meant Church reporting was on hold, so be it." The four Spotlight members, the elite of the paper's investigators, were reassigned to the toughest of the endless stream of story ideas that emanated from the actions of the terrorists. Rezendes went to Florida to retrace the steps of the bombers before they had come to Boston. Pfeiffer found herself writing about the American Red Cross and blood supplies. For their September assignments—the terrorism coverage was orches-trated by Ben Bradlee—team members often were attached to non-Spotlight re-porting teams. Robinson joined a Washington correspondent, writing about var-ious shortcomings of the Federal Aviation Administration, while Carroll applied his CAR skills in 9/11 story after 9/11 story.

It wasn't for another month, in mid-October, that team members would return to the Church project. Nothing of their work on the topic would be published by year-end 2001, and thus nothing would be eligible for the 2002 Pulitzer Prizes.

And what of the prizes that *were* awarded? Not surprisingly, the nominated work would overwhelmingly reflect coverage from the 110 days between the Sep-tember 11 attacks and December 31. The selections of the Pulitzer Prize Board, meeting six months after 9/11, included eight terrorism-related winners, repre-senting more than half the fourteen journalism categories.

The *Globe* and its Spotlight Team members—like so many past incarnations of their beloved Boston Red Sox, the perennial baseball also-rans cursed by the 1920 sale of Babe Ruth to the New York Yankees—would have to wait 'til next year.

For *Globe* readers, Catholics everywhere, and the 2003 Pulitzer Prize Board, it would be worth the wait. The Church coverage, the continuation of which is dis-cussed in Chapter 5, would earn the *Globe* comparisons to the *Washington Post*'s Watergate exclusives by Woodward and Bernstein. The *Post*'s reporting had drawn generations of eager youngsters into journalism careers and transformed the no-tion of newspaper public service. That notion would be transformed again with the *Globe*'s contribution.

CHAPTER 4

A Newsroom Challenged

I have seen reporters crying at their telephones, even as they summoned the professional discipline to keep reporting, keep writing until the task was done. They were inspired and sometimes driven by an awareness of what these pieces had come to mean to the grieving families and friends and to that larger community of Americans who mourned for all the World Trade Center victims, strangers to them or not, just as in an earlier day their parents mourned for the dead of Pearl Harbor.

> —*New York Times* executive editor Howell Raines,
> on the preparation of "Portraits of Grief"

*B*efore work one morning, Gerald Boyd was relaxing in the barber chair. Then the world changed.

The haircut was in preparation for a special dinner party that night. Just five days into his new job as managing editor of the *New York Times,* Boyd would be joining new editorial page editor Gail Collins and executive editor Howell Raines at the home of publisher Arthur Sulzberger. It was also primary election day—a nice little exercise for a Metro desk that had the extraordinary talent of the *Times.* But certainly, there seemed to be nothing on the horizon that warm late-summer morning to jeopardize dinner at the publisher's.

The barber was Haitian and spoke French and Creole, and little English. Boyd liked it that way. "We didn't have to engage in conversations, and he could do his business without talking about world affairs," he said. To catch a breeze, the shop's door was open. "Someone walked in and yelled to the barber, 'Have you heard about the plane that crashed into the Twin Towers?'"

The words were hardly spoken—Boyd leapt from under the scissors. "I ran out with the smock still on, fishing money out for him, saying, I have to go. He didn't understand what I was saying. He said he wasn't finished."

The barber shop was sixty-five blocks north of Times Square, where the newsroom was in desperate need of its new managing editor. Boyd tried the subway. No service. There was a "police action at the World Trade Center," the announcement said. He stopped a gypsy cab willing to make the trip. His fifty dollars and his constant urging for the driver to ignore the speed limit—"If you get a ticket, I'll pay," Boyd shouted—paid off. In fifteen minutes he was in the office. On the newsroom television, he was able to watch early film of the second plane hitting, eighteen minutes after the first strike.

The Culture Kicks In

An outsider looking at the job ahead for Boyd, Raines, and other *New York Times* "masthead editors" might see September 11 as a nearly uncoverable local, national, and global story. But Boyd, who for eight years had served as assistant managing editor and then deputy managing editor before assuming the managing editorship the prior week, saw a ritual play out that was no less amazing because it was expected. At least, it was expected at the *Times.*

"The culture of the *New York Times* kicks in, and that culture is that certain things become automatic," he said. The "A-book"—the paper's first section—was immediately opened up, its ads cleared out. That happened on any huge story: the Berlin Wall coming down, the first Gulf War, the earlier, 1993 attack on the World Trade Center. The A-book had been opened a dozen times since Boyd had been in management.

Planning his staff's day under such pressure, his mind adjusted with each new shock. "As we watched the tube it was soon clear that we were dealing with an incredible story. But what struck me most about it—and it's kind of strange—was when I learned that Air Force One had been zigzagging." Having been a White House correspondent, he knew all that was done to keep the president's plane insulated from the world outside. "I always felt extremely safe, and if they were taking these extreme measures, it made it even more frightening."

Boyd made two decisions within minutes. One was to pull all the staff that had been assigned to cover the election—essentially everyone on the Metro staff—and recapture the space in the paper that was dedicated to the primary. It was a bit of a gamble, but paid off quickly when the crush of events forced the vote's cancellation. ("When I made the call I didn't know that," he noted.) The decision gave the paper a head start.

The second order was to create a series of meetings for the day, to coordinate coverage "and get a handle on what the nature of the story was." That call had been easier given the rapid unfolding of events: the Towers collapsed; thousands feared dead downtown; the president's statement that it was a terrorist attack; the Pentagon being hit; another plane crashing in Pennsylvania (after initial, erroneous reports saying it was in Ohio.) "We knew four planes had been used as guided missiles," Boyd recalled. "That was basically enough for us to begin staking the outlines of that report."

Freeing the A-book of ads had created some immediate needs. "You had twenty or thirty pages that were open. How do you package those pages? And again the culture of the paper was such that we knew how to do that," Boyd noted. "The need first of all is to break down the pages—four pages on collapse of the buildings, four on victims . . . What we had learned to do was to have a packaging meeting that did these kinds of things—to deal only with design, presentation, and look"—keeping design decisions away from the news meetings. "We weren't reinventing the wheel." Amid the chaos, it was a reassuring thought. The questions had been asked before, even if the scale might have been different: "How do we coordinate a Washington staff, a foreign-bureau staff and Metro staff? And how much over-all space to commit?"

As staffers tried to focus fully on the "battlefield coverage" they were suddenly engaged in, personal worries crept in. Boyd was no exception. With phones not working in the city, he could not contact his wife, who worked in the same area, as an editor at *Essence* magazine. "Was she at the World Trade Center or in the vicinity?" he wondered. It would be 5 o'clock before they finally got in touch.

He led the 11 a.m. news meeting. "We didn't talk about stories. We talked about what we knew, what we needed to know, and how we'd get there. Then we came back around noon." That meeting covered story assignments. "Then we had a 4:30 news meeting, and right after that we had our design people begin to lay out the pages." Editors assembled for a photo meeting an hour later, and then for a design meeting. "We had incredible art, and a whole lot of it," said Boyd. Page layouts went on until about 8 o'clock. He was home by 4 a.m.—without a thought, of course, for the cancelled Sulzberger dinner party.

With staffers the caliber of the *Times*'s, great reports were pouring in along with the great pictures. When reporter David Barstow heard about the attacks, he was driving back from Pennsylvania, where he and another writer had been covering a Little League baseball scandal involving an overage player from the Bronx. With the tunnels and bridges into the city closed, they took the Tappan Zee bridge north of the city, then went south into the Bronx until traffic allowed them to go no farther. "I jogged from 243rd Street down to 168th Street, then took the subway to the newsroom," says Barstow. By 8:30 p.m. he was at Ground Zero, having avoided the police who were assigned to keep reporters and others away. He spent the next several days there, he says, "feeding stuff back to the newsroom from the American Express Building while dodging the cops, who were constantly doing sweeps to get reporters like me out of there."

Because such enterprise was going on all around the managing editor, this assessment by Boyd may not sound quite so incredible. "The first night was, in a way, the easiest night," he said, "once we learned the dimensions of the story." Again, that *Times* culture was guiding reporters and editors. Tougher newsroom decisions were ahead.

Breaking Through the Abstraction

Christine Kay, too, would never forget the incongruous scene that got her to bolt for the office without a thought. The enterprise editor for Metro was on her sofa at home in Chelsea with a cup of coffee. She planned to report to work a little later than usual because of the expected late demands of the primary coverage. Her eye half on the TV, she saw what appeared to be some strange movie: a plane, the flames in one of the Twin Towers. "I jumped up and literally ran the twenty blocks north to the office to watch the TV showing the second plane hitting," she says. "And we all started to work."

A former *Newsday* editor who now reported to *Times* Metro editor Jonathan Landman, Kay had been editing a piece on adult homes for the mentally ill. On September 11, it was set aside. She has little recollection of what her hour-to-hour actions were that first day, except that she marshaled forces for Landman and served as a contact for reporters at Ground Zero and throughout the city. And gradually, she began to focus on the victims, taking charge of each missing-person report in those first few days. The identification of the dead would come much later.

Times culture or no *Times* culture, there were really no precedents for the scope of this catastrophe when it came to the newspaper dealing with victims. Not in peacetime, anyway. "I was here for TWA 800," Kay says, recalling the July 17, 1996, air disaster that killed 230 off the coast of Long Island. But those victims were known as soon as the passenger list was in hand. September 11 offered few comparisons. "We had no idea what we were facing," she says. "For the first three days I was coming in to a budget line that said Zero-Zero victims; Zero-Zero firefighters." That meant that even rough estimates of the dead were lacking, both among those who happened to be in the World Trade Center, or those among the first responders trying to save them.

The TWA crash did suggest some obvious approaches to editors looking to help readers grasp a mass-death situation. Even if there are hundreds of victims, "you start writing about them in real ways, intimate ways," Kay says. "You write about the group of school kids who were going to France. You write about the neighbors who were killed, or the husband and wife, or the girls who were left behind. You find small ways to report on it, and there is an immediacy about it."

But in the collapse of the Twin Towers, there were untold thousands of lives lost—with an emphasis, in those early days, on the "untold."

In her role advising Metro on how to develop victim coverage, the challenge was finding an approach that would speak to readers and reduce what she calls the "abstraction" of so many deaths all at once. She tried to plan something, but there was little time. The first thoughts of something like "Portraits of Grief," though not yet by that name, floated to her first on the breeze that carried so many sad, desperate flyers. Posters pleading for information about the thousands missing had started to appear all over the city. A reporter did one story on the phenomenon. "I started to pick them up, and collected them next to my desk in that week," Kay recalls.

"I know people want to hear that we had this thoughtful conversation and sat in a room for three hours, and came up with this magical approach," she says. "But that is not what happened." What did happen was that the pressure built from day to day, with the thought that, "for better or worse, we had to do something about the victims." The challenge for Kay and other editors was to find the time to discuss the various options for their paper to make these victims become real people for readers and to reduce the abstraction of the still-unknown death count. "We'd steal five minutes here and five minutes there," she says. "In one stolen five minutes, it came up that thumbnail sketches had been used before." The *Times* and others had used them in writing about the 168 victims of the 1995 Oklahoma City federal-building bombing, for example. Kay thought a different approach was needed here. She discussed various alternatives with reporter Janny Scott. Previous mass-death treatments were "too telegraphic," Kay says. "They had birth date, where they went to school . . . They weren't impressionistic."

And impressionism, rather than obituary-style detail, was needed to help readers see these victims as real people. Two hundred words seemed a good length to Kay and Scott.

Kay had edited the "Public Lives" profiles that ran in the second section, where she had sought to build impressions of the subjects by using a single character element—a hobby, a passion—and building on it. "I thought one of the most successful things about them was when they luxuriated in one little tantalizing tidbit," she says. To qualify for such a public-lives study, the person, sometimes a celebrity, had to be elsewhere in the news. "The reader got a very intimate profile—

a very distinctive, often one-interview profile that made you feel like you were inside the room with them," says Kay. Maybe something like that could work. But could it be reduced to two hundred words?

The time came for a Metro meeting. "Jon laid some approaches on the table," says Kay. One was the telegraphic bio approach. "Both Janny and I thought that would be very unsatisfying and mind-numbing." Hanging over the editors was the uncertainty of the total count. "We still thought there were ten thousand to twenty thousand dead, and if the goal was to make that less abstract, the bios weren't going to do it."

There was another thought: "What if these people aren't really dead?" The profiles, whatever they were, would have to avoid the feel of an obituary. Kay was after a sense of lives, interrupted. "So we thought, 'What if you just choose one aspect of life. What if you focus on this one woman gardening, one man taking his daughter to ice-skating lessons, or maybe smoking cigars?" Indeed, the definition of the new profile approach grew as much from what it would *not* be. "These are not obits, and this is not about death. This is not about professional achievement. These are not people who would ordinarily appear in the *New York Times* obituary page."

The editors' thinking about a style for the profiles began to take on the feel of a mission to Kay—to design something that would work with the overall coverage approach evolving around them. That coverage reflected "a level playing field," she says. "People who were in the upper echelons of these [investment] trading groups were to be treated in the same way as the dishwashers at Windows on the World."

It was Friday morning, September 14. "I grabbed this bunch of missing posters, which was really handy because they had photographs on them, and I took Janny Scott and five other reporters into Jon Landman's office," according to Kay. "It was very important that they happened to be some of the best reporters in the place. We divided up the posters and they went at it."

On Saturday the first series of mini-profiles—not yet "Portraits"—ran under the heading "After the Attacks: Among the Missing." Below that was the kicker line "The Names," and below that was another headline: "Snapshots of Their Lives with Family and at Work." These paragraphs introduced the first day's collection:

> It has been four days since the World Trade Center was destroyed. Thousands of people who were in the towers at the time are assumed to be dead. But the official body count stands at 124, and the medical examiner has identified only a few dozen victims. It could be months before many of those killed can be officially confirmed dead.

In the meantime, there is the interminable registry of the missing, nearly 5,000 people whose friends and families have reported their names to the police in the hope that they are alive. With each passing day, those hopes grow dimmer. They are fathers, daughters, fiancés and best friends. Bond traders, boxing aficionados and chefs. People expecting babies, planning their weddings, hoping for promotions. Firefighters and police officers who raced to the scene after the first jet crashed. And people who set off for work on a dazzling September morning and met with something unimaginably horrible. Here are glimpses of some of those lives.

The next day, September 16, the rubric "Portraits of Grief" made its first appearance over the profiles. The top half of the page was devoted to a picture layout of the posters; below was the text.

Who had come up with the "Portraits" name? Lots of ideas were bandied about, all avoiding use of "the dead." With the posters in mind, Howell Raines had tossed out "The Street Art of Despair." It was a starting point. As desk editors used the typical process of free association, the word "portraits" seemed to stick, and variations like Portraits of Despair, Portraits of Sorrow, Portraits of Mourning, Portraits of Grief, and Portraits of Loss made the rounds. Recalling the process in an in-house newsletter, Patrick LaForge, then an assistant Metro editor on the night shift, said he flipped "a mental coin" and made Portraits of Grief the front-runner. "I wasn't in love with the phrase, but I figured we could change it." The next day was his day off, so LaForge suggested in an e-mail to the editor on the desk the next night that he think up something else. "Then I went for a bicycle ride, fell and broke my thumb," wrote LaForge. He was in the emergency room, and missed the editor's reply. Things had been so hectic in the newsroom that editors had just continued using "Portraits of Grief."

Birth of "A Nation Challenged"

Well into the first week after the attacks, managing editor Boyd maintained the office meeting routine. It was built around four daily news sessions, with one devoted to layout. But it quickly became clear that the A-book format wouldn't work for the long haul. "We were throwing ads out of the A-book at considerable cost to the paper, so the issue became how long do we want to do this," he said. Advertisers paid up to $100,000 a page for the A-book. There were no notes from the *Times* business side or from the publisher, but editors were aware of the costs, and began looking for an alternative that could be applied right away.

"What was obvious was the need for stories to be packaged together," Boyd said. And a fifth section couldn't be added, because the *Times* had a physical limit of four sections capable of carrying the prior day's news. Besides the normal *Times* A section—including foreign and national coverage—there was a separate Metro section, Sports section, and a fourth section that varied according to day (Science on Tuesdays, for example).

As war began raging in Afghanistan and other reports with ties to 9/11 sprouted around the globe, the nation, and the nation's largest city, the range of stories was vast. Having space for it all was vital. "We wanted an open section—a section without ads—so that we could present the most impressive displays," said Boyd. "The question became what section do we do this in." As the masthead editors met, there was a huge if unspoken worry: If "A Nation Challenged" ended up sharing an editor's section, that editor could lose a front page to the new report.

A brainstorm by *Times* assistant managing editor Tom Bodkin, though, solved the problem of "losing" the page. He proposed that Sports and Metro share a section, but in a peculiar way. Sports would keep its "front" on the back page of Metro—upside down, so that readers would have to flip the section and read toward the center. With that minor adjustment, Sports and Metro readers had their accustomed front pages, while "A Nation Challenged" stood alone, devoid of ads, with two-page spreads for display inside.

On the first Monday after 9/11—the regular meeting day for Boyd and Raines with the publisher—they showed a mock-up of the section to Sulzberger. It was a hit. The section heading, "A Nation Challenged," had been proposed by veteran assistant managing editor Allan M. Siegal. As Siegal recalls it, "I scribbled a few possible section rubrics on a scrap of paper and caught Howell Raines on his way out of the office and asked him to choose." "A Nation Challenged" had been Siegal's favorite, too, he says.

In determining the mix of stories in the newly named section, the guiding principle was to augment and complement what was appearing on page one. "We looked at the stories we had fronted. Then we thought about the front of 'A Nation Challenged,' and how we could use that to make different points journalistically," said Boyd. The approach accommodated each wrinkle as the nature of this gigantic story morphed—war in Afghanistan, anthrax-laced mail, the flow of local profiles. The new section gave editors an accepted alternative to use. Without the section, a major article would probably start with five column-inches on page one and jump inside. Did writers resent losing that front-page display, and instead seeing their stories fronted on "A Nation Challenged"? "There may have been that feeling in the beginning," Boyd said, "but not later on."

No single editor ever ran "A Nation Challenged." Boyd calls the section "a collaboration of numerous editors," over which he and Raines retained the final say.

Besides "Portraits"—the purview of the Metro staff—a feature approach that was Raines's invention took root within "A Nation Challenged." Described by staffers as "all known thought," this journalism form allowed significant issues to be featured in a special, cerebral way. "'Portraits' spoke to the heart and All Known Thought spoke to the mind," according to Boyd. "It proved especially valuable because it became an anchor, and it allowed us to spend a day exploring an issue, like a history of al Qaeda, and produce a comprehensive story that explains it." With all the open pages, the third "anchor" became art—large, well-packaged photos that told a story all by themselves. That the *Times* ended up winning Pulitzers both for Breaking News Photography and Feature Photography was an indication of that success.

A Portrait of "Portraits"

As a daily facet of the section, "Portraits of Grief" took on a life of its own. While missing posters still prompted some vignettes, gradually employee lists from companies at the World Trade Center, and lists of firefighters and police, became available for reporters to use in assembling the profiles. The size of the operation grew. "It became this huge machine. We had ten to thirteen reporters working on it nonstop," says Kay.

Reporters volunteered to contribute, some even coming from Washington to play a part. The items' short length was deceptive. Emotion aside—and it rarely was—they were hard to write. "They were exhausting and absolutely overreported," says Kay, noting that often multiple sources were consulted to get the information right. "There was no glamour here. It was something you didn't have a byline on." Instead, writers' names appeared in a credit box, not even connected to a particular portrait. Yet 143 reporters participated in the project, some for a day or two, others through much of its fifteen-week run.

Subscribers from around the country turned to "A Nation Challenged" first thing after the paper arrived. Or last. One of the many readers who wrote to the *Times* in praise of "Portraits" said she could not drop off to sleep at night without having read them. Jeff Bray of Sioux Falls, South Dakota, wrote: "Nothing—and I mean NOTHING—I have ever read in my life has moved me as much as these riveting windows into the lives of ordinary people." At least one client of the New York Times News Service, the *Oregonian* in faraway Portland, ran "Portraits" in their entirety.

Christine Kay summarizes the feature as delivering this message: "My God, New Yorkers are just like the rest of us. They take their kids ice-skating, and they like Bart Simpson, and they play soccer. Those New Yorkers, they're really Americans."

Still, as one of its editors, Kay did hear complaints—from relatives of those featured in the columns. "Some were upset that we weren't talking about more traditional things," she says. "We weren't talking about the accomplishments, but things that they perceived to be trivial or prosaic. Or a mother was upset that we took what the daughter-in-law remembered, or vice versa." Editors would explain that the idea had been to focus more "on the passion than the professional accomplishment."

Most were moved by the collective power of "Portraits," however. Wrote Howell Raines in his foreword to the book *Portraits 9/11/01:* "These lives, bundled together so randomly into a union of loving memory by those terrible cataclysms of September 11, remind us of what Walt Whitman knew: 'The United States themselves are essentially the greatest poem.'" Metro editor Landman "resisted any suggestion that we abandon our rhythm of a page or two pages every day until the end of 2001." Raines added:

> Among the reporters, another kind of democracy—the democracy of craftsmanship—came into play. Often, on so huge a story as the World Trade Center disaster, the writing of shorter pieces falls to younger reporters. On the "Portraits" project, it became an emblem of pride to join in the largely anonymous labor of creating these pieces; some of our most senior correspondents insisted on participating.

From an editor's view, there were some rules to consider. "We tried never to mention that day," says Kay. Balance was important from item to item. "You certainly didn't want too many Bart Simpson lovers and too many cigar-smoking stockbrokers in the same day." To help achieve balance without being "formulaic," as she puts it, a large backlog of portraits was collected in the first month, and then grouped to be run.

"It was the ultimate group effort," says Kay, who is still stunned by how the "Portraits" came together. It was a group effort, that is, in every case but one.

In a bizarre footnote, disgraced *Times* reporter Jayson Blair was later to become entwined with "Portraits of Grief"—even though he had not written a single vignette. In the report prepared by the *New York Times* analyzing Blair's errors during his time at the paper before he was discovered in 2002 to be fabricating articles, it was disclosed that he had begged off doing assignments for "Portraits." A cousin of his had died in the Pentagon bombing, he said. It turned out, however, that the cousin had been another of Blair's fabrications. "It's too ugly to even go there," says Kay, who does not like to talk about Blair. (Blair resigned after his false reporting was revealed.)

David Barstow was on the team assigned to look into Blair's record at the newspaper, and thus learned early about the invented cousin. "That tidbit about Jayson hit a very deep nerve inside this building," Barstow says.

"Blair gamed that situation," was how Gerald Boyd put it. "At the publisher's insistence, we put together a list of all *Times* employees throughout the building, to find out who had lost relatives in the attacks. And it was in that sense we were told about Jayson." The *Times* treated employees who had lost loved ones compassionately, and Blair benefited—especially when he started being caught in a series of reporting mistakes, and was given special treatment because of his supposed loss of a cousin. In the wake of the Blair plagiarism scandal, Boyd and Howell Raines both resigned from the *Times* in June 2003. (Boyd, fifty-six, died of complications from lung cancer in November 2006, a few months after being interviewed for this book.)

While the Gold Medal was among the record seven Pulitzers garnered by the *Times* that year, the celebration among editors and staffers was muted. "I had very mixed feelings," said Boyd. "I had seen firsthand the extraordinary job that the staff of the *Times* had done. I knew how difficult it was on people. I knew reporters who lost friends in the Twin Towers. I knew of people who had been down in Battery Park when the Towers collapsed and barely survived. And I knew of people who went to Afghanistan for us and had incredible medical problems that they're probably still trying to deal with." Still, "I also felt that the world had changed in a fundamental way. And so in that sense, all of this was more than just journalism. It wasn't about prizes."

For Christine Kay, there was less conflict. "You want to know my personal thoughts? I wish they'd cancelled the Pulitzers. Certainly one felt good about the effort and how 'Portraits' became this national touchstone. But I think everyone would rather not be standing there at all."

While few newspapers will ever confront a challenge like 9/11 and its aftermath, many will face the shock of a sudden community crisis that requires total staff commitment at a moment's notice—whether a raging storm, a horrific accident, or a major crime. In such instances, "A Nation Challenged" may offer some lessons. "Editors should understand that inspiration comes from a lot of different places, and you've got to have a mechanism that encourages people," said Boyd. The section and its "Portraits" feature served to inspire staffers, just as it inspired readers. "I was always amazed how on a given day, someone I never would have thought of would have a brilliant idea. There was really a belief that people could be heard."

In his mind, the *Times*'s performance also underscores the value of avoiding the kinds of severe retrenchments that weaken a staff's ability to react to major events. "As executives and editors try to balance the cost of good journalism with the need for profits, they should think about a couple of things," according to Boyd. When "A Nation Challenged" began, "the circulation of the newspaper went up a hundred thousand copies. The public was saying, If you are relevant, if you are trying to address things we care about, and if you are doing it in a way that provides quality, we'll come along."

2002—*New York Times:* For "A Nation Challenged," a special section published regularly after the September 11 terrorist attacks on America, which coherently and comprehensively covered the tragic events, profiled the victims, and tracked the developing story, locally and globally.

Tuesday, September 18, 2001, the first day the "A Nation Challenged" section ran in the *New York Times*. Used by permission.

The *Times*'s "Portraits of Grief" label first appeared on September 16. The series rarely mentioned the World Trade Center in talking about the lives of the victims of 9/11. Used by permission.

New York Times managing editor Gerald Boyd steps to the microphone with publisher Arthur O. Sulzberger's encouragement on the day of the 2002 Pulitzer Prize announcements. To the right, executive editor Howell Raines looks on. Others present include Jonathan Landman (behind Boyd) and, next to him, Thomas Friedman. Photo by the *New York Times.*

CHAPTER 5

Epiphany in Boston

In fact, the investigative staff of the *Boston Globe* has done the Catholic Church an enormous favor. . . . They were the good guys, the guys in the white hats as opposed to the bad guys in the red hats.

—Father Andrew M. Greeley

*B*y the end of October 2001, work on the Catholic Church story—shelved while *Boston Globe* Spotlight Team members threw themselves into projects stemming from the September 11 terrorist attacks—could wait no longer.

Team leader Walter Robinson was burning to follow up on the meeting he had had with two secret sources less than a week before 9/11. The session had yielded thirty-five or so names of priests, and his sources suggested that the Church had been making widespread use of private settlements to avoid the embarrassment of lawsuits filed by victims. Robinson talked with Ben Bradlee Jr. The decision was made to resume.

Just as suddenly as the work had stopped five weeks before, Spotlight Team members Matt Carroll, Mike Rezendes, and Sacha Pfeiffer rejoined Robinson on the case. They refreshed the suspect-priest database and picked up the pieces of interviews abruptly interrupted a month earlier. When they broke off the reporting they had been investigating the Church story along two tracks. The first involved developing the already long list of priests who were objects of abuse allegations, and learning how and why the Church allowed accused priests to stay in parish work while often paying parents of victims to keep them from pursuing lawsuits. The second track followed John Geoghan, the defrocked priest whose trial for sexually abusing children was approaching in January.

The Church directories, a major contributor to Matt Carroll's database, con-

72

tinued to provide good leads. A priest listed as having been placed on sick leave "became a person of interest to us and we went through every directory for every year to chart his entire career," says Robinson. "We did it with every priest, and it was extremely time-consuming. It took us several weeks, and at the end of that we had a list of well over a hundred priests, including almost all of the thirty-some for whom we knew there had been secret settlements."

The database got another boost when Robinson checked out his own backyard. A Church facility that he knew of in suburban Milton—a Google satellite map showed it was three hundred yards from Robinson's home as the crow flies—had long been known as a place to warehouse priests with alcohol problems. But that was only half the story. "Some of these priests who were in residence at this facility had been kind enough to fill in residency cards for the town of Milton," he says. And sure enough, nearly a dozen were already in the Spotlight computer, suspected of sexually abusing young parishioners.

Bradlee was encouraged about the interviews and the backlog of data coming together along the two tracks. He had been Metropolitan editor in 1992, when the last big Church sexual-abuse case had broken, involving Fall River's Father James Porter. Bradlee had felt that there was a lot more to the Porter story than the *Globe* had been able to report. He wanted the Geoghan story to say more about the prevalence of pedophilia in the Church, if possible, and how the hierarchy was dealing with it. The Porter story "hit the wall" because there was little evidence to support the claims of victims, Bradlee felt. In that case, too, the lawsuits had been sealed at the Church's request. "What was missing there was the paper," Bradlee says. "There were a bunch of plaintiffs who had gotten together and threatened to sue, but no suits."

Lack of documentation would not handicap the Geoghan story for long.

"He Knew!"

While Massachusetts Judge Constance Sweeney was considering the *Globe*'s request to unseal the Geoghan records, attorney Mitchell Garabedian found a way to make public—seal or no seal—some damning information about how the Church had protected the priest. And Mike Rezendes, once again absorbed in his self-described obsession with finding Church documents, quickly got a payoff for the close bond he had built with Garabedian and his clients.

The lawyer reminded the *Globe* reporter of the slovenly Paul Newman character in the movie *The Verdict*. "You would go into his crappy little office and there'd be no receptionist, and cardboard boxes overflowing with documents and empty Styrofoam coffee cups. The place was a mess," Rezendes says. He believed that

Garabedian appreciated the sensitivity Rezendes showed when talking with clients who were abuse victims. But the reporter was working the lawyer, too. "I tried to romance him and be the best friend he ever had," Rezendes says. "It's kind of an art form, getting people to tell you things. And it's as important as finding documents."

It was working. To get Rezendes the critical documents that both men wanted public, the lawyer attached them to a formal response that he was making to a filing by Church lawyers. In a sealed case, attorneys are allowed to file unsealed attachments in specific instances. A document to support such a formal response is one such case.

As Rezendes sat in the Spotlight office looking through this windfall, one of Garabedian's attachments "just exploded in my mind." It was a 1984 letter from Bishop John d'Arcy to Archbishop Bernard Law—still a few months from being elevated to cardinal—warning him about Geoghan's "history of homosexual involvement with young boys," and noting that the parish to which he was being assigned was already "divided and troubled" by other matters. "If something happens," Bishop d'Arcy wrote, parishioners might be "convinced that the archdiocese has no concern for their welfare and simply sends them priests with problems."

Rezendes was stunned. "All Law's public statements to that date were that we didn't know that much about pedophilia. It was that kind of response." Sitting upright in the Spotlight office as he read the letter, "I said to myself—I think out loud—He knew!"

Rezendes also noted in one of the Church directories that in 1984 Geoghan had been reassigned to a parish in Weston, where one of his duties was working with altar boys. "At that point I knew this was a monumental evil that we were dealing with," Rezendes says. "As a story, it was going to be huge."

Technically, the documents Garabedian had filed were just as available to the rival *Boston Herald,* the *Phoenix,* or others in the press. But Rezendes believed that the court file for the Geoghan case—covering eighty-four separate lawsuits against the former priest—was so overwhelming that the competition would not be able to find the meaty unsealed material on their own, let alone make sense of their part in the overall case. And he was confident that the lawyer would not tell other reporters. So rather than prepare a spot story, Rezendes proposed that the documents become part of Spotlight's plan for publishing a major feature on the Geoghan case. The plan was for the Spotlight feature to run no matter what happened in the final court ruling on the *Globe's* challenge to the sealing of the documents. Rezendes guessed right; the paper would be first to use the d'Arcy letter.

Meanwhile, the effort by Albano to unseal the entire Geoghan file also was advancing without the competition taking much note. On November 20, Judge

Sweeney delivered a bombshell to the archdiocese—he ruled in favor of the newspaper. The Church appealed, but a month later, on December 21, it lost the appeal as well. The release of ten thousand pages associated with all those Geoghan suits was scheduled for late January, roughly two weeks after the trial's projected start date. The next strategy of Church lawyers was to write a letter threatening the *Globe* with legal action if it published material taken from records that were still confidential. Indeed, the letter said, sanctions would be sought even for asking questions of the priests involved.

The Spotlight Team proceeded undeterred, following the pedophile priest story along its two tracks: the Geoghan path and the trail of the secret settlements. The latter was the team's priority. Evidence of the multiple settlements that Robinson had unearthed, and that the team's reporting had confirmed and expanded, gave the lie to the Church's longstanding position that the problem was narrow and undeserving of attention from either the press or the archdiocese.

In mid-December, though, Bradlee ordered a shift in the planning for the stories. With the Geoghan trial approaching, he moved the settlements story to the back burner and aimed Spotlight's primary resources at preparing a curtain-raiser. The story would spell out what Spotlight knew about the Geoghan case, and the role played by Cardinal Law in keeping him in circulation. Envisioned originally as a single three-thousand-word piece, the Geoghan coverage soon took on a life of its own. Certainly, there was too much powerful material for a single pretrial story. The paper set January 6 and 7 as target dates for a two-part series. As Matt Carroll's database continued to burgeon, it was about to become a hot January for Spotlight.

A Clerk, a Court, and a Clicking Clock

Just after New Year's Day, Rezendes got another break thanks to Garabedian. While the actual court-ordered unsealing of the Geoghan court documents was still three weeks away—a delay to allow for the documents to be "redacted" for release, with victims' names removed, for example—Garabedian quietly told Rezendes about some *new* Church documents to be filed the next Friday, January 4. Under terms of the state court order lifting the seal, new filings were immediately to become public. The documents sounded most intriguing. They included psychiatric notes on Geoghan and statements the priest had made to doctors, and they contained material that the Church had weighed, and rejected, in deciding to reassign him to other parishes. In addition, some actual, detailed claims against Geoghan were in the files. If the *Globe* could get the documents before the competition did—and if Garabedian had not told the *Herald* and *Phoenix* of his Friday filing plans—the *Globe* would have a pretrial exclusive that would enhance the first Spotlight stories significantly. It would put much of the past several months' reporting in a meaningful context.

The timing seemed to work, though just barely. The Sunday story on January 6 would concentrate on the question of why it had taken thirty-four years, and a succession of three cardinals and many bishops, to place children out of Geoghan's reach. The Monday story would liberally use the documents that Garabedian was to file on Friday. It would offer a timeline of Geoghan's abuses and provide shocking details of just how he turned the children in his care into his victims.

Incorporating notes from his teammates, Rezendes started drafting the Sunday story in advance for Spotlight editor Robinson to edit. It would run with all four team members identified in a byline box, and Rezendes listed as writer. "Our plan," Rezendes says, "was to get these documents, go over them, and work all weekend." Sacha Pfeiffer would write the Monday piece. To get the promised copies of the documents Garabedian filed on Friday, Rezendes and Carroll would show up at the court clerk's office at 4:15 p.m., forty-five minutes short of closing time. The reporters planned to get them from the clerk, quickly copy them, and head back to Morrissey Boulevard to help crash out the two-parter. These would be the first Spotlight stories to appear since the Church project was authorized five months earlier.

But suddenly, maddeningly, the courtroom clockwork took on the misshapen quality of a Salvador Dali painting. "What I didn't realize was that nobody knew we'd won our case," he says. The favorable ruling just before Christmas—and the effect it had of making all newly filed Geoghan documents instantly a matter of public record—seemed foreign to the court clerk. As the minute hand sped south, she refused to make them available.

"I believe in pampering clerks, so I very politely asked if there was someone else I could speak to," Rezendes recalls. "Yes there was, but it took a while to get her supervisor to the counter, and the clock was clicking very loudly here." The supervisor, also unaware that the filings should be open, had a suggestion: Tell it to the judge.

Off the two Spotlight reporters went to the chambers of the Honorable Vierra Volterra—"whose name I will never forget," Rezendes says—cooling their heels briefly in the jury box of an adjacent courtroom while he became available. "It was getting close to 5 o'clock. Matt and I went in to talk to him, and he had the documents on his desk. He said, 'These are very sensitive documents.' And I said, Yes, judge, they are. And he said to me, 'Where is the editorial responsibility in publishing these documents?'"

Rezendes tried not to sigh too noticeably. "I didn't believe I was going to have to get into a philosophical conversation with this judge." But by then, word had gotten to Robinson to rush a fax of the appeals-court order to the courthouse. As Rezendes explained how responsible the *Globe* intended to be, the court clerk reappeared, fax in hand. "To his credit, the judge glanced at the appeals court ruling and just said, 'Yep, that's it. You can have it.'" After then managing to get the clerk to stay forty-five minutes late so Rezendes and Carroll could copy the documents—"We thanked her profusely," says Rezendes—the reporters grabbed a cab back to the *Globe*. Their long weekend was just beginning.

At the chancery, Cardinal Law had been asked weeks before to provide the Church's side of the Geoghan story to the *Globe,* beyond the position it had taken in court. The cardinal had been silent. Now, told that an article was within a day or two of running, he called Baron directly to tell him that there would be no comment. He didn't even care to see the questions the *Globe* offered to fax him.

Down in the Spotlight office, the focus was on writing and editing stories over a nonstop weekend. Drafts went from Robinson to Bradlee, and then across the newsroom to Baron's office.

Robinson was impressed with what Baron sent back down to Spotlight. "Marty is a very quick, astute editor," he says. "I have a memory on that first story that it was three or four thousand words, and Marty came back in about a half-hour's time with a dozen fairly critical questions, including things that had not been addressed." Robinson saw Baron's repair work as reflecting the time Baron had spent as night editor at the *New York Times*. There, he had been the editor assigned to call reporters at home, often during the dinner hour, to interrupt their evenings with discussions about last-minute fixes.

"The stories I received were excellent; the reporting was superb. Standard practice for editing: That's what I did," says Baron. "I'm accustomed to getting long, complex stories late in the process." His main role, he says, was to "look for holes, watch for tone, language, readability, inconsistencies, or anything that might raise questions about our credibility or objectivity."

On Sunday, the Feast of the Epiphany in the Church calendar, *Globe* readers had an epiphany of their own. The story that morning ran on page one under the headline "Church Allowed Abuse by Priest for Years; Aware of Geoghan Record, Archdiocese Still Shuttled Him from Parish to Parish":

> Since the mid-1990s, more than 130 people have come forward with horrific childhood tales about how former priest John J. Geoghan allegedly fondled or raped them during a three-decade spree through a half-dozen Greater Boston parishes.
>
> Almost always, his victims were grammar school boys. One was just 4 years old.

Then came last July's disclosure that Cardinal Bernard F. Law knew about Geoghan's problems in 1984, Law's first year in Boston, yet approved his transfer to St. Julia's parish in Weston. Wilson D. Rogers Jr., the cardinal's attorney, defended the move last summer, saying the archdiocese had medical assurances that each Geoghan reassignment was "appropriate and safe."

But one of Law's bishops thought that the 1984 assignment of Geoghan to St. Julia's was so risky, he wrote the cardinal a letter in protest. And for good reason, the Spotlight Team found: the archdiocese already had substantial evidence of Geoghan's predatory sexual habits.

The front-page article jumped to two pages inside the paper, quoting from Bishop d'Arcy's 1984 challenge to Law's decision to move Geoghan to another parish. There was also one woman's "poignant and prophetic" 1982 letter to Cardinal Law's predecessor "expressing incredulity that the church to which she was devoted would give Geoghan another chance"—after he had molested seven children in her family. A powerful interview with a victim, twenty-six-year-old Patrick McSorley, vividly detailed Geoghan's abuse of him as a twelve-year-old, and said that to "find out later that the Catholic Church knew he was a child molester—every day it bothers me more and more."

Monday's story ran under the headline, "Geoghan Preferred Preying on Poorer Children," and included descriptions in Geoghan's own words, explaining why he was "affectionate" with certain children. It laid out the psychiatric debate about the priest, again all from Church records, for readers to evaluate. A timeline pieced together from the records recounted multiple complaints, filed with various Church leaders from 1962 to 1995, by parents who reported the molestation of their children. For the most part, the complaints were met with inaction, or resulted in Geoghan being transferred to other parishes, ultimately to rape and molest more youths.

Both stories carried a "Contact the *Globe*" box with the Spotlight telephone number, a separate confidential hotline, and an e-mail address. The hot line was to get a lot of use—and almost none of it the carping about an "anti-Catholic" bias that many staffers had expected.

Indeed, Mike Rezendes feared that he would come into work to a demonstration at the door. "This is, after all, the most Catholic city in America," he says. Instead he encountered "an eerie quiet—no protestors, nothing." Then all at once, it seemed, the lines clogged with calls of an unexpected kind: "People were incredibly angry, yes. But not at us. It was at this institution that they loved." Or they called to report new cases of abuse. Checking the names of priests the callers named, Spotlight found that nearly all were mentioned already in its now-bulging database.

"Looking back, I believe the reason for not blaming the messenger was that we had the goods," Rezendes says. "We did not use anonymous sources. It was irrefutable. It was completely locked tight. There wasn't a fact in it that was wrong." And the documents, either quoted in the article or put online in their entirety, "were riveting and appalling."

As the new editor who was ultimately responsible, Marty Baron breathed a sigh of relief. Another followed when the usually combative Cardinal Law held a press conference a few days later. Far from attacking the *Globe,* the cardinal actually apologized to his flock. "It was clear that our stories were uncontestable, because he didn't contest anything," the editor says. "There was no fact that he challenged. And that alone added enormous weight to our coverage." Other newspapers around the country, seeing the Church's apologetic response, not only carried stories of the Boston paper's disclosures but also slowly began launching investigations of their own local parishes.

The *Globe* stories had been written and edited to display what Baron calls "a highly dispassionate tone," even at times "deadpan." The intention was to unburden the stories of any language that even hinted at an agenda. "We knew as a fact that the story would be explosive enough," he says. "If we started characterizing it, and using highly descriptive terms and adjectives, then that itself was going to become a target. There was no purpose served in turning over ammunition to people." Spotlight reporters would eventually adopt that tone on their own.

Robinson later hinted that Baron had done at least his share of toning down the final drafts, though. "Somewhere within sight of this newsroom," he was to joke the day the Pulitzer Prize was announced, "there has to be a closet-full of adjectives he excised from these stories."

"This Is Different"

Globe investigative specialist Stephen Kurkjian, a former Spotlight Team member, had recently been more of a "lone wolf," engaged in one-man projects for projects editor Bradlee. Kurkjian, especially, was stunned by what the team had come up with in its first take-out on Geoghan. "I read the story in Sunday's paper and I said, 'This is different,'" he intones in his own attempt at deadpan. For Kurkjian, the observation had a deeper meaning, since he himself had led the paper's last deep dive into the issue of sexual abuse by priests—the 1992 stories about Father Porter in the Fall River diocese. Kurkjian could see that the Church's own documents, liberally referenced in the first two stories, confirmed how much Cardinal Law and others knew of Geoghan's rampant child abuse in the 1980s, and that they had ignored candid warnings from Church subordinates and parents of victimized children. As Ben Bradlee had intended, the documentary evidence took these new stories to a level beyond what had been possible with the Porter stories. "The Geoghan case shook everyone up and gave them the confidence that victims could speak up and be believed," Kurkjian says. "That wasn't the case in 1992." Neither was it clear back then whether the Church was actively involved in relocating the priest to avoid a scandal. "We did two or three stories about how Porter had been moved around from one place to another, but you didn't have the hierarchy involved."

Three days later, after Kurkjian saw Cardinal Law's press conference, the reporter became even more fascinated at the new dynamic between the paper and the Church. "I had thought, he's going to be a tiger, talking about how anti-Catholic the *Globe* is." Why wasn't the cardinal his old self? Kurkjian asked Bradlee, his immediate boss. The explanation: "The story was so tight that the cardinal couldn't deny it."

There was no time to rest on laurels. The Geoghan trial was three weeks away, and the week before it opened, the ten thousand pages of unexamined court documents were due to inundate the *Globe*. Spotlight felt it had to stay ahead of its rivals, who all would have access on the same schedule. In addition, nothing had run yet on the story that once had been the team's prime target: the secret settlements that the Church had signed to protect so many other priests.

In preparation for the flood of Geoghan documents, Robinson managed to get the first of four additional Spotlight reporters who would be assigned for the duration of the Church stories. It was Kurkjian.

The veteran investigator had had one question before saying yes to the job. "My fear was that I was going to have to go digging deeper and deeper into Geoghan," he says. Kurkjian was eager to be involved only if Spotlight was targeting other abusive priests. "Robby said to me, 'There's lots more.' Would you be interested?' So after working out a schedule with Bradlee, I said, sure, let me give it a chase." Eventually, one of his specialties would become the serious financial threat to the Church posed by the tens of millions of dollars sought in lawsuits, and by the waning support for Cardinal Law among the wealthy Catholic laity—which was not unrelated to the money crisis. By next December 1, Robinson and Kurkjian would be writing a page-one story headlined, "Archdiocese Weighs Bankruptcy Filing."

But first, there was the crunch on the Geoghan case. A January 24 front-page story, written by Robinson and Matt Carroll, with Kurkjian joining the team names in the credit box, contained a penetrating analysis of the volumes of documents in the Geoghan case. The story was an exclusive; the paper had gotten documents a day ahead of the general release. Robinson says the team talked Garabedian into providing material early. That "beat" on its rivals reinforced the sense that the paper was invincible on the Church coverage.

The next *Globe* blockbuster—on Thursday, January 31—was the long-awaited piece on the secret settlements that the Church had signed, covering an estimated seventy or more priests. Headlined "Scores of Priests Involved in Sex Abuse Cases; Settlements Kept Scope of Issue Out of Public Eye," the article was accompanied by thumbnails on twenty-three accused priests. The paper described the database that the *Globe* had assembled, and how the Church's own directories had tipped the paper to suspected molesters.

Running as an inside sidebar was Sacha Pfeiffer's harrowing tale of Father Paul Shanley and some of his victims from long ago in Boston. It began:

> Handsome and charismatic, he wore his hair long, growing thick sideburns and shedding his Roman collar for plaid shirts and jeans. He openly questioned church teachings, particularly its condemnation of homosexuality, clashing often and publicly with his superiors . . . .
>
> He espoused radical views in a city deeply wedded to tradition, and his was a voice of defiance in an institution where obedience is sacred. Known as Boston's street priest in the 1960s and '70s, he created a "ministry to alienated youth" for runaways, drug abusers, drifters, and teenagers struggling with their sexual identity.
>
> But in the parishes and counseling rooms where desperate and troubled young people sought his help, the Rev. Paul R. Shanley was a sexual predator. In interviews with four people who said they were abused by Shanley, as well as their families and lawyers who have settled at least three sexual abuse claims against him with the Archdiocese of Boston, the same stories repeatedly emerged: rape, molestation, and coerced sex in which Shanley used his power and authority to prey on those who came to him for guidance and support.

By then Pfeiffer was already toning down her prose to reflect the direction from above to be careful with inflammatory words. "We learned to do that ourselves," she says. "We were aware how delicate this situation was." Still, she remembers losing a few words to Robinson's editing. "It was probably a little overdramatic in my original," she says. "I had had something in there about his being 'one of the most egregious offenders.'" Since that was obvious in the charges, Robinson excised it. "It was just a little too much," Pfeiffer now agrees.

Her reporting style drew out victims to tell their stories in intimate detail. It awed other Spotlight members, who all were facing extraordinary challenges in the victim interviews that were increasingly becoming vital to the coverage now.

In a way, she helped make it harder for herself and her teammates, she acknowledges, by pushing for explicit language to describe what had gone on between priests and their victims. "You couldn't just continually use the word molest, because this meant a world of things. And it was important for readers to understand in more detail what had happened," she says.

That put Pfeiffer in the position of pressing victims to detail the sex acts that the priest forced on them—an uncomfortable position for interviewee and interviewer alike. "You're dealing with a very delicate issue with very fragile people, but sometimes you would need to be firm with them," she says. "You need very specific kinds of information about what happened to them sexually, because you need to figure out if this was a rape case, or touching—if you're talking about criminal allegations."

She took to spending extra time explaining why she was asking such detailed questions. "It's invasive," she says. "So I would be very open and say, I'm sorry to have to ask this; I know it's very personal, but I need to understand what exactly happened, because I need to understand if it's a criminal act. Sometimes you'd have to hold your breath a little bit as you asked the questions." The answers often knocked her over.

Pfeiffer also was worried that readers simply would disbelieve such sordid truths. "Some people were resistant to the idea that a kid could be repeatedly molested by a priest. They thought that if something happened repeatedly, that meant it was consensual," she says. "We needed to explain to them how it was possible, how the psychology works, how a friendship can be very carefully turned into a sexual relationship." A manipulative power figure could do it, and it was important for readers to understand how even a child who sensed that something was not right could be persuaded to keep doing it.

Pfeiffer and other Spotlight reporters found themselves almost in a counseling role, something they were not trained for. But she feels proud of the sensitivity that reporters displayed toward all sides, and especially the concern that came through in the victims' stories. (It was concern that would continue long past the winning of the 2003 Pulitzer Prize. On August 23, 2003, Geoghan was murdered in his prison cell. And Patrick McSorley, a Geoghan victim identified early in the *Globe* coverage, later committed suicide.)

If Robinson had one complaint about the way the *Globe* dealt with this multidimensional story, he says, it was the slowness with which reporters were added to Spotlight. "We were working sixteen-hour days and weekends. The phone wouldn't stop ringing." And the newly public Geoghan papers were an avalanche. "We went through that first month, and certainly through the huge Geoghan 'document dump,' with just the four of us." Kurkjian had reported for duty on the day the ten thousand pages of records arrived.

Reporters Kevin Cullen and Thomas Farragher joined at the end of January. They hit the ground running. Among Farragher's contributions was a February 3 study of the Church's "culture of silence" in dealing with sexual abuse among priests. Cullen's contributions included a May 12 analysis of how the scandal was eroding the traditional deference that many Catholics had for their Church.

As personal as the issue of priest abuse was for reporters on the Spotlight Team who had been raised Catholic, it was especially so for Farragher, himself a former altar boy. "My mother thinks priests walk on water," he says. One day he was at home with her when his sister brought news that their own family priest—the clergyman who had married Farragher and his wife—had been alleged to be an abuser. (The report first appeared in the *Herald,* as it scrambled to get at least a few news crumbs against the banquet being served up by its overpowering rival.) "You build up a hard exterior and become numb to it. Then, unexpectedly, it would affect you," says Farragher. In general, he adds, the scandals "upset me more as a father than as a Catholic."

Like all good reporters, Spotlight members created a high bar for sources on all sides, making sure that the claims of the victims held up and questioning the lawyers' motives, as well as laying out cases in which Church officials turned their backs on suffering parishioners. A June 3 story headlined "Critical Eye Cast on Sex Abuse Lawyers" was written by Pfeiffer. "Some lawyers initially might have seemed heroic, because they were representing victims. But actually, many of these guys had been settling cases for years, and had this lucrative little niche. It was a cash cow," she says. "We were tough on the bishops. We were tough on the lawyers. We were tough on victims who we thought had filed false allegations." Such range also showed "that the *Globe* had no self-interest in this. We were not after the Church; we were simply printing every aspect of the story."

At times, pure pathos flowed from the *Globe's* pages. Take the February 3 story by Robinson. It began:

> Like other victims of pedophile priests, Tom remembers vividly what happened just after he was molested in a dark corridor at Immaculate Conception School in Revere by the Rev. James R. Porter. It was 1960. He was 12. But he still recalls running.
>
> He ran, and then he hid. Under a desk in a second-floor classroom, frozen in terror as Porter called out for him. And then he ran again, out of the school and home.

Chris was victimized about 12 years ago. He remembers struggling as the Rev. John J. Geoghan groped him in the rectory at St. Julia's in Weston before he squirmed out of Geoghan's grasp. As Geoghan yelled after him, "No one will ever believe you," Chris ran from the room. He ran from the rectory. He ran behind the church—and cowered there until his father came for him. Geoghan was right; Chris never said a word.

Now Tom and Chris have stopped running. Thomas R. Fulchino, the father, and Christopher T. Fulchino, his son, are victims of Massachusetts' two most notorious priest pedophiles—three decades apart. For their family, lightning struck twice.

"It was such a tragic story," the team leader says. "To sit with the father and listen to what happened to him, and how he had gradually come to trust the Church again. And then to hear what the mother had gone through when the family almost came apart again. It was a story you couldn't over-write."

Enter: The Beat Reporter

The final addition to the Spotlight crew—and a vital one as the story expanded to require more analysis about the impact on the Church—was religion reporter Michael Paulson, who had been left out of the first wave of articles. Paulson, too, had been consumed with special projects after September 11. That too had been a major story for religion reporters.

Just after the first Spotlight Church stories ran, Paulson contributed occasional stories for the scandal coverage, although his chain of command remained through the Metro desk in the upstairs newsroom. But soon it became difficult answering two masters, as he describes the arrangement. "I was trying to juggle regular religion reporting and my role in the unfolding crisis," he says. So he approached Bradlee about becoming Spotlight's eighth member, and was added to the team.

He quickly became a key participant. "One of the things that made our coverage so much more distinctive than just being investigative revelations was Mike's ability to step back and bring the whole Church into the context of the story," says Robinson. Paulson—who kept his desk upstairs in the newsroom, closer to Bradlee—soon found himself writing more scandal-related stories than anybody. He wrote about the world's view of the American Church scandal, the action of bishops against priest sexual abuse, and, on December 14, a story headlined, "A Church Seeks Healing: Pope Accepts Law's Resignation in Rome." The continuing stream of Church stories has remained a major part of his beat since Spotlight was finally pulled off the Church story in 2003.

"Lots of other religious denominations have been forced to rethink the way they prevent and handle abuse, too," Paulson notes. The national price tag of abuse settlements in 2005 had passed one billion dollars—most of that after the first *Globe* story was published. And deeper questions continued to develop for Catholicism. "I think it will be a century before we really know how it all plays out. Does the American Church become smaller? Do people simply leave? Or does the universal church change more readily than people expect? It's not on the American news cycle that the Catholic Church changes," says Paulson. "When you think about the impact of this crisis, most of it couldn't have been known to the Pulitzer Board" when it made the decision on the Prize.

But much *was* known, as Marty Baron's nomination letter for the Public Service Pulitzer noted at year-end. "By year's end, the scandal had forced the removal of four-hundred-fifty accused priests nationwide," he wrote. What had emerged, Baron pointed out, was "a nationwide pattern within the Catholic Church of concealing abuse by priests and a practice of shuffling abusive priests from parish to parish." The editor also quoted Father Andrew M. Greeley as writing that without the *Globe* accounts "the abuse would have gone right on. There would have been no crisis, no demand from the laity that the church cut out this cancer of irresponsibility, corruption, and sin, and no charter for the protection of children."

When Public Service jury chair William Ketter, editor of the Lawrence, Massachusetts, *Eagle-Tribune*, met with fellow jurors in March 2003, there was agreement that "it was the *Globe's* year in public service," he says. "It was a sort of slam dunk." There were ninety entries to review, and no major natural disasters that had put newspapers in that kind of service role. Along with the *Globe*, jurors selected Florida's *Pensacola News Journal* for a series on county-government corruption and the *Detroit News* for a series on defects in the criminal justice system.

For the Pulitzer board members who convened at Columbia, too, the Church scandal "was obviously the big news of the year," says *Oregonian* editor Sandra Mims Rowe, who was on the board. "You knew the *Globe* was going to end up being a contender long before you got to the meeting." But under the board's analysis, it was anything but automatic. In her term as a board member from 1996 to 2004, Rowe says, coverage of major stories often was faulted for flaws that turned up under intense review. "You'd see things and say, Boy, in the right hands, this could be wonderful, but the quality of the work just is not there," she says. In the *Globe's* case, though, "the caliber of the journalism and the execution were something rare."

That opinion extended far beyond the board. "In some ways, the clerical abuse scandal has become a journalism textbook. Consider the elements: power, corruption, intrigue, tragedy, sex, betrayal, money—and an institution that dates back

2,000 years," *Los Angeles Times* New England correspondent Elizabeth Mehren wrote in a study of the crisis for Nieman Reports. "The villains are despicable. Meanwhile, the proverbial quest for truth and justice—what brought us all into this line of endeavor, after all—is always at the forefront."

Like the *New York Times* award the year before, the Pulitzer board's selection of the *Globe* for the Gold Medal was hardly a surprise. On Pulitzer Monday the *Globe* staff—which for purely superstitious reasons had avoided using "the P-word," as Robinson put it—congregated in the newsroom to watch the 3 p.m. news cross the wires. Then began a forty-five-minute love fest. At the beginning of the eighteen months spent studying the claims against priests, the paper couldn't know the magnitude of the problem or the depth of the scandal, Baron said. "And now it's nine hundred stories later, and many hours of very hard work later. And now we know. We know that the Church covered up. We know that known abusers were continually placed in positions where they could abuse again. We know that victims were ignored or dismissed. We know that abusive priests were coddled. And we know this because of what was done here, in this newsroom and by our colleagues."

Baron had also learned for sure that being a New York Times Company operation did not mean losing stories to its mighty big sister, even if Times Company policy did require the *Globe* to consult corporate lawyers before planning court filings. (Later, Baron says, he was told by "insiders" that *Times* executive editor Howell Raines "was annoyed that we were onto the biggest story of the year and seemingly headed to a Pulitzer. He then put a lot of resources—think 'flood the zone' philosophy—on the story, with the hope that the *Times* could garner the national reporting Prize" while the *Globe* pursued the local story.)

"There's No Harder Target"

Just when did the *Globe* team members first sense that the story had the potential to be a blockbuster, and perhaps a recipient of the Public Service Pulitzer? Matt Carroll admits to acknowledging the prospect of a prize during the April 2002 Pulitzer announcements, when the *New York Times* and its staffers walked off with their seven awards, including the Gold Medal. "I remember thinking, Gee, I wonder if they'll be announcing our names next year," he says. "It's one of the things you dismiss, and then move ahead."

Ben Bradlee had a feeling after he observed the lack of negative reaction to the first *Globe* stories from among the Catholic community, and from Cardinal Law himself. It was then that he had told Baron that the story had hit a home run. "We struck a nerve," the projects editor says. "You never know when a story is going to have that kind of Zeitgeist." He and his famous father at the *Washington Post* checked in regularly with each other as the Church story developed, although they each say that they never compared the unfolding Church scandal to Watergate.

Comparisons of the two scandals come naturally to others. In some ways, notes Steve Kurkjian—veteran of three *Globe* Pulitzer-winning teams—the Church stories may have hit harder than Watergate, because there was little surprise that Washington politicians, even at the highest levels, would lie to protect themselves. With the Church story, "never have you had an institution with this vaunted an image taking such a blow."

The *Globe*'s reporting and the *Post*'s Watergate coverage both focused on cover-ups, Robinson adds. He believes the Church's deceit was far more troubling than the crime. "It facilitated further abuse over the years, by the same and other people," he says, "and it undermined the integrity of the institution in ways from which it will never recover."

Robinson also notes an ironic connection that arose between the Church story and the *Globe*'s last Public Service Prize, in 1975, for its coverage of school integration and busing—a story he worked on as a cub reporter at the paper. "A lot of people who were aggrieved by the *Globe*'s coverage of busing happened to be both Catholic and conservative," he says. They saw the paper as taking a pro-busing stance to promote integration in their white communities, creating "a large generation with a grudge against the *Globe*." After years of thinking the paper elitist and snobbish, many of those same critics, he believes, now credit the *Globe* with protecting innocents in the Church and cleaning house of abusive priests. "To me," Robinson says, "that's been gratifying."

From Bob Woodward comes high praise for the *Globe,* along with a warning for the media about how few other papers assume the same kinds of risks that the *Globe* and the *Post* did. "It takes a particular kind of energy and courage on the part of editors and publishers to support daily incremental coverage," Woodward says. Too many projects today involve "low-hanging fruit," subjects that reporters and readers already know are tinged with scandal. "I worry sometimes that we don't pick the really hard, important targets that have much broader implications," he adds. "That's where I take my hat off to the *Globe,* because there's no harder target than the Catholic Church."

2003—*Boston Globe*: For its courageous, comprehensive coverage of sexual abuse by priests, an effort that pierced secrecy, stirred local, national, and international reaction, and produced changes in the Roman Catholic Church.

The *Globe* began its series with this front-page article on January 6, 2002. Used by permission.

The *Globe*'s 2003 Pulitzer Gold Medal, front and reverse.
Photos by Essdras M. Suarez, *Globe* staff. Used by permission.

The *Globe*'s Spotlight team on the deck of editor Martin Baron's home. From left,
Thomas Farragher, Michael Rezendes, Kevin Cullen, Michael Paulson, Ben Bradlee Jr.,
Walter Robinson, Sacha Pfeiffer, Matt Carroll, Martin Baron, and Stephen Kurkjian.
In the background is the Cathedral of the Holy Cross, Cardinal Bernard Law's home
church in the Boston diocese. Photo by Essdras M. Suarez, *Globe* staff. Used by
permission.

CHAPTER 6

From *Times* to *Times*

It's not enough to be good at what you do. You want to be part of a team that's winning. And this was like the Red Sox beating the Yankees. Winning those Pulitzers gave them the sense that they themselves were being validated, as well as the paper.

—*Los Angeles Times* editor John Carroll, on staffers earning five 2004 Prizes to the *New York Times*'s one

As the Pulitzer Prize selection process began in 2004, another New England paper seemed hotly competitive for the Gold Medal. While there was none of that same unanimity about whether a Pulitzer would recognize the *Providence Journal*'s coverage of the Station nightclub fire in nearby West Warwick, Rhode Island—a terrifying February 2003 flash-over blaze that killed one hundred rock-concert attendees—the paper's coverage certainly seemed to have a lot going for it.

Journal executive editor Joel Rawson was proud of his Public Service entry. It showed the paper being ahead of fire officials in determining the exact level of overcrowding in the club and in establishing that the eventual victims had only 102 seconds to make an escape. The paper designed elaborate computer simulations, using news film from inside the nightclub conflagration and creating a digital program. It then coordinated survivor accounts and other information into a vivid recreation of events. In terms of impact, the stories led to regulatory changes and fire-code revisions to require sprinkler systems. "With Public Service you're supposed to demonstrate the full use of the paper's resources," says Rawson. "We certainly did that."

In March, the Pulitzer Public Service jury agreed that the *Providence Journal*'s work deserved consideration, forwarding it as a finalist to the Pulitzer board along with a *Louisville Courier-Journal* series on flaws in the Kentucky criminal justice system, and a *Seattle Times* exposé of sexual misconduct by male high school coaches. Because of the work of the Cabal—a group of journalists dedicated to spreading word about the finalists prematurely—the selection of Rawson's paper was not a secret. Part of the Cabal's philosophy is that finalists deserve "their time in the sunlight," instead of being kept confidential until the actual Pulitzer Prize announcement—when nonwinners are automatically branded as also-rans. Disclosures from the Cabal usually are made via an e-mail network and through Web sites, fostering a wave of industry rumors.

The View from Times Square

David Barstow of the *New York Times* was also following the rumor mill closely. The *Times* had entered, in both Investigative Reporting and Public Service, the workplace-safety coverage he had produced with Lowell Bergman for the paper. The *Times*'s entries focused on company safety lapses and the government's inability to deal with fatal plant accidents.

The *Times* work was not among the jury's finalists in Public Service, Barstow suspected from the rumors. That left Investigative—a tough competition based on his reading of one supposed finalist, the Toledo *Blade*'s stories about long-ago Vietnam atrocities committed by a unit called Tiger Force. Barstow was proud of his *Times* work, but the *Blade* material impressed him, too. It certainly had the look of a Pulitzer winner. He hoped that the next rumor would be a good one.

It was. When the *Times*'s own source of behind-closed-doors reports kicked in, Barstow learned that the Pulitzer board had reached into the Investigative finalist pool and picked the *Times* workplace series for the Public Service Prize. The *Providence Journal*, *Courier-Journal*, and *Seattle Times* were all finalists. Close but no champagne.

What had happened was this: During the jury deliberations, the Investigative and Public Service panels had decided between them to nominate the Barstow-Bergman *Times* entry only in Investigative, even though both juries loved the series. (Had Barstow been concentrating on the Public Service competition, that would have seemed an uphill battle, too. "If I'd read the Providence stuff, I'd have said there was no chance in hell. That work was fabulous," he says.) But as the board pondered the six finalists spread across Investigative and in Public Service, it saw the workplace-safety story as being a better fit for the Gold Medal than anything on the jury's Public Service list.

Most board members had already read the *Times* workplace reports—a "familiarity" edge the *Times* has each year—and the stories had left a strong impression.

The board then reviewed the Investigative jury's report. "Thanks to the indefatigable investigative reporting of the *New York Times,* the American public now knows that too many employers force countless workers to toil in conditions so unsafe that many consider themselves fortunate to survive the workweek," the panel wrote. "The *Times* investigation has led to widespread cries for reform; a searching government investigation of its own conduct; and has already resulted directly in several criminal indictments." While a finalist in Investigative, the story had the ring of a Public Service winner. And that is how the board voted, while selecting the *Blade* for the Investigative Prize.

Like David Barstow, Joel Rawson got the early word that none of the three jury-voted Public Service finalists would win any prize at all. Dejectedly, he prepared his staff for the Pulitzer announcements to come. It was a blue Monday in Providence. The *Journal*'s first Public Service Prize—and its first Pulitzer of any kind since 1994—would not be forthcoming for 2004.

The Pulitzer-day joy was keen in Times Square, though. Without this prize, the *Times* would have been shut out of Pulitzers for the first time since 2000. As a Gold Medal, it was special, too. The *Times*'s fifth, it tied the paper with the *St. Louis Post-Dispatch* for the most ever won by a newspaper. (The *Times*—which won Gold Medals in 1918, 1944, 1972, and 2002—had collected by far the most overall Pulitzer awards: ninety through 2003.)

The *Times*'s first three-part workplace project, a January report called "Dangerous Business," had begun with a tip received by investigative reporter Lowell Bergman. The tip had a 9/11 connection. Bergman, a former CBS *Sixty Minutes* producer/reporter who had joined the *Times* as an investigative reporter in 1999 and was jointly serving as a producer and correspondent for Public Broadcasting's *Frontline* program, had been grounded on a flight just after the terrorist attacks on New York and Washington. While waiting for flights to resume, he got to talking with a federal Justice Department source who was looking into the death of a worker at a Texas company called Tyler Pipe. A question the source asked Bergman piqued his interest: "Did you know it's only a misdemeanor to kill a worker?" The Tyler worker, Rolan Hoskin, had been crushed to death while working near an unprotected conveyor belt. Eventually, Bergman was teamed to do the three-part investigation of Tyler with Barstow, who also had come to the *Times* in 1999, and had joined its investigative desk in 2002.

At first Barstow saw the Tyler Pipe story, with the death of a single worker, as having small dimensions—at least relative to his recent assignments. "I'd spent months and months dealing with widows and widowers, and confronting mass death," he says. Not only had he reported regularly from Ground Zero and written a number of the Portraits of Grief vignettes, but he had developed a specialty:

investigating payments flowing to the 9/11 victims. "I was charting all kinds of screw-ups and inequities and other problems that plagued the entire messy process," he says.

One early interview about the workplace situation in Tyler, with an old-timer who had forty years as an iron-pourer, changed everything, though. "It was a real lightbulb moment." The man, with his forearms covered with scars, told of the pressure Tyler had been under since Birmingham-based McWane Inc. bought the plant in 1995. The company had laid off half its workforce, including maintenance employees and, critically, extra "relief" workers for men on the line in the 130-degree summer heat in the plant.

"You have to have breaks if you're going to keep the line going," Barstow says. "You need to stay hydrated, with lots of fluid, and that means lots of bathroom breaks." But with new managers cutting back on replacement workers, there were fewer breaks. "Workers couldn't leave or they'd be disciplined," the reporter says. "Many workers had no choice but to pee in their pants." Such a predicament among the husky iron-workers dramatized the situation for Barstow. Some employees would not be quoted for the record, since talking about having to urinate while on the plant floor, for example, was humiliating. Still, the number of such off-the-record reports suggested it was safe to use.

If that image drove his initial interest in the story, the broader implications of the McWane/Tyler case soon gripped him as well. Barstow and Bergman's reporting was backed by their computer-assisted analysis of the more than 200,000 on-the-job deaths reported over the twenty-nine years between 1972 and 2001. Only 151 of those deaths had been referred for prosecution of a company, and a mere eight cases had resulted in prison sentences over that long span. When a sentence was imposed, the longest was six months.

Barstow saw a strong international economic angle behind the numbers. American businesses were being pressured to adopt minimal safety levels as a cost-cutting technique to stay competitive in the new global environment. If they didn't cut costs enough, they lost out in the marketplace. If they trimmed safety measures, and workers died, the price was not as severe. Regulators at the Occupational Safety and Health Administration (OSHA) were soft, and companies had the upper hand. In the first series, McWane's safety violations were compared to those of other big pipe companies, showing it to have a significantly worse record.

One morning, "probably in the shower," Barstow says, he came up with a line to describe the scene that the series was painting: "part Dickens and part Darwin." Along with the story of Rolan Hoskin's death, that became the opening of the first story on January 8. "In writing that lead, I was trying to get at it as vividly and powerfully as I could," he says. The reporters and their editor, Paul Fishleder, agreed to start the series with an anecdotal account. In Barstow's experience writing multiparters, such an organizational approach seemed inverted. "An overview usually comes first, with the series then broken down into parts. But in this case I was worried about connecting with the readers," he says. "So Day One was just the story of what happened when McWane took over this plant. Day Two we stepped back and looked at who owns the plant. Day Three was what does the government do about it." It was not doing much, the third story maintained, with OSHA records supporting that conclusion. Fishleder, as the primary editor, became the sounding board as Barstow shaped the series and each story in it.

Along with Fishleder, Barstow credits executive editor Howell Raines and deputy managing editor Andrew Rosenthal for early support of the story idea. The editing—and self-editing—challenges were enormous, since Barstow estimates his rough draft of the first article alone at thirty-five thousand words. He cut it first to fifteen thousand, then whittled it into a more polished seven thousand. "This means that an awful lot of great material ends up on the cutting-room floor. Believe me, every word in the final piece was scrutinized for whether it absolutely had to be in the story." The old lesson still holds: "Make the point, make it with power and precision, then move on. Don't make the reader read one word more than necessary."

A television documentary version of the three-part report was to appear on Public Broadcasting System's *Frontline* program. And Barstow found some advantages in having a film entourage around him as he conducted some interviews. "A big project is like running a small business, with the photographer and all the others on the team. These can be great for extending the reach of your eyes and ears," he says. "You grab resources from wherever you can."

He had been apprehensive about the TV element at first because of bad earlier experiences. "But the partnership on 'Dangerous Business' worked really well. It did give us more firepower, crucial on a story with so many tentacles," he says. Along with those additional staffers available for research, though, came one negative. "Television's needs slowed us down because we often had to 'redo' interviews for the benefit of the cameras—that is, go back with a camera crew after I had already interviewed someone for the newspaper," according to Barstow. "It also added greatly to the administrative burdens of the story: more meetings, more coordination required to sync up the stories."

The TV-print connection reflects the future of investigative reporting, he says. "It will be multiplatform, multimedia, with TV, print and Web integrated for the biggest possible bang." And this project showed how the two forms actually could benefit from each other. (The Pulitzer board says that only the print version was reviewed during the jury and board deliberations. Still, some board members suspect that such joint entries may one day qualify for their own category.)

Needed: A Second Series

When the three parts ran in the *Times* in January, and even later when reforms were proposed and indictments were sought against some McWane managers, Barstow found his feelings were mixed. While pleased with the series, he says, "I worried that some folks might walk away assuming McWane was some sort of anomaly." The question of why workplace deaths usually go uninvestigated needed attention. That unanswered question paved the way for months more of work, and eventually the second series in the Pulitzer package, "When Workers Die."

The regulators were at the center of the second series, which Barstow handled as the lone reporter, with research assistance from Robin Stein. One focus was the paradox represented by the law that created OSHA. The law established that an employer's worst offense could be to cause a fatality by willfully violating safety rules. Yet the *Times*'s analysis of the data—"almost certainly the first systematic examination of these worst workplace deaths," the paper said in its Pulitzer nomination letter—found that OSHA doesn't even ask prosecutors to consider filing charges in 93 percent of cases.

This series, too, began with a graphically portrayed accident, following Barstow's sense that a strong connection with the reader was needed to tell the story. The first installment was headlined "A Trench Caves In; A Young Worker Is Dead. Is It a Crime?" It began:

> CINCINNATI—As the autopsy confirmed, death did not come right away for Patrick M. Walters. On June 14, 2002, while working on a sewer pipe in a trench 10 feet deep, he was buried alive under a rush of collapsing muck and mud. A husky plumber's apprentice, barely 22 years old, Mr. Walters clawed for the surface. Sludge filled his throat. Thousands of pounds of dirt pressed on his chest, squeezing and squeezing until he could not draw another breath.

The story went on to point out that Walters had spoken often to his family about his fear of being buried alive. That was because his company, a small, family-owned outfit called Moeves Plumbing, frequently sent him into deep trenches without safety equipment. Local OSHA officials were upset, too, because Moeves had been implicated in a "nearly identical" worker death thirteen years earlier. The *Times* article compared those two cases, and pointed out the lack of OSHA action to correct the unsafe conditions.

The second story, headlined "U.S. Rarely Seeks Charges for Deaths in Workplace," gave stark statistics showing how few prosecutions resulted from fatalities caused by workplace safety violations. Charts and graphs showed how the various states stacked up in enforcement, and one particular passage stood out:

> For those 2,197 deaths [in U.S. workplaces between 1990 and 2002] employers faced $106 million in civil OSHA fines and jail sentences totaling less than 30 years, The Times found. Twenty of those years were from one case, a chicken-plant fire in North Carolina that killed 25 workers in 1991.
>
> By contrast, one company, WorldCom, recently paid $750 million in civil fines for misleading investors. The Environmental Protection Agency, in 2001 alone, obtained prison sentences totaling 256 years.

The third installment aimed for one bright spot in an otherwise bleak picture, as newspapers often seek to do. It involved the approach of one state that has taken on the duty of fighting for victims when workers are killed on the job. The headline: "California Leads Prosecution of Employers in Job Deaths."

The *Times*'s entry got the typical polish that the paper applies when it submits work for the Pulitzers. The submission was a seventy-six-page, eleven-by-fifteen-inch spiral-bound book presenting not only the original articles and editorials supporting them but also readers' opinions and letters from officials heralding the two series, along with descriptions of the *Times* online multimedia presentation, with Barstow's audio commentary, and a description of the *Frontline/New York Times* report.

As Barstow looks back at that time when the Pulitzer rumor mill was grinding, the thrill of getting the award for Public Service seems all the sweeter. "It was a wonderful shock to learn that not only did we win, but we won in the best category of all, against really amazing work."

It certainly was nicer than his experience in 1998, when he was with the *St. Petersburg Times.* Advance word came that he was among the finalists in the Explanatory and Investigative categories. But an editor who had been clued to the Pulitzer board's decision "took me out to lunch and said, 'David, I feel certain you're going to win a Pulitzer Prize some day, but it's not going to be this year.'"

2004—*New York Times:* For the work of David Barstow and Lowell Bergman that relentlessly examined death and injury among American workers and exposed employers who break basic safety rules.

A Medical Center's Maladies

While the *New York Times* won the Gold Medal, the *Los Angeles Times*'s overall performance was at least as noteworthy. Its staffers won a total of five Pulitzers, including prizes for teamwork in Breaking News and National Reporting. Remarkably, *Los Angeles Times* people had been finalists for four other Prizes.

Some staffers gloated about the "five-to-one" score over their New York rivals. And a rivalry it most certainly was. For years, the West Coast paper had complained that it failed to receive the respect it deserved from the "Eastern press establishment"—particularly at Pulitzer time. Still, New York's Gray Lady *had* won that 2004 Gold Medal.

Even as editor John Carroll acknowledged the prior year's bounty, though, he had his eye on a developing story with Public Service possibilities for the next year's prizes: a complex analysis of operational troubles, with racial complications, at Martin Luther King Jr./Drew Medical Center on the edge of the Watts section of Los Angeles.

When they began studying the Los Angeles County hospital system in 2003 with a broader story in mind, *Times* health-care reporters Tracy Weber and Charles Ornstein did not think that a look at the King/Drew part of the system had much promise. Their impression was that the story had "been done." And it had. Fourteen years before, in a Pulitzer Prize category then called Specialized Reporting, *Times* reporter Claire Spiegel had been a Pulitzer finalist with a powerful three-part series about King/Drew that concentrated on the lack of resources available to the hospital. By then, the medical center already had garnered the unfortunate nickname of Killer King. King/Drew had been created after the 1965 Watts riots, with a largely black and Latino medical staff. There were problems, but the community was extremely defensive about King/Drew.

In 2003, John Carroll and managing editor Dean P. Baquet had backed Weber and Ornstein's vision of a far-reaching story highlighting patient-care comparisons among all the county's medical facilities. The impetus for that story had been a front-page study the two reporters had done early in the year. It cited a lawsuit in which doctors had pointed to specific cases of patient deaths resulting from long waits for care. The delays in question had not been at King/Drew, but at another facility.

Julie Marquis, the deputy Metro editor who had been assigned to manage Weber and Ornstein's work, says there was another reason to avoid focusing on King/Drew in their new examination of medical care. It was "like shooting fish in a barrel," she says. "We did not regard that as the most challenging investigative project we could do. One had a sense there was nothing you could do about it. And, of course, there were reasons not to try: a lot of political and racial associations with that hospital that the other county hospitals did not have."

In early May Weber and Ornstein started gathering data, including malpractice suits against each county hospital. "It became clear really early on that King/Drew's problems were much greater than those at the other county hospitals—even the ones that were two or three times larger—so both of us went back to John and said we need to focus on King/Drew first," Ornstein says. At the same time, King/Drew found itself in the news independent of the *Times* reporters' project. It was learned that two patients had died because nurses had overlooked the readings on patient heart-rate monitors. Then, the hospital lost its accreditation to train surgeons because of its problems—"a huge deal for an urban hospital," adds Weber.

The "Grim March"

An internal hospital-faculty meeting at King/Drew, attended by Ornstein and Weber, first brought home the depth of the hospital's story. As the expected complaints arose about how the medical center was underfunded, the director of the health department—who was white—countered that this was not true. Funding was sufficient, he said. The problem was the staff misspending what it received, under the hospital director's leadership. The hospital director was black. "A faculty member got up in the back of the room and said, 'The black overseer always whips harder than the white master.' And everyone in the audience got up and started clapping," according to Weber. "Charlie and I said to each other, This is more than just about a bad hospital. It has all sorts of other overlay."

The more they compared King/Drew to the other medical centers, the more they saw how severely out-of-step it was. Slowly, the case for taking a broader health-care approach eroded. King/Drew was just too important a story on its own. "It was initially perceived as a patient care story," says Marquis. "Strangely enough, after we decided that, we began to accumulate a lot of data on how badly run the hospital was, and how it squandered money, and not so much about patient care." As the reporting continued, though, the theme of poor patient care resurfaced. The story would have a patient-care dimension as well.

In October 2003—fourteen months before the series was published—Marquis and Weber and Ornstein wrote a memo outlining a project they envisioned. The project was between four and six parts, and looked at the problems of King/Drew one by one. When Carroll read the memo, he saw the potential for something special. His vision would confront head-on the complexity and the racial sensitivity of the situation. "He wanted to meld together the political, medical, historical, and social aspects of this hospital," Marquis says. "He was trying to find a way to tell this story without making it seem the standard investigative story on a hospital's medical foul-ups."

The *Times* decided to add to the Weber-Ornstein team, a decision the two reporters supported because "we knew we couldn't do it all ourselves," Ornstein says. Marquis and those she reported to—Metro editor Miriam Pawel and managing editor Baquet—called on Mitchell Landsberg, who was fresh from having worked rewrite on the team that had covered the year's devastating California wildfires. (That coverage would win the 2004 Breaking News Pulitzer.) Steve Hymon, who had moved onto the health-care beat when Ornstein and Weber teamed up to investigate King/Drew in earnest, also was added, along with reporter Daren Briscoe. Briscoe, the lone black team member, was selected in part because of the racial insights he might be able to provide in such a sensitive story. "I'm not sure it was easier for him," says Weber. "He had a difficult time as an African American reporter working on the story." (Briscoe would leave the paper about midway through the project to go to *Newsweek* magazine, and the paper decided not to replace him.)

Carroll, who checked in from time to time on the team's progress, was impressed with the team spirit among the reporters. In his experience with staffers pursuing such complex stories, he says, "often there is kind of a grim march to get them done."

Grim or otherwise, the marches he had helped supervise stretched back to the 1970s, when he honed his editing skills at the *Philadelphia Inquirer* with executive editor Gene Roberts. Carroll first had seen a Pulitzer Gold Medal project take shape as he worked on a police-brutality investigation that won a Pulitzer for the *Inquirer* in 1978. In a sense, though, he had even grown up with public-service journalism. His father, Wallace Carroll, had been a Pulitzer board member in the 1960s, and Wallace Carroll's North Carolina newspaper, the *Winston-Salem Journal and Sentinel*, had won a Gold Medal in 1971 for its environmental coverage.

In the years before coming to the *Los Angeles Times*, John Carroll had served as editor with the *Baltimore Sun* and with Kentucky's *Lexington Herald-Leader*, where he had become skilled not only at supervising projects but also at doing the final write-through of the stories. As a Pulitzer board member himself from 1994 to 2003, he also had an insider's sense of what the members might like in a Public Service candidate.

Working for him at the *Los Angeles Times* were a number of veteran editors, including managing editor Baquet, who had started his career in New Orleans and worked for a time with Jim Amoss at the *Times-Picayune*. Baquet had covered health-care issues himself for the *New York Times*, and previously had served on a

Pulitzer-winning investigative team at the *Chicago Tribune*. In June, longtime editorial page editor Janet Clayton succeeded Pawel as Metro editor. Both Clayton and Baquet are black. Clayton was particularly attuned to the community aspect of King/Drew from her editorial page experience. "She knows everything about the history of L.A. and all the players in our story," says Weber. It was not a simple history. The black community took great pride in having King/Drew there, even if, paradoxically, the facility was sometimes feared because of its care deficiencies.

While the reporting and editing teams did not include a physician, reporters constantly sought out doctors to review cases and the medical files, says Weber. To help reporters understand the case that eventually was to become their lead example—involving second-grader Dunia Tasejo, who had died after being hospitalized for injuries from a minor car accident—"we had not only the head of [the pediatric intensive care unit] from Stanford, we had a couple of other doctors look at it to make sure we understood our way through the file." The reporters' understanding was that Dunia had died from a mind-boggling progression of hospital mistakes.

The team often had trouble getting the data they needed for their analyses. While some difficulties stemmed from the federal privacy act, which allowed hospitals to deny certain information to reporters, there was a special problem in getting material from King/Drew administrators. "They hated our guts," says Weber.

At the same time, though, the team found other records that it never thought it could get. "We learned there were a lot of public records that we didn't know were public records," Weber says. "Who knew that you could get a record of every surgery at the hospital that every doctor had done?" They tracked the records down. Further, workers' compensation cases became public records if the case had been appealed to the state Appeals Board. Within those cases, personal medical records and psychologist reports, too, became public. And even if reporters were not prepared to cite certain records in the series, the documents often corroborated strange accounts that the team's reporting was turning up—accounts about staff accidents and brawls that ran up costs at King/Drew.

"If you were going to write a show like *Scrubs*, you couldn't make up all this stuff that actually happened at King/Drew," says Weber. "There was this one story about a nurse slugging another nurse during surgery." Other times, staffers were selling things in the hallways. Fleshing out the original October memo, the team began assembling drafts of a multipart series for Carroll in March 2004, realizing that he was planning to do the final writing himself.

Carroll loved such project management above all his many other *Times* duties. "I get a greater satisfaction from these gigantic things, and figuring out what they're trying to say," he says. "It's inevitable that people who are writing these stories and gathering vast amounts of information get awfully close to it. And I've never seen one of these stories come in a publishable form."

He had learned the rewriting trade in his *Inquirer* days, working with gifted rewrite man Steve Lovelady, himself a veteran of page one editing work at the *Wall Street Journal.* "Lovelady was unlike anything I'd ever seen in terms of what he understood about the possibilities of creative editing, and not just making sure everything was spelled right," says Carroll. "He opened my eyes." In fact, he describes his work on the King/Drew series as "the Lovelady job."

True to the form that Carroll had observed over the years, he saw that even the excellent job of reporting on King/Drew was going to need serious organizational help. "Very often you need to think through fundamental questions like, What is this about?" he says. "You have to do a lot of work to get a reader through a long story." And the King/Drew epic was developing into a long story. Each of the eventual five parts would fill two or more inside pages, although much of the space reflected lavish use of photographs by Robert Gauthier. "We wanted to make sure the photographer was plugged in fairly early, and was a full-fledged member of the team," says Carroll.

The first installment of "The Troubles at King/Drew" ran on December 5, 2004, under the headline "Deadly Errors and Politics Betray a Hospital's Promise." It began with a patient-care horror story:

> On a warm July afternoon, an impish second-grader named Dunia Tasejo was running home after buying ice cream on her South Los Angeles street when a car sideswiped her. Knocked to the pavement, she screamed for help, blood pouring from her mouth.
>
> Her father bolted from the house to her side. An ambulance rushed her to the nearest hospital: Martin Luther King Jr./Drew Medical Center.
>
> For Elias and Sulma Tasejo, there was no greater terror than seeing their 9-year-old daughter strapped to a gurney that day in 2000. But once they arrived at King/Drew, fear gave way to relief.
>
> Dunia's injuries were minor: some scrapes, some bruises and two broken baby teeth. The teeth would have to be pulled.
>
> "They told me to relax," Sulma recalled. "Everything was fine."
>
> At least it should have been.
>
> What the Tasejos didn't know was that King/Drew, a 233-bed public hospital in Willowbrook, just south of Watts, had a long history of harming, or even killing, those it was meant to serve.

What happened to Dunia, in brief, was a bewildering series of medical errors that eventually cost her her life. She was first accidentally oversedated; then hooked up to a ventilator to deal with the paralysis the oversedating caused; then starved for oxygen by incorrect ventilator settings; then taken off a breathing tube too early; then left unmonitored as her vital signs were worsening and she started calling "Mama." Eventually declared brain dead, she was removed from life support two days later.

As the *Los Angeles Times* team had planned through so many rewrites, the first story was used to outline much more than the issues of medical errors and neglect that made King/Drew the state's top payer, per patient, of medical malpractice. The piece noted that whole "departments are riddled with incompetence, internal strife and, in some cases, criminality." It maintained that lack of money wasn't at the root of this evil; rather, poor spending practices, "abnormally high salaries for ranking doctors," and swollen workers' compensation claims drained more from King/Drew than from the other county general hospitals. And finally, the story promised that the series ahead would explain how for years the governing county board of supervisors had "shied away from decisive action in the face of community anger and accusations of racism."

The other four parts solidly backed up the outline. In an eyebrow-raising passage in the second part of the series published on December 6—a section headlined "Under-funding Is a Myth but the Squandering Is Real"—these paragraphs appeared on the first jump:

> Vast sums at King/Drew go to workers injured in encounters with seemingly harmless objects.
>
> Take, for instance, the chair.
>
> Employees have been tumbling from their seats at King/Drew almost since it opened its doors. The hospital's oldest open workers' compensation claim involves Franza Zachary, now 71, who sprained her back falling from a chair in October 1975—costing the hospital more than $300,000 so far.
>
> The bills for two other chair-fallers have topped $350,000 each, county records show.
>
> Between April 1994 and April 2004, employees filed 122 chair-fall claims at King/Drew, more than double the number at Harbor-UCLA. And King/Drew has spent $3.2 million—and counting—to pay for them.

The final part "laid bare the racial dynamic between the community and the Board of Supervisors," according to the *Times*'s Pulitzer nomination letter. "Readers noted the newspaper's clarity and directness in explaining issues that had paralyzed the county's leadership for 30 years. The Supervisors were left with no choice but to face up to their own failure." While some local politicians remained critical—even angry with the *Times*—Supervisor Gloria Molina told colleagues at a board meeting: "We should be embarrassed, all of us collectively, because we have failed the community." The supervisors eventually put the hospital under the management of an outside firm and voted to close its expensive trauma unit, using the resources to save the rest of the hospital.

Says Marquis of the final piece in the series, written by Landsberg: "He's a gifted storyteller, and he just provided a nice contrast to the maiming and killing aspect of the story." She had had her doubts early on about whether a story on the politics of King/Drew—which Landsberg wrote and Carroll edited—was the right way to end the series. "But now I think it was," she says. The story "took known facts, and wove them together in a way that let you know why all of the previous four parts had occurred."

Editing from the Top

Several team members had been apprehensive at first at the thought of their top editor running the series through his computer. "Demanding is not an adequate word to describe his editing," says Mitchell Landsberg of John Carroll. Landsberg says others who had been rewritten by Carroll had told the team it was in for a torturous time. "You're going to have days when you'll wish you'd never gotten started with this," Landsberg was told. "But in the end he'll make sure it's the best story it could possibly be." Landsberg, the son of a veteran Associated Press Sacramento reporter and World War II correspondent, says that after reading the final version he realized that "everything they said was true."

One thing that helped, adds Weber, was that the very final draft again became a collaboration. "Actually, he ended up being remarkably approachable about things you didn't like."

Based on what he had learned serving on the Pulitzer board, says Carroll, "I think King/Drew was a good candidate for the Public Service category because it not only involved very hard digging and investigative work and very careful accusations drawn against doctors and all sorts of people, but it also involved explaining a very sensitive racial dynamic in local politics that had caused the community to tiptoe around this issue for thirty years. We sort of broke the rules by discussing it very directly, and pulling no punches. The political discussion in that story was nuanced, but very hard-hitting."

The board also had an appreciation for risk-taking—something the *Times* was certainly doing in the King/Drew series. A hostile community of King/Drew supporters, says Carroll, would have objected strongly if they found "any chinks in the story, or anything was untrue."

There were risks, too, simply in the writing style. "Racial stories have to be written in the most precise terms. There's a tremendous potential for community anger, and picketing, and even community violence," he says. As he crafted the stories he tried to be aware of "the belief on the part of many that the white establishment is trying to take away this hospital, and has been for years."

Marquis sees the King/Drew series as an effort by the *Times* to spread its investigative skills to new areas. "The paper had successfully done some projects in other departments, but we hadn't done one in the Metro department for a few years," she says. Unlike the *Boston Globe,* with its Spotlight Team, when the King/ Drew coverage started the *Times* did not have a formal, standing investigative unit—at least outside Washington. (In February 2004, the paper added one with a reporter hired from the *Washington Post.*) Generally, the *Times* had chosen to build ad hoc investigative teams around particular stories, like King/Drew.

When *Times* parent Times Mirror Company had been acquired by the Tribune Company in 2000, there were fears that the prize-winning level of its reporting might be hurt. The paper's 2004 and 2005 performances seemed to illustrate that those fears were exaggerated. After winning the 2005 Gold Medal—the fifth for the 123-year-old *Los Angeles Times*—Carroll credited publisher John P. Puerner and the Tribune ownership for providing "nothing but the strongest support."

A year later, though, John Carroll was gone, lamenting that the promised support from top Tribune officials had evaporated after Puerner, a longtime Tribune official, failed to deliver a high enough level of cost cuts. "They said he'd gone native," according to Carroll. "He was under increasing pressure and ultimately he decided to leave. That was one of the reasons I left." Tribune's change of heart had robbed his paper of a tremendous opportunity, in Carroll's view.

"If left alone we could have clearly established the *L.A. Times* as the best paper in the country," says Carroll. "In order to do that, you have to have good public service year in and year out."

2005—*Los Angeles Times:* For its courageous, exhaustively researched series exposing deadly medical problems and racial injustice at a major public hospital.

New York Times reporters David Barstow (left) and Lowell Bergman are applauded by members of the newsroom after learning of their Pulitzer Prize. Photo by Ruby Washington, the *New York Times*. Used by permission.

John Carroll, having announced that he was leaving his post as *Los Angeles Times* editor a few months after the paper won the 2005 Gold Medal, watches as his successor, managing editor Dean Baquet, talks to the staff. Photo by Al Seib, *Los Angeles Times*. Used by permission.

The *Los Angeles Times* team that prepared the King/Drew series was composed of (standing, from left) editorial writer Mary Engel, reporter Mitchell Landsberg, photographer Robert Gauthier, reporter Steve Hymon, and editor Julie Marquis, and (seated) reporters Charles Ornstein and Tracy Weber. *Los Angeles Times* staff photo. Used by permission.

Part Two

Coming of Age

CHAPTER 7

First Gold

The medal is most artistic in design, and very precious, as it is an award for distinguished public service by a high court of public opinion.

—*New York Times* publisher Adolph S. Ochs,
to the Pulitzer Advisory Board, July 8, 1920

*W*ith the Pulitzer Prizes today signifying the pinnacle of excellence in both journalism and the arts, it is hard to imagine Columbia University's new awards struggling to get off the ground. Yet, unheralded and overshadowed by world war, the selection of the first winners was barely noticed in 1917. Two months earlier, President Woodrow Wilson had declared war on Germany. And even the Pulitzer Advisory Board did not seem much interested in the awarding of the first prizes. Only four of the ten board members joined Columbia president Nicholas Butler in the school's Low Library to make the May 24 selections.

Not that the jurors had given them many nominees to consider. The jurors for the nonjournalism categories, who had been chosen from the American Academy of Arts and Letters, and who included literary lights from Yale and Harvard universities, made only a few recommendations. And the board voted no award at all for Novel or Drama that first year. For the American History Prize, the winner was not an American at all, but the French ambassador, Jean Jules Jusserand, for his book *With Americans of Past and Present Days*. A Biography Prize was voted for *Julia Ward Howe*, written by the daughters of the lyricist of "Battle Hymn of the Republic."

In the journalism categories, small juries of Columbia faculty members had been set up, with Journalism Dean Talcott Williams serving on each. It isn't clear whether jurors simply lacked energy for the job or just found the prior year's journalism unworthy. But they forwarded only two works for consideration—and none at all for Public Service. The two nominations that the jurors did send to the board reflected both the wartime environment and their own eastern backgrounds. From the *New York Tribune* there was an anti-German editorial published on the anniversary of the sinking of the Lusitania, and from the *World,* a series of dispatches by Herbert Bayard Swope titled "Inside the German Empire."

As Pulitzer Prize historian John Hohenberg put it: "The Advisory Board, concluding that first rather desultory session on the prizes, quietly voted the recommendations of all the juries." That meant no recipient for the Public Service Prize that first year. For the few literature and journalism prizes that *were* awarded, Columbia adopted a deliberate policy of restraint, and barely promoted them. For the most part, only newspapers that won them said anything about the prizes.

In a strange way, Columbia's early low-key approach to the Pulitzer Prizes may have helped establish them for the long term. The prizes provoked little criticism, and certainly there was no hint of their being cheapened by excessive touting. As Hohenberg wrote, "Outside the garish spotlight of public cynosure, and relatively free of critical inspection, the system for determining the awards was molded into a reasonably efficient operation." In later years, as word began to get out about quality journalism being recognized, the board's secrecy about the process added to the intrigue.

It would not be until the 1920s that the journalism prizes began to attract significant attention and draw larger numbers of nominations. By then, they were benefiting from their association with great early literary winners like Eugene O'Neill, Booth Tarkington, Edith Wharton, Willa Cather, Edna Ferber, Sinclair Lewis, and Thornton Wilder.

It was just what Joseph Pulitzer had wanted.

The *Times* at War

By failing to select a Public Service winner in 1917, the advisory board had stumbled in the inaugural Pulitzer award process. But as the board left its infancy and stepped haltingly into its second year—another year clouded by the war in Europe—it made a choice for its first Gold Medal that could not have been more propitious, either for the recipient, or for the Pulitzer Public Service Prize itself.

While there are no board minutes available to prove it, those first members must have engaged in serious debate about just what Joseph Pulitzer had meant by newspaper public service. Was the award intended to honor a series of stories? Or could a campaign of some sort—or perhaps even a philosophy that might be expressed by a public-spirited style of coverage—qualify as a "disinterested and meritorious" contribution to society? After all, hadn't Pulitzer himself served the public by using his paper to allow Lady Liberty to raise her lamp over New York Harbor?

In 1918, the advisory board cast a vote for a winner that reflected both fine reporting *and* a new philosophy of coverage. In selecting the *New York Times,* the Pulitzers also happened to acknowledge one of the day's meteoric newspaper success stories. The award, in fact, may well have been meant to recognize the international-reporting phenomenon that the *Times* had become since the war in Europe started, and even before. The paper had changed the nature of overseas newspaper reporting.

Joseph Pulitzer himself had been sharply at odds with Adolph S. Ochs in Ochs's first years after buying the struggling nine-thousand-circulation *Times* in 1896. Rapidly, Ochs remade it into a daily that would appeal to the thinking person, just as Pulitzer had successfully played to passions and to fascination with public crusades. Editorially, the *World* called the *Times* a creature of the trusts, and Ochs the "keeper of the deficit." Meanwhile, the *Times* opposed both Pulitzer and Hearst for practicing "freak journalism" as they beat the drum for war with Spain.

Ochs had worked wonders with the *Times,* not only building circulation to more than one hundred thousand copies in eight years but also hiring extraordinary journalists who saw balanced, in-depth coverage of a range of topics as the desperate need of a growing class of sophisticated New Yorkers. Surreptitiously, Pulitzer joined them. In the thaw that Pulitzer initiated with some rival publishers after the yellow-journalism period ended, Pulitzer invited Ochs for a visit to his Chatwold residence in Bar Harbor, writing: "You may not know that I have the *Times* sent to me abroad when the *World* is forbidden, and that most of my news I really receive from your paper."

With good reason. A 1951 corporate history by celebrated *Times* reporter Meyer Berger noted that "Ochs had a genius for picking men of stature as aides, and he gave their talents free rein, in the newsroom or in the counting room." One such choice was managing editor Carr Van Anda, an Ohioan who joined the *Times* in 1904 from the *Sun,* and immediately began to give meaning to Ochs's new slogan, "All the News That's Fit to Print." Wrote Berger: "There may have been somewhere in newspaper history a more perfect publisher–managing editor team than the Ochs–Van Anda set-up, but none comes to mind." Both loved science, and especially new discoveries, and both believed a wide swath of New Yorkers hungered for their new approach. "There were many in the trade, and out of it, who preferred garnished fact and the literary touch—the journalistic cocktail—to the news that Van Anda served straight. They found the *Times* stuffy and elephantine in pace, even if it was complete, and honest."

Those readers had plenty of alternatives at the *World, Herald, Sun, American,*

Press, and others. "The years were to prove that the Ochs and Van Anda formula was best for the long haul, that an intelligent reading public bought newspapers—strange as it seemed to some—to read the news," according to Berger.

When it came to covering science, the paper not only excelled, but it used technology for its own purposes. A decade before the war, Ochs's *Times* had carried the "First Wireless Press Message across the Atlantic," as the paper's own headline proclaimed on October 18, 1907. The technology gave the *Times* an edge over the competition for years, especially in wartime.

There were lapses. But what history later exposed as one editorial blunder offers a fascinating insight into the *Times* and into the era before the war. A piece of *Times* lore has its roots in a June 1908 interview that correspondent William Bayard Hale conducted with Kaiser Wilhelm II on the imperial yacht *Hohenzollern* off the coast of Norway. It was six years before European hostilities were to begin, and the German leader's thoughts were largely unknown. But in a two-hour diatribe, he told Hale that blond, Protestant Anglo-Teutons from northern Europe were destined to rule the world. "It is a mistaken idea that Christianity has no countenance for war. We are Christians by reason of forcible conversion," he said to Hale. "The Bible is full of good fighting—jolly good fights."

The reporter, who hadn't dared take notes, madly assembled a long memorandum. Afraid to send it by cablegram, Hale told his editors: "Result so startling that I hesitate to report it without censorship of Berlin." When they finally saw it, Ochs and a collection of *Times* editors that included Van Anda and Charles Miller considered it potentially world-shaking. For the sake of national interest, though, they decided that Hale should go to Washington and show it to President Theodore Roosevelt. Calling it "astonishing stuff," Roosevelt said it should not be run. "I don't believe the emperor wanted this stuff published," he told Hale. "If he did, he's a goose." Roosevelt had no power to block the *Times.* But Ochs, agreeing that this particular news was *not* fit to print, locked it in his private safe. There the memo stayed, incredibly, for thirty years, coming out only in an article appearing in the *Times* Magazine in 1939. There, it was cited to compare the Kaiser's ranting to that of the German leader of the time, Adolf Hitler.

If the *Times* ever regretted the decision not to give the world an early peek at the Kaiser's warmongering, there wasn't much time for second-guessing. Soon, it was telling readers of impending war in four-column headlines like this, from July of 1914:

AUSTRIA BREAKS WITH SERVIA;
KING PETER MOVES HIS CAPITAL;
RUSSIA IS MOBILIZING HER ARMY;
BERLIN AND PARIS MOBS FOR WAR

Three years later, on April 3, 1917, above the full text of President Wilson's address to the nation in six columns, another headline appeared in the familiar eight-column banner format:

PRESIDENT CALLS FOR WAR DECLARATION,
STRONGER NAVY, NEW ARMY OF 500,000 MEN
FULL CO-OPERATION WITH GERMANY'S FOES

That headline surely was on the minds of the five advisory board members as they assembled at Columbia for the first Pulitzer Prize decision in May 1917. Meeting again the *next* May, though, that *Times* war-declaration story and others that followed it were certainly part of the deliberations that led the board to awarding the 1918 Gold Medal to the New York newspaper.

One way Van Anda had made the *Times* unique was by using the paper's established edge in cable to saturate readers with dispatches, giving them the ability to judge for themselves what diplomats and leaders were saying in Europe, even as *Times* reporters covered the same ground in their balanced way. Ochs freely bankrolled it. The *Times* figured that it spent fifteen thousand dollars a week for cable use alone, for example, more than Ochs's predecessors had spent on foreign coverage altogether.

Three years after the Gold Medal was awarded, *Times* reporter Elmer Davis, who later gained fame as a broadcaster, wrote this to express the paper's philosophy during the war years:

> The editors of the *Times* believed that their circulation contained an unusually high proportion of readers who were willing to give the time to reading long speeches and long documents, not necessarily because they had superfluous time on their hands, but because they realized that in a war of this kind full understanding required careful study, and that study of the evidence was the most important business of any intelligent man. The editors thought, too, that the *Times* more than any other paper was read by people who were capable of forming their own opinions from study of the original evidence in full, and who would rather have every word available for their own study than accept a summary made by somebody else.

Did the coverage formula work for the *Times,* other than winning for it the first-ever Pulitzer Public Service Prize? Its circulation skyrocketed during the war to 323,000, with annual advertising linage—2.2 million lines when Ochs bought the paper—surging to 23.4 million lines.

Van Anda's legend would continue to grow. In 1919, the *Times* copyrighted a story stemming from a meeting of astronomers in London, discussing findings from a May 29 solar eclipse that proved a little-known scientist's theory that starlight did not travel to earth in a straight line, but instead curved around the sun. The *Times* thus introduced Americans to Albert Einstein.

A later Van Anda–Einstein story involved the editor's reading of one of the physicist's lectures at Princeton. "It came at a time when relativity was only understood by Dr. Einstein and by the Deity," according to a fellow professor who told the tale. ". . . Dr. Einstein had already lost even the professorial mathematicians who were here to hear him, but the *Times* called me before going to press to ask whether there was not some mistake in the figures . . . . Mr. Van Anda thought one of the equations was wrong." The professor checked, found that the *Times* had accurately presented what Einstein had said, and decided to check back with Einstein himself. When Einstein was consulted he was astonished. He scanned the notes and replied, "Yes, Mr. Van Anda is right. I made a mistake in transcribing the equation on the blackboard."

It was also Van Anda who "went feverish over an Egyptian King who had slept some 3,500 years and restored him and his times with great fidelity and journalistic art." What had fascinated the editor, of course, was archaeologist Howard Carter's November 1922 discovery of King Tutankhamen's tomb. The original 250-word Associated Press story was all but ignored by the rest of the press. But Van Anda lined up an exclusive relationship through *The Times* of London to give his *New York Times* rights to the story. Its front-page article pointing out the "incomparably magnificent and wondrously beautiful" throne, among other things, helped start a national King Tut craze.

A Precious Medal

The decision to forgo that first Gold Medal in 1917 eliminated a potential problem for the Pulitzer board: no medal yet existed, nor had it even been designed.

Columbia president Butler commissioned sculptor Daniel Chester French to design a Pulitzer medal in the fall of 1918, paying him one thousand dollars. At the time, French was best known for his Minute Man statue in Lexington, Massachusetts, created in 1875 when the sculptor was twenty-five. (His statuary masterpiece, the seated Lincoln in the Lincoln Memorial on Washington's Mall, would not be dedicated until 1922.) But he had also designed a series of impressive commemorative medals. Today his nine medals are considered classics of the form, although by far the best known is the Joseph Pulitzer Medal. French worked with apprentice Augustus Lukeman on the medal, initialing it with DCF/AL just behind the left foot of the printer on the reverse.

Originally there was no printer. Butler had ordered the likeness of Benjamin

Franklin on one side—French apparently chose to base his Franklin profile on a bust by Jean-Antoine Houdon—and a simple inscription on the other: "For the Most Disinterested and Meritorious Public Service Rendered by Any American Newspaper during the Year . . . . . ." But as they made their clay mock-ups, French and Lukeman thought the reverse too plain. French wrote to Butler that "interest would be increased by introducing an early press with a figure of a printer at work. I hope you may think so." The Columbia administrator called it "a little touch which is quite a stroke of genius." (In early designs the printer wore a shirt and printer's cap, although the final medal has him bare-chested with his shirt draped across the far end of the press.)

The first medal, not minted until the year after the announcement of the *Times's* Public Service Prize, took even longer to make the sixty-block trip from Columbia to Times Square. The *Times's* files show that publisher Ochs acknowledged its receipt by hand-delivery on July 8, 1920, with a two-paragraph letter noting its "artistic design."

An even more surprising delay may be the twenty-six years it took for a second Gold Medal to find its way to Times Square. The *Times* would not win another Public Service Prize until the *next* world war, in 1944. In other areas, though, the paper became a Pulitzer-winning machine—capturing thirteen prizes during that span.

1918—*New York Times:* For its public service in publishing in full so many official reports, documents, and speeches by European statesmen relating to the progress and conduct of the war.

In Defense of "Americanism"

If board members chose the *Times* in 1918 for its objective and thorough presentation of the combatants' original documents, their 1919 choice reflected quite a different approach to wartime coverage. Indeed, the board unanimously voted to give the Gold Medal to a newspaper that had engaged in a long struggle to oppose "Germanism in America." That effort had included blocking the teaching of German-language courses, opposing anti-war legislators like Senator Robert La Follette, and defending the reputation of its state, Wisconsin, against detractors who claimed that anti-war sentiment there emanated from its heavy German-American population.

The paper was the *Milwaukee Journal,* edited by Lucas Nieman, whose next seventeen years at the paper would be dedicated to keeping the news free of special interests—in an era when partisan advocacy was a feature of many other papers. Nieman later would become the benefactor of Harvard's Nieman Foundation.

The jurors, again Columbia professors, made their nomination "tentatively," until they could conduct "investigations to confirm or disprove our present impression as to the risk and effectiveness of this service, pending the result of which we do not feel able to make a positive recommendation." That is how the jury system was working back then.

A spokesman for the board, the AP's Melville Stone, explained why it honored the Milwaukee paper, remarking that "in a city where the German element has long prided itself on its preponderating influence, the *Journal* courageously attacked such members of that element as put Germany above America." President William Howard Taft was among those congratulating the paper on its award.

According to a 1982 history of the *Milwaukee Journal:* "Privately, Nieman and his staff were jubilant," creating a slogan for the paper: "First by Merit." More jubilation grew from the paper's achieving both record advertising linage and circulation after the prize. Said a *Journal* editorial: "Wisconsin, which has been so misrepresented and so maligned and so misunderstood, is awarded the Pulitzer Medal for its patriotism in the Great War."

1919—*Milwaukee Journal:* For its strong and courageous campaign for Americanism in a constituency where foreign elements made such a policy hazardous from a business point of view.

Joseph Pulitzer I, nearly blind, strolls along Fifth Avenue with oldest son Ralph of the *New York World.* Used by permission, *St. Louis Post-Dispatch.*

Joseph Pulitzer II, at age four, helps lay the cornerstone for the *World* building, 1889.
Used by permission, *St. Louis Post-Dispatch*.

The Chatwold estate near Bar Harbor, Maine, with its "tower of silence," right. At Chatwold, Joseph Pulitzer developed the idea for the Pulitzer Prizes.

Joseph Pulitzer II (left) and brother Ralph communicated frequently by letter before Pulitzer judging time. Here they are hunting together in a duck blind in 1934, three years after the *World* failed. Used by permission, *St. Louis Post-Dispatch.*

The New York Times.

PRESIDENT CALLS FOR WAR DECLARATION,
STRONGER NAVY, NEW ARMY OF 500,000 MEN,
FULL CO-OPERATION WITH GERMANY'S FOES

ARMED AMERICAN STEAMSHIP SUNK; 11 MEN MISSING

Text of the President's Address

MUST EXERT ALL OUR POWER
To Bring a "Government That Is Running Amuck to Terms."

The War Resolution Now Before Co[...]

The *New York Times* of April 3, 1917, was
already printing full texts of documents, such
as President Wilson's declaration of war. Used
by permission.

Carr Van Anda, managing editor of the *New
York Times* when it won its first Pulitzer Gold
Medal. From the *New York Times* photo
archives. Used by permission.

CHAPTER 8

Reporting on the Roaring

The Jazz Age had had a wild youth and a heady middle age . . . the most expensive orgy in history . . . . It was borrowed time anyhow—the whole upper tenth of a nation living with the insouciance of grand ducs and the casualness of chorus girls.

—F. Scott Fitzgerald

The Pulitzer Prizes for journalism entered the new decade like a child prodigy in that period of early, awkward adolescence. As an institution it had its brilliant moments—certainly, one was the choice of the *New York Times* for the 1918 Gold Medal—but it was still quite immature.

Again, no award was voted in the Public Service category for 1920. (The board would skip the category in 1925 and 1930, too.) But the board took one step that was to have great long-term significance for the prize process, adding thirty-five-year-old *St. Louis Post-Dispatch* editor Joseph Pulitzer II to its ranks.

Together, Ralph Pulitzer and his idealistic younger brother would infuse the prizes with their father's principles, as well as with the benefactor's ambition for the prizes to become a major part of the national scene. Public service stories that displayed real courage in the telling would get extra attention from the board with these New York and St. Louis newspaper executives in the room. So would any coverage that brought about significant benefits to society. J.P. II, especially, launched a flurry of personal correspondence with other board members before each meeting, encouraging nominations and seeking their thoughts about how the Pulitzer Prizes in general were doing. He was frustrated by the lack of entries from newspapers around the country, and hated for the board to have to pass over a category for want of good candidates.

The board started to take its job seriously. More members showed up to select prize winners, and they began strenuously debating those nominations that were forwarded from the Columbia journalism faculty members. Frequently, the board reversed the jury recommendations.

Further, the board began to see that if it found a truly exemplary work to honor—particularly with a Public Service Medal—it could provide a much-needed model of excellence for the industry, and could also boost the image of the Pulitzers themselves. This was an important development, coming at a time when the prizes still had almost no public image at all. The number of entries began to grow slowly, often because jurors and editors brought to the table candidates that they had read themselves during the prior year. The time when newspapers clamored to nominate their own best work was still in the future.

Meanwhile, as the war began to fade as a dominant story, front pages reflected the emergence of disturbing social problems: the tenacity of racial hatred and the flourishing of political graft and corruption. Battling these evils would become central for Pulitzer board members selecting the Gold Medal winner.

A Story for the Jazz Age

The national mood also was undergoing a swift, if not altogether clear, transformation as the 1920s began to roar. For many people, the former idealism about the turn-of-the-century world veered toward cynicism. A strange, frantic self-indulgence took hold. After the horrors visited on the battlefields of Europe, immediate gratification made more sense to some than did sacrifice. But it was also a time filled with paradox. Newspapers often saw themselves as standard-bearers for old national ideals, even as they began to reflect the new era's hedonism in their pages.

There could not have been a better newspaper story for the Jazz Age—or one that grew more powerfully from the anything-goes spirit infecting America—than the story that the Pulitzer board cited in its 1921 Public Service award.

For once, the board had a real choice in the category. Meeting in early April, a jury of three Columbia journalism professors offered the board two possibilities. One nomination was for the *New York Evening Post,* which had brought attention to "the shortcomings of the Government work for the relief and rehabilitation of the soldiers of the World War," according to John W. Cunliffe, the new director of Columbia's journalism school, and the leader of each of the juries. It was, the jury had noted, a project benefiting "a great number of deserving men to whom the country owed a debt that was being neglected." The stories had been written by Harold Littledale, who had won a Reporting Pulitzer in 1918. Indeed, the jury helpfully suggested that when the board compared it with the other nominee, "in case of performances of equal intrinsic merit, it may perhaps be good policy to broaden the scope of the School's relations to the newspaper world and especially not to confine its awards too closely to metropolitan papers."

The remark was something of a slight to Boston, home to the other nominated newspaper: the *Boston Post*. That city also thought of itself as metropolitan, and the *Post,* its largest paper at the time, actually sold more copies than the *New York World*. The *Post*'s nomination was "for the pricking of the Ponzi financial bubble, in investigating his claims to be operating in foreign exchange and throwing doubt on him at a time when the public officials were inactive and other newspapers were either ignoring him or treating him as a genuine financial wizard." The work was undertaken "at great risk of incurring heavy damages." If the jurors saw a negative in this story winning the Public Service Prize, it was that—unlike the veterans who were helped by the New York paper—"the persons chiefly benefited by the exposure of Ponzi were foolish persons who were seeking something for nothing, and who were entitled to little sympathy."

The nomination did not have to identify the "Ponzi" involved. It was celebrated huckster Charles Ponzi. During an exhilarating summer the previous year, the bombastic Italian immigrant had devised a get-rich-quick scheme that captivated the nation's attention—and made Ponzi a cult figure. In a Ponzi scheme, as such enterprises are now known, early investors receive hefty payouts from the funds provided by subsequent investors, although the schemer puts in place no fundamental profit-making machinery. The success of early investors builds publicity for the investment ruse, although it ultimately peters out when not enough later investors can be found to pay off earlier ones. Investors demanding their money back find that there is no cash.

The *Boston Post* work already had a powerful supporter on the Pulitzer board in Robert L. O'Brien, who called it "a piece of newspaper enterprise of the first importance." That opinion carried extra weight because O'Brien edited the rival *Boston Herald*—which had been thoroughly whipped on the story by the *Post*. And he was far from alone as a fan. Calvin Coolidge, then the Massachusetts governor, praised the stories, as did a host of local politicians, many of whom had been flat-footed in their enforcement role while the *Post* unmasked Ponzi's duplicity.

The jury wrote in its nomination letter that the jurors were "in doubt which of these enterprises was more deserving of the Prize"—the *New York Post* or the *Boston Post*—but the board saw a clearer choice. The Ponzi reporting was simply the perfect Joseph Pulitzer–style campaign: Great reporting of hard-to-get information, helping protect the "common man" from scams, and taking the form of shocking front-page news that stirred terrific controversy. The investigation also had required editor Richard Grozier, son of publisher Edwin A. Grozier, to face serious financial risk from the brazenly litigious Ponzi, and from legions of adoring followers who saw the *Post* as out to hang their innocent hero. These fans were ready to drop the *Post* as a result, especially as rival papers were proclaiming Ponzi a financial wizard well into the *Post*'s investigation.

The *Post*'s work also drew on the expertise of Clarence W. Barron, who had started the successful Boston News Bureau in the city's financial district. In 1902 he had spread his influence south to New York by buying a company called Dow Jones and its main product, the *Wall Street Journal.* Barron, whose name lives on in the weekly Dow Jones paper *Barron's,* and whose descendants controlled Dow Jones for 105 years, until 2007, was to be both an expert source for the *Post* and something of a guest columnist as the paper broke news in the Ponzi case.

Clipped by Coupons

Edwin Grozier, after working for a time under the *Boston Globe*'s Charles H. Taylor, had actually served the first Joseph Pulitzer at the *World* in the pre-yellow-journalism years. Grozier loved Pulitzer, describing his mind as "like a flash of lightning, illuminating the dark places." But eventually Grozier left the editorship of the *Evening World* to return to Boston and buy the troubled *Post,* asking Taylor's permission, in that age of gentlemanly exchanges. "If you have even the slightest objection," he told Taylor, "I won't consider purchasing the paper." Taylor responded that if Grozier "can gather up any of the crumbs that fall from the Globe's table, you're welcome to them"—to which Grozier retorted: "If I can, I shall go after the cake, too!"

Grozier saved the paper with a series of Pulitzer-like stunts and promotions, such as printing the names of every child that contributed to the *Post*'s campaign to buy elephants for the local zoo. Like Pulitzer, he played up murder and mayhem, winning subscribers with the heavy coverage of Lizzy Borden and other grisly crime stories. He also promoted Irish causes, which stuffier Boston papers did not, and he cut the price to one cent from three. In time, the paper's circulation overtook that of the *World,* with its much larger market. When Grozier took ill in 1920, though, it was his son Richard who proved himself by challenging the Ponzi phenomenon as it swept his city.

The thirty-eight-year-old, slight-of-build Charles Ponzi, nattily dressed in his trademark boater hat and cane, had a flair for selling and a wonderful head for business—as long as that business was crooked. Unbeknownst to Bostonians who first heard his get-rich-quick promises in early 1920, he had a past full of fraud and forgery, having served prison terms in Montreal and Georgia. Almost as ardent a stamp collector as he was a con artist, he had devised a plausible-sounding investment plan—with implausible returns of 50 percent in ninety days—based on foreign exchange rates in the postwar Europe of collapsing currency values.

To get those returns for investors, Ponzi pledged that he would put their dollars into humble-sounding instruments called "International Reply Coupons," or IRCs. These actually did exist; IRCs had been created by a global agreement before the war to help governments fix values at which their nation's postage stamps would be redeemed. Countries designed coupons with floating redemption rates, reflecting what currency was being used in the transaction, to allow the international mailing of letters. Thus, mail posted at a certain rate in, say, the United States would be delivered to Spain or Italy, no matter what happened to rates in those countries when the U.S. mail was sent.

In 1919, Ponzi examined one of the IRC certificates that an associate in Spain had sent him, and began to think. We know something of his thought process because of accounts he gave later about his adventures. As Boston journalist Mitchell Zuckoff writes in his 2005 book *Ponzi's Scheme,* "in a flash of insight, some might even say genius, Ponzi saw something more, a global currency whose value fluctuated wildly depending on where it was used." Ponzi did some calculations: If one U.S. dollar could purchase five IRCs in Boston, it could buy sixty-six IRCs in Rome once the dollars were exchanged for the severely devalued Italian lira.

It was a moment reminiscent of *The Producers'* Max Bialystock, plotting with Leo Bloom how they might make more money with a play that flopped than with one that became a Broadway hit. To make money with this kind of exchange himself, Ponzi would have to start with a hoard of original dollars to buy the IRCs in countries with devalued currencies—a hoard he did not have. Then he would have to buy and transport the huge bundles of coupons that would have to be involved if any meaningful profit was to be produced. That's if it was even legal. "But those critical details would wait for another day," Zuckoff writes. Ponzi decided instead to use his brainstorm to sell others on investing in Ponzi's own securities. That would get him his bankroll. He would then deliver the promised returns by paying them off with the investments of later investors.

His international trade in IRCs never began. What did begin was a promotion based on persuading others that Ponzi could manipulate the system to turn a huge profit for them.

For fifty cents he registered the name of a new company at the end of 1919: Securities Exchange Company—a name that existed over a decade before a federal government "Securities and Exchange Commission" was created to *protect* the investment community from scams like Ponzi's. Shamelessly, Ponzi began building a foundation for his scheme that was designed to insulate him from the authorities. At the police commissioner's office, he made a point of putting money in the Boston Police Relief Association, and promised more.

Just for fun, he put out feelers with postal officials about whether the exchange he had dreamed up for IRCs might actually be possible. Could he redeem IRCs for cash—a key part of his scheme—if he had them? No, he was told. But by that time the promotion was already going crazy, with ninety-day, 50 percent Securities Exchange Company notes flying out of his downtown Boston shop. The post office began examining his scheme. It would "begin" for many months, without result. But Ponzi was bringing in thirty thousand dollars a week at the start. Then more, and more, both in tiny investments and, soon, in ten-thousand-dollar chunks.

He also was digging himself deeper into a hole each day, of course. Each coupon was a debt he had no hope of repaying without plundering later investment dollars. As his secretary kept doling out the company promissory notes, she wrote investors' names on index cards. The names multiplied as quickly as the incoming cash. From 1,525 investors he brought in forty thousand dollars during May. Ponzi bought an expensive house in the suburbs and a fancy car for the commute. His lifestyle was lavish. New ways had to be found to keep drawing investors, and Ponzi found them. He cut the payout time in half, and touted that "a little dollar could start on a journey across the ocean and return home in six weeks, married and with a couple of kids."

"Can It Be Real?"

Enter the newspapers. On June 9, the *Boston Traveler* was first to promote Ponzi in the news columns, with an all-capital headline saying: "WE GUARANTEE YOU 50 PERCENT PROFIT IN 45 DAYS." The postal inspector that a *Traveler* reporter questioned failed to signal any problem with the investment, and added a tantalizingly mysterious note: "We haven't figured out how they make their enormous profit, but they seem confident of their ability to do so." That triggered more investor interest. But basically, newspapers didn't pay much attention for a few more weeks. There was lots of news cramming the front pages: Nationally, Prohibition had gone into effect in January. States also were debating another constitutional amendment that would give women the right to vote. In Massachusetts, a murder in a Boston suburb was being blamed on two Italians, Nicola Sacco and Bartolomeo Vanzetti. The governor, Calvin Coolidge, was considering a run for vice president. Further, notes journalist Zuckoff, sports pages were full of Babe Ruth, "pounding home runs for the New York Yankees after his stunning sale the

previous winter by the Boston Red Sox. The Babe's move fueled the question of
whether New York City might eclipse Boston as the 'Hub of the Universe.' Most
Bostonians doubted it."

It was July 4 before the *Boston Post* got involved, beginning a two-month flurry
of stories about Ponzi. It started with a courthouse reporter's piece about a million-
dollar lawsuit that a Ponzi associate had filed against him. The plaintiff couldn't
be found to comment, but Ponzi, as usual, had plenty to say. It was just a case of
someone wanting money from him because he was so wealthy, Ponzi said, and any
legitimate claim would be "satisfied because I have got two million dollars over and
above all claims of investors against me in this country." The article then went on
to note that Ponzi "is today rated as worth $8,500,000—purchaser of business
blocks, trust companies, estates and motor cars." To the question of "Can it be
real?" posed by the story, federal, state, and city authorities were said to be answering "that they have been unable to find that he is doing anything illegal."

Richard Grozier was incredulous at the 50 percent profit claim, though. He
asked *Post* city editor Edward J. Dunn to have some reporters look into Ponzi and
his company more closely. One worry on Grozier's mind was that a number of *Post*
employees, mostly in the press room, were investors with Ponzi. Various investigations also had started, to go with the postal probe, and bank examiners were talking with Ponzi's bankers. Using investor money, Ponzi set up a $1.5-million short-
term certificate of deposit at the bank to placate inspectors.

The *Post* clearly had been able to dig up very little of a skeptical nature. But
what it had, for some reason it chose not to run in the first of the two front-page
articles it planned, one for Saturday, July 24, and the other for the next day. The
headline on the Saturday story read:

DOUBLES THE
    MONEY WITHIN
        THREE MONTHS
50 Per Cent Interest Paid in 45 Days
By Ponzi—Has Thousands Of Investors
        Deals in International Coupons Taking
        Advantage of Low Rates of Exchange

That was, essentially, what the un-bylined page-one story said—little more, in
fact, than what had appeared in the July 4 lawsuit story. But it said it in bold on
page one. The July 25 story was different. Headlined "Ponzi Has a Rival Next Door
to Him," the article began with a reference to a federal investigation that "is being
pushed with vigor." The first story caused a rush on Ponzi's offices by people want-

ing to buy more notes. And despite the change in tone of the second article, the rush continued the next day.

But at least the *Post* was on the story.

City editor Dunn had two reporters, Principio "P. A." Santosuosso and Herbert L. Baldwin, on the case, trying to push it beyond what little they had. They turned to Clarence Barron as a source. Barron, short, bearded, and weighing 330 pounds at age sixty-five, had established himself as quite a Boston character. He had a reserved suite at the Ritz Carlton, across from the Boston Public Garden, to go with his Beacon Hill home and an estate in the posh South Shore community of Cohasset. The page of news his Boston News Bureau provided was aimed for Boston's high-finance readers, who paid the princely sum of one dollar for it. But Barron had strong views about Ponzi and his popularity, and the journalist was a great interview. The *Post* article featuring Barron ran under the headline:

QUESTIONS THE MOTIVE
BEHIND PONZI SCHEME
Barron Says Reply Coupon Plan
Can Be Worked Only In Small Way

Identified as being "recognized internationally as among the foremost financial authorities of the world," Barron was quoted as saying: "No man of wide financial or investment experience would look twice at a proposition to take his money upon a simple promise to pay it back with a 50% increase in three months." Barron further raised the question of whether there could possibly be enough supply of postage to soak up the millions that Ponzi said was being invested. While "there is now probably opportunity for people to deal in a small way under these postal arrangements so as to make money out of the fall in foreign exchange," he said, "it is unreasonable to ask anybody to believe that any large amount of money can be so invested. If a man were to go down to the Boston post office to invest millions in postage stamps he would very soon exhaust the supply and it might be a long time before the paper mills and the factories could turn out a new supply." Ponzi then was given several paragraphs at the end to recount his supposed investment strategy.

The public reaction to all this cold water on the hot investment? The biggest rush yet from people wanting to *buy*. When Edward Dunn walked around the corner from the *Post* to check on the scene, his observation was: "Pigs being led to the slaughter."

The scenario was to play out for several more weeks, each new skeptical story seeming to stimulate business rather than stifle it. On July 30, New York's postmaster was quoted as saying that the small number of postal reply coupons in existence made it "impossible" that a multimillion-dollar fortune could be created from them. Barron sharpened his old charges about it being a case of "robbing Peter to pay Paul," adding some sarcasm about the possibility that Ponzi could apply his investment formula to solve all of Europe's woes. "Surely," he said, "the allies could spare him a million and within three years clean up that debt tangle." *Post* cartoons pictured a worried-looking Ponzi trying to keep his "pot of gold" boiling. An editorial by Grozier said, "It Cannot Last."

But the charming Ponzi, now identified as a man of the people, was past criticism to many. In fact, the heavier the attack, the more his cult-figure status seemed to grow. He milked it unmercifully. In one of his frequent impromptu speeches to crowds, he said, "Now please don't think that I'm boasting, but I have forgotten more about foreign exchange than C. W. Barron ever knew." When someone in an audience suggested he was the greatest Italian in history, he responded, "No. I am the third greatest." He rated Columbus and Marconi higher. Finally, to shouts of "Ponzi for mayor!" and "Ponzi for governor!" he suggested, in a comment sure to win him fans, that he might throw his support to an anti-Prohibition candidate. The *Boston Traveler,* ever the Ponzi supporter, ran a sports column comparing him to Babe Ruth. The bankers are trying to retire Ponzi "with the banks full," the writer said. "Just like trying to retire you with the bases full, hey Babe?" The *New York Times* observed that in the city to the north, "public distrust seems to be shifting from Ponzi to his critics and assailants."

Recalled *Editor & Publisher* in its later account of the *Post's* reporting:

> The first steps taken against Ponzi seemed to lead up against a blank wall. The cheerful "wizard" was apparently entirely frank, and talked very openly. He showed a quarter of a million dollars in bills crushed into two suit cases and another quarter of a million of Liberty Bonds, to impress the Post reporters with his financial ability to meet an attack upon his establishment. . . . Ponzi had won the first round in the contest between him and the Post.

But the *Post* wasn't finished. Its reporters were still gathering information, and sources were starting to step forward in response to its stories. It delivered a one-two punch.

What a PR Man Owes the Public

First, when Ponzi's own public relations man, William McMasters, a former *Post* reporter, became suspicious of his boss, he did some snooping around the office and found incriminating information—which he offered to Grozier. The *Post* editor paid $5,000 for it, something the ensuing article did not disclose. Under McMasters's own byline, the article said that Ponzi had earned nothing from investments outside the United States and was at least $2 million in debt. His article ran on Monday, August 2, under the page-one headline:

DECLARES PONZI IS NOW HOPELESSLY INSOLVENT
Publicity Expert Employed by 'Wizard' Says
He Has Not Sufficient Funds to Meet His Notes—
States He Has Sent No Money to Europe nor
Received Money from Europe Recently

Why had McMasters chosen to speak up? "As a publicity man," he wrote, "my first duty is to the public." While that statement might have stopped a few readers in their tracks, more than a few others believed the rest of his claims. At last, investors lined up outside Ponzi's office with withdrawals in mind, pulling out $400,000 on Monday alone. But some Ponzi fans still weren't convinced. That would take one more *Post* story.

On August 8, Ponzi was comfortable at home in his bathrobe as he settled in for two hours with *Post* reporter P. A. Santosuosso. The questions were about his life before coming to Boston. There were holes in the story—holes that Santosuossa was looking for, because he had heard rumors that Ponzi had a criminal record in Canada. Still, the reporter didn't have enough to confront Ponzi about it. After the interview was over, though, the *Post* Montreal correspondent provided the tip the paper had been itching for: that someone named Charles Ponsi, spelled with an "s," had been imprisoned there a decade earlier for forgery. The charge had stemmed from his employment at Banco Zarossi. Santosuossa called Ponzi back at home with his follow-up. Ponzi laughed off the direct question of whether he was the same Ponsi, who also used the alias Bianchi. Had he been in Canada at that time? Yes. Had he worked at that bank? "I might have."

For the *Post,* the next step was immediately dispatching a reporter to Montreal—it was Herbert Baldwin—to nail down the report once and for all. His interviews were successful, bringing numerous confirmations from the Ponzi photo Baldwin displayed. With the addition of a mustache, he was told, it was the same man: the forger Ponsi, alias Bianchi. Or, as one said, "Bianchi, the snake!"

Being Ponzi, the trader still made efforts to deny it, even after a bylined story by Baldwin ran August 11 with the headline "Canadian 'Ponsi' Served Jail Term" and with details of the forgery conviction. When he was told what the story would say, and was asked to comment, Ponzi told the *Post* reporter: "Then you are going to get the presses ripped out of your building." But the bravado didn't last. Just over a month had passed since the unquestioning July 4 story in the *Post*. Now, Ponzi's life unraveled fast.

"It was this revelation that finally burst the bubble," said the *Post* in its nomination letter to the Pulitzer board. "Practically the last doubts were swept away." From the arraignment on through trial, conviction, and sentence, any remaining doubts certainly vanished. As the authorities swarmed, Ponzi admitted having served the Georgia prison term as well.

Ever chatty, Ponzi said to the *Post*'s Baldwin at a moment toward the end of the trial: "You did a fine job on me. If it hadn't been for that story in the *Post*, maybe things would have been a lot different for me today." Much later, Ponzi was to detail the entire scam. "My business was simple. It was the old game of robbing Peter to pay Paul," he said. "The whole thing was broken."

In *Editor & Publisher*'s June 4 recap, the magazine said that from his first inkling that Ponzi was dishonest:

> . . . Richard Grozier felt that, whatever the cost, whatever the danger, the real facts of the Ponzi scheme should be obtained and the wily plan exposed for the good of the public who were being befooled and upon whom he believed were daily falling tremendous losses. Such action on the part of Mr. Grozier called for strong courage and a high sense of newspaper duty, since if he were unsuccessful in finding the flaw then he was bringing a very grave danger to a great newspaper property.

The Public Service Pulitzer was to be the highlight of the next three decades for the *Post*. A long period of decline began. Edwin Grozier died in 1923 and Richard Grozier died in 1946. The next Gold Medal to a Boston publication would be the *Globe*'s Pulitzer, won in 1966. That was ten years after the *Globe* had bought the *Post*'s library and the rights to its name.

1921—*Boston Post:* For its exposure of the operations of Charles Ponzi by a series of articles which finally led to his arrest.

Swope's *World*

If Charles Ponzi was the perfect charlatan for the Jazz Age, the *New York World*'s Herbert Bayard Swope may have been the perfect journalist to represent the forces of truth, justice, and the American way.

The winner of the very first Pulitzer Prize—in 1917, for his reporting on the

German empire from Europe in the early years of the war—Swope was thirty-eight when he returned to the United States in 1920 and became a key player for Ralph Pulitzer's paper. With all his gifts, Swope was in a good position to help keep the *World* competitive in the changing mix of New York City newspapers. In postwar America, the *World* occupied much the same place that the *New York Times* does today, attracting many of the best journalists from around the country. And Swope was one reason. The tall, red-haired reporter had moved to New York from St. Louis, and the *Post-Dispatch,* much earlier. But even as a young man he had approached the status of legend for his driving desire to get a story, solving crimes ahead of the police and putting his personal mark on every story he covered. In Europe, besides winning the first Pulitzer Prize, he was best known for having donned tails and top hat to crash the Versailles peace talks—to which no reporters were invited—getting crucial, exclusive details for the *World.* He brought that same outrageous flair to editing once he returned to New York.

"What I try to do in my paper," Swope once said, "is to give the public part of what it wants to have and part of what it ought to have, whether it wants it or not."

Even finding a job title for Swope became an adventure. In the internal political structure of the *World* in the early 1920s, the editorial page editor carried the title of editor, and Ralph Pulitzer was the publisher. The managing editor thus was the most powerful person in terms of running the day-to-day news operations. Because of Swope's outsized reputation, managing editor wasn't an appropriate title for him, Ralph Pulitzer and Swope decided. The position of "executive editor" was created. Swope was the first person at a newspaper to have such a title, which is now nearly as common as editor-in-chief. (He sometimes referred to himself as Chief Executive Editor, only half-jokingly.)

One Joseph Pulitzer aphorism that Swope favored was "Every reporter is a hope, every editor a disappointment." But Swope attacked editing with the eye of a reporter, albeit one who knew how stories should be packaged for the front page.

Under his guidance, the paper would win two Public Service awards for the *World* in three years. The first Gold Medal, however, was the greatest. Coming in 1922, it started a pattern that would prevail for decades—honoring stories for the Public Service Prize that pointed out racial injustice. Swope had decided that the *World* would take on the Ku Klux Klan.

The Klan of that day had risen to a level of prominence very quickly. The groups of hooded vigilantes that fought Reconstruction in the South and border states after the Civil War, making the lynching of freed blacks and cross burnings their symbols, had died out before the 1870s. But seemingly from out of nowhere, a national KKK revival had occurred just before the United States entered World War I. Among racists, the rituals and mysteries of the organization made it attractive in an almost romantic way. It was estimated to have half a million members in both cities and rural areas around the country, spewing hate at Catholics, Jews, and other minorities, as well as blacks. Little had been written about the new rise of the Klan, however.

Swope himself tracked down the individuals who had created the new KKK. As it turned out, the Klan's twentieth-century origins were largely as a money-raising scheme, although as World War I approached it also grew by building its isolationist appeal. It was actually formed in Georgia in 1916 as a chartered secret fraternal organization. Swopes began to strip the mystery away. He assigned *World* staffer Rowland Thomas, a part-time novelist and one of the paper's best writers, to write a series that would turn out to be twenty-one parts long. Swope was the editor for the stories, which ran without a byline, something not unusual for that day.

The sources tapped for the project included Henry P. Fly, a former Klan member who had become disenchanted with its message of hatred. Before leaving the Klan, Fry had risen to the rank of "Kleagle," as local leaders were called. In June, he delivered files to Swope that included a membership list and details of how the Klan operated, from its terrorist tactics to its secret handshake. Swope had another, less-expected source in the person of his friend Walter White, leader of the National Association for the Advancement of Colored People. White, it seemed, had been writing letters back and forth to William Joseph Simmons, the former Methodist minister who had first formed this new Klan. White had pretended to be a white Southerner living in the North, interested in the KKK's ways, and Simmons had "blabbed all sorts of incriminating confidences that he would not, had he known his communicant's identity, have told to one of the country's most militant Negro leaders," wrote E. J. Kahn Jr. in his biography of Swope.

The first of the World's twenty-one straight days of articles began with an eight-column banner headline proclaiming:

SECRETS OF THE KU KLUX KLAN EXPOSED BY THE WORLD;
MENACE OF THIS GROWING LAW-DEFYING ORGANIZATION
PROVED BY ITS RITUAL AND THE RECORD OF ITS ACTIVITIES

Through three weeks of stories, the evil of the organization came alive. The series began:

What is the Ku Klux Klan?
    How has it grown from a nucleus of thirty-four charter members to a membership of more than 500,000 within five years?

How have its "domains" and "realms" and "Klans" been extended, until they embrace every state in the union but Montana, Utah, and New Hampshire?

What are the possibilities of a secret organization that practices censorship of private conduct behind the midnight anonymity of mask and robe and with the weapons of whips and tar and feathers?

What ought to be done about an order whose members are not initiated but "naturalized," whose oaths bind them in obedience to an "Emperor" chosen for life?

What ought to be done about an organization with such objects, when the salesmen of memberships in it work first among the officers of the court and police departments, following them with the officers on the reserve lists of the military and naval forces?

At the end of months of inquiry throughout the United States and in the performance of what it sincerely believes to be a public service, the World this morning begins the publication of a series of articles in which answers to these questions will be offered, set out against the vivid background of as extraordinary a movement as is to be found in recent history.

To give a flavor of the approach, the September 9 installment of the series talked about Klan recruitment and how it raised money for Simmons through membership fees, while the September 10 installment discussed the racial and religious hate tests that prospective members had to pass, and broke down such Klan titles from Klaliff (vice president) to Klexfer (outer guard.) Included with the writing were cartoons by the paper's Rollin Kirby, including one on September 11 that showed Uncle Sam with his own noose, chasing a rope-wielding Klansman. The caption: "Reversing It." Yet other stories described lynching and tarring-and-feathering episodes, the innocent victims, and the fear that the Klan had instilled in communities.

For the *World*, it was a phenomenal circulation booster, adding about sixty thousand readers during the run of the series. New Yorkers stood in line to wait for copies that rolled off the presses just after midnight. Swope also arranged for wide syndication, reaching two million readers through eighteen papers, mostly in the North and West.

The Klan series was also the unanimous choice of the Pulitzer jury, again a group of three Columbia faculty members led by John Cunliffe. While the board enthusiastically approved and chose the *World* for the 1922 Gold Medal, strangely, the pick was not unanimously applauded around the Pulitzer newspaper empire. The *Post-Dispatch,* in St. Louis, had been chilly to the project, with some editors thinking it overdone as a twenty-one-part crusade. At the *Evening World,* the independently edited sister of the New York paper, managing editor John H. Tennant was so disappointed that the board passed over his own paper's work on slum housing that he broke down and wept.

Analyses of the results of the Klan crusade, done in the years since it ran, have suggested that the *World* actually may have built up the Klan's popularity among some white-supremacist factions. Others have said that the *World* series contributed to the decline of the KKK, helping to make it be seen as something of a national joke.

1922—*New York World:* For articles exposing the operations of the Ku Klux Klan, published during September and October 1921.

∽∾∾∽

As the *World* Returns

The next year, the *Memphis Commercial Appeal* won the Public Service Prize largely for its cartoons challenging the Klan in Tennessee. (And two more papers in the 1920s—the Columbus, Georgia, *Enquirer Sun* in 1926 and the *Indianapolis Times* in 1928—would win wholly or in part for campaigns reporting on the Klan in their areas.) In 1924, the *World* won again, for a Swope-led project of a different kind.

For the first time, the board overruled the jurors in selecting a Gold Medal winner. A letter from the three professors recommended the prize for the *Fort Worth Press* exposé of fraudulent oil promoters, which had helped convict promoters. Others in the Columbia journalism school, though, had suggested consideration of "the work done by the *New York World* in exposing the peonage system in the prison camps of some of the Southern states." In the end, the *World*'s stories won over the board.

One of Swope's many credos was that one should "boil over whenever wrong is done the little fellow." And coverage of the "peonage evil" involved such a case. Martin Tabert, a North Dakota boy who had left the farm to seek work in Florida, had traveled by rail without buying a ticket. Arrested, he had a choice of paying a twenty-five-dollar fine or spending ninety days in a country jail. But the money his family sent never got to him. Instead, Tabert became one of the prisoners leased out by the sheriff to a lumber camp. There, he was horsewhipped to death, although his family was told he had died of malaria and pneumonia. When the State of North Dakota tried in vain to get Tabert's death investigated, Swope's *World* took over.

Tracking down some fellow lumber-camp inmates—including one from Brooklyn who had kept a diary—reporter Samuel Duff McCoy worked the story for two months. Among his findings was that a Florida state senator owned a turpentine camp that benefited from convict labor. Even from far-off New York, the *World* managed to get results. The man who had used the horsewhip on Tabert was indicted on a first-degree murder charge and the Florida legislature passed a statute forbidding whipping, though the vote was close.

Swope would leave the *World* in the late 1920s, frustrated with how poorly Ralph Pulitzer and his brother Herbert were managing the paper. (It was to fold in 1931.) His deep involvement with the city's and the nation's arts scene as well as the news scene—as a confidant of the powerful in both fields—was to continue. A story related by biographer Alfred Allan Lewis has Swope, in his last years at the *World,* seeking help from a psychoanalyst. Characteristically, he required that the phone be moved closer to the couch, however:

> "Now, then, where shall we begin" [asked Swope.] "I was born in St. Louis—" The phone rang, and the doctor answered it. It was Governor [Al] Smith for Mr. Swope. For the rest of the hour, it rang incessantly, with Mayor [Robert] Walker, Bernard Baruch, and George Kaufman all on the wire for Swope. The doctor's incredulity grew with each call. When his time was up, Swope leaped to his feet and shook the doctor's hand energetically. "Thanks, Doc. You don't know how much better I feel." And in a long stride, he was gone.
>
> When the physician called for a diagnosis, the analyst replied, "It's simple. The man has delusions of grandeur."

1924—*New York World:* For its work in connection with the exposure of the Florida peonage evil.

A Martyr for the Truth

In 1926, *Canton Daily News* editor Don R. Mellett had been doing the nitty-gritty work of dedicated editors everywhere. A newcomer to the eastern Ohio town, he decided to keep track of local underworld figures and to try to make their operations known. It was work in the tradition of watchdog journalism. For a criminal with a house to plunder, however, the first step is often to kill the watchdog.

Mellett, one of seven sons in an Indiana newsman's family, arrived in Canton in 1925 as the business manager, and then as publisher of the paper. Its owner, former Ohio Governor (and 1920 Democratic presidential candidate) James M. Cox, had wanted Mellett, then thirty-four, to help the paper narrow the circulation gap with the market-leading *Canton Repository.* Mellett proceeded to do just that with a series of promotional stunts, like hiring the "Marvel Man," a lip-reader, to go from place to place and listen in on conversations. (One story reported that the words actually spoken by Douglas Fairbanks in a silent film were "What the hell is the matter with you?" and not the subtitled "Anyway, I love you.") In one story, though, the Marvel Man discovered an ugly truth about Canton. He lip-read a drug deal between an addict and a pusher. A headline appeared that said "Traffic in 'Dope' Uncovered."

Crime was no stranger to Canton, as Mellett found in pursuing stories about various unsavory characters in town. While not a crime center like Chicago, Cleveland, Detroit, and Pittsburgh, Canton was considered a "hideout" for criminals on the lam from those cities. And Canton had its own bootlegging, gambling, and prostitution underworld, managed by a character named Jumbo Crowley. With the combination of visiting thugs hiding out and local crooks running their rackets, Canton was a nest of vipers.

On January 2, 1926, Don Mellett stepped right into that nest. His editorial started:

> It is the opinion of The News that Canton needs cleaning up. Bootlegging, gambling, and houses of prostitution are running wide open, in flagrant violation of the law. If [Police] Chief [Saranus] Lengel denies this, proof is available to him. If he states he cannot clean up these vice conditions upon proof of their existence he should step aside and permit some one who can to do so.

The final suggestion was, "Get busy or get out." He could have been tougher, but Mellett was still getting to know the town. But Chief Lengel was kicked out by the reform mayor the paper had supported. (He was later reinstated by the civil service commission.) And as the publisher's knowledge grew, so did the boldness of his editorials. The March 1 paper carried an editorial with the headline, "Vice Cleanup Only Started; Climax Coming." It began:

> Canton's clean-up of vice conditions has only just started. The dismissal of the chief of police was necessary, it appears, as the first step toward building a more militant aggressive police department. With a determined police department on the job organized liquor, and dope traffic cannot operate, nor can gambling. Without protection, directly or indirectly the underworld cannot exist. And already the slight changes made in the police department are beginning to bear fruit. The fear of God is beginning to creep into the hearts of the law violators and a break-up is on the horizon.
>
> . . . Jumbo Crowley must be put out of business. His every place must be stopped and kept dark . . . .
>
> Liquor law violation is only part of the vice. Dope and gambling are contributing a big share to making Canton's underworld a place to be reckoned with.

During the last six years there have been committed nearly fifty murders in Stark County. Of these only two convictions were obtained. It is a common thing, rather than the exceptional, for a murder to go unexplained rather than to obtain a confession or apprehend the murderer . . . .

He went on, naming names—a dozen more in this editorial, and in later ones—for four-and-a-half months. While the *Daily News* did sell more papers, the attack on graft didn't make him popular in much of the town of 107,000. Mobsters were upset, of course, to see themselves identified by name, with their supposedly shadowy exploits spread across the front page for all to see. But town leaders, too, were displeased that their town was portrayed as crime-ridden. It was bad for business. When Mellett criticized Price Janson, a local businessman who served on the civil service commission, for supporting Sheriff Lengel, Janson was removed from the commission. He answered Mellett's criticisms in a letter, and on July 12, the day of Janson's ouster, publisher Mellett gave him his say on page one, if only to show readers the split that existed in the community:

> Mr. Mellett not so long ago blessed the State of Indiana by leaving it and brought to Canton a mouthing, slobbering, overworked jawbone and by his blackguarding, muckraking tactics has caused Canton unmeasurable harm by his publicity of scandalous matter and given to Canton an unfavorable name which the facts and the truth of the situation do not warrant—a man whose civic pride all rests in his jawbone. In a less refined, civilized society than exists here in Canton the community would have purged itself of this nuisance by riding him out of town on a rail amidst the praise and applause of the enraptured multitude.

Mellett's response to Janson the next day was tame. "Certainly there should be no division of the good citizens while the forces of the underworld stand united, ready and willing to confuse the fight for their abolishment."

After he and his wife returned from a dance, Mellett was putting his car in the garage when he was shot three times, once in the head. He died instantly.

Newspapers around the country ran the story of this new martyr to the cause of using the newspaper to speak out for the community. Under the page-one headline, "We Carry On," the *Daily News* ran an editorial saying: "Like a captain in battle leading his forces Don R. Mellett, publisher of the Daily News, has fallen—a sacrifice to the cause he waged against vice, and what he believed efforts to corrupt the city government. Wanton murder stalked at midnight into his home . . ."

Wrote Cox in a tribute to Mellett: "How foolish were the assassins and those who goaded them on! The taking of a single life in the present circumstances is of no avail. When a general falls at the head of his army, the spectacle of sacrifice moves his followers onward to increased devotion in the cause."

Enduring Mysteries

The local police, not surprisingly, were somewhat lax in their investigation of the crime. Chief Lengel had been reinstated earlier, and a local grand jury failed to bring any indictments. It took the intervention of a special investigator from Chicago to get five men arrested, tried, and convicted. One was Chief Lengel, and another was an out-of-town mobster named Patrick "Red" McDermott, both eventually convicted of first-degree murder. McDermott said that a plan to beat up the publisher had escalated into a shooting.

Chief Lengel, however, was eventually granted a new trial and freed when a witness against him at the first trial refused to repeat his story. Even now, there is uncertainty about who fired the fatal shot, and who else might have been involved in the killing.

Of course, there was no Don Mellett to hammer away at the need for results. And soon, there was no *Daily News* either. While the Gold Medal was sealed in the cornerstone of a new building for the paper, Cox sold both the *Daily News* and the building three years later, and it was combined with the *Repository*, which took over the new building.

Another mystery was the reaction of the community. Even in its shock over the murder, Canton's citizens were cool to Mellett. Journalists doing anniversary stories much later noted that Canton—whose drive to build up local businesses has been crowned with the National Football League Hall of Fame—played down the Mellett case. Some people still had the feeling that Mellett was more interested in building circulation than in cleaning up government. And most did not want the old stories of Canton's sordid past brought up again.

But to the nation's journalism community, the *Canton Daily News*'s Pulitzer always will serve as a stark reminder of the ultimate price that editors and reporters can pay for working on behalf of the public.

1927—*Canton Daily News:* For its brave, patriotic and effective fight for the ending of a vicious state of affairs brought about by collusion between city authorities and the criminal element, a fight which had a tragic result in the assassination of the editor of the paper, Mr. Don R. Mellett.

"Pulitzer Prizes for Pulitzer Papers"

When the *New York Evening World* won the Gold Medal in 1929 for a series of criminal justice–related campaigns, it was the third Public Service Prize awarded to Pulitzer-owned newspapers and their twelfth Pulitzer Prize overall. Only forty-one journalism prizes had been awarded, making the Pulitzer papers in New York or St. Louis the owners of more than a quarter of them. Beyond that, most of the prizes had gone to eastern newspapers.

The board members—and especially the Pulitzer brothers—certainly had not intended for the prizes to favor Pulitzer newspapers. Joseph and Ralph were very sensitive about the appearance of favoritism when the *World* papers and *St. Louis Post-Dispatch* won. And for the Pulitzer Prizes to be accepted nationally, they knew, the awards had to recognize journalism excellence from coast to coast. In 1928, J.P. II had written to Columbia president Nicholas Butler: "If we cannot manage to get more entries and thus very largely widen the field, I seriously fear that the Pulitzer Prizes in Journalism will come to be regarded as sad jokes by American newspaper men in general, indeed, I have reason to believe that this tendency is already under way."

In November 1929, the Pulitzer Advisory Board's executive secretary took a thirty-two-city tour of newspapers outside the East and made a disturbing report. The "indifference and apathy encountered are too generally prevalent," he said. "Many frankly admitted that they had ceased making nominations because they had concluded that the awards were generally made to the metropolitan newspapers of the east. Frequently allusions were made to the regularity with which the prizes were given to the Pulitzer newspapers."

The Pulitzer brothers quietly agreed that their papers would withhold making any entries for the 1930 prizes. They then withheld entries again in 1931, and perhaps in later years as well.

Another way to approach the problem was to encourage nominations from outside the East, and then to make sure the board gave them due consideration. In the 1930s, many more midwestern and western papers would be honored as winners, in Public Service and in other categories as well. The Pulitzer Prizes benefited from the diversity.

For all the perceived questions about favoritism, the Public Service Prize had at least been defined in the 1920s. No longer did editors wonder what kinds of stories the Pulitzer board would recognize with Gold Medals. Unfocused collections of articles, no matter how good, went out of favor as Public Service Prize candidates as the 1930s approached. By its acknowledgment of the Canton murder case, the Ponzi exposé, and campaigns against the Ku Klux Klan, the board showed that physical courage and financial risk-taking were qualities it prized, along with success in bringing about positive changes in the community. And the board clearly liked a powerful investigative story.

Boston Post editor Richard Grozier, who had his staff pursue the Charles Ponzi scandal. Photo courtesy of the *Boston Globe*.

The *Boston Post* of August 11, 1920, discloses the Canadian record of Charles "Ponsi." Used by permission of the *Boston Globe*, courtesy Boston Public Library.

The next day's *Post* shows how Ponzi would look with a moustache painted on, à la the Ponsi mug shot above. Below the clean-shaven Ponsi is another big news story for Boston: "Ruth Injures Knee Sliding."

The *New York World* begins its series on the Ku Klux Klan, September 6, 1923. In the lower right it notes that eighteen publications around the country are also carrying the stories. Courtesy of the New York Public Library.

World executive editor Herbert Bayard Swope on the cover of *Time,* January 28, 1924.
Used by permission of *Time* magazine.

The front page of the *Canton* (Ohio) *Daily News* on July 16, 1926, banners the news of editor Don Mellett's murder. Reprinted by permission of the *Canton Repository*. Page provided courtesy of the Stark County District Library.

CHAPTER 9

From Depression to Wartime

[In the 1930s] the Pulitzer Prizes in Journalism became an intrinsic part of the profession in the United States. If they were not perfect, they were at least respected. Their permanence was not questioned.

—John Hohenberg, Pulitzer Prize administrator
and secretary, 1954–1976

*A*lmost on cue in October of 1929, the bubble burst for the Roaring Twenties. Still, it took Americans a while to shake the notion that Charles Ponzi might have been right—that maybe everybody *could* get rich quick, magically and without effort. In the 1930s, the Great Depression and its constant companions, graft and crime, provided the backdrop for much of the newspaper public service that the Pulitzer Prizes honored.

While the Pulitzer Advisory Board was eager to name winners in all the journalism prize categories, it sent a signal in 1930 that only top-notch entries deserved the Gold Medal. The board turned down all five jury selections, without explaining its reasons, and voted to give no Gold Medal at all that year. The three Columbia faculty-member jurors had considered nineteen entries before unanimously recommending Maine's *Portland Evening News* for "its successful campaign against the exploitation of hydro-electric power from the State of Maine"—coverage that showed "unusual courage and independence." The other four: the *Brooklyn Daily Eagle* and *New York Telegram* for unearthing city scandals, the *Detroit News* for promoting a reforestation project, and the *Cleveland Press* for a war on machine politics.

The advisory board gave no Pulitzer for Editorial Writing, either. It saved all its journalism plaudits for Reporting, where it again acknowledged the global coverage of the *New York Times.* Technology was a factor, as it had been in the 1918 Public Service Prize. The *Times's* winner was Russell D. Owen, for reports on Admiral Richard E. Byrd's Antarctic exploration. The journalist had submitted his reports by radio transmission.

The next year was a sad one for Ralph and Joseph Pulitzer. In February, the *New York World* folded after years of losses and was merged into what became Scripps-Howard's *World-Telegram.* Ralph continued on the Pulitzer board as chairman. (J.P. II would take over after Ralph's death in 1939.) With the disappearance of the New York paper, concerns about Pulitzer Prizes for Pulitzer papers diminished. In the 1930s through the early 1950s, however, the *St. Louis Post-Dispatch* became an even greater Pulitzer-winning force than the *World* had been, especially in the Public Service category.

Standing Up to Mob Rule

After honoring three solid cases of local watchdog journalism from 1931 to 1933—the work of the *Atlanta Constitution, Indianapolis News,* and *New York World-Telegram*—the Pulitzer board faced a tough choice in 1934. The jury, considering twenty-three nominations for the Gold Medal, offered the board a mixed recommendation that proposed no single winner. In what seemed a peculiar proposal, two jurors recommended that the press as a whole be recognized with a Gold Medal, while a third juror opined that no entry was worthy of the prize.

Board members, unmoved by either argument, dug into the entries on their own and found a winner in Oregon's 4,440-circulation *Medford Mail Tribune.* The *Mail Tribune* had courageously challenged a local demagogue who had used mob tactics—and his own newspaper—to try to overturn the town's government. In the end, he had sought to protect his power base by killing a local constable.

Llewellyn A. Banks, a wealthy orchard owner and alleged bootlegger who had moved to Oregon from California in the 1920s, formed around him a group of extremist supporters to help him control local officials, including the Jackson County sheriff. The miseries of the Depression created a fertile environment for Banks to incite rebellion against the town government. In 1929 he had bought a newspaper, the *Medford News.* In the next few years he published invented charges about a "gang" that had "fattened at the public purse for fifteen years." Starting an organization of local ruffians he called the Good Government Congress, Banks used his newspaper and meetings of the group to push the area toward martial law, threatening existing officials with horsewhipping or hanging.

As the community became more divided, *Mail Tribune* publisher Robert W. Ruhl challenged Banks, warning that the Good Government Congress was aiming to spark a local revolt. After a February election in which a close vote threatened to unseat Banks's choice for sheriff, the ballot boxes were stolen and Banks was charged for the theft. While state police issued a warrant for his arrest, Banks boasted that he would kill any arresting officer. On March 16 he made good on the promise. As constable George Prescott stood outside the door with his warrant, talking with Banks's wife, Banks shot him through the heart with a hunting rifle.

The day after the killing, Ruhl began his editorial, "The Challenge Is Accepted!" this way:

> Do the people of Jackson County want more innocent officers shot down in cold blood behind the skirts of some woman?
> Do they want continued lawlessness, continued pillaging of court houses, and burning of ballots?
> Do they want this reign of terror followed by another, until this community is reduced to a shambles and advertised far and wide as a place where crime is encouraged, sedition lauded, and murder condoned?
> If they do, then that is precisely what they are going to have. All they need to do now is to lie down and take it.

Banks eventually was sentenced to a life term for murder, and some associates went to jail. In nominating his paper for the Gold Medal, Ruhl wrote that "the show is over, the play is played out! But it was a close call!"

Inside the Advisory Board

Why was the Pulitzer board left by jurors to identify this story on its own?

The jurors—*Philadelphia Public Ledger* editor Charles Munro Morrison, *New York Times* Sunday editor Lester Markel, and Columbia dean Carl Ackerman—became embroiled in a debate about President Franklin Roosevelt's National Recovery Administration, the New Deal effort to get business on track by setting wage and other standards for industry. Publishers across the United States sought a waiver from NRA guidelines, contending that applying government standards to newspapers violated the First Amendment. Of course, a waiver also would mean that publishers could pay workers less.

A group of editors and publishers had nominated America's newspaper publishers in general for the Public Service Prize for standing up to the president. Morrison and Ackerman agreed in their jury majority report, saying that "the 'most disinterested and meritorious public service' rendered in 1933 was not by any single newspaper, but by the press as a whole in safe-guarding the freedom of the press in a national emergency." The report suggested that "the Gold Medal be placed in the permanent custody of *Editor & Publisher*," and circulated among members of various press associations.

Some journalists did not see quite the emergency that concerned the two jurors and the publishers. A strong dissent came from Markel, who questioned "the advisability—and, more, the propriety—of that award." He continued:

> What are its implications? Simply this: that, had it not been for the defence [*sic*] of the First Amendment to the Constitution made by the publishers, the President would have acceded to a breach of that Amendment. Whether that danger existed or no (and there are strong opinions on both sides), it does not seem to me fitting for so grave a charge to be leveled against the President, even by implication, in the form of a Pulitzer award. Such action, I feel, runs counter to the whole spirit of the Pulitzer plan.

Markel was equally tough on the other entries in arguing that no medal be awarded. He wrote:

> In what was without doubt the greatest news year in the country's history, there was surely some outstanding newspaper performance of reporting or illuminating the stirring succession of national events that deserves commendation. Yet all of these twenty-three exhibits deal with local matters.

Through a communication from Ralph Pulitzer to his brother Joseph, it is possible to enter the board's inner sanctum at Columbia that year. J.P. II, who was not able to attend the 1934 board meeting, insisted on a full accounting of the proceedings. He got it in a May 2 letter from his brother, the board chairman.

Ralph's reply detailed the reasoning of the board in rejecting the jury recommendation and in selecting the *Mail Tribune*. His letter also sheds light on the selection process of that time, while demonstrating the strong commitment that the Pulitzer sons felt to their father's original goals in establishing the prize, and particularly the Gold Medal. It was clear that in their minds, giving the Public Service Prize to a group of publishers was not appropriate. Wrote Ralph:

> At the meeting I first stated my personal objections (1) that it departed from J.P.'s terms in giving it not to a newspaper but to a group of newspapers; (2) that it departed from those terms since they stated it was to be for a disinterested service, and the fight of the papers could not be called a disinterested service, whether one believed in it or not; (3) that although I was fully aware that many of the men who fought for the freedom of the press clause were actuated solely by patriotic or unselfish motives I was equally aware that many were actuated by motives the

very reverse, and that I thought under these conditions if the press pinned a medal on itself it would become a laughing stock.

I then asked each of the members to state their own personal objections which they did, and without any discussion it was decided not to bestow the gold medal as recommended by the majority report of the sub-committee.

However, the board also "overwhelmingly" voted to reject Markel's proposed withholding of the prize altogether. As entries were then considered one by one, Ralph first favored the *New Orleans Picayune* for its fight against the crooked populist governor of Louisiana, Huey Long. Then another board member brought up the *Mail Tribune* "as having rendered a remarkably courageous public service in fighting a powerful and dangerous bootlegger who had come into that town from California and introduced criminal practices." Continued Ralph Pulitzer's letter:

> At the risk of his life, the editor made a fight against this man and his gang and finally succeeded in having him sent to prison and the gang dispersed.
> The point was made that a service of this kind in such a small town as Medford involved much more danger and courage than in a city like New Orleans. I was won over to this point of view and the Board unanimously voted for the Medford Mail Tribune.

Markel was correct that most entries covered largely local issues, and that the crush of national and global events in 1933 might have produced journalism to merit consideration for the Public Service award. The advisory board's choice seems an early sign that local and regional stories, rather than national or global ones, would tend to be favored for Gold Medals.

Yet, in many ways, newspaper readers may have understood the Depression best as a series of local stories about a national and global economic condition. In addition to the New Orleans and Medford papers, other journals nominated for the Public Service Prize helped settle strikes in New Jersey, fought labor-union crime in Cleveland, exposed sweat shops in Pittsburgh and Scranton, showed up bankruptcy-process irregularities in Wilkes-Barre, and described the life of the unemployed in California.

The Pulitzer Advisory Board was not happy with the 1934 jurors. It asked future jurors to list three to five examples, in Public Service and the other classifications, without making recommendations of their own. The board would do the selecting.

1934—*Medford Mail Tribune:* For its campaign against unscrupulous politicians in Jackson County, Oregon.

A Dust Bowl Primer

Public Service jurors called it a tie in 1938. After looking at thirty-three Public Service entries, they picked two to forward to the board, "because both campaigns deal with extremely important matters and because both newspapers used great versatility and tenaciousness over a long period of time." One nominee was the *San Francisco News,* for fighting vice and police graft. The other was North Dakota's *Bismarck Tribune,* for a series called "Self Help in the Dust Bowl." The advisory board, however, saw the Dust Bowl project as something special for the age.

It was the work of publisher and editor George D. Mann, who died before the paper entered the Dust Bowl series for the Pulitzer. Managing editor Kenneth W. Simons took over as editor. He described the entry as an attempt "to aid the people of the Great Plains to restore prosperity and to forever abandon dependence upon relief systems, public or private." It said the project was aimed at eight million farmers victimized by the Dust Bowl.

The *Tribune's* Pulitzer entry summarized the agricultural history of the Dust Bowl, helping readers understand what had befallen the farmers on the Great Plains:

> The northern great plains have been semi-arid for untold centuries.
> Drouth cycles were known and prepared for by the Indians, long before the careless and avaricious white man settled here. The evidence of aridity was here for all to see . . . . White settlement commenced in 1870 despite warnings that agricultural practices of Iowa, Indiana, Ohio and Pennsylvania were not adaptable in the northwest . . . .
> Through all the years the few men who could see the cumulative effects of blind land management were ignored when they uttered warnings of future disaster. The ground was fertile. The rains fell. Crop prices made more and more wheat farming profitable.
> Then came 1929. A drouth cycle commenced. Sixty years of soil exhaustion, sixty years of unscientific farming, began to take their toll. Farmers failed. Business failed. The regional economy tottered on the brink of destruction.

The Dust Bowl forced 130,000 families to flee the region, the stories said. But the *Tribune's* coverage told the story "of the courageous people who have remained there to fight out their battle, one of the greatest in the history of our country."

The program that it promoted called for farmers to stop single-crop planting, and to restore grass in place of grain on the ranges, replenish natural water reservoirs, and reforest areas that had been cut for crop planting. Overall, the philosophy "substituted the doctrine of self-help for that of government bounty," a drive that the paper said had won "partial acceptance."

The paper produced sixty-nine editorials to go with its news coverage. One editorial, titled "What Is News?" can be read as an early defense of such explanatory journalism. News, wrote the editors, includes the "new things being originated by men of science, the practical application being given to both old and new ideas in the face of changing conditions."

> Upon such things the very life of the community depends. We live in an area in which rainfall is admittedly deficient, at least under the old systems of farming. The people of this region have had warning to either change their habits or move out. Things are not like they used to be and probably never will be again.
>
> The greatest human story ever written on these prairies is that of the struggle of the people for a living; their efforts to maintain the civilization which they built when times were better and when nature smiled upon this region more benignly.
>
> It is an epic tale, worthy of the pen of a Homer. It contains the elements of great achievement and high tragedy, everything needed to move the mind and heart to understanding and new endeavor.

The series covered success stories of farmers who had used enlightened cultivation techniques, and it celebrated the strengths of the midwestern farmers who chose to hold their ground in the Dust Bowl. This July 22 story by reporter Gordon Mac-Gregor began:

> If there is any dominant trait that marks the people of western North Dakota apart from their brothers in other regions it is tenacity.
>
> Here on the northern great plains the tenacious Indian made his last great stand against an overwhelming wave of whites who coveted the soil where the buffalo grew fat.
>
> Here the tenacious ranchers who first settled the country struggled to keep open a range against a flood of peoples with plows who yearned for the free soil that Uncle Sam unwisely opened to farming.
>
> Here the tenacious farmers have clung to their homesteads against implacable drouth and hordes of insects.
>
> All of them—Indian, rancher and farmer—allowed that tenacity to blind them to facts that might have kept them individually and as a class from the brink of destruction to which they were at last inexorably drawn.

Various community and government programs were adopted to support the *Tribune* recommendations. Simons was appointed a member of a new state water conservation commission. In broader terms, the paper argued in nominating its articles that the series served to bring "hope to a people sorely in need of hope; to restore confidence to a people who had become apathetic; to spread the doctrine of self-help and governmental common sense in a land where grasping for political panaceas has been an inevitable result of the devastation which has affected both the land and the people."

The *Tribune,* now owned by Lee Enterprises, keeps the Gold Medal in a vault but has its Pulitzer Prize certificate on display in the newsroom and in the publisher's office. One editor in recent years noted that in North Dakota, the long-ago accomplishment may now be overshadowed by a 1998 Public Service Pulitzer won by the *Grand Forks Herald* for its coverage of a disaster caused by flooding, fire, and blizzard. "We bring up the Pulitzer less with every passing year," *Tribune* editor Dave Bundy said in 2006. "I'm very proud to be editor of a Pulitzer Prize-winning paper and we're proud of the role we've played and will continue to play in our community, but with Grand Forks winning a Pulitzer less than a decade ago, touting an almost seventy-year-old award seems to be resting a little too long on our laurels."

Still, viewed historically, the honor for the small paper's Dust Bowl coverage was an early statement by the advisory board about the major public service that environmental reporting can perform. Decades later, environmental journalism would be a staple of the Pulitzer Prizes.

1938—*Bismarck Tribune:* For its news reports and editorials entitled "Self Help in the Dust Bowl."

Flunking History

While its war coverage again was superb in the 1940s, the *New York Times* won its second Gold Medal by focusing on a home-front issue: deficiencies in the teaching of American history. The idea for the project came from publisher Arthur Hays Sulzberger's wife, Iphigene Ochs Sulzberger. A former history student at Barnard College, she feared that testing American young people about U.S. history would show their ignorance on the subject. Her hope was that exposing the level of the problem would lead to a drive to improve teaching requirements.

The survey was planned by distinguished Columbia history professors Hugh Russell Fraser and Allan Nevins, and coordinated by *Times* education writer Benjamin Fine. Among its more shocking results: 30 percent of the students questioned did not know that Woodrow Wilson was president of the United States during World War I. In the middle of another global war, the story took on a new significance because of what it said about young Americans' poor knowledge of their own country.

Fine's April 4, 1943, story was headlined:

Ignorance of U.S. History
Shown by College Freshmen
Survey of 7,000 Students in 36 Institutions
Discloses Vast Fund of Misinformation
On Many Basic Facts

The *Times*'s nomination letter for the 1944 prize noted that a number of colleges introduced American history after the article ran, and that the states of Illinois and Pennsylvania passed their first requirements for U.S. history to be taught.

There had been plenty of controversy over the story. Four days after the series ran, the *Times* carried a story saying that the *Harvard Crimson* student newspaper had called the test "one of the greatest hoaxes in American history." According to the *Crimson,* many students answered the questions facetiously, while the *Times* took their responses seriously. The *Times* stood by the story, and so did the Pulitzer Advisory Board. Thirty-two nominations in Public Service had been submitted that year, and the jury had designated several favorites—with the *New York Times* history study *not* among them. The board, however, saw clear education value in selecting the *Times*'s work.

1944—*New York Times:* For its survey of the teaching of American History.

Corruption in Lansing

Political graft and crime did not take a holiday during World War II. In fact, toward the war's end several newspapers won Gold Medals for exposing corruption. One was the *Detroit Free Press.*

The *Free Press* had been reporting regularly on statehouse abuses in Lansing, which a judge was investigating in the form of a one-man grand jury. The paper closely followed Republican boss Frank D. McKay, who was suspected of involvement in much of the state's criminal activity. Veteran crime reporter Kenneth McCormick, just back from a Nieman Fellowship at Harvard, had a close relationship with the judge, Leland W. Carr. The case had become bogged down, and the prosecution was left in the hands of an attorney general who was one of McKay's closest associates.

Reporter McCormick's stories, supported by *Free Press* editorials, pushed for a special prosecutor. When one was named, numerous indictments followed. Before the story was done—and McKay was indicted—the paper saw a sign of how great the danger to McCormick was. State senator Warren G. Hooper, a witness in the conspiracy case against McKay, among other related cases, was assassinated in a small Michigan town. The murder is unsolved to this day. McCormick's story on the killing, on January 11, 1945, ran too late to be part of the 1945 Pulitzer entry. But the attack on Hooper provided a sobering backdrop for the board about the environment in which McCormick and the *Free Press* had been reporting.

On the Pulitzer board, chairman Joseph Pulitzer II had seen 1945 as an unusually strong year for Gold Medal contenders. On March 29 he wrote a letter to fellow board member Arthur Krock of the *New York Times,* suggesting that Krock should write an article in the *Sunday Times Magazine* about the strength of all the entries. (The two board members were then in the process of reviewing submissions in advance of their April meeting.) Pulitzer's letter said:

> I am much impressed by this year's entries for the Pulitzer Public Service Prize. If the claims are valid, and I don't doubt they are, the record makes a fine showing for the public service rendered by our much-abused newspapers. In these days when everybody takes a shot at the press, I really believe it would do the public good to be reminded what the press does for it. This year's list ranges all the way from pacifying a dangerous mob of penitentiary prisoners to upholding Japanese-American civil liberties to preventing the abuse of power by the police in the case of an humble citizen to checking an outbreak of typhus. These are just a few.
>
> In a word, it is a damn good record and I, for one, would very much like to see you write about it. Clearly, the piece would carry much more weight under your name than under mine, so please don't think I am passing the buck.

Krock wrote back that he liked the idea of an article. He suggested another writer, though:

> Despite your modesty the name of Joseph Pulitzer attached to the article would attract a hundred-fold the readership which any piece of the kind by me could summon, and the explanation for that is simple. It is the name of the founder of the awards and a celebrated journalist and citizen of the past. It is also the name of an eminent and successful journalist of the present, an enlightened one, too, I may add.
>
> So you must do the article, Joe, and buck-passing is neither your motive nor mine in this discussion.

Pulitzer pondered the proposal for a while, characteristically asking his own *St. Louis Post-Dispatch* managing editor, Benjamin H. Reese, if he agreed with Krock. "If so, I shall need a ghost writer who would have to do quite a bit of research, examining the material submitted and checking it to make certain that the claims of public service rendered are well founded." The paper did assign a staffer, Pulitzer Prize–winning reporter Alvin Goldstein. When Pulitzer did not like the resulting article draft, however, the idea of a Joseph Pulitzer–bylined article was apparently dropped.

1945—*Detroit Free Press:* **For its investigation of legislative graft and corruption in Lansing, Michigan.**

Back to the "Society Page"

On the home front, World War II impacted American journalism in many ways. So, too, did its conclusion. Men who had left their newspapers for military service came back to the newsroom battle-hardened. They had a new model for getting journalism jobs done: a military model, with mission-oriented teams that answered to higher authority. In some newsrooms, that military model already existed. In others, reporters turned to team investigations for the first time.

In another major shift in newsroom demographics, the war's end displaced thousands of other qualified reporters: women. Many had finally gotten a chance in the 1940s to do serious newspaper journalism, and now found themselves forced to go back to the "women's page" or the "society page." It would not be a long-term exit. Women would stream back into hard-news reporting in the 1950s and 1960s and begin winning their share of Pulitzers, including Gold Medals for their papers.

The front page of *Bismarck* (N.D.) *Tribune* from July 22, 1937, carries one of the "Self Help in the Dust Bowl" stories that won it the 1938 Pulitzer Gold Medal. Its headline: "Tenacity Is Trait of North Dakotans." Reprinted by permission.

CHAPTER 10

A Handful of Gold

I know that my retirement will make no difference in its cardinal principles, that it will always fight for progress and reform, never tolerate injustice or corruption, always fight demagogues of all parties, never belong to any party, always oppose privileged classes and public plunderers, never lack sympathy with the poor, always remain devoted to the public welfare, never be satisfied with merely printing news, always be drastically independent, never be afraid to attack wrong, whether by predatory plutocracy or predatory poverty.

—Joseph Pulitzer's *St. Louis Post-Dispatch*
"Platform," April 10, 1907

How would one go about identifying the finest local newspaper staff ever assembled? Since newsrooms do not have the "all-century-team" distinctions that are so popular in the sports world, Pulitzer Prizes leap to mind as one suitable metric for the task.

If the yardstick was the winning of Pulitzer Gold Medals, though, the runaway choice would have to be the *St. Louis Post-Dispatch* from the mid-1930s to the early 1950s. The paper won five in the fifteen-year period from 1937 to 1952, a record total that stood for fifty-two years. When the *New York Times* won its fifth in 2004, and the *Los Angeles Times* followed the next year, the achievements of those two papers covered work done over eighty-six and sixty-one years, respectively. Making the *Post-Dispatch* performance even more remarkable was that it bracketed World War II, when more than half the paper's staff was serving in the military. Not counting the four war years, it won the Gold Medal every other year during that fifteen-year stretch.

Its winning journalism was eclectic, ranging from the exposure of local voter frauds and federal government corruption to an environmental project that helped cleanse its hometown's filthy air. The repercussions were significant, too. The clean air drive, for example, provided a model for blighted cities from Pittsburgh to London. The paper's revelation of federal tax–related payoffs sparked high-level government resignations in 1951 and led to civil service being installed at the agency formerly known as the Internal Revenue Bureau. Quite literally, then, taxpayers have the *Post-Dispatch* to thank for the Internal Revenue Service.

How did one midwestern paper launch so many Gold Medal–winning crusades in so few years?

For one thing, the paper's long investigative reporting tradition, dating back to the first Joseph Pulitzer, attracted great editors and reporters from around the country. Its record of impressive reporting had continued through the 1920s because of writers like Carlos F. Hurd, John T. Rogers, and Paul Y. Anderson. (In April 1912, Hurd had been the only reporter on the *Carpathia,* the *Titanic's* rescue ship; Rogers and Anderson each won early Reporting Pulitzer Prizes—Anderson in 1929 for helping expose the Teapot Dome oil-reserves scandal.) The *Post-Dispatch* was especially well known in the 1930s and 1940s for its managing editors, first Oliver Kirby Bovard and later Benjamin Harrison Reese. Both had an almost military approach to running a newsroom, but also inspired reporters to perform to the best of their ability.

O. K. Bovard personified the newsroom "field general" who instilled both loyalty and fear in his troops. O.K.B., as he signed his memos, lived for a good scoop and insisted on reporters who could dig deep and pursue stories tenaciously. Failure to get a story was not an option. Because he liked to build reporting campaigns around the accumulation of seeming minutiae, he hated "minor errors." He was known to fire reporters for getting a middle initial wrong. His biographer, James Markham, called him a "one-man journalism school," and wrote that a reporter "had only to show that he had worked under Bovard on the *Post-Dispatch,* and he could get a job almost anywhere."

Some of the paper's scrappiness reflected a deeply rooted institutional inferiority complex. The first owner of the *Post-Dispatch,* after all, had left what he called "provincial" St. Louis for the East and the *World,* recognizing New York as the center of national and international influence—and of big circulation. (Not coincidentally, it also offered huge journalistic targets as the seat of some of the worst corruption in America.) The first Joseph Pulitzer often shortchanged his midwestern paper, especially by transporting its talent eastward.

To succeed Pulitzer as editor of his flagship *World* he designated his oldest son, Ralph, while second son Joseph Pulitzer II eventually was relegated to the post of editor and publisher of the St. Louis paper. In no small measure, however, the designation of J.P. II to run the *Post-Dispatch* became a key ingredient in the paper's rise to greatness.

J.P. II has sometimes been pictured as the Pulitzer son least likely to succeed, at least in his father's eyes. (His third and youngest son, Herbert, also worked at the *World*.) And a disappointed Joseph Pulitzer did indeed pull the struggling young Joseph out of Harvard in 1906, and sent him to work in St. Louis almost as chastisement.

But the patriarch's thoughts about his middle son were more complex and conflicted than that. J.P. II had trained for years at his father's side at the Chatwold estate in Bar Harbor and elsewhere, and had worked both at the *Post-Dispatch* and the *World* before being sent to St. Louis with the idea of preparing to take over that business. Young Joseph's biographer, Daniel Pfaff, believes that he almost certainly "was in Pulitzer's opinion the most promising of his three sons." Unlike the quiet Ralph, "Joseph was robust and outgoing, and had his father's vigorous confidence—minus the piercing style of command." And indeed, young Joseph eventually might have taken over both the *Post-Dispatch* and the *World* had he not been scorched by his mercurial father's remarkable change of heart about him. The father's reversal is reflected in the 1909 revision of his will, which reduced J.P. II's stake in the earnings of both newspapers from 60 percent to 10 percent while boosting to 80 percent the share assigned to Herbert and Ralph. (The remaining 10 percent went to top editors and managers of the papers.) As Pfaff describes it:

> The precipitating episode occurred while [young] Joseph was working at the *World*. One evening during dinner at the family's New York mansion on East 73rd Street, Pulitzer—whose hearing was extremely sensitive—erupted at his daughter Edith for making too much noise carving her squab. Joseph came to her defense saying he'd seen enough of his father's bullying and was leaving home for good. He left, but returned about a week later after accepting a compromise his father had offered: He would stay at the *World* a while longer with the possibility . . . of being permanently assigned to St. Louis.

Joseph Pulitzer II unquestionably loved both St. Louis and the *Post-Dispatch*, and the paper thrived with J.P. II as editor and publisher. He saw the rivalry with the *World* as a challenge to make the Gateway City paper even better. The editor was a vital ingredient. Unlike his bombastic father, this Pulitzer had a management style combining relentlessness with gentle persuasion. One of American journalism's underrated figures—perhaps because he liked to work out of the spotlight—the younger Pulitzer clearly outshone his brother Ralph as a manager. By studying the *World*'s problems closely as it slid toward its 1931 demise, Joseph learned how to build journalistic excellence without sacrificing profitability. In his view, intelligently investing in news coverage was the path to financial success. That meant paying editors and senior reporters well, handing out bonuses for good work, and gently but firmly prodding top editors.

Such prodding usually came via his "yellow memos," typed on his own special tinted newsprint stock. Dubbed "the yellow peril" by editors who got them, the notes actually were written with deference in most cases. A typical opening for a yellow memo featuring Pulitzer's dispute of some decision might be, "You'll pardon my disagreeing, but . . . "The modesty was genuine, built on respect for his editors. Yet it ran deeper; beneath the patrician exterior and wealth, Pulitzer was an insecure man.

The extent of that insecurity emerges in an oral-history interview he gave in 1954, a year before his death. His candor may be partly explained by the condition that the interview would not be released during his lifetime:

> [T]his is probably a stupid thing to say—but I always felt as a kid that my lack of intellectual attainment might not prove to be a serious handicap after all, but might give me a sense of what is generally popular, what the people want to know about. I don't know whether that makes good sense or not. I always had confidence that I could do something in the way of getting out and selling a newspaper. . . . I'm not a flaming first-page editorial writer and I'm not a great reporter and all that. I have never uncovered a great crime and I'm not a genius of the business office or anything of the kind. As a friend of mine at home says, "I do the best I can with my shaped head."

A Force Was with Them

The staff also was guided by an inspirational written force: the eighty-two-word statement of principle known as the *Post-Dispatch* platform. Originally written by the first Joseph Pulitzer on his sixtieth birthday in 1907, it marked his retirement from active management of the paper he had founded in December 1878.

William E. Blundell, a retired *Wall Street Journal* reporter and editor who makes the newspaper circuit as a writing coach, has an axiom to describe the soaring quotations he sees etched in stone at America's journals. "The more inspiring the inscription in the lobby," says Blundell, "the worse the paper." At the *Post-Dispatch* under J.P. II, however, the platform was used as a practical tool to keep the paper aiming high.

Editors and reporters identified certain projects as "platform stories." Staffers knew that they would get a warm reception for any crusade that aimed to right wrongs on behalf of people with no voice of their own. The platform's leading proponent was Pulitzer himself. "I'm afraid I'm not as religious as I would like to be but this platform is literally my Bible. As it is a Bible, I hasten to add, for every man on the *Post-Dispatch*," he told the oral-history researcher. "That's true of every cub reporter that comes on the paper. . . . There's no funny business about it. There's not a trace of demagoguery or anything like that." In looking back on his long career at the paper, retired managing editor Ben Reese added this note in talking with the same researcher:

> There was one thing about the *Post-Dispatch,* there were no sacred cows. I think I ought to say right here that I think a great thing about the *Post-Dispatch* was the fact that it had one guide, and that was the platform. When Bovard resigned and I was named managing editor . . . I had this platform reproduced in forty-eight point letters, and put at the top of it, "The *Post-Dispatch* platform is my guide and my only guide. Joseph Pulitzer." I had it framed and put it on a wall near my desk.

Pulitzer's humility kept all this high-mindedness from lapsing into arrogance. He may have been the leader of a great newspaper—and of the vaunted Pulitzer Prize Advisory Board, which he chaired from 1940 until his death in 1955—but he did not see himself as particularly powerful. His own insecurity, along with his divided loyalties to the *Post-Dispatch* and to the prizes, help explain the dilemma that Pulitzer constantly faced. While he feared that a Pulitzer-owned newspaper winning too many Pulitzer Prizes would undercut the image of the broad national awards program that his father envisioned, he also wanted the *Post-Dispatch* to win them.

That conflict explains the running tabulation he kept of *World* and *Post-Dispatch* Pulitzers in the 1920s, which continued for the *Post-Dispatch* alone after the *World* was sold in 1931. He wanted to make sure his paper was not winning *too many* prizes. It also explains the continuing schizophrenia he had about Pulitzer Prizes. Entering the 1930s, J.P. II ached for his paper to win a Gold Medal, yet he worried how it would look in journalism circles if that happened.

Much later, after the *Post-Dispatch* had won its five Gold Medals, Ben Reese would describe the conflict he observed in his boss: "As a matter of fact, he really hates to see the paper win the public-service prize, but he insists that we make entries. He's very anxious for wide participation, wide nominations" among the nation's newspapers.

Pulitzer's agonizing over whether the *Post-Dispatch* was winning too much would reach a peak between 1937 and 1952—to the delight of the rest of the staff.

The "Ghost Voters"

What Selwyn Pepper remembers most about the summer of 1936 is the sweltering heat—to this day, still one of the hottest St. Louis summers on record. But for Pepper, the summer also stands out because of a story he was assigned to help cover in his first year as a *Post-Dispatch* reporter.

In six days—starting on July 22 under the headline "Wholesale Frauds Found in Primary Registration in City," the paper presented evidence that precinct by precinct, and even building by building, thousands of names were listed fraudulently on the voter rolls for the August 4 primary. That first day, the accounts of the reporters who had canvassed the city ran alongside photographs of clearly unoccupied stores or flop-houses where dozens of "ghost residents" were registered to vote. Together, the page-one stories and pictures underscored the absurdity of the claims that voters lived at the locations.

The paper had been tipped to the impending fraud by the activist head of an organization called the Citizens' Non-Partisan Committee, who relayed evidence to Bovard of a 1935 fraud that had occurred during the approval process for a $7.5 million city bond issue to develop the riverfront. With the system gearing up to conceal fraudulent registrations again in 1936, Bovard established a separate task force under city editor Ben Reese to attempt to document this attempt at election-stealing.

Pepper, then twenty-one, had been among those armed with registration lists and dispatched by Ben Reese and assistant Raymond Crowley to check various buildings and see who actually lived there. At one flophouse along the Mississippi riverfront, Pepper encountered a man who had no problem confirming that everyone on the reporter's list was a resident. Recalls Pepper: "He kept saying yes to everything. So I asked if Ben Reese lived there. And he said yes. Did Raymond Crowley live there? Yes." After sweating through the interviews, he came back to the office and fed his notes to a rewrite man.

Pepper's technique caught on. One follow-up story mentioned that a reporter had used such a trick with a woman hotel manager who had suspiciously confirmed all the registered voters on the *Post-Dispatch* list. "Her glibness in replying," said the story, "led the reporter to recite a list of names of prominent St. Louis attorneys. She assured him that each one lived there, too."

Pepper summarizes the entire effort as he remembers it nearly seventy years later: "It was thrilling, and also exhausting."

As evidence piled up, the newspaper declared that there was "a vicious conflict between two factions of [Democrats] to carry a vital primary election by fraud." After first laughing off the investigation as mere "newspaper talk," the bipartisan board of election commissioners, sworn to conduct honest elections, eventually relented. The board members ordered an official recanvass at the behest of the governor who had appointed them. On July 31 the *Post-Dispatch* carried the results: 46,011 phony names, nearly 15 percent of the legitimate city registration—clear evidence that party hacks were getting set to throw the election with last-minute votes they already had in their hip pockets. Six weeks later, the governor fired the election board.

Another staffer put on canvassing duty, Wayne Leeman, remembers doing voter interviews with a notary in tow—and thinking how much that was costing the paper. Whatever the price, J.P. was paying it. Perhaps Reese was thinking of the fraud exposé when he later said of Pulitzer's management of the paper: "There's no story in the world too expensive for us if we really want it."

As was typical of such campaigns at the *Post-Dispatch,* and at many other newspapers of the day, none of the stories carried bylines. (Even in the paper's own Pulitzer Prize entry, and its eventual coverage of the award it received, individual reporters and editors were not mentioned by name.)

The editorial page, run by Charles G. Ross—the Correspondence Prize winner in 1932 for writing about the Great Depression—hammered home the temerity of the registration fraud. Cartoonist Daniel R. Fitzpatrick pictured ghosts lining up to haunt a voting booth. Even the front-page "Weatherbird," a tiny cartoon fixture at the paper that makes comments on the day's weather and news, contributed. "Little Hotels Have Big Registers," he chirped, as drops of sweat flew from his feathered brow.

The next question for J.P. was whether to enter for the Gold Medal, given his conflicting desires. A yellow memo to Bovard, dated January 19, 1937, indicates that the editor signed off on the entry—but cautiously:

> Memo for O.K.B.:
> This entry appears to be well worth making. Let me say, however, that I should really prefer to have nothing further to do with our entries so that I can go into the meeting and say that . . . all I did was to lift the ban against them in the belief that the paper and its staff were entitled to consideration. J.P.

Of the twenty-one entries received in Public Service, the Pulitzer jury ranked the *Post-Dispatch's* first among its five finalists. The board, without J.P.'s participation, voted the same way. As usual, none but the winner was identified publicly by the advisory board.

1937—*St. Louis Post-Dispatch:* For its exposure of wholesale fraudulent registration in St. Louis. By a coordinated news, editorial, and cartoon campaign this newspaper succeeded in invalidating upwards of forty thousand fraudulent ballots in November and brought about the appointment of a new election board.

⸺⚬⚬⚬⸺

St. Louis Quits Smoking

When Bovard left the *Post-Dispatch* in 1938 in a dispute over control of the editorial page, it was a huge loss. But new managing editor Ben Reese had learned Bovard's ways, as had the new city editor, Raymond Crowley.

Pulitzer himself inspired the campaign that won the second Gold Medal. Awarded eight months before Pearl Harbor, this prize would recognize a *civic* war against an enemy that faced cities across the country: smoke. The plague had made St. Louis perhaps America's filthiest city.

In making the regular trip between St. Louis and his father's old Chatwold estate in pristine Bar Harbor, Maine, Pulitzer was increasingly shocked to return to a Mississippi River industrial town so clogged with pollution. For decades, cleanup plans had been ineffective. The *Post-Dispatch* supported some well-meaning proposals, but these invariably dissolved amid finger-pointing by city leaders.

In 1939 a statistic appeared in the paper that shocked St. Louisans: For the first time since 1764, St. Louis's population was falling. Some experts blamed it on the city's abysmal air quality.

The paper assigned reporter Sam J. Shelton to study the problem, assemble information, and make a recommendation. He worked closely with Reese, Crowley, editorial-page editor Ralph Coghlan, and cartoonist Fitzpatrick—who excelled in using his charcoal to depict the smoke-plagued city. The research approach "followed the traditional Post-Dispatch method of thorough preparation, clear exposition, [and] aggressive and intelligent advocacy."

On Sunday, November 26, 1939, a long editorial appeared, tamely headlined "An Approach to the Smoke Problem." It began: "St. Louis has been talking about smoke for 50 years. Now let's do something about it." The accompanying Fitzpatrick cartoon showed the city literally in the grip of smokestack emissions. It was captioned, "Can't Go On Forever." The *Post-Dispatch* plan called for the city to ask producers of smokeless fuels to bid for St. Louis's business. The city would acquire clean fuel and sell it to individuals and licensed dealers.

There was nothing tame about the outflow of reporting work that followed, much of it directed by Shelton. The stories were read with urgency because of particularly bad atmospheric conditions that winter. On some days St. Louisans looking out their windows saw only soot and darkness.

On Monday a page-one headline proclaimed: "St. Louis Chokes in Smoke." A photograph of City Hall, taken at 9:30 a.m., appeared all black, except for the barely discernible outline of a statue of General U.S. Grant—looking like he was leading troops into some awful smoky battle. Stories focused on a phenomenon called "midnight at noon." At one point, a picture was published of Carl Milles's then-new "Meeting of the Waters" fountain, which had been criticized by prudish St. Louisans for a lack of drapery over its nude figures. The forms were no threat to decency in the thick smoke. The caption: "No Veil Needed."

The newspaper's coverage effectively combined the visceral and the visionary. But it also had to explain what smokeless fuels were; St. Louis was a slave to the cheap high-sulfur soft coal mined across the Mississippi in southern Illinois. St.

Louisans who thought about energy at all considered cleaner gas, oil, coke, and new-technology products an impossible luxury.

Shelton scoped out the problem from numerous technological and financial angles, often disregarding conventional wisdom—and ignoring the city's many hopeless hand-wringers.

The city and its smoke-regulation commissioner, Washington University mechanical engineer Raymond R. Tucker, welcomed the *Post-Dispatch* plan to buy and sell smokeless fuels, and used it to launch a campaign of cooperation with industry. Authorities named a new seven-member committee, and the paper kept it focused by continually publishing news stories, editorials, and cartoons. All the while, Shelton and other reporters added information about smokeless fuel research. Articles paid special attention to technologies for making Illinois coal cleaner, recognizing the threat that alternative fuels posed to a major regional industry.

An ordinance was enacted to "rid the city of the smoke nuisance" in three years by phasing in clean-fuel requirements. It met with vehement objections, first from coal-fired railroads. But the barrage of newspaper stories made the public impatient with industry delays. A Fitzpatrick cartoon showed the city "Going *Down* in Smoke." The *Post-Dispatch* also let industry play good-guy for a change, creating an "Anti-Smoke Roll of Honor" that listed companies agreeing to comply. When victory was finally declared toward the end of 1940, 841 companies were listed.

In something of a one-year test in the winter of 1940, the paper used "before and after" pictures to help tell the story. Days with similar weather conditions, but a year apart, were chosen. Pictures taken through the same lens showed a remarkably improved air quality that readers could see for themselves. In December, Fitzpatrick drew eerie ghost-shaped clouds hovering over other cities across the river and asking of the clear St. Louis skyline: "How Did You Manage to Quit Smoking?"

The city remembered Raymond Tucker's role in the cleanup. After becoming Washington University's engineering-school dean, Tucker was elected mayor in 1953 and served twelve years, being twice reelected. The *Post-Dispatch* offices, formerly on Main, today are located on the renamed Tucker Boulevard.

An Afterthought

Strangely, given the involvement of Joseph Pulitzer II with the Pulitzer Prizes and the constant stream of entries over the years by the *Post-Dispatch*, entering the anti-smoke campaign for the Gold Medal appears to have been an afterthought. Indeed, Pulitzer and Reese were prepared not to enter anything in Public Service. Then, in a telegram just before the March 1 entry deadline, J.P. reconsidered, proposing that they enter the anti-smoke campaign either for the Gold Medal or as an Editorial Writing entry for Ralph Coghlan. He also mentioned another prize entry, for editorials and cartoons that had fought a contempt-of-court citation against the paper.

Pulitzer's telegram included a surprisingly derogatory reference to other Pulitzer board members, most likely in jest:

> Although I do not believe there is one chance in a million that it will win, I do think that in fairness to yourself and in fairness to the Post-Dispatch and in fairness to the Pulitzer Prizes, your original antismoke editorial should be submitted for the Editorial Prize. . . .
>
> Is there any good reason why we should not, in addition to entering your editorial for the Editorial Prize, enter for the Gold Medal Public Service Prize which goes to the newspaper rather than to the individual (A) Our entire editorial, cartoon, reprint and news column smoke campaign and (B) our contempt of court case. Admittedly if you boys go to jail we members of the Advisory Board might have a hard time rewarding you for being contemptuous. Even so I think the paper has a right to be proud of that entire campaign and that we might very well enter it. . . .
>
> Ben and I must have both been asleep at the switch when we canvassed the Prize situation some time ago and concluded that we had nothing to enter this year. On the contrary I now think we have a great deal to enter and plenty to give [Pulitzer board administrator] Dean [Carl] Ackerman and some of the boobs on the Advisory Board to think about. . . .

At Columbia, the choice of a 1941 Gold Medal winner was not easy. With both Pulitzer and *New York Times* representative Arthur Krock out of the room, the "boobs" had three jury recommendations: *New York World-Telegram* columnist Westbrook Pegler's articles on labor scandals, the two *Post-Dispatch* campaigns (anti-smoke and the contempt-of-court fight), and the *New York Times*'s "comprehensive coverage of news of the war and world events." The board chose the anti-smoke campaign for Public Service, and gave Pegler the Reporting Prize.

The jury had noted that the *Times* rested "its nomination not upon a newspaper campaign, but simply upon its 'coverage of world events in 1940.'" It was impressive, the jury said, and "comparable to that when The Times was awarded the first Public Service Prize for its publication of the full text war documents and speeches. With the lamps of information going out one by one, this year's Times coverage would seem to deserve the prize at least as much as in 1918."

But once again the board passed over an international story and picked the paper that had helped clean the air.

1941—*St. Louis Post-Dispatch:* For its successful campaign against the city smoke nuisance.

———— ◦◈◦ ————

Disaster in Centralia

Twenty reporters returned to St. Louis from World War II still hankering for a fight. Ben Reese soon gave them some domestic enemies to attack. Across the river, the Illinois administration of Republican Governor Dwight H. Green was rife with graft and cronyism. On a March 1947 day in a remote southern Illinois town, a catastrophe occurred that at first seemed unrelated to the governmental corruption.

It wasn't.

Selwyn Pepper and Roy J. Harris (this author's father) had both served in the Pacific—Pepper on General Douglas MacArthur's staff, and Harris as an Army major who had been through the kamikaze attacks of the Okinawa campaign. On the evening of March 25 both got urgent calls at home from city editor Ray Crowley. Remembers Pepper:

> . . . [H]e said there'd been an explosion in a coal mine in Centralia, Illinois. Get over there as quickly as possible. At the time I wasn't feeling very well. I was coming down with a cold or something. But a word from the city editor was a word from God, and you didn't dare say, "I don't feel well, I don't think I ought to go." You went. It was [first] a matter of finding out where Centralia was . . . And finding the mine. But once I got there, there was the whole tableau sitting right in front of me: All the wives of miners under the lights, trying to find out what was happening. And it quickly became apparent that the miners were trapped down below, and might not get out alive.

By late in the day, the tableau also contained half a dozen *Post-Dispatch* staffers, with Harry Wilensky as leader. Six days earlier Wilensky had written a front-page story out of the state capital, Springfield, about a "shakedown" of Illinois coal mine operators for political contributions. The state department of mines and minerals was raising funds for the Chicago Republican mayoral campaign, and mine inspectors were threatening to enforce safety regulations—unless operators contributed.

The *Post-Dispatch* therefore saw in the wrenching disaster an additional element of graft—an element that other journalists hardly touched. On that first day, a Wilensky bylined story started this way:

> CENTRALIA, Ill., March 26—The Centralia Coal Co., operators of the mine in which 104 miners are trapped 540 feet below the surface near here . . . had been warned repeatedly by the Illinois State Mine Inspector to improve conditions

which constituted an "explosion hazard." Warnings of the danger due to an excessive amount of dust in the mine were posted in inconspicuous corners of the mine washrooms.

Wrote Pepper in his sidebar:

A closely grouped, strangely silent crowd stood in the sunshine near the mine entrance today. They were first-aid workers, mine officials, and relatives of the trapped miners, waiting for the appearance of any possible survivors of the disaster, and of the bodies known to be below ground. Wives of some of the miners standing behind the first row of men, were weeping after an earlier showing of restraint.

It set the stage. The next day Wilensky dropped a bombshell, although his story inexplicably carried no byline:

CENTRALIA, Ill., March 27—Workers in the Centralia Coal Co. mine from which bodies are now being removed begged Gov. Dwight H. Green of Illinois more than a year ago to "please save our lives" by making the State Department of Mines and Minerals enforce safety regulations in the mine. . . . The four signers of [the letter to the governor] all were in the mine when the explosion occurred. [One] was brought out alive a few minutes after the blast. [Another] was killed, his body having been brought out last night. The other two signers . . . are unaccounted for.

Pepper remembers that Wilensky had found the save-our-lives memo in the dark, under glass on a bulletin board near the entrance to the mine. The day that the story ran, a Fitzpatrick cartoon starkly depicted a giant skeleton, with a mining helmet on his skull, somberly addressing a mine inspector and a coal-company official: "You Gambled But I Paid."

The Competition Vanishes

This doubled-edged coverage—with compassion for the victims and outrage over the corruption—captured the key elements of this tragedy. Pulitzer wanted the reporting to say more, though. He saw a moral obligation for the paper. One yellow memo to Reese said:

The Post-Dispatch having so often had to damn the miners and their leader, John L. Lewis, I somehow feel it is our peculiar duty to turn ourselves inside out to get to the bottom of what clearly appears to have been faulty inspection of the Centralia mine, to the end that safe conditions can be assured for the future, those responsible . . . be brought to justice . . . and that we undertake to do whatever we can do to help the prospects of the bereaved families.

Pulitzer proposed tying the whole story together, words and pictures in one section. "This may take a full page or for all I know a dozen full pages. It may take a staff of a dozen men," he wrote. Reese began making the assignments.

As the rescue workers finished their grim task—111 miners in all eventually were confirmed dead—something strange happened. The Centralia disaster had been a major story for the U.S. press, even if it was not being covered with the insight that the *Post-Dispatch* reporters displayed. But suddenly, says Selwyn Pepper, reporters from around the country abandoned the story, leaving the "wrap-up" largely to the *Post-Dispatch*. He still does not understand why. But the paper began to deliver some of its best exclusives at that point. It located letters that dying miners had left in a corner of the pit:

> Dear Wife and Sons: Well, hon, it looks like this is the end. Please tell mom and dad I still love them. Please get the baby baptized and send [the name was withheld] to the Catholic school. . . . Love to all of you.

Another said simply, "Dear Wife: Goodbye. Forgive me. Take care of all the children."

Stories from the scene by Wilensky and Pepper, Harris, Evarts Graham, and Robert Dunlap, and from George Hall in Washington and Spencer McCullough in Chicago, also took aim at the political conniving. In a midnight interview at his home, mine inspector Driscoll Scanlan, who had refused to participate in that earlier shakedown of mine operations, told Wilensky that the mine department had "played politics with the lives of the miners." Scanlan had begged the department's director, Robert M. Medill, to close the mine because of the explosion danger—drawing from Medill the callous rejoinder: "We'll have to take that chance." Scanlan's problem, said Medill, was that he was "too damned honest."

On April 30 the paper ran Pulitzer's special section, edited by pictures editor Julius Klyman, and distributed sixty thousand copies free through the Illinois coal country and to Illinois legislators and state and federal agencies.

The nomination letter for the Pulitzer Prize described "a long and hard-fought campaign to change existing conditions in mine fields with the view of saving the lives of other miners in the future." The campaign had sought:

> . . . four necessary changes: 1) Take mine inspectors out of politics; 2) Outlaw political contributions by Illinois coal companies and all other corporations; 3)

Make failure to comply with state safety laws a felony; 4) Bring the guilty to justice.

There was little jury debate over its 1941 recommendation. Of sixty-two entries considered, it wrote, "the St. Louis Post-Dispatch handling of the Centralia, Illinois, mine disaster was so superior to any of the other entries as an illustration of the integrated use of spot news, features, editorials, photography and cartoons as to leave the others far behind." The board agreed, giving the *Post-Dispatch* its third Gold Medal.

1948—*St. Louis Post-Dispatch:* **For the coverage of the Centralia, Illinois, mine disaster and the follow-up which resulted in impressive reforms in mine safety laws and regulations.**

"Gravy-Train" Editors

In August 1948, Ben Reese assigned Roy Harris to become Springfield correspondent. It was a critical time for Illinois. Republican Governor Green was coming up for reelection in November, and the paper felt a duty to keep exposing the corruption that it knew pervaded his administration. For Harris it was his first out-of-town duty station since returning from the Pacific.

Springfield was a busy state capital for reporters interested in administration scandals. Harris's stories were about how prison wardens got luxury furnishings in their quarters and thousands of Green cronies were rewarded with "special investigator" badges. As the reporter made a routine check of state payroll data at one point, he became suspicious as names of some Illinois editors cropped up, seemingly as state employees. A small story appeared in October. The number of such minor scandals multiplied by the November election. Green was trounced by Democrat Adlai Stevenson, although President Truman's margin over Republican Thomas E. Dewey was extremely narrow. Even without Green, much of the wrongdoing from his administration lingered in Illinois government.

George Thiem, a reporter for the *Chicago Daily News,* also took an interest in the editors-on-the-payroll story. As representatives of one-person bureaus for papers that did not directly compete against each other, Harris and Thiem decided that they would be able to get more accomplished if they pooled their resources on the story.

"About the end of March, a Statehouse employe [*sic*], chatting with Thiem and me, recalled the mention of newspapermen in the October [*Post-Dispatch* story] and suggested that further investigation might be productive," Harris later told

Editor & Publisher magazine. "The job would be a tedious one, as I had learned last fall, but we decided to make a stab at it."

Tedious indeed. The state tracked its thirty-five thousand employees by county, listing them in numerous volumes. It took the two men more than two weeks to root through them all, with one reporter handling card files that listed Illinois newspaper staffers and reading off names, while the other checked the payroll.

Because they had other statehouse coverage responsibilities as well, the two found collaboration on the project a godsend. "I seriously doubt that either of us would have dug up the payroll story, working alone, because of the grueling detail and extra hours involved," said Thiem. "We knew we were handling delicate if not libelous information and we had to be accurate. By the time we discovered ten names, we realized we were on the way to a good story." Added Harris, "Each of those names represented a million-dollar lawsuit"—if for some reason the information was incorrect.

While it was perhaps a rare reporting arrangement, Thiem saw the teaming of journalists from different papers, but with similar interests, as a natural if it was done carefully. "I've been impressed by the need for newspapermen to work together more closely to accomplish something for good government and the welfare of the taxpayers generally," he told *E&P,* "rather than to struggle for individualist scoops."

For a time, the two were pulled away by a tragic hospital fire in the town of Effingham in which about seventy people died. When the reporters returned, their list of editors who possibly were on the payroll began to grow—and then shrank, as the double-checking of names, through legislators and others, reduced the count.

When they finally had the story, the two men sat together at separate typewriters in Harris's room at the Leland Hotel, writing late into the evening of April 13. It was nearly midnight when they filed their dictated stories by phone for their afternoon newspapers. Harris's April 14 story began:

> SPRINGFIELD, Ill.-Editors and publishers of at least 32 downstate Illinois newspapers were carried on the state payroll during the administration of Gov. Dwight H. Green, collecting more than $300,000 in salaries, inquiry by the Post-Dispatch revealed today. Most of them held "gravy train" jobs like "field investigators" and "messenger clerk."

Some actually did work at their state jobs, but the chief function of many editors "was to print canned editorials and news stories lauding accomplishments of the Republican state administration."

Surprisingly, to Harris at least, the *Post-Dispatch* ran the story on page three. He knew it was a major scandal. One St. Louis competitor played it on the front page, even though it was a rival's exclusive. (The *Chicago Daily News* spread it across page one as well.) Reese, or someone else on the desk that evening, likely had made the placement decision.

Chances for rectifying the "inside play" came soon, as Harris and Thiem built up the list of editors in increments, eventually confirming fifty-one on the payroll, with the total of payments to them reaching $480,000. Those stories ran on page one. A strong editorial also ran in the *Post-Dispatch,* along with a Fitzpatrick cartoon showing editors tracking sludge across the good name of the press.

At first, few other newspapers around the country paid much attention to the Illinois stories. Then a *Washington Post* editorial took the press to task:

> At best, this looks like crass indifference to a particularly juicy bit of news. At worst it looks like a cover-up of scandal within the family. The newspaper press claims special status as a pillar of free and honest government. By the same token it has special obligations. Among these is the duty not to keep its own dirty linen from public view.

Uncharacteristically, Pulitzer himself personally nominated the work, in both the Reporting and Public Service categories. (It was, perhaps, easier for him because a second newspaper was involved in the project, as well.) The Public Service jury picked six of the seventy entries, listing the *Daily News/Post-Dispatch* stories first. The board kept them first, awarding each paper a Gold Medal, and citing Harris and Thiem for the work, only the second time individuals had been noted in a Public Service citation.

1950—*Chicago Daily News* and *St. Louis Post-Dispatch:* For the work of George Thiem and Roy J. Harris, respectively, in exposing the presence of thirty-seven Illinois newspapermen on an Illinois state payroll.

The Tax Man Taketh

Theodore C. Link returned to the *Post-Dispatch* in 1945 with a wound received as a Marine sergeant at Bougainville, and threw himself back into the job with war-like fervor. Long known for his shadowy underworld sources, Link began writing stories about Illinois gangs as well as abuses in the Green administration. Sometimes he toted a gun, for his own protection.

In early 1951 Link was tipped about federal tax cases in Missouri being fixed at high levels of the federal Internal Revenue Bureau. Federal agents were open to letting companies and individuals off the hook by reaching under-the-table deals. After pitching the story to managing editor Ray Crowley, who took over when Reese retired, Link quickly expanded the story beyond his home state. Selwyn Pepper worked rewrite for Link, who throughout his career rarely wrote his own stories. Sam Armstrong, the new city editor, directed the campaign.

The resulting articles disclosed that case-fixing had become almost routine among influential lawyers with friendly ties to public officials in Washington, St. Louis, and elsewhere. In one year, 63 percent of the tax cases approved for federal prosecution had been killed by internal-revenue regional counsels, or by people inside President Truman's Justice Department.

A federal grand jury in St. Louis at one point received a U.S. report saying there was no evidence of tax fixing, although the judge did not believe it, and told the grand jury so. Link was able to learn that the report to the grand jury had been written at the suggestion of Truman's attorney general, J. Howard McGrath. A national scandal erupted over how Washington had withheld evidence.

One major case involved American Lithofold Corporation, a St. Louis printer with government contracts. The *Post-Dispatch* reported that the company's federal tax collector was on the American Lithofold payroll. Further, William M. Boyle, the chairman of the Democratic National Committee, served on the company's board. Boyle had been instrumental in helping American Lithofold win government loans.

The paper's editorial page, under its editor, Irving Dilliard, backed the developing stories. One Fitzpatrick cartoon pictured bureaucrats falling like grains of salt from a dollhouse-like Internal Revenue building. The caption: "Shake 'Em All Out."

The new Internal Revenue Service almost did just that. By year's end, eight revenue collectors were fired or forced to resign, and two ended up behind bars. In all, there were 380 discharges or resignations, and more than a dozen employees were indicted. Truman also fired his attorney general.

When the Public Service Prize was announced, the *Post-Dispatch* installed its fifth Gold Medal with the four others on the wall of the publisher's private office. Apparently, there was no ceremony to recognize that the *Post-Dispatch* staff had just achieved something unique in American journalism.

In October 1953, *Arizona Daily Star* editor William R. Mathews, a fellow member of the Pulitzer Advisory Board chaired by his friend J.P., answered a Los Angeles editor who had written to Mathews questioning the frequency—and propriety—of the *Post-Dispatch*'s winning Pulitzer Prizes. "There is just something about the newspaper of the founder being considered which makes some people wonder," wrote Virgil Pinkley of the Los Angeles *Mirror*. Mathews replied: "You will be interested to know that Mr. Joseph Pulitzer has several times expressed the same opinion that you have, and in a way that showed he meant it, but we have overruled him in each instance by the vote of all of the members of the board, Mr. Pulitzer not voting."

The letter was copied to J.P., and remains among his collected papers.

1952—*St. Louis Post-Dispatch:* **For its investigation and disclosures of widespread corruption in the Internal Revenue Bureau and other departments of the government.**

Joseph Pulitzer II and son Joseph Pulitzer Jr. in the late 1940s with bust of Joseph
Pulitzer. Used by permission of the *St. Louis Post-Dispatch.*

The front page of the *St. Louis Post-Dispatch* from July 22, 1936, exposes the scope of the city's election fraud. Reprinted by permission.

Selwyn Pepper. Photo by
St. Louis Post-Dispatch staff.
Used by permission.

Sam J. Shelton. Photo by *St. Louis Post-Dispatch* staff. Used by permission.

HOW DID YOU MANAGE TO QUIT SMOKING?

Fitzpatrick cartoon "How Did You Manage to Quit Smoking?" in the *Post-Dispatch*, 1939.

A Daniel Fitzpatrick cartoon for the *Post-Dispatch,* "You Gambled but I Paid," illustrated the role of the mining company in the 1947 Centralia mine disaster. Reprinted by permission.

Harry Wilensky. Photo by *St. Louis Post-Dispatch* staff.
Used by permission.

Joseph Pulitzer II (center) and Ben Reese (right) greet staffers at Pulitzer's sixtieth
birthday party, 1945. Used by permission.

The *Post-Dispatch* announcement of the 1950 Pulitzer Prizes (for work done in 1949) features information on staffer Roy J. Harris and *Chicago Daily News* reporter George Thiem, who revealed a press scandal in Illinois and won Gold Medals for both papers. Reprinted by permission of the *Post-Dispatch*.

Post-Dispatch reporter Roy J. Harris in a 1949 staff photo. Used by permission.

Post-Dispatch reporter Ted Link in a 1952 staff photo. Used by permission.

CHAPTER 11

A New Stew of Issues

Somehow, some time, every Arkansan is going to have to be counted. We are going to have to decide what kind of people we are—whether we obey the law only when we approve of it, or whether we obey it no matter how distasteful we may find it. And this, finally, is the only issue before the people of Arkansas.

—*Arkansas Gazette* editor Harry S. Ashmore,
September 9, 1957

As the Pulitzer board searched for its Public Service medalist each year, the goal was to find the very best story—not to go out of its way to achieve a broad mix of winning news organizations. Had variety been the aim, of course, the *St. Louis Post-Dispatch* likely wouldn't have been a five-time recipient in so short a span. Likewise, board members were not looking to honor a diversity of story types that might be viewed as ideal in some broad sense. With a half-dozen or so finalists forwarded by each Public Service jury, the board members had enough of a challenge just selecting the year's strongest candidate.

But as the nation's editors continued to tackle the topics that gripped the communities around them in the postwar years, the Public Service Prize winners did indeed manage to touch on many of the major themes of the age.

Papers that exposed the grit of corruption and graft got their share of honors, recognizing that important duty of the watchdog press. Other Gold Medal selections in the 1950s and 1960s, though, began to explore compelling social issues—from racial integration of schools to legislative reform to drugs, sex, and the environment.

By 1950 the number of journalism categories had increased to seven, with the old Reporting award being broken by the Pulitzer board into local, national, and international divisions. Cartooning had its own prize, and so did photography. During the next two decades, in an expansion to eleven categories, some unwieldy category names were chosen—such as Local Investigative Specialized Reporting (later called Investigative Reporting). Photography was divided into Spot News and Feature Photography.

In the enlarged deck of awards, the Gold Medal sometimes began to take on the look of a "wild card"—with the board seeming to use the designation to mark what it considered to be simply the best effort of the year. Increasingly, though, the members began to see the Public Service award as a way to honor the special case of a newspaper that reached across the classic Pulitzer Prize divisions, or perhaps that said something totally new to benefit the community.

During the 1930s and 1940s, the word "coveted" routinely began to be associated with the Pulitzer Gold Medal. Again, it showed that the prizes were on the track to elevating the profession in ways that Joseph Pulitzer would have approved.

A Klan Reprise—and Finale

In 1953, the *Whiteville News Reporter* and the *Tabor City Tribune* got special attention because they were the first weeklies ever to win "the coveted Meritorious Public Service awards," as *Editor & Publisher* magazine called them. (It was another case of two newspapers winning in the same year for writing independently about similar topics.) But far more important was their success in attacking a North Carolina rejuvenation of the Ku Klux Klan.

Over the course of the papers' campaigns, more than a hundred Klan members, including Imperial Wizard Thomas L. Hamilton, had been convicted of various crimes because of what the Whiteville and Tabor City papers wrote. The papers, whose editors were personal friends, were only twenty miles from each other, and were close to the boundary with South Carolina, the state where Klan activity was most vicious. KKK terrorism, including beatings of both blacks and whites by night riders, had spread in 1950 and 1951.

The fears in the community were sometimes matched by fears in the newsroom. "I would be lying if I said I haven't been afraid," *News Reporter* editor Willard Cole said to *E&P,* "but the mission of a newspaper editor is to voice convictions, not to exhibit his own misgivings." Cole, who earlier had worked at the *Winston-Salem Journal,* kept three guns because of threats he had received. As the two newspapers attacked the Klan violence, county, state, and federal agents moved in. When the prizes were awarded in May 1953, Cole called the North Carolina Klan "as dead as a door nail."

Cole's wife, a teacher, also got some credit for finding a way to break through

the silence among frightened victims that had hampered investigators and reporters alike. "She listened to children gossiping at school and learned of three
beatings," the Associated Press reported in its coverage of the Pulitzers. "The information was relayed via Cole to the authorities who pried the information out
of the reluctant victims."

Tribune editor W. Horace Carter, too, admitted being terrified for his wife and
two young children as cars drove past his home at night. At one point, his four-
year-old son asked him, "The Klan gonna come and get you, Daddy?"

1953— *Whiteville News Reporter and Tabor City Tribune:* **For their successful
campaign against the Ku Klux Klan, waged on their own doorstep at the risk of
economic loss and personal danger, culminating in the conviction of more than
one hundred Klansmen and an end to terrorism in their communities.**

"Alicia's Toy" No More

The New York suburbs gave rise to a new kind of journalism in the 1940s. Publisher Alicia Patterson had begun molding *Newsday* into both a community voice
and an enemy of corruption, especially the labor rackets.

Being taken as a serious publisher had not been easy. She was the great-grand-
daughter of *Chicago Tribune* owner Joseph Medill and the daughter of Joseph
Medill Patterson, founder of the *New York Daily News* and benefactor of North-
western University's Medill School of Journalism. But ever since buying the Garden City–based paper in 1940, Alicia Patterson had had to live down the sexist notion that *Newsday* was just "Alicia's toy."

The story that carried *Newsday* to its first Pulitzer Prize—and a new sense of
pride—was inspired by managing editor Alan Hathway. He had assigned reporter
Helen Dudar, among others, to investigate Nassau County construction-trades labor czar William DeKoning Sr.

While individual names are not generally associated with Public Service Prizes,
Dudar may be the first woman journalist involved with winning one. But bylines
did not show her role. The editors, feeling that bylines might expose reporters to ret-
ribution from the individuals they were writing about, kept her name off her stories.

Dudar had started at *Newsday* as an advice columnist while she attended classes
at Columbia. She displayed special skill in crafting complex stories, although her
role in the DeKoning investigation was to follow Hathway's instructions closely.
As early as 1950, Dudar and other staffers found a nest of wrongdoing involving
an area trotting racetrack where DeKoning also was involved. The paper kept up
the pressure. Along the way, a number of its news tips came from New York City

Anti-Crime Commission investigator Bob Greene. Eventually, DeKoning went to prison for extortion—and Greene jumped to *Newsday* as a reporter.

The state investigation turned the *Newsday* stories into convictions. It was the work of Governor Thomas E. Dewey, who had so narrowly lost the presidential election to Harry Truman in 1948.

Newsday's victory over the labor boss was all the sweeter because some New York City papers had knocked their new rival as a "soggy suburban"—and largely ignored the DeKoning story. The *New York World-Telegram* played down the Pulitzer news that year, and for what it *did* run it ordered up an article "belittling *Newsday* and saying that the Pulitzer Prize committee was crazy for not giving it to the Telegram." That assessment came from a reliable source: Fred Cook, the unfortunate *World-Telegram* reporter who was ordered to write the derogatory story. "I had to do it. I sure did hate it," he said. "It was buried in the paper somewhere. It was a disgusting performance."

In a statement after the prize was announced, Patterson credited Hathway, who "spent more hours, more effort, more energy on the story than any other *Newsday* member. It was he who was cited by David Holman, DeKoning's attorney, as the man most responsible for DeKoning's downfall."

Newsday's greatest successes in the Public Service arena were ahead of it, however. The successes would be largely of Bob Greene's making. In ten years, Greene would become a legend in investigative team reporting.

1954—*Newsday:* For its exposé of New York State's racetrack scandals and labor racketeering, which led to the extortion indictment, guilty plea, and imprisonment of William C. DeKoning, Sr., New York labor racketeer.

Leadership in Little Rock

Despite the inspirational work of the *Arkansas Gazette* in leading its community through the Little Rock school desegregation crisis of 1957, there is still an aura of sadness in looking back at that time.

The most dramatic element of its coverage sprang from the September 2 decision by Governor Orval E. Faubus to call out the National Guard and state police to surround Little Rock Central High School, preventing fifteen black students from registering for classes. The front page soon carried pictures of black students being turned away from the schoolhouse door, with white students taunting them. Then came the violence.

Editor Harry S. Ashmore and the *Gazette* had spent more than a year trying to avert such a collision. They had worked closely with the governor, whom the paper had helped elect. The *Gazette* had promoted a "ten-year plan for desegregation"—one opposed by the National Association for the Advancement of Colored People as too slow. But that plan, the *Gazette* contended, was within the spirit of the "deliberate speed" that the Supreme Court had sought in its 1954 *Brown v. Board of Education* ruling. Days before September 2, Governor Faubus had said he would keep his word, and would not intervene to prevent black children from enrolling. That had led the *Gazette's* Ashmore to editorialize optimistically on September 1. Headlined "A Time of Testing," the editorial said the paper was confident "that the citizens of Little Rock will demonstrate on Tuesday for the world to see that we are a law-abiding people."

When Faubus called out the National Guard, though, all bets were off.

"Little Rock was actually a progressive city whose citizens were headed off at the pass by the governor," says Gene Roberts, who covered civil rights for the *New York Times,* and later took the *Philadelphia Inquirer* to greatness as executive editor. There in Arkansas, "you had a civil rights conflagration at a time when there was progressive civil rights leadership at the paper. Other places, papers were mediocre, and part of the problem, rather than the solution."

The *Gazette* dutifully had been publishing both pro-segregation and anti-segregation views in its news columns. A story that was part of its Pulitzer Prize submission, for example, was headlined, "Petition Adopted at 'Mothers League' Meeting Asks Faubus to Prevent Integration of School." The unbylined story said: "The petition was approved by a standing vote of most of the 250 men and women present at the second meeting of the League. . . . It heard impassioned pleas from several segregationists, including one from Texas, to fight the integration of Little Rock Central High School."

But racist opinions could not stand up to the eloquence of Ashmore's reasoned editorials. On September 4 he wrote one headlined, "The Crisis Mr. Faubus Made." It began:

> Little Rock arose yesterday to gaze upon the incredible spectacle of an empty high school surrounded by National Guard troops called out by Governor Faubus to protect life and property against a mob that never materialized.
>
> Mr. Faubus says he based this extraordinary action on reports of impending violence. Dozens of local reporters and national correspondents worked through the day yesterday without verifying the few facts the governor offered to explain why his appraisal was so different from that of local officials—who have asked for no such action. . . . On Monday night he called out the National Guard and made it a national problem.
>
> It is one he must now live with, and the rest of us must suffer under. If Mr. Faubus in fact has no intention of defying federal authority now is the time for

him to call a halt to the resistance which is preventing the carrying out of a duly entered court order. And certainly he should do so before his own actions become the cause of the violence he so professes to fear.

On September 25, another major episode in the struggle was recorded in an editorial headlined, "The High Price of Recklessness." Wrote Ashmore:

> This is a tragic day in the history of the republic—and Little Rock, Arkansas, is the scene of the tragedy.
> In one sense we rolled back our history to the Reconstruction era when federal troops moved into position at Central High school to uphold the law and preserve the peace.
> Yet there was no denying the case President Eisenhower made in solemn words on television last night.
> Law and order had broken down here.

The lawlessness and disorder were captured also by AP reporter Relman "Pat" Morin, who won a 1958 National Reporting Pulitzer for his news reports on mob violence in Little Rock.

As for the Pulitzer Public Service prize, jurors gave the board a choice among the *Gazette* coverage and a wide range of other entries, including several old-time political graft stories and the *New York Journal American*'s coverage of a "mad bomber" in the city. The board recognized, though, what an extraordinary and courageous statement the *Gazette* had made in its reporting of the desegregation crisis.

Roberts observes that this was the only Pulitzer Gold Medal awarded to a southern newspaper during desegregation in the region, making the joint recognition for the newspaper and Ashmore—in Public Service and Editorial Writing—all the more significant in journalism history. "I personally think that the so-called southern liberal editors during this period collectively made it the brightest era for editorial writing ever in America," says Roberts, whose book *The Race Beat: The Press, the Civil Rights Struggle, and the Awakening of a Nation,* cowritten with Hank Klibanoff, won the 2007 Pulitzer Prize for History.

Some *Gazette* readers did what they could to dim the moment, however. Despite the paper's "fearless and completely objective news coverage"—and, in fact, because of it—the *Gazette* suffered a subscriber boycott and pressure from advertisers. During 1957, circulation fell to 83,000 from 100,000, putting it behind its conservative rival, the *Arkansas Democrat.* Fourteen years later it would be forced into a merger, becoming the *Arkansas Democrat-Gazette.* Even today, the *Gazette*'s courageous stand—and its two 1958 Pulitzer Prizes—get scant mention in the now-combined paper's online history.

1958—*Arkansas Gazette:* For demonstrating the highest qualities of civic leadership, journalistic responsibility, and moral courage in the face of great public tension during the school integration crisis of 1957. The newspaper's fearless and completely objective news coverage, plus its reasoned and moderate policy, did much to restore calmness and order to an overwrought community, reflecting great credit on its editors and its management.

⤙⤚

Speaking Above a Whisper

Like many newly hired women reporters of the 1950s, Lois Wille had found herself on fluffy "women's page" or "society page" assignments after getting a journalism degree and joining the *Chicago Daily News* in 1956. Starting as assistant to the fashion editor, she eventually got her wish to move over to the city desk. But at first it wasn't much better. She was one of the "our girl" reporters—getting her picture in the paper "powdering my nose in a flight suit" after she flew with the Navy's Blue Angels, for example. Soon, however, she began making her own breaks. In 1959, she hid in a laundry truck to get close to Nikita Khrushchev on the Soviet premier's 1959 tour through the Midwest. She got her interview.

By 1961 Wille was covering poverty and public-aid issues, and latched onto one issue that at first was a hard sell with city editor Maurice "Ritz" Fischer. The public health agencies in the area "all had a policy of not giving out any information about birth control to indigent women—much less services," she says. The need for birth-control services was discussed often among public-health workers, "but it was never written about"—especially in heavily Catholic, conservative Chicago. "Ritz had given me a free hand to explore the issues," but this one seemed to sit on his desk without a decision. Then, Fischer went on leave for some surgery, and his assistant, Robert Rose, took over.

"Rose was fearless," Wille recalls, "and he thought it would just be a hoot anyway to work on this story while Ritz was gone."

The story she prepared was balanced, examining the economic and social reasons advanced by proponents, who claimed that offering the services would "reduce the rolls of those who receive public aid and rely on public funds for medical care." They argued, too, "that those Chicago families who can least afford to provide for children are reproducing at high rates, thus contributing to delinquency and other social ills," according to the Pulitzer Prize entry by the paper. On the other side, birth control was "considered immoral by a large number of taxpayers."

Said the *Daily News:* "Behind closed doors of conference rooms, in private gatherings of social workers, among clergy of various denominations, these issues were debated and discussed over and over again.

"But in whispers."

Wille did not whisper. After intensive research and interviewing, in which people had to be persuaded to speak for the record, she pulled together the cases and the arguments she needed. At that point, the Pulitzer entry letter said, "a disheartening problem thrust itself into the picture. The Catholic laymen and clergy she talked with gave her little sermons on why The Daily News should forget the whole thing." Indeed, the Church would not even offer a comment on the controversy.

City editor Fischer, now back at his desk, took it seriously that the Church was not planning to participate in the series. He arranged several meetings with Catholic leaders. And at one point, without Wille's knowledge, he even passed her story to a Church leader of his acquaintance, Monsignor John J. Egan.

"I figured, This could not be good," Wille recalls, although, "back then I wasn't as appalled as I might be today." Father Egan, though, was one of the more progressive priests in Chicago. He suggested some changes, but also made sure that the Church would offer a detailed statement of the Catholic position to appear in the articles.

The eloquence of Wille's writing—and of the people she got to speak to her—gave the series special power. In one story, Wille began:

On a hot Saturday morning in August, Mrs. Sandra Allmon, 26, walked into Newberry Settlement Houses just off Maxwell St., waited in line with about 100 other women and poured out her story:

"I asked about it at County Hospital when my youngest was born, and everybody shut up like a clam.

"I've got seven now, I told the doctor. And he said, 'Well, you're healthy enough for seven more.'

"I asked my ADC man, and he just says he didn't know anything about it.

"When I took my baby to the Welfare Station, I asked them—and when you bring THAT up, why, they act like they don't know you.

"I heard about you people from a neighbor. It was just like a miracle. I couldn't believe it. You're the only ones who will talk to me about it."

It was a story that was told in scores of different ways that morning to Mrs. Virginia Hackmer, social worker.

"The faces change," she said, "but what they tell me is essentially the same—nobody else will help them."

"I have to credit Ritz," says Wille. "When he came back from his surgery he pushed it forward."

Still, the reporter also found herself assigned to write her own Pulitzer Prize nomination letter early the next year, something she remembers dashing off before she and her husband left for a vacation to the Mediterranean. When someone asked her if she expected to win, Wille laughed, "Don't be silly; this is just something I have to do. It's routine." And she believed it.

Told after a day of touring Egypt that several cables had arrived for her, "I thought someone had died," she recalls. "Why else would we be getting cables?" Her husband checked it out, and came running down from the cable office shouting, "You've won!"

Wille was to champion the hiring of women reporters at the *Daily News* until the paper closed in 1978. She then became editorial-page editor of the *Chicago Sun-Times,* leaving that paper when Rupert Murdoch bought it in 1984, and moving to the *Tribune.* She won her own Pulitzer for Editorial Writing at the *Tribune* in 1989.

1963—Public Service—*Chicago Daily News:* For calling public attention to the issue of providing birth control services in the public health programs in its area.

Highway Robbery

A February 1963 telephone tip to *St. Petersburg Times* Tallahassee bureau chief Martin Waldron suggested that fiscal controls over turnpike-related spending were abysmal. Huge amounts of public monies were being wasted. The call kicked off a six-month investigation of fraud in the state turnpike authority.

The authority had been created during the 1950s to operate more than 100 miles of toll roads from Miami to Fort Pierce, and in 1960 Governor Farris Bryant supervised the sale of $157 million in new bonds for an extension that would make the whole road more than 260 miles long. But the system was rife with waste and abuse.

Waldron's team included reporters Jack Nease, Don Meiklejohn, and John Gardner, and they were supported by editorial writer Warren Pierce and photographer Johnnie Evans. The team leader was a fearless but somewhat happy-go-lucky character, as associates described him. And to the serious business of investigating, Waldron introduced lighter moments. One was his decision—with the help of Meiklejohn and *Times* accountants—to test just how much two people would have to eat to run up one of the huge meal tabs that turnpike-authority employees were submitting.

In the "time capsules" that many of these long-ago Pulitzer-winning efforts represent, today's inflated dollars sometimes make the amounts of money seem laughable. This case is a prime example. The outrageous-looking meal tabs for two ran to $30—at a time when half as much could buy an elegant two-person dinner, complete with drinks and generous tip. Waldron and Meiklejohn picked Pierre's

Restaurant and Lounge in Miami for their experiment. As Waldron later told it, the job was grueling, requiring the two to start with several martinis and whiskey sours, followed by a Caesar salad, double sirloin, and cherries jubilee, and topped off with two brandies. When they failed initially, managing only a $23.10 bill, they stepped up the effort.

"Another glass of brandy will cost what?" Waldron asked the waiter, only to be told that it would add just $1.10 more. After figuring a $5 tip, they did not manage to hit $30 until they bought the glass that their beverages came in—for $1—proof positive that the turnpike officials had been taking advantage of the lax oversight.

As a result of the paper's stories, the state legislature created a bond review board to regulate bond issues and a state audit was ordered, where previously the authority's own auditors had been in charge. Turnpike authority chairman John Hammer resigned; there was a full investigation, and members of the authority were stripped of their unlimited expense account privileges.

1964—*St. Petersburg Times:* For its aggressive investigation of the Florida Turnpike Authority that disclosed widespread illegal acts and resulted in a major reorganization of the state's road construction program.

Zoned Out in California

Like many investigations that lead to Gold Medals, the *Los Angeles Times*'s successful investigation into the sleazy side of city government grew over several years. In 1966, Metro editor William F. Thomas had received a telephone tip about abuses by city officials. "It was a zoning story, and a hell of a good one," he says. Officials were taking bribes to make zoning changes, especially for the corners where the city's many gas stations were located. Property owners paying the bribes were profiting from the increase in values that resulted.

"I didn't want to form an investigative team," recalls Thomas, who had a low opinion of reporters who called themselves investigators rather than journalists. "So I gave the calls to George Reasons, who had been an education writer. I told him not to be a policeman, or I'd pull him off. He did become a policeman, but he listened to reason."

At the same time, Thomas listened to Reasons. When the reporter said he needed help with the expanding assignment, the Metro editor created a team with reporters Art Berman, Gene Blake, Robert L. Jackson, and Ed Meagher.

A barrier had to be surmounted before any rooting out of corruption could be done, though: the *Times*'s lawyer. As Bill Thomas was rising in the editing ranks at the Metro section, he saw the attorney blocking good work time after time. "I refused to send my stories up to him because they'd get killed if they had any hint of possible legal action," Thomas says. "This was a very careful newspaper. It didn't take any chances." At one point, however, the *Times* named a new general counsel, and arrangements were made for the paper to be represented if necessary by a trial attorney with the big firm of Gibson, Dunn and Krutcher.

Thomas recalls his apprehension when he first attempted to get one of the tough zoning stories past an attorney in this new system the *Times* had created. When the editor handed the piece over for a reading, the lawyer started chuckling. "And I'm thinking, He's going to shoot this down," Thomas recalls. But then, going point by point down the pages, "he started saying, 'We can win that . . . We can win that . . .'"

While the relationship eased the way for the stories by Reasons and others to appear, Thomas was not sure what impact the work would have. "They really didn't seem to be blockbusters," he says, "but they were really hard-work stories." Many of the abuses were extremely small, with some officials taking bribes of as little as $2,000. "That always amazed me," he says. "Why in the hell would they risk it for that much? Why wouldn't they hold out for $10,000?" Eventually, he figured it out. The local politicians thought it was something everyone was doing, and that this protected them from exposure. "And for $2,000, maybe you wouldn't have such a guilt feeling."

The guilt feelings would come, however, courtesy of the *Times* articles. Incrementally, the stories "just kept unfolding, and then you'd run into a roadblock," Thomas says. Then "finally you figured you had enough to do a series." Taken together, the small exclusives painted the picture of a corrupt administration.

The paper could have won a Pulitzer for its work on the project in 1967, Thomas believes. But in the third year, 1968, the paper got both another crop of great stories and significant results. The stories that year concentrated on the harbor commission and the recreation and parks commission. Three harbor commissioners were convicted of bribery; a $12 million city contract for a world trade center was cancelled; and, in recreation and parks, two commissioners resigned and a golf course contract was cancelled.

Times editor Nick Williams wrote in his Pulitzer Prize entry letter, "There can be no doubt that without the disclosures made over the past two years by The Los Angeles Times none of the above reforms, indictments and changes in the Los Angeles City government would have taken place."

Looking back, even Thomas sounds amazed at how rapidly the *Times* was able to create such a reporting powerhouse in the 1960s. "The *Times* came out of nowhere—one of the ten worst, as *Time* magazine supposedly said—and in a period of ten years it became among the top three and stayed there."

Thomas largely credits publisher Otis Chandler and editor Nick Williams, whom Thomas would soon replace. By the time Thomas retired as editor in 1989 the *Times* had won twelve Pulitzers, including another Gold Medal in 1984.

1969—*Los Angeles Times:* **For its exposé of wrongdoing within the Los Angeles City Government Commissions, resulting in resignations or criminal convictions of certain members, as well as widespread reforms.**

⸺◦◦◦⸺

Alicia Patterson on the cover of *Time*, September 13, 1954. Used by permission of *Time* magazine.

Arkansas Gazette editor Harry Ashmore in 1957. Used by permission of the *Arkansas Democrat-Gazette.*

The front page of the *Arkansas Gazette* from September 4, 1957, showed Little Rock in crisis, and featured an editorial by Ashmore. Reprinted by permission of the *Arkansas Democrat-Gazette.*

Chicago Daily News reporter Lois Wille in 1962. Used by permission.

Part Three

The Golden Seventies

CHAPTER 12

Secret Papers, Secret Reporting

The balance of political power in America is not running with the press or the Congress but with the President. . . . Somewhere there is a line where the old skeptical, combative, publish-and-be-damned tradition of the past in our papers may converge with the new intelligence and the new duties and responsibilities of this rising and restless generation. I wish I knew how to find it, for it could help both the newspapers and the nation in their present plight, and it could help us believe again, which in this age of tricks and techniques may be our greatest need.

—James Reston, the *New York Times,* Pulitzer Prize
Fiftieth Anniversary Dinner, May 10, 1966

When the Pulitzer Prizes celebrated their fiftieth year in 1966, only thirty-three newspapers—a diverse collection of large and small journals from across the country—could boast having a Pulitzer Gold Medal. A mere handful owned more than one. The *New York Times* had two, one short of the number earned by the *Chicago Daily News,* a paper that would not survive the next decade. The *Washington Post* had none.

In the 1970s, so much would change.

Two of the greatest pure newspaper stories of the century broke, one in June 1971 and the other in June 1972. Each was a story that very possibly would not have seen print at all without the vigilance and courage of the paper that took charge of the coverage. First, the *New York Times* published the secret Pentagon Papers, which Neil Sheehan had obtained and a crew of *Times* reporters and editors had analyzed. Then, the *Washington Post's* Bob Woodward and Carl Bernstein parlayed their early scoops about "a third-rate burglary"—as the Nixon administration portrayed the Watergate break-in—into an investigation that gradually exposed White House involvement in that crime and many others.

With their work, both the *Times* and *Post* created models of public service for decades to come. Both papers won Gold Medals. Yet shockingly, for different reasons, each came very close to being shut out of the Pulitzer Prizes altogether.

It may be a journalistic article of faith that Woodward and Bernstein by themselves suddenly created a nationwide investigative reporting mania. For years before Watergate, though, newspaper investigations had been gaining popularity around the country. A decade after winning the 1954 Gold Medal, *Newsday* was using team techniques that eventually would help it capture the Public Service Prize in 1970 and again in 1974. And papers like the *Boston Globe* had moved toward team investigations.

For his part, when Bob Woodward hears Watergate cited for boosting investigative journalism he redirects some of the credit to the Vietnam War and the distrust of government that grew from it. Driving the spirit among reporters "was the back-to-back nature of Vietnam and Watergate," he says. "If Watergate had been isolated, the impact wouldn't have been the same." In Southeast Asia, journalists had dealt with official deception on many levels. Seymour Hersh won the 1970 International Reporting Pulitzer for his work uncovering the massacre of civilians by American troops in the village of My Lai. His stories had been carried by the small, Washington-based Dispatch News Service, but had been published by newspapers around the country.

At home, war protests created divisions in the media just as they widened the schism between Americans. During that time—marked by the tumultuous 1968 Democratic National Convention and shootings of Kent State University students by Ohio National Guardsmen at a 1970 antiwar rally—many reporters developed a keen "question authority" mind-set.

Still, Watergate certainly played an outsize role in attracting bright youngsters to journalism careers, especially after Woodward and Bernstein's book *All the President's Men,* which was later made into a movie that was a hit in theaters. And for a while at least, public support for the press even increased, where before there had been little. "This didn't last very long—maybe eight or ten years—but it was good while it lasted," according to former *Newsday* editor Anthony Marro, who competed with Woodward and Bernstein for Watergate stories in 1972.

For the most part, *New York Times* editors look back at the Pentagon Papers, not Watergate, as the real journalistic breakthrough of the 1970s. They note that some of the Watergate-style domestic spying under President Nixon was a reaction to Daniel Ellsberg's leaking of the Pentagon Papers to Sheehan and others.

Times associate editor Harrison Salisbury tried to capture the power of the Pen-

tagon Papers in his description of the newspaper's final decision, after weeks of debate, to publish them. (His book *Without Fear or Favor* contains one of the better
remembrances that *Times* editors have produced over the years.) Salisbury set the
stage on "that limpid Sunday of June 13, 1971," when the first so-called Vietnam
Archive installment appeared, just as *Times* publisher Arthur O. "Punch" Sulzberger was preparing for a trip to London:

> As Sulzberger checked over his carefully packed bags he had not the slightest pre-
> monition that publication of the Pentagon Papers story that morning was trig-
> gering a sequence of events which would lead inexorably, step by step, to the
> greatest disaster ever to befall an American president, a disaster so profound, so
> far-reaching in implication that by the time it was over basic relationships in the
> American power apparatus would be changed; the very system would quiver; a
> President would fall; the balance of the tripartite American constitutional struc-
> ture would shift; and the role of the press in America, the role of The New York
> Times, and even the function of the press in other great nations of the world
> would be transformed.

A Newsroom at the Hilton

Fox Butterfield was hardly the typical second-year reporter for the *New York
Times*. A summa cum laude Harvard graduate in 1961, specializing in Asian studies, he had lived abroad and served as the *Times*'s Taiwan stringer for nine months
before the paper hired him full-time to work back home. Still, he was in the position of most other cub reporters when he was called back to Times Square as the
new decade began: he took the assignment given to him. It was covering Newark,
a city still simmering from recent race riots.

In one of his early stories he had covered a stormy teachers' strike with strong
racial overtones. At a particularly contentious city-hall meeting, a band of attendees roughed up Butterfield right in the meeting room and stole his notes, along
with his wallet and wristwatch. He wrote a first-person account of the incident for
the front page, and the paper assigned him a bodyguard. The old newsroom
adage—don't make the news; just report it—had been violated, even if unwill-
ingly in this case.

So Butterfield was uneasy when he got a call from the secretary of *Times* managing editor A. M. "Abe" Rosenthal, telling the reporter to stop by the office one
afternoon. "I could only assume the worst: that they were dissatisfied with my performance," Butterfield says. But the meeting was not what he expected.

Rosenthal asked his reporter, "Do you have any problem working with classified
documents?" recalls Butterfield. "I didn't know what he was talking about. I said,

'I assume you've got them. If *you* don't have a problem, I don't think I would, either.'"

It was the correct answer. Butterfield became the first reporter to join Pentagon correspondent Neil Sheehan in a team writing project that was nearly as secret as the documents they would be describing.

Once again, the *Times* was about to make news, not merely report it. The news would open up government records that officials wanted to keep closed, but it would also reinforce an endangered legal principle at the highest level: that government cannot engage in "prior restraint" of news that it does not want the press to publish.

Why had Butterfield been picked to work on the Pentagon Papers team? He gives two possible reasons. "One was favorable to me: I'd been an undergraduate working on east Asian history, and I'd already been to Vietnam myself. I'd actually been to Hanoi," he says. "Then there was an unfavorable reason: that I was so junior and so unknown that I could disappear from my beat in Newark, and the *Washington Post* would not know that I was gone."

That kind of secrecy played an enormous part in the decision-making at the *Times*. A large team was being assembled in a group of suites on the eleventh and thirteenth floors of the New York Hilton. Joining Sheehan and Butterfield were veteran *Times* reporters Hedrick Smith and E. W. Kenworthy, along with editors Allan M. Siegal, Samuel Abt, and Gerald Gold. The group grew to include five secretaries, a researcher, and a makeup editor, all watched over by *Times* security guards.

It was no secret in journalism circles that the *Times* was working on something special. In his autobiography, Ben Bradlee noted that *Post* reporters were aware that a "blockbuster" was in the works at some off-site location, although "we never found out who was part of the task force, much less what they were task-forcing about." Nat Hentoff wrote in a May 20 *Village Voice* piece about a "breakthrough unpublished story concerning the White House, Pentagon and Southeast Asia." He also noted that there was an internal debate at the paper, and asked, "Is this story going to be published? Or are there still Times executives and editors who might hold back such a story 'in the national interest'?"

The blockbuster taking shape at the Hilton involved an analysis by the reporters of forty-three volumes of an extraordinary government history of America's involvement in Vietnam from World War II to May 1968. The entire forty-seven-volume history—seven thousand pages and 2.5 million words—had been commissioned by President Lyndon Johnson's defense secretary, Robert S. McNamara, after he had become disillusioned about Vietnam. It was classified top secret.

Sheehan's source was a thirty-nine-year-old former RAND Corporation researcher, Daniel Ellsberg, then at the Massachusetts Institute of Technology. Ellsberg, a former Marine who had helped write the history when he worked at the Pentagon, had studied at Harvard six years ahead of Sheehan, and nine years ahead of Butterfield. Ellsberg felt driven to take the Vietnam history public, believing that Americans needed to understand the decades of deception underlying their government's Vietnam policy. He had tried other channels inside and outside the government, but was unsuccessful until Sheehan agreed to copy the documents and prepare them for publication in the *Times*. Sheehan's initial OK came from James "Scotty" Reston, the Washington-based columnist and revered elder statesman and vice president of the *Times*.

Ellsberg held back four volumes as too sensitive, especially with peace negotiations going on in Paris at the time. But on Friday, March 19, in Cambridge, Massachusetts, Sheehan and his wife received sixty pounds of pages from Ellsberg. They lugged them to all-night copying shops over three nights and spent fifteen hundred dollars of *Times* money to make copies before returning the Pentagon Papers to Ellsberg. Sheehan and editor Jerry Gold then spent two weeks sorting through the documents in Washington, discussing alternate approaches that might be taken for publication. Sheehan thought they should run in three parts; Gold thought they should be given as many as twenty. Such decisions, of course, would be made higher up—if the Pentagon Papers were to be published at all.

Punch Tells a Joke

On April 20, at 3 p.m.—coincidentally, just hours after the New York Times Company's annual stockholders' meeting—*Times* top editors met to decide what recommendation to make to publisher Punch Sulzberger. Abe Rosenthal held the session in Reston's cluttered New York office, with senior staffers who included Washington bureau chief Max Frankel, foreign editor James Greenfield, columnist Tom Wicker, and assistant managing editor Seymour Topping. Also present were general counsel James Goodale and Sydney Gruson, Sulzberger's assistant. Sheehan told them what he had, although not the source of the documents. The editors asked how confident Sheehan was that the material was genuine, and whether there was any question of national security being breached by its publication. The assembled journalists could see no potential security violations. This was history, after all. "Not an editor expressed doubt. If the materials were authentic . . . then of course *The Times* had to publish the story," Salisbury later wrote. He continued:

> Frankel then put the key question to his colleagues—journalistically, did the story warrant defying the government and possible government legal action; did the

documents, in fact, betray a pattern of deception, of consistent and repeated deception by the American Government of the American people.

There was agreement in the room that this was precisely what the documents showed. Reston added, "These are the government's own conclusions. This is not only what our article is about—this is its basic concept." . . . It was the lies, the government's lies, continuing one administration after the other, which lay at the heart of the matter.

So, added Rosenthal, this would be the manner in which *The Times* would present the material—it would be *history*. The government's own version of history.

General counsel Goodale felt that the historical approach could be defended legally. He was concerned, however, that too many people had attended the day's meeting, and information leaks about the *Times's* story could give the government a head-start on plans to oppose publication. "Everyone has to remember. Be quiet!" Goodale said as they prepared to leave. "Because everyone in this room may have participated in a felony."

More tough decisions—and intensive study and writing—lay ahead before the scheduled June 13 publication date for the first installment. The paper's longtime outside law firm, Lord, Day and Lord, was firmly opposed to the publication of secret, stolen documents, and told Sulzberger that he could be jailed for authorizing it. This was a time of soul-searching for editors, too. Rosenthal and Topping both considered resigning if the decision was made not to publish. Reston said he would publish the Pentagon Papers in his own small journal, the *Vineyard Gazette* in Martha's Vineyard, Massachusetts, if the *Times* decided not to run them.

They discussed the closest apparent precedents at the *Times,* although the precedents were too old to be of much help. There were the newsroom actions taken before the American-supported 1961 invasion by Cuban exiles at Cuba's Bay of Pigs. The *Times* had toned down its story, citing national security as the reason. It had, however, still published in advance of the invasion. (Later, President Kennedy was to suggest that had the *Times* published more detail, perhaps the ill-fated invasion would have been called off, and "you would have saved us from a colossal mistake.")

The editors also reviewed the 1908 case of *Times* reporter William Bayard Hale's interview of Germany's Kaiser Wilhelm, in which the Kaiser had spewed angry words about England and Japan and supported world domination by white people. The paper had consulted President Theodore Roosevelt first, and then killed the story after he opposed its publication. (It was Punch Sulzberger's grandfather, publisher Adolph S. Ochs, who had locked that interview away in his safe, where it remained until it was finally published in 1939.)

Through May, Sheehan and the Pentagon Papers team kept working at the Hilton while general counsel Goodale debated the outside lawyers, who remained strongly opposed to publication. At a May 12 meeting with Sulzberger, the publisher was noncommittal, but allowed work to proceed, planning to make a final call later. Still, Goodale was concerned that the publisher might follow Lord, Day's legal advice and pull the plug. Word of the internal debate trickled in to the Hilton. The team members worried as they wrote.

On June 10 the publisher reviewed a new opening that was being written for the proposed story. Washington chief Frankel and Sheehan had often been at odds in the *Times* newsroom over the years, but they had been thrown together into this rewrite—"improbable collaborators on what each now saw as *the* story of his time," Salisbury called them.

Editors made last-minute presentations to Sulzberger about how to balance the documents and the reporters' analysis in the series. Should they cut down the number of secret documents reprinted, and run more explanations? That could reduce the risk of the government opposing publication. Their presentations done, they waited for the final ruling from the publisher. He had already made up his mind. But in announcing his decision, Sulzberger didn't make it easy for the editors.

"I've decided you can use the documents—but not the story," he told them. After a moment of silence, it dawned on them that their publisher was joking. Sulzberger was ready to approve the June 13 start of a series with just the balance of documents and analysis that his editors proposed. His major suggestion was for a review procedure to make sure that no military secrets were being published. According to Floyd Abrams, who became part of the legal team defending the *Times* after Lord, Day finally backed out: "In retrospect, the decision [to publish] may seem obvious, but it was by no means an easy one at the time, and it remains one for which Sulzberger deserves enormous credit."

Back at the Hilton, Sheehan had gotten to drafting the third of the installments to run in the series now dubbed Vietnam Archive. The decision had been reached earlier to start the Archive with the 1964 Tonkin Gulf incident, which President Lyndon Johnson had used to widen the war. When the series reverted to a chronology, the earliest chapters would be written by Fox Butterfield.

The first day's thirteen-paragraph introduction, being crafted by Frankel, caused problems for some on the team. "Usually we lead with the strongest thing, but you had to read to the jump to see what it was really about." Butterfield says. "Neil and Rick (Smith) were unhappy with the way it was toned down, too," he adds. "It was as if you'd thrown a grenade in the room and then tried to cover it up." The first day's story ran with a Sheehan byline:

Vietnam Archive: Pentagon Study Traces 3 Decades of Growing U.S. Involvement
A massive study of how the United States went to war in Indochina, conducted
by the Pentagon three years ago, demonstrates that four Administrations pro-
gressively developed a sense of commitment to a non-Communist Vietnam, a
readiness to fight the North to protect the South, and an ultimate frustration with
this effort—to a much greater extent than their public statements acknowledged
at the time.

An accompanying page-one story, by Smith, was headed "Vast Review of War
Took a Year." Even if the treatment was too low-key for some of the writers, the
Sunday blockbuster was at last in print.

Then came the reaction—or, rather, the lack of it. At first, other media did not
seem to notice the *Times's* monumental project. Sunday was the slowest day of the
week. Still, even the wire services left it alone. Had the weak opening fooled readers into thinking this was just another war story?

An exception was the *Washington Post,* which played the story prominently. It
soon became clear that editors there saw themselves as badly scooped. They scrambled to find a copy of the Pentagon Papers for themselves. Finally, one television
network did pick up the story Monday night. Harry Reasoner started his CBS
broadcast with: "*The New York Times* has begun publication of what is an extraordinary achievement in journalism . . ." *Times* staffers at the Hilton watched in-
tently, and felt some relief.

"I Am Not a Weakling"

The Nixon administration, too, had seemed to ignore the Sunday exclusive in
the *Times.* For one thing, the Archive shared the Sunday front page with presidential daughter Tricia Nixon's wedding. For another, Democratic presidents bore
the brunt of the blame for Vietnam deception, since the Archive stopped before
Nixon took office. The Pentagon Papers story was pushed toward the back sheets
of the White House daily news summary. With Monday's second installment in
the *Times,* however, the administration's view began to change drastically.

One account of President Nixon's Monday communications suggested that national security adviser Henry Kissinger, concerned about the Paris peace talks being compromised, created a "frenzy" by playing to his boss's fear of leaks. Kissinger
told the president that permitting publication would "show you're a weakling."
People in the Justice Department took a firm anti-*Times* stand, too.

On Monday evening, a message came to Sulzberger's office from Attorney General John N. Mitchell: publishing the Pentagon Papers was illegal and "will cause

irreparable injury to the defense interests of the United States." Mitchell "respect-fully" requested that no further information from the study appear.

With the Tuesday paper being readied for publication, the *Times* brain trust tried to reach Sulzberger in London. As Rosenthal waited, he considered calling the press room and saying "Stop the presses!" That was something he had never done. Instead, he asked the supervisor to "slow things down a bit." When Sulzberger finally was on the phone, the course of action was briefly discussed. General counsel Goodale was strongly in favor of continuing with publication, as were all the editors. When Sulzberger asked if publication would increase the *Times*'s lia-bility, Goodale answered, "Not by five percent." The publisher gave the go-ahead. First Amendment authority Floyd Abrams and his former Yale constitutional law teacher, Alexander Bickel, were retained to lead the legal fight.

On the day of the third installment, the *Times* lawyers lost their bid to block a temporary restraining order, which the Justice Department had based on claims of irreparable injury to the nation. Prior restraint in the past had been viewed as acceptable only in the case of clear danger to a war effort, such as a newspaper's decision to print troop-ship timetables. Judge Murray I. Gurfein's order, which happened to come on his second day on the federal bench, was the first peacetime application of prior restraint.

Faced with another choice—whether to honor the court order—the *Times* chose to halt publication and prepare a legal fight for the right to publish.

Meanwhile, the *Washington Post* had managed to get four thousand pages of the Pentagon Papers from Ellsberg. An editor had hauled a cardboard box of them down from Boston on an empty first-class seat he bought next to his own. It was a monumental job of reading, sorting, and annotating—done for the most part at Bradlee's Georgetown house—but an installment quickly was prepared for publi-cation. It was ready just as the *Times* interrupted its series. Still, the *Post* needed the go-ahead from its publisher, Katharine Graham. And that decision was every bit as risky as the *Times*'s. The paper's parent company was about to go public. A felony conviction for espionage would chill that prospect, and could also threaten its ability to retain ownership of lucrative television stations. After clearing publi-cation with the *Post* lawyers, Bradlee called Graham. Her answer: "OK, I say let's go. Let's publish."

Hurray for the *Post,* Darn 'Em

Times reporters at the New York Hilton, still pounding out installments that now might not run at all, were torn by the developments. "We were very upset to be enjoined, and then when the *Washington Post* picked them up there were mixed emotions," says Fox Butterfield. "We were amazed that these people could produce stories in a couple of days, when it had taken us months. On the one hand we were cheering them on for continuing to publish. On the other, we felt sabotaged."

Shortly, however, the *Post* was enjoined as well. And a series of court battles began, providing some of the most inspiring judicial language ever about the media. The first such ruling came when Judge Gurfein, a former Army intelligence officer, lifted his restraining order. He had found that, when pressed, the government was unable to identify specific portions of the Pentagon Papers that could injure the United States if revealed. He wrote:

> The security of the Nation is not at the ramparts alone. Security also lies in the value of our free institutions. A cantankerous press, an obstinate press, a ubiquitous press must be suffered by those in authority in order to preserve the even greater values of freedom of expression and the right of the people to know. . . .
>
> In the last analysis it is not merely the opinion of the editorial writer or of the columnist which is protected by the First Amendment. It is the free flow of information so that the public will be informed about the Government and its actions.
>
> These are troubled times. There is no greater safety valve for discontent and cynicism about the affairs of Government than freedom of expression in any form. This has been the genius of our institutions throughout our history. It has been the credo of all our Presidents. It is one of the marked traits of our national life that distinguish us from other nations under different forms of government.

The government appealed that decision, and the Supreme Court set an expedited hearing date. Each day, however, was another infringement of the long-held principle barring prior restraint.

As other papers began publishing parts of the Papers, new injunctions were issued. (Among the papers obtaining their own copies: the *Boston Globe, Los Angeles Times, Chicago Sun-Times, St. Louis Post-Dispatch,* and the Knight newspapers.) Argued attorney Alexander Bickel on behalf of the *New York Times:*

> Prior restraints fall on speech with a brutality and a finality all their own. Even if they are ultimately lifted, they cause irremediable loss, a loss in the immediacy, the impact of speech. They differ from the imposition of criminal liability in significant procedural respects as well, which in turn have their substantive consequences. The violator of a prior restraint may be assured of being held in contempt. The violator of a statute punishing speech criminally knows that he will

go before a jury, and may be willing to take his chance, counting on a possible acquittal. A prior restraint therefore stops more speech, more effectively. A criminal statute chills. The prior restraint freezes.

Even the government prosecutor, Solicitor General Erwin N. Griswold, by then was halfhearted in his argument. (Griswold was to write eighteen years later in a *Post* op-ed piece: "I have never seen any trace of a threat to the national security from the Pentagon Papers' publication. Indeed, I have never seen it even suggested that there was an actual threat.")

The Supreme Court ruled six-to-three in favor of the *Times* and the *Post*, with Justice Hugo L. Black writing:

> [T]he press was protected so that it could bare the secrets of government. Only a free and unrestrained press can effectively expose deception in government. And paramount among the responsibilities of a free press is the duty to prevent any part of the government from deceiving the people and sending them off to distant lands to die of foreign fevers and foreign shot and shell. In my view, far from deserving condemnation for their courageous reporting, the *New York Times* and the *Washington Post* and other newspapers should be commended for serving the purpose that the Founding Fathers saw so clearly. In revealing the workings of government, that led to the Vietnam War, the newspapers nobly did precisely that which the founders hoped and trusted they would do.

Seventeen days after the first *Times* story, the *Times* and the *Post* resumed running the Pentagon Papers. Editors emerged from the experience awed by the Supreme Court's support—and relieved at the bullet the press had dodged. Looking back at the June 15 front page, which had carried the headline "Mitchell Seeks to Halt Series on Vietnam but Times Refuses," managing editor Rosenthal ruminated:

> . . . that if it had said, "The Times Agrees," the history of this paper and I believe of American journalism, would have been radically different. If we had surrendered to Mitchell, and had allowed the government, without a court battle, to dictate to us, I really believe that the heart would have gone out of the paper and American newspapering.

After such a victory, one might expect a Pulitzer Public Service Medal for the *Times* to be nearly automatic. The Public Service jurors saw it that way, unanimously recommending a joint award for the newspaper and for Neil Sheehan. "It is fortuitous that the Pulitzer Prizes can recognize the accomplishments of both the newspaper and of a persistent, courageous reporter, and thus reaffirm to the American people that the press continues its devotion to their right to know, a basic bulwark in our democratic society," the jury wrote.

But the board was divided. Before the session, Ben Bradlee lobbied board chairman Joseph Pulitzer Jr., editor and publisher of the *Post-Dispatch* (and J.P. II's son), arguing that the *Times* and *Post* should both should receive special citations. The *Times* should not win a prize for "anything hand-delivered by a single source to a newspaper," according to Bradlee. (He later relented, supporting the Public Service award for the *Times*.) Leading the forces for the *Times,* and the *Times* alone, to win the Gold Medal was chairman Pulitzer. On the other side was *Wall Street Journal* editor Vermont Connecticut Royster, who had concerns "about the propriety of such an award," according to Pulitzer administrator John Hohenberg. "As the debate flagged, one of the Board's members finally asked Royster with elaborate casualness, 'Vermont, if the Wall Street Journal had had the Pentagon papers, would you have published them?' Without a moment's hesitation, Royster answered, 'Yes.'"

At that point the board decided that its members could agree on the value of acknowledging the *Times*'s public service. The vote was unanimous, although the board worded the citation purely to honor the act of publishing the Pentagon Papers. From the beginning, the jury's proposal for Sheehan to receive his own prize was "set aside as a complicating factor."

Another barrier developed to the *Times* receiving the prize, though: the twenty-two-member Columbia University Board of Trustees. Under the original terms of the Pulitzer Prizes, trustees could disapprove the decisions of the Pulitzer board, although they were not permitted to pick a substitute winner. The trustees had never before given such a disapproval. But on Sunday, April 30, they held a marathon closed session and twice informally voted down the award to the *Times*—along with a National Reporting Prize that the board had recommended for columnist Jack Anderson for work unrelated to the Pentagon Papers. After the voting, Columbia President William J. McGill asked them to reconsider. Finally, the trustees agreed to let the awards stand. Without mentioning specific prizes, the trustees added a statement that had "the selections been those of the Trustees alone, certain of the recipients would not have been chosen."

Awarding the prize to the *Times* in such a way—over the trustees' objection and without mentioning Sheehan—was an imperfect solution. Further, the citation itself said nothing of the journalism that had gone into interpreting the Pentagon Papers. And there was no recognition of other newspapers that had taken up the cause when the *Times* was enjoined, securing their own copies of the Pentagon Papers and publishing them under many of the same threats that the *Times* faced.

For many of those papers, too, it was a defining moment. Ben Bradlee was later to write that with that event "the ethos of the paper changed, and . . . crystallized for editors and reporters everywhere how independent and determined and confident of its purpose the new Washington Post had become." The experience created "a sense of confidence within the *Post,* a sense of mission and agreement on new goals, and how to attain them. . . . After the Pentagon Papers, there would be no decision too difficult for us to overcome together." It would only take a year to test the *Post*'s newfound confidence.

1972—*New York Times:* For the publication of the Pentagon Papers.

New York Times reporter Neil Sheehan in 1972. Photo by Barton Silverman, the *New York Times.* Used by permission.

New York Times front page of June 13 1971. Used by permission.

SUPREME COURT, 6-3, UPHOLDS NEWSPAPERS ON PUBLICATION OF THE PENTAGON REPORT; TIMES RESUMES ITS SERIES, HALTED 15 DAYS

Nixon Says Turks Agree To Ban the Opium Poppy

PRESIDENT CALLS STEEL AND LABOR TO WHITE HOUSE

He Asks Both Sides to Meet With Him Tuesday Before Contract Talks Start

Pentagon Papers: Study Reports Kennedy Made 'Gamble' Into a 'Broad Commitment'

BURGER DISSENTS

First Amendment Rule Held to Block Most Prior Restraints

Soviet Starts an Inquiry Into 3 Astronauts' Deaths

U.S. and Diem's Overthrow: Step by Step

CHOU TIES U.N. SEAT TO TAIPEI'S OUSTER

Also Says Peking Must Have Permanent Council Post if It Is to Be Member

Jim Garrison Is Arrested; U.S. Says He Took Bribes

Cousin Asserts Jerome Johnson Told of Job With Italian League

THE STATES RATIFY FULL VOTE AT 18

Conferees Cut Military Pay Rise As Authority to Draft Runs Out

ACTION BY GRAVEL VEXES SENATORS

False Advertising Laid to H&R Block

New York Times front page of July 1, 1971. Used by permission.

New York Times managing editor A. M. Rosenthal, publisher Arthur O. Sulzberger, and attorney James Goodale hold a press conference after the Supreme Court decided to allow publication of the Pentagon Papers. Photo by Jack Manning, the *New York Times.* Used by permission.

CHAPTER 13

All the Editor's Men

People don't win Pulitzer Prizes by being for; they usually win them by being against.

—President Richard M. Nixon, to the National
Association of Broadcasters, March 19, 1974

*B*ob Woodward had not seen the movie *All the President's Men* for twenty-five years. Then one day in mid-2005 he sat down with his eight-year-old daughter Diana while she watched it for the first time.

Noticing her squirming a bit, the *Washington Post* assistant managing editor asked what she was thinking. "The guy pretending to be you doesn't look like you at all," Diana told him. And what else? "Boring, boring, boring," she said.

"And she's exactly right," Woodward agrees, chuckling—not so much about the movie, but the nature of the Watergate investigation itself. "Because it's about fitting little pieces together. You don't know what you have when you publish a little piece, but you publish it anyway."

Any squirming of his own on the topic of Watergate may have more to do with how often he is still asked to rehash the role of "Woodstein"—as *Post* editors nicknamed the duo of Woodward and Carl Bernstein during their investigation—in the events that led to President Nixon's August 1974 resignation. Just a few months before the father-daughter movie viewing, another flurry of national publicity erupted when Deep Throat chose to identify himself. Woodward's celebrated secret source turned out to be W. Mark Felt, the number-two man at the Federal Bureau of Investigation during the time of the Watergate probe. (A smoke-wreathed Hal Holbrook, stepping from behind pillars in an eerie, dark garage, played him in the 1976 film.)

Alan Pakula's movie—with Robert Redford and Dustin Hoffman as Woodward and Carl Bernstein, and Jason Robards as Ben Bradlee—actually holds up very well. For adults, at least, it now plays as a historical/political thriller. The mystery is not whether the president will fall, but how two reporters and one cantankerous editor can help precipitate it.

The case is so familiar to journalists today that there is little suspense even in that. When the University of Texas created a home for Woodward and Bernstein's Watergate papers, just two months before the Felt/Deep Throat revelation, retired *Newsday* editor Anthony Marro led a seminar in Austin to reexamine some Watergate-related media issues. One question: Just how much credit did the press really deserve for driving a president from office? Marro, who was among a relative handful of reporters competing with the *Post* for early Watergate stories, argued that the media got too much. It had merely played a role in a much broader drama. "The fact is that Nixon was ousted by a constitutional process that involved all three branches of government—criminal investigators, the courts, and the Congress," he told the assembled journalism students.

Woodward himself concedes that the full impact of the *Post*'s reporting cannot be known. But he believes that without press exposure, the White House cover-up well might have succeeded in protecting the guilty, and obstructing justice enough that the facts remained hidden. After the intricate web of the Nixon administration's involvement in criminal activity was exposed, about forty people went to jail, including former Attorney General John Mitchell, Nixon chief of staff H. R. "Bob" Haldeman, and chief domestic adviser John Ehrlichman. "The truth of the matter is that prosecutors had some of this information, but they didn't use it. And we made it public," Woodward says. The *Post* stories—vehemently attacked at the time as biased, shabby journalism by a White House anxious to isolate the paper from the rest of the press—may have directly led federal judge John J. Sirica to put pressure on a key defendant, James McCord. Only in April 1973, when McCord began talking about the burglars' ties to the White House, did the conspiracy of silence begin unraveling, eventually setting off the avalanche of confessions and convictions.

"Pure Opera Bouffe"

Whatever the *Post*'s actual role, it is easy to forget the Watergate story's gradual evolution from humble police-and-courts beginnings to journalism legend, with elements of myth.

No less a personage than former Vice President Al Gore fell victim, Woodward says, when the two men had dinner together in the summer of 2005. Gore—briefly a visiting journalism professor at Columbia University after leaving office, and a reporter with Nashville's *Tennessean* in the early 1970s—"talked about the purity of the Watergate stories. He said, 'Those were so wonderful, and now you write about Bush and you don't nail him,'" according to the *Post* editor. "And I said to him, 'You have consumed the Kool-Aid of the mythology of Watergate.' Because those stories were incremental, they were not perfect. They contained some mistakes, they contained some under-reaching, some over-reaching. It's what you would expect. It's daily reporting. We didn't say, 'In an outrageous violation of all constitutional principle . . .' We just said, 'This happened.' Very bland, bloodless, if you will. Not in the Pulitzer advocacy tradition." And, he adds, perhaps thinking back to his recent movie-viewing experience, "there was no music in the background."

The blue-bound Pulitzer Prize entry folders submitted by managing editor Howard Simons in late January 1973 capture the matter-of-fact nature of the early *Post* coverage, and how it slowly built into a riveting drama. He filed two entries: one on behalf of the *Post* for Public Service, and one on behalf of Woodward and Bernstein for National Reporting.

The *Post*'s bid for a Pulitzer was a tough sell at the time. Many journalists still were suspicious of any stories under the Woodward and Bernstein byline. President Nixon had been inaugurated after his landslide reelection over South Dakota Senator George McGovern. Most Washington correspondents had made the *campaign*, not Watergate, the main story. It had been such a strange contest, with one Democrat after another seemingly stumbling into some great gaffe. First, Maine Senator Edmund Muskie withdrew after being embarrassed on the eve of the New Hampshire primary. The *Manchester Union-Leader* had received a mysterious letter suggesting that the senator condoned use of the slur word "Canuck" for French Canadians. And later, McGovern's vice-presidential choice, Thomas Eagleton, a Missouri senator, withdrew after press reports revealed that he had been treated for clinical depression in the past. A black cloud seemed to hang over the Democrats all the way to their flop at the polls.

Surely, this had been the real story, many journalists thought at the time—far bigger than a peculiar June 17, 1972, attempt to bug the Democrats, which had resulted in guilty pleas by men whose suspected ties to the Nixon campaign were all officially denied.

Simons's nomination letter tried to fit the *Post* entry into the Pulitzer public-service tradition:

> It began as pure opera bouffe—four men, gloved and masked, breaking into Democratic National Committee headquarters in the dark of a summer night,

armed with walkie-talkies and sophisticated electronic bugging devices. They even called it a caper.

But this was the Watergate Case, the biggest political scandal of the decade.

As this is written five men have pleaded guilty. Two more are on trial. A high White House official has been eased out of his job. The treasurer of the Committee to Re-Elect the President has resigned in protest. A Senate investigation is under way. The Administration has been politically embarrassed.

The word "Watergate" has become a symbol for the deterioration of the American political ethic.

All of this has happened as the result of the journalistic efforts of The Washington Post, its reporters—Carl Bernstein and Robert Woodward—editors, editorial writers and its cartoonist . . .

It was a fine nomination letter, but the Public Service jurors were not persuaded. In March they made the *Post* only their third choice. It would take another month of confirming news to create media understanding of the *Post*'s accomplishment. Only then was the full Pulitzer board able to find it worthy of the Gold Medal.

Tip of the Day: Choose the Front Row

The *Post* got onto the story fast that June 17 Saturday morning through a telephone tip to Simons within hours of the burglars' arrest. That call came from attorney Joseph Califano, who had been counsel both to the Democratic Party and the *Post* in the past. Alerted by the managing editor, longtime police reporter Alfred E. Lewis accompanied the acting police chief to the crime scene and spent hours behind police lines. Other police reporters remained outside. Woodward—an ambitious first-year *Post* reporter not particularly enthused by having to cover a hearing related to a local break-in—went to the burglars' arraignment. He was in the front row to hear defendant McCord whisper to the judge his last place of employment. It was the Central Intelligence Agency.

"No three letters in the English language, arranged in that particular order, and spoken in similar circumstances, can tighten a good reporter's sphincter faster than C-I-A," executive editor Ben Bradlee later wrote. Or an editor's. By the end of the day, ten reporters were working the story, including Bernstein, who explored the Miami connections that the burglars seemed to have. Both he and Woodward contributed to the main Sunday story, appearing under Lewis's byline. After that, Woodward and Bernstein were the natural choices to stay with it, at least in the early stages, when it appeared to be the very "third-rate burglary" that President Nixon's press secretary described.

"They got the story assigned to them because they were the first two reporters identifying themselves that Saturday morning," says Bradlee with a laugh. "The big shots don't work on Saturdays." The tougher assignment decision came later: keeping them on Watergate after they began turning up strong White House connections. "There were a few people on the national staff who wanted the story," Bradlee says. "You'd ask them, 'What fault do you find with Woodward and Bernstein, and what reason are you going to give for taking it away from them?' Then, opposition pretty much disappeared."

If the accident of working a Saturday shift brought them together on the story, they quickly made the most of the pairing. Professionally, they complemented each other well despite their many differences. Bernstein's reporting drive was combined with a notoriously mercurial personality that often got him in trouble with editors. There was an office story, for example, about his forgetting a rental car he parked in a garage, running up a huge tab for the paper. For his part, the Yale-educated Woodward, though newer to journalism, had served as a naval officer and had chosen journalism over going to Harvard Law School.

"Both are bright, but Woodward was conscientious, hardworking, and driven, and Bernstein messy and undisciplined. He was, however, the better writer, more imaginative and creative," *Post* publisher Katharine Graham wrote in her 1997 autobiography. "In other ways the relationship was oil and water, but the end product came out right, despite—or perhaps because of—the strange mix."

Woodward describes the imperfect art of newsroom teaming as "assembling the perfect journalistic brain, something no one person has that I know of." He notes, "Carl Bernstein and I never really look at things the same way, even to this day." But there was one big plus to their collaboration, Woodward points out: Total-immersion coverage caused no problems at home. "We were young and unmarried, Carl and I."

Their reporting encountered lots of dead ends, and some smaller threads of information led down curious alleys, but turned up nothing definitive. Still, there were enough exclusives to keep Bradlee in their camp. "They got the White House involvement. They identified the money. They tied the money to the Committee to Re-Elect the President. And this was all Woodward and Bernstein, these nonentity reporters," he says.

The headline on their Monday, June 19, collaboration read:

GOP Security Aide
Among 5 Arrested
In Bugging Affair

Under the heat of a deadline, Bernstein literally snatched the final writing job away from Woodward, who had to concede that his new teammate had a gift for banging out clear, fast copy. The story started:

> One of the five men arrested early Saturday in the attempt to bug the Democratic National Committee headquarters here is the salaried security coordinator for President Nixon's re-election committee.
>
> The suspect, James W. McCord Jr., 53, also holds a separate contract to provide security services to the Republican National Committee, GOP national chairman Bob Dole said yesterday.

After turning in their story on Sunday, Woodward went to McCord's home. He found the lights on, but no one answered the door. The news for Tuesday's paper did not develop until after midnight, when a night police reporter for the *Post*, Eugene Bachinski, called Woodward. A source at the station had told Bachinski of two interesting entries found in notebooks taken from the burglars. The story was another scoop, under E. J. Bachinski's and Woodward's names:

> A consultant to White House special counsel Charles W. Colson is listed in the address books of two of the five men arrested in an attempt to bug the Democratic National headquarters here early Saturday.
>
> Federal sources close to the investigation said the address books contain the name and home telephone number of Howard E. Hunt, with the notations, "W. House" and "W.H."

The world would learn one day that it was E. Howard Hunt, not Howard E. (He gained an infamous Watergate footnote for having performed some political dirty tricks while disguised in a cheap red wig.) To track down Hunt, Woodward first called the White House and got a number where he could be contacted. Finally reaching Hunt, the reporter asked him why his name was in the Watergate burglars' notebooks. Said Hunt: "Good God!" He then mumbled "no comment" and hung up.

Now It Can Be Told

Helping link Hunt to the case was the man Howard Simons had dubbed Deep Throat after a pornographic movie with the same title—and because of the man's arrangement with Woodward that his information would be for "deep background," not publishable unless confirmed independently. His guidance was vital, though. To Woodward, the appearance of Hunt's name in the notebooks was far from proof of complicity. "I called Felt twice that day," says Woodward of the long-secret contact he now can discuss freely. "Felt said to me, 'Don't worry, he's involved. He's at the center of things." The high-level confirmation was what the *Post* needed to run with that story.

In the office, Bradlee was an editorial model of tough love, and he radiated aggressiveness. "It was 'go get 'em, kid; there aren't limits here,'" says Woodward, who had been at the *Post* only nine months the day he called the White House to find Howard Hunt. Amazingly, the cub reporter was not nervous for that first call. "And that's not because of me; that's because of the atmosphere of 'go get 'em, kid.'" Still, Jason Robards got Bradlee's demanding side right, Woodward says. "Those scenes of his slapping the copy and saying, 'You haven't got it, kid'—you want to strangle him, but that didn't mean 'I don't believe it.' That didn't mean 'We're not going to publish it.' It meant 'Work harder; get more sources; make sure it rings with me.'"

The next major exclusive ran August 1. In Miami, Bernstein tracked down an explanation for how a twenty-five-thousand-dollar cashier's check to the president's reelection campaign found its way into the Florida account of a Watergate burglar. Then, on September 17, the reporters established that the fund paying the burglars was controlled by top aides to former Nixon campaign manager John Mitchell. (As attorney general, the same Mitchell had sought to enjoin the *Times* from publishing the Pentagon Papers in June 1971.)

On October 1 came another *Post* blockbuster. Mitchell, while still attorney general, personally had controlled a secret fund for spying on the Democrats. The story quoted Mitchell's response to Bernstein, who called him for comment at 11:30 p.m.:

> All that crap, you're putting it in the paper? It's all been denied. Jesus. Katie Graham is gonna get caught in a big fat wringer if that's published. Good Christ. That's the most sickening thing I've ever heard.

It is well known now that Mitchell actually said that the publisher would get "her tit caught" in that wringer. "Leave everything in but 'her tit,' and tell the desk I said it's OK," the executive editor had said to Bernstein. (The publisher later wrote that Bradlee did not check with her before running the quote—and she added that it was "especially strange of [Mitchell] to call me Katie, which no one has ever called me.")

Nine days later, Howard Hunt's phone records led to another *Post* exclusive. He had made numerous calls to a California lawyer, Donald Segretti, who turned out to be involved in a broad network of campaign dirty tricks. The October 10 Woodward and Bernstein story began:

> FBI agents have established that the Watergate bugging incident stemmed from a massive campaign of political spying and sabotage conducted on behalf of President Nixon's re-election and directed by officials of the White House and the Committee for the Re-election of the President.
>
> The activities, according to information in FBI and Department of Justice files, were aimed at all the major Democratic presidential candidates and—since 1971—represented a basic strategy of the re-election effort.

Included was information tying the White House to a range of tricks, including some involving the Muskie presidential bid that that had come apart in New Hampshire. Mark Felt had been a secret source on this story, as well. The FBI was following the tricksters, too.

To get the demanding Bradlee to sign off on any story that the reporters' digging produced, the *Post* set a tougher-than-usual standard for getting information confirmed before publication. Bradlee required at least two solid, independent sources if the information was from individuals who would not allow their names to be used. "It grew out of paranoia," Woodward says of the rule. "Some source could be spinning you. And a second element was the seriousness of the charges. You're accusing someone of criminal, unethical behavior."

Among perhaps two hundred Watergate stories the *Post* did in 1972, Tony Marro lists only those of August 1, September 17, October 1, and October 10 as breaking "significant new ground." Still, having to follow Woodward and Bernstein on their daily reports was exhausting, says Marro, whose *Newsday* was one of the few papers that tried hard to compete on the story. The paper saw it as part of its investigative tradition, and also felt a duty to extend the previous investigations it had done into President Nixon's personal and business relationships. "You worked all day and all night, and everybody was under a tremendous amount of pressure, and we were still getting beat," Marro says.

Woodward does not disagree that those few 1972 stories stood out. In between them, though, were dozens of smaller ones that would lead the reporters down the path, stone by stone, to the Oval Office.

"There'd be a little story on [page] B-38 about the expensive receiver that the Watergate burglars used to monitor the calls. A $3,000 receiver from a firm in Rockville called Watkins-Johnson—only I remember it," Woodward says. "Now $3,000 for a radio receiver was a lot of money. That story really didn't lead anywhere, except that it told you that this was a really well-financed operation. As you get these details and add them together, the facts created the momentum for understanding what was really happening."

Avoiding the I-Word

Through the summer of 1972, the hours of interviewing and writing were so intense that he and Bernstein gave little thought to how high in the administration the reporting might lead. "You kept your head down and stayed focused on the next story," Woodward says. He does remember one moment, though, just before the October 1 story on Mitchell, when he and Bernstein were sitting in the *Post* cafeteria and Bernstein suddenly said of Nixon: "This guy's going to be impeached." Woodward thought about it and replied, "You're right. But we'll never be able to use that word."

As the pair worked on, Bradlee tried to insulate them from the heat of internal and external criticism. "We knew at the time that people didn't believe what we'd written. Many of our colleagues on the *Washington Post* national staff didn't believe it," Woodward says, recalling how hard that was for a young reporter to accept. Just as hard to accept were the daily Nixon administration denials and attacks on the *Post*. "The effort to discredit our reporting was staggering, unparalleled," says Woodward. "It gets your attention when you turn on the television and there you are, just roundly denounced. And you know what you wrote is right, and carefully done."

Even when things went wrong, the executive editor and managing editor stood up for "Woodstein." Bradlee and Simons had built up a strong editing crew to handle continuing news like the Watergate story. "It takes a particular kind of energy and courage on the part of editors and publishers to support daily incremental coverage," says Woodward. The *Post* at the time did not have a standing investigative team with its own dedicated editors. Such editing—along with the extra time newspapers can give to special-project reporting—sometimes makes catching potential errors easier.

The best known of Woodward and Bernstein's mistakes probably would have slipped through any editing processes. While he was interviewing Nixon reelection committee treasurer Hugh Sloan in late October, Woodward misunderstood what the official said about whether his grand jury testimony included mention of presidential chief of staff Bob Haldeman as one of the five officials controlling the secret fund that financed campaign dirty tricks. Flawed *Post* "confirmations" of what Woodward believed he had heard from Sloan led to an inaccuracy in an October 25 story. Sloan had not identified Haldeman before the grand jury. The error brought ringing denials from all over the administration, and forced the *Post* to pull back to discover what had gone wrong.

It would eventually come out that Haldeman *was* the fifth controlling person, but that the grand jury had not asked Sloan about Haldeman, so Sloan had not mentioned his name. Still, the error gave ammunition to *Post* critics. "You shouldn't make any mistakes, and the Haldeman story was a mistake," says Woodward.

Wrote Bradlee of the error:

> Mercifully for us, on the afternoon of October 26, Henry Kissinger gave a press conference at the White House to announce that "peace was at hand in Vietnam," and that gave us a little breathing room, since it occupied both the press and the Nixon administration.

Soon, Woodward and Bernstein returned to form. They would continue to lead the nation in coverage of Watergate-related stories throughout 1973 and 1974.

"A Pimple on the Elephant's Ass"

Along with the package of news stories in the 1973 Pulitzer Public Service entry, the *Post* submitted a dozen editorials by Phil Geyelin and Roger Wilkins. On the very first day after the break-in, one editorial appeared called "Mission Incredible," opening with the line: "As always, should you or any of your force be caught or killed, the Secretary will disavow any knowledge of your actions. . . ." Among the cartoons submitted in the package, all by Herblock, as Herbert Block signed his work, was one depicting a family on a tour of the White House. The mother had strayed down a stairway leading to a sludge-encrusted basement area filled with "taps," "bugs," "handguns," and "rubber gloves." The caption: "Sorry, Ma'm—The Lower Level Is Not Part of the White House Tour."

None of the five Public Service jurors who convened on March 8 and 9 was from Washington, New York, or Los Angeles, where Watergate stories had been in the news more regularly. One juror was from Portland, Maine, and the others from Chicago, Kansas City, Salt Lake City, and Riverside, California. Their overwhelming first choice was the *Chicago Tribune,* for a probe of primary-election violations that had led to indictments and convictions. Articles on police corruption by the *New York Times,* the previous year's winner for the Pentagon Papers, earned that paper a spot ahead of the *Post,* also.

In notes submitted to the Pulitzer board, the jury said that one juror had ranked it second, and three ranked it third. "However, a fifth juror gave it a substantially lower rating on the ground that the Post had overindulged professional restraints on unattributed information in order to make its point." (Woodward laughs when told of that argument from the work's detractor. "We weren't trying to make a point," he says.)

Beyond that, some jurors felt that office break-ins and campaign slush funds were relatively small potatoes, even if the reporting was correct. One unidentified juror told a Columbia official: "Watergate is only a pimple on the elephant's ass."

The view of the *Post*'s coverage changed dramatically before the Pulitzer board meeting, though. On April 5, Watergate break-in suspect James McCord, the former CIA man, told Judge Sirica that there had been White House pressure to keep the defendants silent. As more high-level figures then became implicated in the break-in and cover-up, others in the media began publishing stories that confirmed much of what Woodward and Bernstein's hard-won anonymous sources had told them months earlier. As Pulitzer Prize administrator John Hohenberg put it:

> It was in this charged atmosphere that the Advisory Board met at Columbia on April 12. The same membership as in 1972 met around the black oval table in the World Room under the lighted Statue of Liberty stained glass window, only this time Messrs. Bradlee and Reston were out of the room . . . . Within a few minutes after Chairman [Joseph] Pulitzer [Jr.] had declared himself in favor of the Washington Post for the public service gold medal, all nine Board members in the room agreed to reverse the Public Service Jury.

The Pulitzer board gave the *Tribune* the Spot News Pulitzer after its members had decided on the Gold Medal for the *Post*.

Bradlee was prepared to resign from the board if the *Post* had not won for its Watergate coverage. But even after the Gold Medal was won, he had a delicate job to do: explaining to Woodward and Bernstein that the Public Service Prize was for the newspaper, not for individuals. Officially, they would not be winning it themselves. In fact, the reporters were not listed in the Pulitzer citation. Woodward remembers Bradlee reassuring the reporters that they should not worry because they would forever be identified with Watergate.

"It was one of his all-time understatements," Woodward says.

"I don't consider myself as having ever won a Pulitzer Prize," he adds, "and that is factually correct." As he thinks about it, the *Post* assistant managing editor believes it is wise for the Pulitzers to have an award acknowledging a paper, and not individuals. "Anything that's a little humbling is a good thing," he says.

The board never gave any explanation for why the two reporters' names were left off the citation. Reporters by then had been identified in citations three times, in 1947, 1950, and 1960. Some board members who have served more recently have viewed the omission of Woodward and Bernstein—as well as Neil Sheehan's exclusion from the 1972 *New York Times* award—as unfortunate mistakes. "It would seem to me to have been entirely appropriate to have named Woodward and Bernstein, and to have named Neil Sheehan. They were central figures and it was their initiatives that led to the Prizes," says Seymour Topping, the retired *New York Times* editor who served as administrator of the Pulitzer Prizes during most of the 1990s.

Gene Roberts, executive editor of the *Philadelphia Inquirer* during the Watergate years, agrees that the Public Service citation should have named Woodward and Bernstein, but adds that individual Pulitzers should have gone to them as well. "It was maybe the single greatest reporting effort of all time," he says. In his nine years on the Pulitzer board in the late 1970s and early 1980s he found the board too reluctant to acknowledge individuals by name when it honored a paper with the Gold Medal. "I think it's wonderful that the paper would win an award," he says, "but it's even more important to the institution of the Pulitzers to take a step backward and always put the reporters first."

Other board veterans don't consider the exclusion of the names to be so serious. "It's not as if either of them failed to get the accolades," says retired *Chicago Tribune* editor Jack Fuller. Besides, "Woodward and Bernstein did terrific work, and it was the centerpiece, but the *Post* stuck its neck out big-time and deserved the Public Service award."

Just how exposed it was became apparent when tapes of conversations in Richard Nixon's Oval Office were released. In one conversation on September 15, the day Hunt and the burglars were indicted, the president told some senior aides:

> The main thing is that the *Post* is going to have damnable, damnable problems out of this one. They have a television station . . . and they're going to have to get it renewed. . . . And it's going to be God damn active here. . . . [T]he game has to be played awfully rough.

What would people have thought of the Pulitzers had the *Post* not won a prize for its Watergate coverage?

Some board members from later years believe the damage could have been severe. "If the Prize had been awarded two months earlier, it would have been extremely embarrassing for the *Post* not to get the Pulitzer," says Gene Roberts. Seymour Topping agrees, and extends that sentiment to the case of the *New York Times*'s publication of the Pentagon Papers the previous year. "Those two achievements were so outstanding that to put them aside would have indicated that there were extraordinary political considerations behind the choices," he says.

Watergate's Legacy

More than three decades after Watergate, few if any journalistic enterprises are studied more than that coverage by Woodward, Bernstein, and the *Washington Post*. For the University of Texas seminar in 2005, retired *Newsday* editor Tony Marro analyzed questions that ranged from the use of anonymous sources to how it was possible that the *Post* could have had the story almost to itself for so long.

Marro noted that the Washington press corps of 1972 was much smaller, and did little investigative reporting, since it was largely dedicated to political and government coverage, such as the election campaign. For those who did want to cover Watergate and its fallout, critical sourcing issues arose. Many of the criminal defense lawyers for Watergate figures also had worked in government. "There were a lot of reporters at the *Post* who knew these people very well," according to Marro. "Most of the reporters for the out-of-town papers didn't know them at all."

Meanwhile, editors back home—like the Pulitzer juror who refused to rank the *Post* entry—balked at trying to follow stories that relied so heavily on unnamed sources that their own reporters could not duplicate. While the *Post* did not disclose its Watergate sources, the administration was very much on-the-record with its vehement denials and accusations against the paper. It took the revelations in Judge John J. Sirica's courtroom to get other papers to take the scandal seriously.

Marro believes that Watergate's greatest journalism contribution was leading newspapers and other media to spend more money on serious investigative reporting. "I think this probably would have happened anyway," he says, "but Watergate speeded it up."

The coverage created mixed blessings, as Marro sees it. Using unnamed sources, something papers had discouraged in the past, became far more common among investigative journalists. "Granting anonymity can be as addictive as heroin," he says. Gradually, sources themselves learn to expect being shielded, making on-the-record material harder to get. Woodward disagrees that there is an over-reliance on anonymous sources, arguing that granting anonymity remains necessary for reporters to get at hidden truths.

In Marro's view, the post-Watergate press also became too confrontational. Reporters quit giving sources the benefit of the doubt, adding a note of negativity to coverage that was overdone, especially in stories about government. "My own experience as a reporter persuaded me that there's at least as much confusion as conspiracy in government," he says.

Criticisms aside, the *Post* got its stories because "Woodward and Bernstein just worked harder than everyone else," according to Marro. They spent "hundreds and hundreds of hours assembling and updating chronologies and files detailing just who had been accused of what, who had admitted to what, who had pointed the finger at others, and who was still out there—a superior or a subordinate or a partner of the accused—who could fill in what pieces of the puzzle."

It was a technique that computers would make considerably easier in the coming decades.

For Woodward, some Watergate lessons were very personal. One was quite recent. Since watching the movie with his daughter, he has resumed doing "night work," as he calls it—going to interview sources at home after-hours, as he and Bernstein had done regularly. "That's where you get people alone, away from the office. Seeing them empty their pockets, as Howard Simons used to say."

He also credits Simons, who died in 1989, with teaching him a broader life-lesson in the wake of Watergate.

Just after President Nixon resigned, Simons "called me into his office with these arm motions that only he could do," says Woodward. On the desk was a reporter's recent obituary. "It had a headline like 'Joe Smith, 80, won Pulitzer in 1947.' And Howard said, 'That's you. This guy won the Pulitzer and you never heard from him again. That's what happens. Always remember, you're never going to have a story that has the impact of Watergate. Never.

"And then he said the most important thing: 'Now get your ass out of here and get back to work.'"

1973— *Washington Post:* For its investigation of the Watergate case.

Washington Post reporters Carl Bernstein (left) and Bob Woodward meet with publisher Katharine Graham during their 1972 Watergate reporting. *Post* staff photo. Used by permission.

Post executive editor Ben Bradlee ponders history in the making. The headline reads "Nixon Resigns." *Post* staff photo by David R. Legge. Used by permission.

CONFIDENTIAL   CATEGORY ONE

REPORT OF THE PUBLIC SERVICE JURY
PULITZER PRIZES FOR 1973

(1) For a distinguished example of meritorious public service by a newspaper through the use of its journalistic resources which may include editorials, cartoons, and photographs, as well as reporting, a gold medal.

To the Advisory Board on the Pulitzer Prizes

We, the members of the jury assigned to making recommendations in the
Public Service category present for your consideration the following entries
in order of our preference:

(1) Chicago Tribune, nominated by Clayton Kirkpatrick, editor: Expose
of vote fraud in Chicago. 116.

The Chicago Tribune by persistent probing uncovered flagrant violations
of voting procedures in the primary election which resulted in indictments
and convictions of a number of persons. This entry was the first choice of
four out of five jurors.

(2) New York Times, nominated by A. M. Rosenthal, managing editor:
Investigation of municipal corruption and the erosion of criminal justice in
New York City. 148.

The Times' articles on corruption in the Police Department, the construction trades and the courts were a courageous and imaginative application of the resources of a large and talented staff.

This entry was the second choice of three of the five jurors.

(3) Washington Post, nominated by Howard Simons, managing editor:
Investigation of the Watergate case. 131.

The Washington Post, despite obstacles placed in its path by politicians
and use of intimidation tactics, continued on a determined course to reveal
the close ties of the Watergate bugging incident and White House personalities.

This entry was the third choice of three of the five jurors and the
second choice of another. However, a fifth juror gave it a substantially
lower rating on the ground that the Post had overindulged professional
restraints on unattributed information in order to make its point.

(4) Wilmington (Del.) Evening Journal, nominated by Leslie E. Cansler
Jr., managing editor: Investigation of narcotics in Delaware. 133.

The Evening Journal did a courageous and thorough job in uncovering
the numerous sources of narcotics in Wilmington and naming the pushers.

This was the first choice of one juror.

(5) Chicago Sun Times, nominated by James Hoge, editor: Series on
Environment: Troubled Waters. 126.

(6) Buffalo Courier Express, nominated by Douglas L. Turner, executive
editor. Investigation of malpractice in city affairs. 137.

Respectfully submitted:

/s/ Arthur C. Deck, executive editor, The Salt Lake Tribune (chairman)
     George R. Burg, managing editor, The Kansas City Star
     Ernest W. Chard, editor, Guy Gannett Publishing Co., Portland, Me.
     Howard H. Hayes Jr., editor and co-publisher, Press-Enterprise Company,
       Riverside, California
     Audrey T. Weaver, city editor, Chicago Daily Defender

The report forwarded to the Pulitzer board by the Public Service
jurors in 1973 recommended the *Washington Post*'s Watergate entry
third, after work by the *Chicago Tribune* and *New York Times*. Report
provided courtesy of the Pulitzer Prizes.

CHAPTER 14

Two Types of Teaming

That's a good paper; it's won a Pulitzer Prize.

—Esther Marro to her son, newly hired *Newsday*
reporter Anthony J. Marro, 1968

Newsday and the *Philadelphia Inquirer*, winners of three of the Public Service Pulitzers awarded in the 1970s, had to break through debilitating handicaps on their way to becoming national models of project journalism.

Truth be told, it was a seriously flawed *Newsday* that won the 1954 Pulitzer Gold Medal. The paper had been responsible for the significant public service of "dethroning DeKoning," as its own corporate history described the exposé that led to William DeKoning's imprisonment. But even that 1990 book, by staffer Robert F. Keeler, notes that personal interests inspired the drive led by managing editor Alan Hathway to get dirt on the area's labor czar.

In the early years after Alicia Patterson took over the paper in 1940, *Newsday* had treated DeKoning with kid gloves, often concentrating on what appeared to be his philanthropic side. But then, Hathway himself became involved with a campaign to build an arena for Long Island. It was a move that, "combined with his private ambition to make some money, overruled journalistic common sense," Keeler wrote. Eventually, Hathway's interests had come into conflict with those of DeKoning, who controlled the workforce that was to be involved in building the arena project. And later, when DeKoning also backed a Republican congressional candidate to oppose *Newsday*'s choice for office, that second conflict became a "triggering event that finally pushed Hathway over the edge, prompting him to convert his files on DeKoning into an aggressive series of stories."

So much for the "disinterested" nature of the journalism that the Gold Medal was supposed to recognize. The Pulitzer board probably had no idea.

The vintage-1954 *Newsday* was a weak journalistic model in other ways, too. "Seizing her newspaper's greatest moment of glory," Keeler writes, "Alicia Patterson decided to use the Pulitzer Prize not as a crown of laurel, but as a whip." Sure, that was partly to discourage staffers at the young paper from becoming smug in their success. But more than that, she considered the paper still "minor league" in its editing and its appearance. The copy desk was almost nonexistent, for example, leading to amateurish style snafus.

After she invested heavily in its improvement, the paper was in much better shape by 1963—the year Patterson suddenly died of a stomach ulcer at fifty-six, leaving her wealthy husband to take over. He was Harry Guggenheim, a mining-family heir whose relatives had founded New York's Guggenheim Museum with some of the family riches.

The Greene-ing of *Newsday*

Of all *Newsday*'s investments after winning the 1954 prize, the best might have been the hiring of Robert W. Greene to run investigations for the paper.

Bob Greene was a born snoop. He had been involved in some type of investigation work since high school, when he was employed as a "sniffer" for a department store, checking out the underarms of fancy dresses that women bought and later returned. His olfactory test proved whether a woman had worn the garment to a party before bringing it back for a refund.

In his early newsroom years at a New Jersey paper, other sniffing around led him toward local corruption that warranted a closer study. But Greene left newspaper work for a succession of government crime-busting jobs, where he sharpened his organizational skills and elevated his promotional abilities. Groups like Tennessee Senator Estes Kefauver's subcommittee studying organized crime, and the succession of regional crime commissions for which Greene worked, were very publicity-conscious. By parceling out information to reporters in the late 1950s, commissions taught the public about "a guy by the name of James Hoffa, who nobody really knew at the time," says Greene. At the New York City Anti-Crime Commission, Greene also had been a major source of scoops for *Newsday*, helping reporters bring down DeKoning when it won its 1954 Public Service Prize.

After a falling-out with New York commissioners in a change of leadership, Greene jumped in 1955 to the paper that he had come to admire for its tenacity, and for its shiny Gold Medal. Quickly, he built a reputation as a unique newsroom character.

At *Newsday,* he was far from the only one. Greene started out answering to managing editor Hathway, a boisterous, profane Chicago-style chief. Greene still laughs when he recalls the strange chemistry in the office during the elegant Mrs. Patterson's frequent visits to Hathway's realm. "He was the barnyard dog. She was the genteel lady," says Greene.

"Whenever Hathway wanted something investigated, he'd come to me," Greene says. Greene was the classic lone wolf at first, working on his own and keeping his sources to himself. Soon, he began to spot ethical problems not only among the people he was investigating, but within *Newsday* itself. He talked about it with other reporters who had observed the same thing. The concerned staffers saw some conflicts of interest involving Hathway. But their greatest concern was with Kirk Price, whose job as Suffolk editor put him in charge of coverage from that graft-ridden Long Island county.

If Greene began to write stories about abuses by officials in Suffolk County, "it was always a dead-end. You had a feeling you were being pulled off and steered in another direction." He suspected that Price was personally invested in some of the deals that staffers sought to investigate. Later, it became more than suspicion. Greene—now retired and teaching college journalism on Long Island—went to Hathway about the problem in the mid-1960s, suggesting that Price be removed from that key job. According to Greene, "Hathway says, 'Absolutely not. Who is telling you this?'"

For a time it created a personal crisis for Greene, who wasn't sure whether to stay at the paper. "So now what do you do?" he asked himself. He felt that he couldn't quit. He had two children, and had just left the crime commission because of unhappiness with management. He decided to stay. Maybe he could be a force for change at *Newsday.*

The "Red Meat" Philosophy

Greene traveled the South in 1964, exposing a yet-again resurgent Ku Klux Klan in a four-part series the tabloid headlined "The Klan Rides Again." In 1967 he went to New Orleans to look into District Attorney Jim Garrison's examination of President Kennedy's assassination. A lover of good food, who weighed in at more than three hundred pounds, Greene liked big expense accounts almost as much as he loved big stories. But because Greene turned up dirt in abundance wherever he went, managers tolerated the size of the invoices he submitted. He was *Newsday's* version of Eliot Ness: untouchable.

Then in 1967, Hathway retired and Kirk Price died, and the investigative environment at *Newsday* changed. Bill Moyers, who had served as press secretary during President Lyndon Johnson's presidency, became the new publisher. Al Marlens, who like Moyers was known in the office for uncompromising ethics, took over as managing editor. The new Suffolk editor was Art Perfall, who also had tried in vain to pursue corruption stories under Price, and had complained that he "could never get any movement from Kirk."

With Greene on the job, stories came furiously, many of them from the town of Islip. But the investigations quickly spread, exploring corruption in a succession of other towns across Suffolk and Nassau counties. Greene's own worries about the ethics of his editors were over.

Instead, he devoted time to selling them on story ideas. Given a few minutes of preparation before talking to an editor, Greene usually found a way. He employed what he calls "the red-meat philosophy," a sure-fire way to win over editors who needed persuading about a story. It worked like this: "You get something really good, and you say, Here's what we have already. That's the red meat. Then you say, If you give me time, I can get more. Editors get comfortable if you've got something in your pocket already."

His Suffolk proposal started with the meat of what they knew already: a *Newsday* editor, now deceased, had been involved in suspect deals in the county. Greene promised that he could prove a bigger scandal. From that small start, the first "Greene Team" soon sprouted.

Working through the Suffolk office of the Garden City–based paper, Greene combed through deeds and mortgages, creating paper trails that appeared to lead to various dirty officials. Greene also had a secret source with the federal Internal Revenue Service. The source, whom he nicknamed Zip, steered him toward more irregularities. "I'm saying, This is coming along pretty good, but I need more people to help me," Greene recalls. "They gave me one, and then one more." News clerk Gerry Shanahan was assigned to the team and became a Greene favorite.

Greene found that he liked leading a crew of reporters, and had a knack for teaching his investigative techniques and interviewing styles, unorthodox though they often were. His information-getting lessons started with a piece of advice: Do enough research so it appears to the interviewee that you already know the whole story. "I like to think I know about 80 percent of the answers before I sit down," he says. Then the subject on the hot seat asks, "Who squealed?" The corollary to this philosophy: "The minute you start asking questions like you don't know the answer, they lie to you."

Shanahan, now assistant foreign editor at the *New York Times,* got her reporting education from the Greene Team. Reporter Kenneth Crowe showed her how to root through documents. "Sometimes you didn't even know what you were looking for, but you'd know it when you found it," she says. "These people had dummy corporations. There was so much land, and they were chipping in together and buying parcels, and then would rezone it so it would become much more valuable. Then they'd sell it."

The Greene Team's first investigation turned up companies that were part of an Islip rezoning scam by officials. The team's stories implicated the late *Newsday* editor, Price. The work was entered for a Pulitzer Prize in 1968. It lost. In October 1968, two of the officials netted in the Islip investigation were convicted, and similar disclosures by the team were made involving the town of Brookhaven. In 1969, *Newsday* entered again. Again, it lost.

Sayonara, Indeed

But the team—which occasionally used the name Greene's Berets, after the crack Army unit in Vietnam—was hardly finished. Greene and his crew found that the Islip and Brookhaven investigation formula could be applied in most other Long Island towns, with the same result.

In 1969 they turned to reports of corruption involving three leading lights of Long Island: state Supreme Court Justice Arthur Cromarty, a major Republican Party leader; Nassau County state Senator Edward Speno; and Babylon Republican leader Fred Fellman. Tony Marro, a Vermonter who had joined the paper in 1968, was added to the team.

"I knew very little about the team," says Marro, who eventually became *Newsday*'s editor. "It was supposed to be an eight- or nine-week assignment. I was basically gone for three years." He learned fast, a requirement in any Greene-run shop. "It was total immersion. You were locked up with a small group of people. You got assignments every day. You had to report what you did every day, and you had to read everybody else's reports." The intense process often produced stunning findings, since few details of the entire three years of investigation ever got totally lost.

Food was often at the center of the job for Greene. As Marro puts it: "Ken Crowe taught me the difference between a mortgager and a mortgagee; Greene taught me the difference between chicken Kiev and chicken cordon bleu." His reporters believed that Greene owed his considerable girth to his taste for eating only the best that restaurants had to offer. The story is told of the boss hosting one group lunch and interrupting a new reporter as he was ordering the Salisbury steak. "When you eat with the team," Greene scolded, "you don't eat chopped meat."

Greene sometimes used reporters as foils during interviews, and he often bluffed. Shanahan remembers a Greene interview with a county judge whom a *Newsday* source had accused of taking bribes to fix zoning decisions. "Greene wrote on a manila folder, 'Tapes'—and had the subject's name on them—to let that guy think we had something." Greene recalls that he had actually made up a reconstruction of what the tape of a conversation about a bribe *might* have sounded like, complete with background sounds of babies crying and screen doors slamming. He then packaged those tapes up as if they were the real thing, and laid the package on the interviewee's desk. "His hands were shaking," recalls Greene. "Then I said, 'Did you know this guy was very much into electronics?' Now he's in shock; he's reaching for his water glass."

Says Shanahan, "He got the truth out of that guy."

If he had 80 percent of what he needed before the interview, that last 20 percent was often crucial. It was the part that implicated others. Greene tells the story of meeting Babylon Republican leader Fellman at a place named, appropriately enough, the Sayonara Motel. They caught Fellman off-guard when Greene spread out six folders on the hotel-room floor. Each contained incriminating documents. He then gave Fellman the choice of admitting his involvement in "three from Column A and three from Column B," in a way that might save him from paying the heaviest amount of back tax. "Bob, can I have it all?" Fellman asked.

"Off the Droshky!"

The Fellman case illustrated an interview technique that Greene's Berets called "off the droshky." The term came from a Russian fairy tale. As Tony Marro described it:

> There are many different versions of this story, but they all have the same unhappy ending.
> It starts with a family—father, mother and several children—traveling through the woods on a cold winter's night. They're riding in a Russian sleigh, which is called a droshky. Suddenly, a pack of starving wolves comes rushing out of the woods and begins to give chase. The horses try to race away, but the wolves keep getting closer and closer. The family becomes frightened, panicked, and desperate. Finally, to save the others, the father throws the youngest child off the droshky, into the jaws of the wolves.

The Greene Team was the wolf pack. When someone like Freddie Fellman admitted to fraud or implicated Judge Cromarty, it was a case of Fellman throwing something off his droshky. "It was always a moment of celebration when a reporter would come back from an interview, give a thumbs up to the rest of the team, and announce: 'Off the droshky!'" according to Marro.

While the information from Fellman tarred Cromarty, prosecutors ended up hitting the judge far more gently than they hit Fellman, who eventually went to prison. "We didn't like it that way," says Greene, since Fellman had cooperated with the team. "But there was huge juice protecting Cromarty." The investigation had produced enough good graft stories and convictions, though, for another try at the Pulitzer.

The third time was a golden charm for *Newsday*. Bill Moyers, who had become handy at writing the publisher's cover letter by that time, was able to note in 1970 that the investigations had led Governor Nelson Rockefeller to form a special commission on ethics. The Pulitzer jurors ranked *Newsday* first "for exposing secret land deals and zoning manipulations by public and political party office holders." The board agreed, adding to the citation the element that the paper's work followed two earlier years of investigations. It was *Newsday*'s second Gold Medal, and the first for a Greene Team project.

(Unbeknownst to the paper, it had come within a hair of winning the year *before*. The Pulitzer Public Service jury recommendation for 1969 shows a tie vote between *Newsday* and the *Los Angeles Times*, which had investigated two city commissions and won convictions for their work. "The jury felt that an edge, if any, should go to the *Los Angeles Times*," the jury report said. "Both newspapers showed what large, well-financed and capably manned newsrooms can do when examples of public misfeasance and malfeasance in office are brought to their attention." The Pulitzer board declared the *Times* its winner. But back then, finalists were not identified, so *Newsday* did not officially know its entry had come so close.)

How strange, then, were the circumstances of the 1970 Pulitzer announcement. The chairman of the company that was the brand new owner of *Newsday*—Otis Chandler of Times Mirror, parent of none other than the *Los Angeles Times*—happened to be in the Long Island newsroom, giving his first pep talk to a *Newsday* staff that was worried about his plans for the paper. As Chandler was talking, the phone rang and Greene answered. "It sounded like he was talking to a beat reporter: 'Yes. Thank you. Good. Fine,'" Chandler recalled in describing the phone call that had interrupted him. The call, however, was to inform *Newsday* that it had won the 1970 Gold Medal. Chandler came to regard that Pulitzer interruption as "a wonderful omen for me, because I think it broke the ice a little bit, gave me a chance to talk a little bit more about editorial quality and our number one interest in maintaining it."

Newsday saw the 1970 prize as honoring all three years of investigation, as the Pulitzer citation noted. It partied three times in celebration. Even one of the crooks it had exposed, Freddie Fellman, showed up.

Greene says that Fellman probably had no idea then that the Republicans had made a decision to toss him from their own droshky—and to protect Cromarty instead. At the party, Fellman lived up to his reputation as a big talker, taking the floor and catching the attention of the assembled journalists. "Wait a second," he said to the surprised revelers. "You couldn't have done this without me!"

Long Island was just that kind of place. Says Greene: "He was a crook, but I liked him."

1970—*Newsday:* For its three-year investigation and exposure of secret land deals in eastern Long Island, which led to a series of criminal convictions, discharges, and resignations among public and political officeholders in the area.

Going Global

Like many stories that involve Bob Greene, the tale of how he wound up in Turkey and France leading the "Heroin Trail" project for *Newsday* is somewhat convoluted.

Greene himself sees the assignment as the simple product of an investigation that had been quashed by higher-ups: a study of President Richard Nixon's Florida ties to his friend Bebe Rebozo. The reporter blames executives of Times Mirror, whose flagship *Los Angeles Times* was a Republican stalwart, for stopping the project. With the Nixon-Rebozo probe entering the 1972 election year, the parent company was afraid the series would seem to be a political vendetta, Greene was told.

Greene was upset, of course. But when new *Newsday* publisher William Attwood suggested that the next team-based story would require Greene to go to Paris and scout the international drug trade's French connection, the reporter decided it was worth a try. "I'd never been to Europe before and, he says, 'Fly first class,'" recalls Greene. They were trying to placate him, he knows, but he willingly let them.

"I laid out the whole thing, to take a team and go to Turkey and go to France. Not with law enforcement, but following the underworld." Eventually, the thirty-two part series would run in February and March 1973, a year after the initial conversation with Attwood, and after reporters Les Payne and Knut Royce served for more than six months overseas with Greene.

The main idea was to test the Nixon administration's claim that paying Turkey to stop growing opium poppies—the U.S. government policy at the time—was drying up the heroin trade. (The team concluded that the payments were not working.) But from the start, the series had strong local and national angles. Readers were introduced on the first day to the drug-shortened lives of three Long Island residents in their early twenties. Other installments, reported by a U.S.-based team headed by Tony Marro, now a Greene Team veteran, concentrated on the New York and Long Island connections in organized crime. Other reporting originated in Washington, Miami, and Mexico.

Marro, who had been in the Washington bureau when he was called for the project, was not at all happy with the assignment. Three years of working under Greene had been enough. And besides, in 1972 he had been in the middle of another little story—one growing out of a bungled burglary at the Watergate complex. "I can't pretend I was breaking a lot of stories on Watergate—I wasn't—but I knew it was a good story," he says. Using Greene's own techniques, Marro even filled a yellow pad full of reasons why he should not be involved, and took a train to Long Island to make his case to his editors.

"I walk in, and there on the wall is this huge picture of Greene and Les and Knut in a poppy field in Turkey," Marro recalls. "I knew I wasn't getting out of this."

Beyond the Marx Brothers

As might be expected of an ambitious global project being run by an investigator who had never ventured east of Montauk Point, this one had its zany moments. Keeler notes that "the *Newsday* invasion of Europe began like the opening scenes of *The Marx Brothers Stalk the Poppy*." Greene's proposal for a Land Rover, to be purchased and hauled to Turkey, was turned down. But he managed to win approval for a cache of weapons to accompany team members overseas, which created a few problems when the guns were transported with them by plane. He also got *Newsday* to pay for a three-week Turkish-language course for team members. (Les Payne, a former Army officer who was among the first African Americans hired by *Newsday,* later would tell of Greene's careful attention to the Turkish words for lamb, eggplant, sea bass, and other delicacies that would be on the menus in Ankara. Payne joked that for his own part, he wanted to learn the Turkish phrase for "Let's get the black guy.")

At one point, when Attwood asked how much Greene's grand reporting plan would cost the paper, he told them fifty thousand dollars, without the Land Rover. Greene now figures he was off by at least a factor of six.

One story from abroad tells of Greene, Payne, and Royce at a European gambling casino the night that the team leader hit it big-time. "He was walking majestically towards the cashier's cage with a large pile of chips in both hands when his pants fell down," says Marro, who heard the tale later. "He couldn't put down the chips without spilling them, so Payne and Royce had to pull his pants up from the rear."

But thanks to the time spent on thorough organization of the international, U.S., and local Long Island elements, the *Newsday* report was clear and detailed. It contributed much to knowledge of how the Turkey-to-France-to-America trail was operating. By way of the old-fashioned results *Newsday* was used to—people convicted, laws passed—the paper couldn't offer much to the Pulitzer jurors. "The results of such a far-reaching series are not immediately measurable," it said in its cover letter. "This is because the information revealed by *Newsday* will provoke eventual counter-measures and it may take several years before these counter-measures take on substantial form." It did note, "At least three of the persons named in the Newsday series as major heroin operators in the New York–Long Island area have since been arrested for narcotics crimes."

Some at the paper felt that the headlong plunge into the Turkish-French connection had missed the bigger drug-trade news: that Southeast Asia had become a heroin hotbed in the Vietnam era, possibly with the encouragement of Central Intelligence Agency agents who were reported in other journals to have been taking political sides among nations in the region. "It was a good story, but not a complete story," says Marro.

If it wasn't complete, at thirty-two parts it was certainly long. Had Marro himself read it all? "I don't think anybody did," he says with a laugh, "except Joel Kramer, who was the copy editor."

Greene-less Teams

However much of it the Pulitzer jurors read, they liked it just fine. It was their unanimous choice, beating out a *New York Times* enterprise on art thefts and a *St. Louis Post-Dispatch* project that took an altogether different look at the drug trade: defending the constitutional rights of suspects against "high-handed government agents."

Bob Greene went on to hold a succession of jobs at *Newsday*. He also led another investigation, a national collaborative effort to solve the murder of *Arizona Republic* reporter Don Bolles in 1976. As it reported on the crime as part of Investigative Reporters and Editors' "Arizona Project," this Greene team consisted of thirty-six journalists from twenty-three news organizations. He considers that work, which certainly promoted the cause of investigative journalism nationally, his proudest moment professionally. (While many stories were written, the case was never completely resolved.)

The Greene Teams, which for a long time kept that name, continued with distinction under various Greene successors. Former team reporter Brian Donovan joined Stephanie Saul in a project that won a Pulitzer for Investigative Reporting in 1995, exposing abuses of disability pensions among police. Marro, by then the paper's editor, proposed that story. Joe Demma, another longtime Greene Team member, was responsible for leading post-Greene teams through numerous projects. (Marro also brought Greene back to head the team for several years before his retirement.)

When Greene was not at the helm, though, the investigative style changed—and expense accounts shrank. "People who worked on the Greene Team ended up running other parts of the paper, and the Greene commitment to investigative reporting spread to other parts of the newsroom, not just the team itself," Marro says. At one point, editorial-page editor Jim Klurfeld, foreign-desk chief Les Payne, Washington bureau chief Jim Toedtman, labor reporter Ken Crowe, and education reporter John Hildebrand all were team veterans.

Having led two teams to Public Service Pulitzers, Greene occasionally thinks how strange it is that reporters instrumental in the prize-winning—like himself, Tony Marro, and others—so rarely receive specific credit in the case of the Public Service Medal. Had the prizes been in the Investigative category, individual reporters likely would have been named. But in the case of individuals working on a Gold Medal project, "when their grandchildren go to look it up," Greene says, "there's nothing there."

Greene once had a discussion about it with the *Washington Post*'s Ben Bradlee, who told him how Woodward and Bernstein had puzzled at why the 1973 prize for their Watergate reporting did not cite them specifically. But Greene says he's dealing with it. "I think of myself as a Pulitzer Prize winner," he says, "whether I'm listed or not."

1974—*Newsday:* For its definitive report on the illicit narcotic traffic in the United States and abroad, entitled, "The Heroin Trail."

———oᴐᴐo———

Policing the Philly Police

The *Philadelphia Inquirer* was a grand experiment for Eugene L. Roberts Jr., the North Carolina–born editor whom the *New York Times*'s Harrison Salisbury once called "the best journalist living and breathing in the U.S.A. and probably the world."

Roberts had moved north to Knight Ridder's *Detroit Free Press* as labor reporter, and later Metro editor. He then jumped to the *Times* in 1965, where he covered the civil rights movement with insight and intelligence, served as a Vietnam correspondent, and was promoted to national editor. Knight Ridder executive Lee Hills had tried to woo back Roberts since he left Detroit. In 1972, Hills made Roberts an offer he couldn't refuse: take over the *Inquirer*. It was a job most sane editors would have refused in a heartbeat.

Roberts had half-jokingly told Hills over the years that he would leave the *Times* only to run some newspaper that the world thought was beyond rescue. At lunch one day, remembers Roberts, Hills said to him: "I have the very newspaper for you."

Steve Lovelady, a *Wall Street Journal* page-one rewrite specialist who was among Roberts's first Philadelphia hires, recalls that the new executive editor used a variation of Hills's same improbable "lure" to get him to move from the *Journal* to the *Inquirer*. "It was a terrible paper, just an awful paper," says Lovelady. "It was so bad that after he talked me into going to work there, and then sent me a week's worth of papers, I was appalled and called him up to renege. I told him, Nobody, not even you, can salvage this dog."

Responded Roberts breathlessly, "Yeah, isn't it great!"

Then he turned up the heat on Lovelady. "You've already worked on a great newspaper; anybody can do that," Roberts told him. "This is the only chance you'll ever get to take a piece of shit and turn it into a great newspaper." The *Journal* rewrite man sat with those slowly drawled Roberts words for a minute. "It was a pretty compelling argument, if you bought the premise that he was going to succeed," says Lovelady. "But the first year I was there, there wasn't a day that went by that I didn't think, What have I done?"

During the eighteen Roberts years, the *Inquirer* did plenty. The paper or its journalists won seventeen Pulitzers between 1975 and 1990—including two Gold Medals, in 1978 and 1990.

Inside the "Roundhouse"

Bill Marimow still recalls the strain of climbing to the common-pleas courts building's ninth floor—and the smell of the clerk's foul cigar—even though it has been nearly thirty years now. There in the fetid haze of Room 951, Marimow and fellow *Inquirer* reporter Jonathan Neumann slogged through records of "suppression hearings," showing how many confessions had been thrown out against defendants on trial for murder.

A source had given them a computer print-out—a somewhat novel document for reporters in 1977—listing instances of judges approving defense motions because they believed the cops had beaten confessions out of the suspects. Mostly, the beatings were administered in small interrogation rooms of "the Roundhouse," as police headquarters is known.

While that is how the *Inquirer* story started, underlying the investigation was Gene Roberts's newsroom management approach. Roberts encouraged and supported reporters who came up with enterprise stories that could make a difference in the community.

Marimow had been hired by Roberts's predecessor, John McMullen, a good editor who for two years was in the unenviable position of "shrinking the paper to greatness," through cutbacks ordered by Knight Ridder, as the reporter puts it. (The technique would be tried again in the years before Knight Ridder sold out to McClatchy in 2005.) Roberts, though, was unique. As a newsroom presence "he was an unadulterated pleasure," Marimow says. "I always used to wonder why he wasted so much time talking with me, one of the least-experienced reporters at the *Inquirer*." When Marimow was on the labor beat, Roberts once spent forty-five minutes explaining how, in his Detroit days, he used to carry four separate notebooks into meetings with the United Auto Workers leader. The notebooks helped him prepare for various profiles or analyses he had in the works. "I remember thinking, 'This guy is crazy; I'm never going to be able to do that,'" says Marimow. "The fact that I can remember the talk with such specificity, though, tells you about the influence he had."

Any reporter bringing a good story idea to Roberts or Metro editor John Carroll would get time to pursue it, says Marimow, who after working as vice president of news at National Public Radio has now returned to Philadelphia as the *Inquirer*'s editor. (After his first *Inquirer* stint, Marimow would later work with Carroll again at the *Baltimore Sun* where Carroll was editor before his move to the *Los Angeles Times*.) Younger reporters like Marimow and Neumann, then in their twenties, also had no fear of their story being assigned to others with more experience.

The police brutality story came up from the beat. "Most of the best journalism is bottom-up, rather than top-down," says Roberts. "That means that, as an editor, you have to have a sense for listening, as opposed to simply giving assignments." Keeping the original reporter on the story simply follows—as it did for Ben Bradlee in letting two young *Washington Post* reporters keep plugging on Watergate. "If you steal that story, and give it to a senior reporter, you could imagine what's going to happen," says Roberts. "People aren't going to come up with ideas."

Neumann and Marimow each had been involved with earlier stories analyzing court issues and police problems, and Marimow recently had covered a murder trial during which the defendant confessed and was convicted—before someone else admitted to the killing. Police, it seemed, had beaten a confession out of the defendant, and also had beaten various witnesses to make the case stick. (A federal grand jury eventually began looking at the wrongful conviction.)

Marimow had moved to city hall from the courts during the trial, with Neumann taking over. So they both had that bizarre case in their minds—along with lots of other ideas about the dysfunctional Philadelphia police force. "Toward the end of 1976 Jonathan and I put our heads together. What he had seen covering the courts, and what I had seen, suggested a closer look." And in January 1977 they began reporting what became known as the Homicide Files.

They knew that records could help them document the cases being thrown out because suspects were beaten into confessing. Marimow visited a common-pleas-court source to see if such records might be available. "Presto, bingo, ala kazam, my source gave me a computer print-out." It was something new to him.

The print-out showed that 17 percent of cases involved an illegal interrogation. So Marimow and Neumann began their climbs up to the ninth floor to that smoky records room to read transcripts of the actual suppression hearings.

Beatings, threats, medical records, eyewitness testimony—all of it was revealed in the files. "Interestingly, most of the judges never ruled on whether there had been abuse," Marimow says. Instead, they ruled out the confessions as the inadmissible "fruit of the poisoned tree," without disciplining the abusive police. Marimow then began interviewing judges to establish why.

The two reporters also realized the need to understand the pressures that homicide detectives faced, on the street and in the station house. Some abhorred the brutal police tactics but lived with them anyway. Selecting three interviews from a number they conducted, the reporters assembled a sidebar for the first "Homicide Files" installment on April 24. Under the headline "At the Roundhouse: How Detectives Compel Murder 'Confessions,'" the article began:

> It can be said with certainty that two things happened in the 22 hours between Carlton Coleman's arrest and his arraignment last October.
>
> One is that he was interrogated by homicide detectives. The other is that his health went from good to poor. When it was all over, he spent the next 28 days hospitalized for injuries of the abdomen, arms, shoulders, chest, calf, spine and back.
>
> Medical problems are not rare among those interrogated by the Philadelphia Police Department's 84-member homicide division. In fact, a four-month investigation by The Inquirer has found a pattern of beatings, threats of violence, intimidation, coercion and knowing disregard for constitutional rights in the interrogation of homicide suspects and witnesses.

Two paragraphs later came a statistical hook: "From 1974 through this month, judges of the Common Pleas Court have been asked to rule in pretrial hearings on the legality of police investigations in 433 homicide cases," the story said. "In 80 of those cases, however, judges have ruled that the police acted illegally during homicide interrogations," with documentary evidence of coercion from X-rays to photographs cited as evidence.

Metro editor Carroll's editing of the story had been heavy but effective. "When Jonathan and I drafted part one, John Wardlow was the case we started with. He became the last anecdote," says Marimow. The top twenty paragraphs of the story reflected Carroll's deft touch.

Carroll says he had a secret weapon: rewrite expert Steve Lovelady. "We worked very closely on that story," says Carroll. Adds Lovelady, who later became managing editor of the daily Web site of the *Columbia Journalism Review:* "John rewrote it, but as he did so he passed along the rewrite, literally page by page, to me, and I offered suggestions and contributions."

The edited copy from Carroll was then reviewed and approved by the reporters "up until about 8:30 the night before the story ran," Marimow says. Such thorough processing, Lovelady notes, "was pretty much par for the course on the *Inquirer's* big ambitious efforts in the 1970s and 1980s."

A Powerful Image

Gene Roberts had been struck from the beginning by an anecdote he heard from the reporters about a case in which "the interrogating officers had an old ornamental sword, and stabbed a person in the testicles with it," he says. "It sounded so outrageous and bizarre that you know that if we could definitively prove it, it would certainly get people's attention." The sword incident appeared in the thirty-ninth paragraph, but jumped out at readers. It was explained that a twenty-three-year-old black suspect had been "stabbed in the groin with a sword-like instrument and blackjacked on his feet, ankles and legs until the blackjack broke in two." The four detectives doing the interrogation, as well as the suspect, were all named in the article.

The sidebar containing the detective interviews, which like all the stories carried the Neumann and Marimow bylines, presented mixed reactions from detectives. All had agreed to talk only if their names were *not* used. Said one:

> It's a fight every day. The homicide detective must fight the lawyers, the judges, the Supreme Court—and he must fight crime . . . not to mention newspapers . . . A homicide detective must know the law as it is now, and he must know the law as it is going to be interpreted five years from today . . .

But, according to another:

> I'm not going to defend the Police Department now. No way. I work on my own.
> There're people there (in the homicide division) I'd refuse to work with.
>
> We've got a new breed of guy now. Years ago we'd sit there (in the interrogation
> room) and talk with the defendants. The detectives used to think with their heads,
> not their hands. They were good, damned good, and they got the evidence clean.
>
> Now, all they care about is statements (from suspects). I think statements are
> bull——.

Part two was headlined "How police harassed a family." It started with the amazing case of a home invasion—conducted by law officers—and it was accompanied by pictures that a family member had taken of a stormtrooper-like entry by armed police. Parts three and four examined the reasons police were not being charged with beating suspects, even when the evidence was overwhelming. "Interviews with defense attorneys and judges show that many are aware of crimes committed in the interrogation room. But, because the practices are so deeply rooted in Philadelphia, few have tried to do anything about them," the story said.

In a box with the first day's story, an "official reply" quoted the police commissioner: "I emphatically and categorically deny this allegation" that there is a pattern of illegal interrogations by homicide detectives. But he refused to allow an interview, as did Mayor Frank L. Rizzo (a former police chief) and others. Additionally, the officials would not allow any of the thirty-one police officers mentioned in the series to be interviewed—although the *Inquirer* noted that a number *were* quoted, just not by name. "All 31 were asked for interviews by certified mail," the story said.

Editorial support was powerful. The first day, an editorial headlined "Homicide in Philadelphia: A Cry for Federal Action" was written by Michael Pakenham. It began:

> On Page One of today's Inquirer there begins a series of articles on the Philadelphia criminal justice system and murder. It is a horror story. It demands community action. It cries for federal investigation and criminal prosecution.

How were things on the Philadelphia police beat that week? Don't ask Marimow and Neumann, who had been working from the city hall bureau when they prepared the series. It wasn't much fun, recalls now-retired police reporter Robert J. "Bo" Terry. "I took a lot of grief from a lot of the detectives on the stories about the homicide detectives," he recalls. "One detective would say, 'You work for a Communist newspaper; you're just like Marimow.' My stock answer to them was, 'You're next.'"

He was joking, of course. Terry was not in a position to get any officer mentioned in Marimow and Neumann's story. But he had worked with the two reporters, supplying Marimow with "incident reports" that would allow the team to understand what police records said about the detectives' activities, for example. The police reporter specifically requested that he not be mentioned or given any byline credit, in fact. "I said, Bill, I don't want my name anywhere, because I have to face these guys every day."

Terry also took special pains to assure the officers that he had nothing to do with the coverage. "I asked them, Do you see my name on the story?"

In the mind of many police reporters of that era, thanklessness often came with the territory. It was a quality that some willingly accepted. (Terry was pleased, he says, with how profusely Marimow thanked him after the *Inquirer* won the Pulitzer.) "Look at Watergate," says Bo Terry. "It was the police reporter who gave that information over to Woodward and Bernstein, and look what they did with it." (The reporter in question was the *Washington Post*'s Alfred E. Lewis.)

Neumann and Marimow weren't finished after their four-parter ran. Reader response to the first series assured that. "We were deluged with calls about police in Philadelphia just beating people up on the street," Carroll remembers. Adds Marimow, "People were saying, You guys missed the boat. You ought to take a look at what's happening on the street." As the second series showed, what was happening was as severe as the Roundhouse beatings. Yet a federal prosecution against three police officers, which grew from that second series, and was supported by numerous witnesses, resulted in the police officers' acquittal.

"Jonathan and I were devastated, because we believed the citizens were telling the truth." In yet another measure of Roberts's commitment to supporting his reporters, he and Carroll took the two staffers to a consolation dinner. "Gene was talking to us about how during the Civil Rights movement in the South juries were returning verdicts that had nothing to do with reality."

Other things were competing for Roberts's attention. Mayor Rizzo "virtually declared war on the paper," the former editor says. Further, a union sympathetic to the mayor and the police was jamming truck bays to keep the paper from getting out. These became supporting arguments to be included in Roberts's Pulitzer Prize entry—as were the columns in the rival *Philadelphia Bulletin* that had ridiculed the *Inquirer* reporting, and sided with the police.

Ignoring the Cutting Edge?

The *Inquirer* kept up its war against abusive police for years. In 1985, Marimow won an Investigative Reporting Pulitzer in his own name for a series exploring the high incidence of police dogs attacking suspects. But Marimow saw the Pulitzer Prize for his and Neumann's work as the highest vindication after all the opposition they had endured. He took special pride that the award was for Public Service, "the greatest among equals."

Marimow and Neumann were not named in the Pulitzer Prize citation. But above his desk at home, Marimow keeps a framed replica of the Joseph Pulitzer Medal with an inscription from Roberts crediting the two reporters. What about the individual prize that *is* in his name? "That's in a desk drawer. No one's ever seen it," he says.

For Roberts, the *Inquirer's* first Gold Medal was particularly sweet because it recognized the entire staff's work turning around the paper. Individuals had won three Pulitzers by then, but the paper had missed out on Public Service—the category that Roberts associates with the courage displayed by southern editors who opposed the Ku Klux Klan and who supported the law during school desegregation.

The irony, he says with a laugh, is that the *Inquirer's* accomplishments, in a way, sprouted from the depths that the publication reached in the 1960s. He never would have had a free hand to test his managerial vision at a successful paper, Roberts says, because "success breeds conservative thinking and non-risk-taking. Nobody wants to screw up a good thing." In Philadelphia, "they were willing to try anything," he says.

"It's wonderful when newspapers are desperate enough to try good journalism."

1978—*Philadelphia Inquirer:* For a series of articles showing abuses of power by the police in its home city.

Newsday reporters behind investigative team leader Bob Greene in 1970 are (from left) Gerry Shanahan, Anthony Marro, Jim Klurfeld, and Ken Crowe. *Newsday* won the 1970 Gold Medal for their work. *Newsday* staff photo. Used by permission.

Newsday reporters Les Payne (left) and Knut Royce stand next to team leader Bob Greene in a Turkish poppy field during their reporting of the Heroin Trail story, Gold Medal winner in 1974. *Newsday* staff photo. Used by permission.

Philadelphia Inquirer
executive editor Eugene
Roberts in 1977. *Inquirer*
staff photo. Used by
permission.

Inquirer reporters
William Marimow (top)
and Jonathan Neumann
being informed that
the paper won the
Gold Medal for their
work in 1978. *Inquirer*
staff photo. Used by
permission.

CHAPTER 15

Davids and Goliaths

Kay Fanning knew that a newspaper is a public trust, and she published hers in an unrelenting quest for the public good. I don't know if she was a student of James Madison, but I know she embraced the ethic of which he spoke when he observed, "Knowledge will forever govern ignorance, and a people who mean to be their own governors must arm themselves with the power which knowledge gives."

—Howard Weaver, McClatchy Co. vice president/news

*W*ho doesn't love the story of the pathetic ninety-pound weakling thumping the muscle-bound bully; of the overmatched Rocky Balboa humbling the hulking Russian Ivan Drago, or the scrawny David felling the mighty Goliath with his meager stone? Journalists certainly do. After all, they all grew up in a profession where "man bites dog" is a three-word definition of news. And it's bigger news when the dog is a pit bull.

The increasing popularity of investigative reporting fostered several classic David-and-Goliath battles involving smaller press organs in the 1970s. If relentless *Post* journalists were a match for a secretive Nixon White House, so too were some small-town scribes taking on major adversaries in the far reaches of Alaska and rural east Texas.

In a way, another big-versus-small contest took place at Columbia University as Pulitzer jurors and board members weighed epic public service efforts by the *Los Angeles Times, Philadelphia Inquirer,* and *New York Daily News* against the work from those pint-sized Alaska and Texas papers. There, too, the little guys won.

Bob Woodward proposes that "degree of difficulty" should be factored into the standards used for the Public Service Prize—the way Olympic judges add points for a dive or floor exercise. To some degree the Pulitzer board already does that when it considers the long odds faced by a small newspaper. On the frontiers of journalism, where a newspaper may lack a battery of in-house lawyers, or even a security guard at the door, challenging wrongdoing is a risky undertaking. The adversary may have the power—legally or illegally—to shut down well-meaning journalists in an instant. Or to do even worse.

Bringing Gold to Alaska

Howard Weaver was twenty-five when his editors at the *Anchorage Daily News* teamed him with relative veteran Bob Porterfield in pursuit of a story on the mightiest institution in Alaska: Teamsters Union Local 959. Unlike the kinds of team-formation decisions being made at larger, investigation-minded papers, the choices were fairly simple for executive editor Stan Abbott and managing editor Tom Gibbony. There were only a dozen staffers.

Compared to mainstream American newspapers there was also a sense of remoteness in the forty-ninth state, which was literally a place apart in 1975. "You could not watch Walter Cronkite live in Alaska," says Weaver. "They videotaped it in Seattle, flew it up, and showed it at 11 at night."

The Anchorage-born Weaver felt close to the latest trends in investigative journalism, though. A year earlier he had attended a ten-day American Press Institute reporting seminar at Columbia. Inspired, he did not see a story on the Teamsters as particularly daunting. After all, he had been exposed to *New York Times* reporter David Burnham, whose stories had covered Frank Serpico, the cop who blew the whistle on widespread payoffs in the New York Police Department. Weaver had read the *Newsday* stories of Bob Greene from just across Long Island Sound, considering that paper "a well-oiled machine that could get to the bottom of things." And Watergate stories, reflecting the best of recent investigative journalism, were still in the news.

Looking back now, he sees that he probably should have been a bit daunted. The *Daily News* was the number-two paper in Anchorage. Its thirteen thousand subscribers gave it less than a third the circulation of the *Anchorage Times,* which owned the building and leased its smaller rival space under a joint operating agreement. As for Teamsters in Alaska, there were twenty-three thousand of them—more than the number of registered Republicans in the state.

The *News* did have something special going for it: publisher Kay Fanning, whose idea it had been to throw the paper's resources into finding out what made the Teamsters tick. She had also authorized Weaver to attend the Columbia investigative seminar. To her, Weaver was a logical choice for the Teamster assignment.

Fanning, in the mold of fellow publishers Katharine Graham and Alicia Patterson, had newspaper lineage, credentials, and instincts. After divorcing her first husband, Marshall Field IV, publisher of the *Chicago Sun-Times,* she married newspaperman Larry Fanning and persuaded him to buy the *Anchorage Daily News.* She took over after he died. "Kay simply couldn't see any reason why Anchorage ought to be backward," according to Weaver. "The phrases 'good enough for Anchorage' or 'just as nice as Seattle' didn't figure in her landscape."

Her presence in the newsroom kept the staff from feeling too provincial. "Kay Fanning knew Mike Royko, and Ann Landers. Newt Minow was her lawyer. She'd eaten dinner at the White House and been to opening nights at the Met," according to Weaver. He remembers once waiting for her in her living room, marking time by thumbing through the books on her shelves, "and noticing that most were autographed to Kay from the authors. I didn't know anybody else in Anchorage of whom those things were true, and neither did most other people."

So when she targeted the Teamsters for coverage, it seemed natural enough. Now, Weaver reflects, "It was a very brave thing for her to do. Remember that the head of the union was also on the board of the largest bank in town. There was no real labor-management distinction; it was all about power. And the Teamsters had a lot of it, and Kay Fanning didn't have much of it." Of the project with so much potential to damage her little paper, he notes, "it would have been easy to duck."

A Bubble of Dues Money

Fanning had not ordered up a Teamster story because of a tip about wrongdoing or fallout from some breaking news event. Rather, she believed readers needed to know more about the most powerful institution in the state. Weaver, for one, had been on good terms with the union and had even been a dues-paying Teamster at one time. "I had no animosity," says Weaver. "Au contraire, I saw unions as a social benefit." In fact, Weaver used his union history as an icebreaker in interviews.

The reporters did not feel they needed to turn up a scandal in order to give readers a fascinating story. In a mere eighteen years, through Alaska's meteoric oil boom, Jesse Carr's Local 959 had swelled up like a balloon over the Macy's Thanksgiving Day Parade—maybe menacing, maybe just big, but clearly hovering above everything else in the state. Teamsters in Alaska had the best health club in town, prepaid legal benefits, and other advantages. They had every benefit known to man. And it was all fueled by an enormous infusion of pipeline workers paying dues. The Teamsters Union was big news nationally, too, and not only because of the specter of former convict/former union leader Jimmy Hoffa, who was to disappear in mid-1975. Labor reporters like the *New York Times*'s Wallace Turner had been following the Teamsters and their pension funds for years. Hoffa's predecessor, Dave Beck, was also mentor to Jesse Carr.

Alaska's Local 959 leadership knew that few of its strapping young members would ever retire as Teamsters—not in their state, anyway. They would move on, leaving behind much of the money they had pumped into the benefit pool. "It created this huge bubble," says Weaver—a bubble of dues money. The *Anchorage Times* wrote of the union providing cradle-to-grave coverage. "We were a little racier, and referred to it as womb-to-tomb. But the Teamsters referred to it as erection to resurrection."

As Weaver and Porterfield began their investigation, they found Local 959 entwined in the overheated Alaskan economy through a web of investments, often through complex trusts. It was easy to find individual Teamster investments, but it seemed impossible to grasp the whole picture of what they controlled.

The reporters immediately noticed the role of property. They discovered real estate investments in California, especially. But they also found that few were willing to discuss the Teamsters' investments, or to be identified with any story that might be seen as negative to the powerful organization—especially if written by a news outlet that was roundly perceived as weak.

Even while the reporting was unfocused, the reporters adopted a system and applied it relentlessly. "I was single, and Bob was married but soon to be single. We worked constantly on this story," says Weaver. "We developed these voluminous files, and had to make up filing systems to keep up with all this, because of course there were no computers. We'd make index cards, and we had big charts with four-colored pencils tying things together. This guy's on this board, and that guy's on another board." Jim Babb was added to the team, and was assigned to work on sidebars on the operation of the pension fund and the legal structure of the investments.

Were the Teamsters breaking the law? Nowhere that they could see clearly. Yet their money and power were everywhere in the state. It was still a big story.

Another Goliath, Big and Gray

If the Teamsters Union was Goliath, the *Daily News* was about to face a second giant as well. The *Los Angeles Times* was coming to Alaska to write about the union.

"That really panicked us. It was shadowy," says Weaver, who learned that three or four reporters from Los Angeles had come to town and also interviewed people in Juneau about the union. The *Daily News* investigators, whose material was still unfocused, worried that they might have to rush something into print prematurely to beat or match the *Times*. "In the end, we decided that we had to do our thing as best we could, and that we couldn't do what the *Times* did," Weaver says.

Then came the shock of seeing the *Times*'s story in November, a couple of weeks before the *Daily News*'s projected first installment. The headline read "Crime Wave Strangles Alaska." The *Times* led with: "Widespread lawlessness, a helpless government and the stranglehold of a single Teamsters Union chief severely threaten a state crucial to the nation's future energy independence."

Recalls Weaver, "We just about freaked out. We hadn't found anything like that." He and Porterfield read below the strong language of the opening paragraphs, though, and determined that the paper had fallen back on generalizations, failing to make the case. "I don't want to 'dis' the *L.A. Times*, particularly because we won the Prize and they didn't," says Weaver, "but we thought, 'That's the way you write it if you're from out of town.' We live here, and that's not the story we're going to write." While other Alaskans conceded that the *Times* was correct in its conclusion that the oil-pipeline boom had increased crime, there was a wide sense that the paper had overstated the case. (Governor Jay S. Hammond wrote that "most Alaskans [don't] believe a midnight stroll down Cushman in Fairbanks [is] fraught with half the hazards faced on L.A.'s Sunset Strip at high noon.")

Says Weaver, "I suppose it's easier to be bold when your newsroom is 2,300 miles away."

The *Times* had its reporters working in pairs because of fears of Teamster reprisals. Weaver, too, had some worries as he pursued the stories—especially one day when he found that his Volkswagen Beetle had caught fire in his driveway. (It was accidental.) "But the genuine bravery involved," according to Weaver, "was that of the beleaguered small-town publisher playing You-Bet-Your-Newspaper on a daily basis."

The Alaskan reporters did find suspicious information about the North Star Terminals on the south edge of Fairbanks, an operation led by a man who had been sentenced to a year's probation in California in the 1950s. On the one-hundred-person payroll under him were about forty individuals who had been convicted of murder, burglary, robbery, drug crimes, and other offenses. Three of the top six Teamster officials listed on the terminal roster had criminal records. The *Daily News* also concentrated on potential conflicts of interest involving union lobbyist Lewis M. Dischner.

But the reporters found little direct lawbreaking. Rather, their work concentrated on how the Teamsters were amassing enormous clout for an organization in a sparsely populated state, with a power structure that could exercise power far beyond the normal checks and balances of the union-versus-management environment.

The series moved toward a powerful conclusion, too: that the inflated organization the Teamsters had set up in Alaska could not last. At his McClatchy office in Sacramento, Weaver points to a page of notes from the reporting that he still has tacked to his wall. "IMPLOSION" is written across the top. The Teamsters union would indeed see much of its power collapse in the years after the story ran. "But they were still in their muscle period then," says Weaver.

The reporting at the *Daily News* had not been closely monitored by editors, but Stan Abbott challenged the writing to make sure the conclusions at the top were supported deeper down in the stories. "You don't know enough to say that," the editor said over and over, leading Weaver to rewrite one of his lead paragraphs thirty times. "I'd write it as tough as I could every time, and he'd challenge me," he says. "I wanted it to be more sweeping, and he wanted it to be more specific." The series, "Empire: The Alaska Teamster Story," ran through December, with organizational charts on trusts and funds and investments spread across pages.

Compared to the *Los Angeles Times*'s Crime-Wave-Strangles-Alaska take, this series was characterized by a low-key approach. The first-day story by Weaver and Porterfield was headlined "Teamsters: How much power?" It started:

> Teamsters Union Local 959 is fashioning an empire in Alaska, stretching across an ever-widening slice of life from the infant oil frontier to the heart of the state's major city.
>
> Secure under the unquestioned leadership of Secretary-Treasurer Jesse L. Carr, the empire has evolved in just 18 years into a complex maze of political, economic and social power which towers above the rest of Alaska's labor movement—and challenges at times both mighty industry and state government itself.

A Standing-O in Juneau

While the *Daily News* was proud of the project, a Pulitzer Prize was hardly something it expected. For one thing, no Alaskan paper had ever won one. For another, the project itself was mainly explanatory, with no laws passed and no one convicted as a result. There had been some wrongdoing noted, but its real service was in giving shape and dimension to something that was previously unknown. "The union was big and powerful, but it existed only in myth," says Weaver. "How big? Once you gave it an actual shape, by describing the extent of its investments, the cross-directorships that they occupied, the techniques they used for negotiations, then it became real."

In preparing the Pulitzer entry, Fanning and her editors had aimed for Investigative Reporting. But at Columbia University, the Investigative jury handed it off to Public Service. The Public Service jurors had some very strong entries that year. In their top three were the *Chicago Tribune,* for detailing $4 billion of waste and inefficiencies in the federal Department of Housing and Urban Development and the Federal Housing Administration, and the *Detroit News,* for showing that four men had been wrongly sentenced to death in a murder case. They made a fourth pick: the *New York Daily News,* for a probe of the New York state lottery.

Their first choice, though, was the *Anchorage Daily News,* which "drove its way into the operations of the powerful Teamsters Union in Alaska to show the union's impact and influence on the whole spectrum of the economy and the politics of the state at a critical time of booming growth. The presentation was made fairly and dispassionately and without sensationalism, well conceived, well written and well presented. It is a remarkable performance by a small but vigorous daily newspaper."

Had the jury report been made public, the next sentence would have particularly cheered the Anchorage staff. "Our jury for Category 1 [Public Service] also had an entry by the Los Angeles Times covering essentially the same subject—the Teamsters in Alaska. However, it was our conclusion that the Anchorage Daily News' performance and product was the more meritorious and did qualify more fully for the Prize that we are recommending."

In remarks he prepared for a book of recollections about Kay Fanning, Weaver recalled what it was like in the office on Pulitzer Day, 1976:

> A ringing telephone in the second-floor newsroom . . . conveyed the unimaginable news that a tiny, struggling daily on the edge of North America had won not just a Pulitzer, but the celebrated Gold Medal prize for Public Service. The paper was among the smallest ever to have captured the award, its staff one of the youngest.

Champagne in the newsroom began a three-day celebration. Then came a standing ovation in the House of Representatives in Juneau when the award was announced. "For Alaska to win a Pulitzer was a big deal. The other paper even wrote a very generous editorial congratulating us," he says. "I bet even Jesse Carr loved the idea that he was a big enough dude to lead to a Pulitzer."

Kay Fanning's courage in taking on the project, and the Teamsters, became clear only later. At Pulitzer time she was actually a few months away from an announcement that the paper was nearly broke. "Still, instead of kissing up to the power structure in Anchorage, she gave us a flashlight and sent us looking in the shadows," according to Weaver. He believes that the Gold Medal "probably saved the *Anchorage Daily News,* because I'm not sure McClatchy would have bought it if it hadn't noticed it for its Pulitzer-winning."

Soon, the *Daily News* would pass the *Times* to become the state's largest paper. "And the *Daily News* staff would learn, by winning another Pulitzer, that lightning really can strike twice," he says. The second prize, also a Public Service award, would come in 1989, for a very different kind of story.

1976—*Anchorage Daily News:* For its disclosures of the impact and influence of the Teamsters Union on Alaska's economy and politics.

A Trainee Dies, the Marine Corps Lies

Editor Joe Murray was in a grumpy mood when he walked into his east Texas office at the *Lufkin News* early on Monday morning, March 15. It was supposed to be his day off, but work beckoned. And there in the waiting room outside his office was an old advertiser, probably with a gripe. "I'm thinking, 'Oh, man, whatever goes on in the paper, they come to the editor.' We'd probably run his ad upside down or something," Murray recalls. But it was not about an ad at all.

J. A. "Bo" Bryan was a relative of a Lufkin Marine recruit who was the subject of an obituary about to be published in the *News*. Bryan believed that the truth of his relative's death was being covered up by the Marines.

The official word was that twenty-year-old Private Lynn "Bubba" McClure had died from head injuries suffered during close-combat training at the San Diego Marine recruit depot. "But Bo Bryan starts telling me this story, and it's a horror story," says Murray. It started with the description of his grand nephew, who had never succeeded in anything and quite possibly was retarded, but who had inexplicably been accepted by the Marines. Family members, told that it was a simple training accident, didn't believe it—in part because of the extent of the injuries that had killed young Bubba. And the injuries that Bubba's stepfather had observed when he visited McClure in San Diego before he died didn't seem consistent with a simple training accident.

"I was sitting there listening to him, and thinking, 'What am I going to be able to do about this? I'm just one person. We're just one little paper. How long is this guy going to keep talking? I'm a busy editor,'" says Murray. But then Bryan paused and looked right at him. "I'll never forget that moment, and what he said: 'They beat that boy's brains out—literally.' It sent a cold chill down my spine."

Bryan had been selected to represent Bubba's extended family because he was one of the few relatives with an education, and had gotten results from Murray before. Years before, when Bryan's home-building enterprise had run into some environmental problems, the *Lufkin News* had run an item recounting the state's complaint. An unhappy Bryan had come to the office to tell his side, and had gotten satisfaction. He trusted Murray to do the right thing again.

Maybe there was something the *News* could do. The editor assigned reporter Ken Herman to look into the situation.

"We used to joke about how there were only two people there—me and Dwight Bailey—and they don't usually let the janitor write stories. So it was me," says Herman. Murray made a joke of it, too, remarking that he only had three reporters, so he had assigned one-third of his staff to the case.

Oft-Told Tales

Murray and Herman have recounted the tale many times. Pulitzer Prize projects quickly become the stuff of legend at a newspaper—and especially at a small one like the *News,* part of the Cox newspaper chain. Still, each telling can bring out powerful emotions about events that moved people long ago.

Herman remembers vividly standing beside Bubba McClure's open casket as he was reporting on the funeral. "He was a slight young man, and he looked very un-Marine-like," says the reporter. "The feeling was of this child in the proud uniform of the United States Marines." Herman was just a year older than Bubba McClure. His first story, that Tuesday, was fifty-four short, hard-hitting paragraphs appearing under the headline "Marine McClure Buried: He Died Trying to Prove He Was One of Those 'Few Good Men.'" It began:

> Lynn (Bubba) McClure, 20, joined the Marines to become a man and make his family proud of him.
>
> "I can't wait to show you my uniform," he had written his mother.
>
> Today, wearing that dress blue uniform, he was buried in a flag-draped casket.
>
> As he was lowered into his grave, two questions puzzled his family and those who knew him.
>
> —How did the tenth-grade dropout, considered "slow" by those who recall him, pass the Marine Corps entrance exam?
>
> —What drew this slightly built youth into the rigors of Marine Corps boot camp where he was fatally injured in a training exercise?
>
> Those who knew him said his brief life was scarred by failure and frustration.
>
> Apparently he saw the Marines as the end of that failure. But three weeks after arriving at the San Diego Recruit Depot his hopes ended.

Based on interviews with family and friends, the story examined the strange circumstances of the enlistment of the five-foot-six, 125-pound youth who seemed to have significant disabilities. It quoted Bo Bryan: "When I first heard he was in the Marines, I thought they meant the Merchant Marine." McClure also had been in trouble with the law, with a police record for reckless damage and public intoxication. The record should have turned up on a Marine background check and kept him out of the service, Herman and Murray knew, even if he had somehow managed to pass an entrance exam.

McClure had failed both Army and Marines exams eighteen months earlier. Details of his enlistment, and the test that he apparently passed, were not available. The Marines would not comment except to provide bare details of the training accident. In another section, the story offered heart-wrenching snippets of four letters home that McClure had "scrawled in a childlike penmanship." The first announced his enlistment to his unsuspecting mother. The last arrived the same day they were notified of his injury. He had written, "I been in boot camp about two weeks and it's making a man out of me quick . . . "

A Cover-Up Unfolds

The *News* kept its focus local, and sensitive to the family. The un-bylined piece the next day said that the prior article had been "authorized by the young man's mother"—a notation, says Murray, reflecting some readers' concerns that the paper appeared to be playing up McClure's disabilities. The story also quoted local congressman Charles Wilson, an Annapolis graduate, who took a deep interest in the case. In talking with Representative Wilson, Herman got the feeling that McClure's death reflected what Wilson saw as weaknesses in the all-volunteer military.

The next Herman byline quoted a private investigator, retained by the family, who said McClure had been beaten to death with "continued blows." In pugil-stick fighting, recruits wear protective gear, including football helmet and face mask, although the gear is no guarantee against injury. The circumstances of McClure's enlistment, which involved his passing a second recruitment test in Austin, remained a mystery, although the story did note that a General Accounting Office study just released had raised questions of "recruiter malpractice and fraudulent enlistment."

The next *News* story, reported and written by Murray, sprouted from a moment of competitive exasperation. It also added a dramatic national angle. Herman was off for the weekend when his editor saw an Associated Press story come across, saying that Marine investigators were blaming the town of Lufkin's law enforcement community for withholding information that could have invalidated McClure's enlistment.

"You cannot imagine how the ground was cut out from under me when that story came out of the AP from Washington," Murray says. The *Lufkin News*'s treatment of the McClure case and the congressional studies had by then attracted some national press. But the *News* had not expected to lose its edge like this. Murray's obvious next step: "We had to find out who the Marines had been talking to here."

The answer astounded him. He reached a Marine public affairs officer in New Orleans. "It was a Saturday," says Murray. "I got him at home, and he came in from his yard. By then I was real disgusted, but his job was to make the media happy." And in a convoluted way, he did that with the *News*.

Going into the office and checking the records to show who in Lufkin had been contacted about McClure, the public affairs man called Murray back with the information. A "Johnson" in the sheriff's department and a "Ms. Walker" at the Lufkin police station had provided the confirmation that McClure had no police record. Murray called the local police and sheriff himself to ask these Johnson and Walker characters how they could have gotten it wrong.

"There wasn't anybody by those names," he says. Someone in the Marine recruiting office had made Johnson and Walker up to cover the fact that no call had ever been placed to check on McClure's record.

When it turned out the Marines had lied on the report, Murray says, "you can imagine how I felt," Murray says. "I thought, I had 'em."

It is a cautionary tale for journalists seeking the truth, as well as for bureaucrats trying to cover their tracks. "Had the Marines taken that one more step and called to check themselves, they would have found out," Murray says. "But they stopped asking questions when they heard what they wanted to hear."

The headline on his story read "Fake names found in Marine reports." It began:

> The use of fake names has opened up the possibility of a cover-up in the investigation, and U.S. Rep. Charles Wilson said Saturday he would seek to find out if the recruitment records were deliberately falsified to protect those responsible for McClure's recruitment.

The story delivered another detail: Not only had McClure passed a second recruitment test in a second city—after dismally failing the first, in Lufkin—but his score on the second test had been so high that McClure "was put in charge of the recruit detachment sent from San Antonio to San Diego." The *News* never figured out how the high score occurred, but clearly, says Murray, either someone took the test for him, gave him the answers, or changed his score. "We know his IQ didn't increase."

As the reporters did further interviews and private and government investigations continued, a complex picture of malfeasance began to take shape. The young Marine with the learning disability had found himself placed in a "motivational platoon" in San Diego, where punishment was meted out through heavy menial labor and pugil-stick-fighting sessions. On the day Bubba McClure was injured, he had been forced to fight seven men. No officer was present, as Marine regulations require. Eyewitnesses said that McClure had refused to fight, while a drill instructor goaded the other recruits to pound him from all directions until he curled up in the dirt screaming, "God, make them stop." Knocked unconscious, he had a five-gallon bucket of water poured on him in an attempt to revive him. He remained in a coma until he died, more than three months later.

Two Big Career Boosts

Murray wrote editorials that conveyed a personal, small-town feel in siding with the family in its search for the truth beyond the lies. Ken Herman resumed his coverage on the news side. It was to have a bitter ending. While Congress launched hearings on recruitment techniques—and eventually tightened standards for the military—a Marine court-martialed in McClure's death eventually was acquitted on charges of "involuntary manslaughter, assault, maltreatment of a recruit and violating an order to conduct close combat drills only with supervisory officers present."

Says Murray, "Maybe it was the biggest lesson in life I ever had." No matter how well you do in your job, the results in a courtroom can turn everything around.

Murray entered the McClure series in a statewide competition, and got a good result: second place. (The editor of the winning Texas paper later jokingly told him, "We should have entered for the Pulitzers, too.") But the Lufkin stories had attracted the attention of Pulitzer Prize administrator John Hohenberg, who wrote to the *News* suggesting that it enter. The letter amazed the newsroom. "You simply don't ignore that kind of letter. In fact, we have it framed in the newsroom," Murray wrote in submitting the entry before the February 1 deadline. The submission barely was postmarked on time. The paper did not have a copier, and Murray had to poke a pocketful of dimes into the machine at the library.

The Public Service jurors unanimously picked the *Lufkin News* over the *Philadelphia Inquirer,* which was number two for its reporting on a state hospital for the mentally ill. "A small newspaper, with limited resources, chose not to settle for the official explanation of a local Marine's training camp death," jurors said of the *News*. "What might have been a routine obituary became instead a search for better answers and, in time, because of the newspaper's efforts and determination, the cause of fundamental reform in the recruiting and training practices of the United States Marine Corps." The board agreed with the jury's first choice.

By the time of the Pulitzer announcement, Herman had taken a job at the Dallas office of the Associated Press, and was home with his parents. The timing is now meaningful to him since he was to lose his father not long after the prize was announced. "It was a grand moment," Herman says. On top of that, the job offers began to come in from other news organizations, including the *Philadelphia Inquirer*. Ultimately, he decided to stay at the AP, although he since has rejoined the Cox organization, covering the White House.

The Brooklyn-born Herman, who had only been in journalism for six months when he started working for Joe Murray, credits his old boss with bringing out the best elements of Herman's youth, yet teaching him to temper his emotions for the sake of the story. "This is what Joe did," Herman recalls. "He kept me thinking that there is another side, or two or three, to this. Maybe I went a little far in drawing this emotional picture. It was a matter of not piling it on. You don't have to keep hitting people with it."

He would have been happy with any Pulitzer, Herman says, "but I happened to know that this was the Pulitzer of Pulitzers. It's the same one that Woodward and Bernstein got."

In fact, the movie version of *All the President's Men* had just come out when the *Lufkin News* won. Murray remembers attending an editors' conference in Hawaii and meeting Ben Bradlee and his wife, Sally Quinn, often in the news themselves after Watergate. "We're all gee-whiz when Bradlee and his wife walked in," recalls Murray, "and he comes over to the table and says, 'I want to introduce myself. I'm Ben Bradlee. I sure admire what you did.'"

The prize, which often boosts the careers of the reporters and editors who do the work, certainly gave a lift to Murray's and Herman's careers. Cox named Murray the Lufkin paper's publisher, after which he promptly restored the newspaper's original name, *Lufkin Daily News*. It sounded more formal to him, especially for a paper with a Pulitzer Prize. In the years before Murray's retirement at age sixty, Cox had him travel the world, where he made a specialty of writing homespun articles on Communist nations from Cuba to Eastern Europe.

Ken Herman, just back from a Middle-East trip with President George W. Bush, chuckles at the tone that his former boss used to set when he wrote pieces from behind the Iron Curtain: "It came down to every story saying, 'You know, they don't have grits in Yugoslavia; they don't have grits in Russia.'"

1977—*Lufkin News:* For an obituary of a local man who died in Marine training camp, which grew into an investigation of that death and a fundamental reform in the recruiting and training practices of the Marine Corps.

Anchorage Daily News publisher Kay Fanning (left) learns of the paper's 1976 Pulitzer Prize with reporters Jim Babb, Bob Porterfield, and Howard Weaver. The paper won for its series on the Teamsters Union. *Anchorage Daily News* staff photo. Used by permission.

Lufkin News editor Joe Murray (left) and reporter Ken Herman at a celebration in their honor after the east Texas paper won the 1977 Gold Medal. *Lufkin News* staff photo. Used by permission.

CHAPTER 16

Mightier than the Snake

God, I thought, wouldn't it be amazing to win? If the miracle should happen, I don't want to be photographed looking like I just came off a ski slope. You're a country editor—dress like one, I thought, and took off the turtleneck and tucked a favorite red-plaid shirt into my blue jeans.

—Dave Mitchell, from *The Light on Synanon*, 1980

"Today is the first day of the rest of your life" hardly seems a sentiment to strike terror in the heart. Coined by Synanon founder Charles Dederich, the aphorism expressed the healing, New Age image he wanted for his commune of rehabilitated drug addicts. Behind its guarded gates in California's bucolic west Marin County, though, Synanon was changing in the 1970s. It was becoming a brutal armed camp.

In 1977—two years after Dave and Cathy Mitchell paid what was then a princely forty-five thousand dollars for the tabloid weekly *Point Reyes Light*—the young owner/editors did not know that. Synanon had owned property in their county north of San Francisco since the mid-1960s, they knew, and had been around for twenty years since its founding in the Los Angeles–area beach community of Santa Monica. The group planned to move its headquarters to Marshall, just a short drive up Route 1 from Point Reyes Station, a charming but ramshackle town of 425. The Mitchells expected it would be a small news story for them.

Dave Mitchell had visited the Synanon property just after buying the *Light*, and not thought much about it. A commune was hardly strange for northern California, home to all sorts of alternative lifestyles by the 1970s. Mitchell described his readers at the time, and the community in general, as "fairly evenly divided between longhairs and cowboy hats." But he had come away from his tour with an itchy feeling that he couldn't quite describe. In his first stories, he tried. It had something to do with Synanon's size. "Above all it is big—much bigger than most people imagine," he wrote. "Synanon boasts a fleet of about 400 vehicles, not including scores of motorcycles. It also has three large boats moored in Tomales Bay, with more on the way, and six airplanes tied down at Gnoss Field in Novato." And its computer center was "appropriate for a large corporation." Mitchell also took note of how Synanon residents—nine hundred of them, on three properties—worked the phones from cubicles, promoting various gift items and offering premiums to raise money. The overall impression, he said, was of "happy, articulate people seemingly living productive lives. Many of those I talked to told of drug and criminal problems before joining Synanon."

In retrospect, Mitchell calls his early visit "the Potemkin Village tour of Synanon," masking dark secrets behind the false front of industriousness on behalf of charity. The real story was deeper. Dederich led the public into believing he ran a nonprofit, in Mitchell's view, "but it was really a corporation in the greediest sense of the word." Mitchell's skepticism showed through in his story. "They weren't happy with the story I wrote," he says. In 1978 they were to get a lot unhappier.

"Be Conservative"

The Mitchells had met as communications graduate students at Stanford in 1967 and gotten married. After several journalism and teaching jobs in the Midwest—and one unhappy reporting gig in central Florida, where the paper refused to examine the community's racial strife—they returned to northern California. They bought the *Light,* "convinced we would make it the *New York Times* of West Marin," they said in their 1980 book *The Light on Synanon,* written with psychology professor Richard Ofshe of the University of California, Berkeley.

It was far from the *Times.* The Mitchells had one full-time employee, four part-timers, and twenty-six hundred readers. But the paper won numerous state and regional journalism awards in those early years—one about a tribesman of the local Miwoks, "virtually the last Indian done out of his land by the white man," according to Dave Mitchell.

Toward the end of 1977, rumors circulated about strange events at Synanon. At a dinner party at Dave and Cathy Mitchell's isolated hillside cabin off Route 1, just north of Point Reyes Station and a few miles south of Synanon's new headquarters, one guest suggested that Dederich was "going crazy" as he neared his sixty-fifth birthday. She did not want to talk much about Synanon, but she had heard that some members were frightened. Others at the party had seen Synanon criticized in *Time* magazine and the *Los Angeles Times.*

The next day, Cathy suggested that it was time for an in-depth Synanon story in the *Light*. But before they got too far with the discussion, the Mitchells took off for a long-planned January vacation in Mexico.

The *Light* had a history of bad luck when the Mitchells were away. Once, a fill-in editor had written "that there wasn't a place to get a decent meal in west Marin," leading all the restaurant advertisers to cancel ads. Another time, an assistant had gratuitously insulted the area's real estate agents. Winning back offended advertisers was hard work for a tiny weekly. So the Mitchells had two words of advice as they left reporter Keith Ervin in charge: "Be conservative."

Ervin did have one Synanon story to follow while the Mitchells were gone. Cathy had seen a report on a San Francisco television channel that Synanon had purchased sixty thousand dollars' worth of guns and ammunition from a Bay Area gun dealer. It was already in the news, the Mitchells figured, and couldn't cause much of a local stir. They took off for Mazatlan.

But Keith Ervin got a new Synanon story to report: an armed altercation on a local road between two groups, one of them Synanon members in a van. Hearing about it on the police-monitoring scanner, Ervin arrived in time to take a photo of three men spread-eagled for a weapons search. Synanon members said the three were hassling them, while the three men, who had a pellet gun with them, said it was the other way around. Deputies filed no charges, but noted in the police report an ominous uttering from one Synanon member: "People cannot hassle Synanon residents and get away with it."

Ervin, recalling the Mitchells' admonition, ran the February 2 story on the bottom of page one below an article on property taxes. But he had heard a story from a disgruntled neighbor of Synanon, Alvin Gambonini, about the help he had rendered to runaway Synanon youngsters trying to reunite with relatives. Gambonini said he had been roughed up by Synanon members two years earlier for his efforts. But Ervin didn't print anything about Gambonini or the runaways. Instead, his story combined the highway altercation with news of the weapons cache. Synanon refused to comment for the story. The sheriff's spokesman, who told Ervin that the arms purchases were legal, said the sheriff had "pretty good communications" with Synanon. Still, the reporter wrote, "Local reaction to Synanon's arms buildup was almost universally negative."

Dave Mitchell was happy with the coverage when he returned, since it gave thorough treatment to the "armed camp" issue. He turned his attention instead to a big twenty-four-page, thirtieth-anniversary special. It ran on March 2—the Mitchells' last quiet week for a while.

A Grand Jury Speaks

Each county in California empanels grand juries to hand up criminal indictments, and to act as a watchdog over county government departments. The Marin grand jury had checked out Synanon in 1976 and actually criticized the county's probation department for not sending young delinquents there for rehabilitation. Note was taken of runaways from its compounds, but Synanon's explanation satisfied the grand jurors: children ran away because the program was so rigorous.

Since then, however, Los Angeles attorney Paul Morantz had been representing parents who believed their children, Marshall-based Synanon members, were being mistreated. Morantz was friendly with many reporters in southern California, and had worked in the past with *Los Angeles Times* reporter Narda Zacchino. Morantz wanted to make public what he knew about the abusive group he believed was evolving into a dangerous cult. "I instituted warrant proceedings to get the children brought back to Santa Monica court," the lawyer says, "and then I did something borderline unscrupulous." He called reporter Zacchino and alerted her to the filings. The resulting *Times* stories on runaways and alleged abuses created an unflattering picture of Synanon, and the Associated Press picked them up. The *Time* magazine coverage in December 1977 referred to "a once respected drug program" that had become "a kooky cult."

The next year's Marin County grand jury took a tougher look at Synanon. Its report on March 3, 1978, criticized public officials for failing to regulate it, and noted that "the runaway problem, the lawsuits against Synanon to obtain the release of children and others, intemperate statements by Mr. Dederich, the arming of Synanon people, the altercations with neighbors at Marshall, [and] the reports of child abuse have placed Synanon in the public limelight."

In a *Light* story headlined "Grand Jurors Blast Synanon," Dave Mitchell balanced juror claims against a retort from Sheriff Louis Mountanos, who had found only encounter sessions and other "games" at Synanon. Encounter sessions "have long been the organization's primary way of shaping members' behavior," the sheriff said. But in a Keith Ervins sidebar headed "Underground railroad for Synanon runaways," Synanon neighbor Gambonini told a different tale:

> "The kids that come here—every one—said the adults [at Synanon] told them we'll shoot them. But one girl came in here at two in the morning, and she told me, 'What have I got to lose?'"
>
> Most of the runaways are between ages 11 and 20. Usually the Gamboninis let the kids call their parents. The sheriff's deputies are notified, and they often take the youngsters to Juvenile Hall.
>
> Gambonini's wife, Doris, keeps a collection of letters from grateful parents

whose children have returned home from Synanon. . . . An earlier runaway complained to Mrs. Gambonini, she says, that he had been boxed on the ears for bad behavior. "I can hardly hear," she quotes him as saying.

Now that Synanon has bought weapons to defend members, Gambonini says he's scared to plow his fields near his border with the rehabilitation center.

Mitchell's next editorial was headed "A County/Synanon Alliance?" It pointed out how defensive various county agencies became after the grand jury criticized them for supporting Synanon or even merely for ignoring it. The strongest Synanon alliance seemed to be with Sheriff Mountanos, who actually employed two of its members as "reserve deputy sheriffs."

Mitchell was friends with a member of the sheriff's top brass, Art Disterheft, who ran the sheriff's substation, and they often chatted on Tuesday nights when the Mitchells were "pasting up" pages. (Dave had page negatives made on Wednesday for a press run and distribution the next day.) Disterheft was unhappy both with Synanon and with the sheriff who played down the organization's violent side. And on one March evening, he let slip to Dave that there was an assault case he might look into—one that Disterheft had been told not to discuss with the press. Mitchell found a report on file about a "split-ee," as Synanon members called those who left the organization, being beaten because he was suspected of spying for *Time* magazine.

A New Source of Income

Synanon went after *Time* in court as well, with a $76 million lawsuit over the story that called it a kooky cult. KGO-TV's owner, ABC, had been hit with a $42 million suit, and the Hearst Corporation faced a $40 million action stemming from a long-running dispute over 1972 coverage calling Synanon a "racket." The *Los Angeles Times* and the *Light* had not been sued, although the Mitchells half-expected it at any time. It wasn't something they looked forward to; without a staff lawyer of their own, they would have had to arrange for outside legal coverage.

Despite the exposure, the paper's reporting toughened and broadened. On April 6 it ran financial details researched from state records. Synanon's assets were about $20 million, and Dederich had been granted a $500,000 "pre-retirement bonus."

The organization could afford it, and it was soon to get even richer. Hearst settled its Synanon suit out of court for $2 million. (Apparently, Synanon had found out that two hired men had stolen tape recordings from the organization for the Hearst defense, and that negative information had led Hearst to settle with its accuser.) News of the $2 million deal spread quickly in the media.

The strength of community weeklies, as Mitchell sees it, involves persistence: keeping tabs on subjects continually, rather than doing an entire issue on them. Such coverage often brings out sources who might not otherwise talk. That is what happened with the *Light's* weekly Synanon stories, which drew the interest of UC-Berkeley's Richard Ofshe. He had done a year's research on Synanon several years before, and former members were telling him about growing violence that echoed what was reported in the *Light*. Ofshe agreed to serve as an unpaid consultant for the Mitchells. Others, too, told them about new cases of Synanon violence, along with potential irregularities on the business side. One government official who offered the *Light* information—but asked anonymity—was dubbed "Green Door" by Dave Mitchell, in deference to Bob Woodward's Deep Throat source. (*Behind the Green Door,* like *Deep Throat,* was a pornographic movie that caused an uproar in the 1970s.)

Attorney Paul Morantz, whose Synanon-related cases had multiplied, remembers talking to Mitchell nearly every day as the *Light's* coverage intensified. "Dave and I are similar kinds of personalities," he says. "We're knowledge-driven. Once he knew about Synanon, he couldn't go back."

As the *Light* kept up the weekly drumbeat about Synanon's abuses, the Mitchells felt increasingly isolated. Not only were the police laying off but the northern California press had become uninterested as well. Those multimillion-dollar lawsuits were having a chilling effect, the Mitchells worried.

Then in late September they learned of another beating. The organization reportedly was ordering members to get vasectomies as a means of controlling their sexual lives, and one who disagreed with the policy had been treated for a skull fracture after a fight. Dave's editorial was headed, "Is anyone listening?" It ended by asking:

> Each case of violence by Synanon members is treated as unrelated to every other case. Marshall residents say they are intimidated; the county tries to solve the problem with better zoning.
>
> West Marin residents have a significant problem with Synanon. But like rancher Gambonini we wonder: is anyone out there listening?

The tone of despair in the editorial may have reflected something in the editor's personal life as well. His and Cathy's marriage had been off-and-on, although they were constantly together in the little newsroom. He ran the journalism side of the Synanon story, she the business side. (After the Mitchells' permanent split, Dave would later discover that he was suffering from clinical depression, and needed medication.)

Opponents of Synanon were making some gains, however. Paul Morantz won a $300,000 September court victory in Los Angeles on behalf of a woman whom Los Angeles County had referred to Synanon's Santa Monica facility for counseling. Synanon had not allowed her to leave, shaved her head, and psychologically abused her.

One day as Mitchell was reporting on Synanon, the *Light*'s receptionist alerted him that Morantz had called with an urgent message. Synanon members were being urged to attack Morantz, he said, and the lawyer's home address was being aired over the organization's closed-circuit radio station, called "the wire." The broadcast used terms like "break his legs." The attorney had called the police, bought a gun, and called the *Light*. The same day, as Mitchell was discussing this with one of the friendlier sheriff's department officials, the officer told the editor: "I don't want to alarm you, but you ought to let somebody besides your wife know where [your notes] are. If any harm should come to you, those notes will at least give us an idea about where to start looking."

That evening, Ofshe gave the Mitchells his reading on what this all might mean. "Dederich usually telegraphs his punches. He has to because he almost never gives a direct order if he can avoid it," the psychology professor said. "It's a device to put distance between him and the act, so that afterward he can deny responsibility if he wants to."

Mitchell then asked Disterheft whether a "goon squad" was being formed at Synanon, as he had heard. Disterheft called an acquaintance with the state attorney general's Organized Crime Bureau, and soon they had an answer. Synanon had started an internal group called "the Imperial Marines." Also, the Crime Bureau had opened an investigation of Synanon beatings reported in the *Light*.

"They Got Morantz!"

On Wednesday, October 11, Mitchell had driven the week's *Light* negatives to the printer and was heading back to the office. Under the page-one headline, "State Probe of Synanon Widens," the paper carried this line: "Among the allegations being investigated is a threat against attorney Paul Morantz, who has represented a number of Southern California clients in disputes with Synanon." Half-listening to the car radio, "a sudden excitement in the announcer's voice caught my attention," Mitchell recalls. Morantz had been bitten by a four-and-a-half-foot rattlesnake hidden in his mailbox.

Mitchell concedes that—for the moment at least—he reacted "with unmixed joy," stopping to call his wife from a pay-phone and shouting. "They got Morantz!" At last, the world would start paying attention to the *Light*'s story. Cathy was more terrified than elated. She was going to have to drive past Synanon to get to her teaching job. But if she stayed home, she worried that she might be attacked there. After paranoia, she later recalled, "my second reaction was, How stupid! There's no way Synanon can get out of it this time."

What had Morantz himself gone through? On October 10 he had tickets for a World Series game at Dodger Stadium, but had been kept late at his office by a meeting with agents from the state's Crime Bureau. The topic was the danger that Synanon presented to him. Too late to make it to the ballpark, he headed home to watch on television instead. With the Crime Bureau meeting fresh in his mind, he redoubled his attention to the routine he already followed: examining his car before he got in it, for example. Once home, "I got into my house by opening the door, letting it swing back, and looking both ways. If my dogs didn't bark when I came home, I didn't go in the house." Still, "not in my wildest imagination was I thinking of the possibility of a rattlesnake being in my mailbox."

He brought some groceries to the kitchen, and let his collies out. "I remember thinking something odd was stuffed in my mailbox," according to Morantz. The box was built into the front wall, accessible inside through a grill door. He wasn't wearing his contact lenses as he approached the flap from the side, and he reached in thinking he was retrieving a package, or perhaps a mass like some kind of scarf that had been stuffed in. When he had the mass in his grasp, he unthinkingly pulled it out. The snake's rattles had been cut off. "I actually saw the head strike out and bite me. As it happened my left hand swung into the air, and the snake went into the air and landed on my floor." He screamed, then thought of his dogs outside, and slammed the door as the snake recoiled. Running out the back door, he yelled to neighbors, "Call an ambulance! I've been bitten by a rattlesnake. It's Synanon."

Paramedics and firemen arrived together. The firemen killed the snake with a shovel, while the medics treated Morantz's painfully swollen and blistered left arm. Neighbors reported a suspicious car that had been spotted in the area. Some had written down a license number. The plates were registered to Synanon in Marshall.

A Clean Scoop

The *Light* story, which seemed prescient when the weekly hit the street, was very old by the weekend. Two Synanon members were arrested, one of them the son of band leader Stan Kenton. The news was everywhere. Walter Cronkite intoned that the crime was "bizarre, even by cult standards."

The Mitchells planned five stories for the October 19 issue, harboring little il-lusion that they could have anything fresh in their weekly. Dave had interviewed

Jack Hurst, a former Synanon president now out of the organization. While shocked by its gradual turn toward violence, he had declined to be interviewed in the past. Now he was ready. "I feel very badly about this," he told Mitchell. "I'm doing something I swore I would never do: turn against Synanon." But he also was frightened. His dog, purchased for self-protection, had been mysteriously hanged. "They're heavily armed and very dangerous—and specifically trained in terrorist activities," he told Mitchell. "I think I'm next."

During the interview, the editor learned that Hurst lived with a recent Synanon split-ee named Mary Inskip, who had told Los Angeles police that Dederich personally had urged members to attack Morantz. When Mitchell called her, she confirmed it, providing specific language that the leader had used. The *Light* could quote her by name.

It would be the paper's lead piece, although he wanted to run it by a lawyer first. "When I wrote the story, I knew that potentially someone might go ahead with a libel case," he says. For pro bono advice he called an attorney friend from Stanford, Ladd Bedford. (His "pay" was a couple of pizzas Mitchell brought for munching during their consultation.) Bedford suggested one critical word change in his lead. "The lawyer said, 'You've written here that Dederich called for the attack on Morantz. You need to write that he called for *an* attack on Morantz. We don't know he specifically called for this one. And that would be hard to prove.'" (They even discussed the veiled order England's twelfth-century King Henry II gave for the killing of Thomas à Becket: "Who will rid me of this meddlesome priest?")

Once Mitchell cleared the wording he slapped a "Special Synanon Issue" on page one, and printed four hundred extra copies. With so much new competition, could the Dederich story possibly be exclusive?

It was. Mitchell later learned that other papers had trouble getting reports of Dederich's attack order confirmed. In the case of the *Los Angeles Times*'s Narda Zacchino, she had received information from Mary Inskip, too, and had it confirmed. But *Times* lawyers spent several days checking it over before it was finally cleared. Eventually, the *Times* ran the story on Halloween.

Different Spouses, Different Fears

The *Light* became a primary source for the nation's newly interested press. The Mitchells continued to have original information each week.

As the rattler attack spread fear among other Synanon enemies, Dave Mitchell was strangely unworried. "If anyone physically attacked us, everyone would know," he says today. "That's the difference between being a small-town editor, where everybody in town knows the guy and what his battles are, and being someone like

Paul Morantz, who's in a large metropolitan area where few people know what he's doing." Still, Art Disterheft ran extra patrols at the Mitchell house. And the night Dederich was arrested on a conspiracy charge, Disterheft spent the night there.

The moves were wise. Cathy believed that their hillside cabin sat far enough from neighbors, and from the road below, that the couple was vulnerable. "Dave was more macho than I was," she recalls from her office at the University of North Carolina at Asheville, where she is a professor specializing in media history. Disterheft's patrols only added to her panic level. "Coming up the long winding driveway, you'd hear this car and think, 'Oh my god, they've come,'" she remembers. "We asked them to stop the patrols because they were doing more harm than good."

Dave Mitchell had one scare: a late-night encounter that almost turned tragic, then ended up comic. "Cathy and Richard and I were going down Highway 1 through Marshall and were just about to pass the Synanon facility when a Synanon van, with twelve people in it, made a turn across the road right in front of me," he says. "I locked up my wheels and I stopped a few feet short of hitting them." Says Mitchell, "They never knew it was me. Still, that would have been something, to plow into a bunch of Synanon members on their doorstep in the middle of the night. It would not have been a good thing. It was the only time I was really physically afraid of Synanon."

The Mitchells' aggressive coverage continued through the end of the year, with one late-October editorial blasting Sheriff Mountanos and another story analyzing the legal case against Morantz's attackers. On December 28 the *Light* proclaimed Dederich its "Man of the Year," recounting his rise and fall.

Like Joe Murray at the *Lufkin News*, Dave Mitchell had problems getting his Pulitzer entry in the mail. The *Light* had left the task to the last minute, and with the deadline bearing down, Mitchell found himself "driving a million miles an hour" to get to San Rafael, the only Marin station that could postmark an envelope late.

The Public Service jury had the *Light* tied with the *Chicago Sun-Times* and its series on profiteering from abortions. The board went with the California weekly.

When a Washington reporter called the Mitchells early on Pulitzer Monday to say he had heard a rumor that the *Light* might have won a Pulitzer, the initial shock quickly gave way to fear—that the weekly's onerous deadlines might make it miss its own award announcement. "We picked up the production schedule," says Mitchell. "If by chance we did win, it wouldn't screw up production." The story made it into the paper.

Later, after the marriage broke up and Cathy moved to Asheville, Dave continued to run the *Light*, becoming something of a journalistic guru. The paper, however, remained marginally profitable at best. In 2005, Mitchell sold it to Robert Plotkin, a former Monterey County deputy district attorney with a Columbia University journalism degree. As a consideration in the sale, Mitchell kept the Gold Medal. Prior to a falling out in 2006 between Mitchell and Plotkin, the former editor also continued to write his *Light* column, "Sparsely, Sage and Timely."

The new owner immediately began modernizing the newsroom and planning staff additions. Though new to Marin, he has grand ideas. "This is the place where the new literary movement is about to happen," he says. "This is going to be the Paris of the twenties. This is going to be the Beats of San Francisco in the fifties." Talent will gravitate to the *Light*, he says, because it is still known, even back East, as the little California paper that won the Pulitzer Prize.

Mitchell, though, will never forget how strange it felt to have been so small, and to have won so big: "It's like being out playing touch football and making a good catch, and somebody says, 'You could play for the 49ers with a catch like that!'"

1979—*Point Reyes Light,* a California weekly: For its investigation of Synanon.

Point Reyes Light owners Dave and Cathy Mitchell in front of the office after the paper won the 1979 Pulitzer Prize. Used by permission.

SPECIAL SYNANON ISSUE

October 19, 1978   25¢

POINT REYES LIGHT

Vol. XXX, No. 27, Point Reyes Station, California   West Marin's Community Newspaper

Lawmen told of

Alleged call for attack on atty.

By Dave Mitchell

Los Angeles police and Justice Department investigators have received information from ex-members of Synanon alleging Synanon founder Chuck Dederich earlier this year repeatedly called for an attack on atty. Paul Morantz.

Morantz on Oct. 10 was bitten by a 4½-foot rattlesnake placed in the mailbox of his Pacific Palisades home by two men. Their car's registration was traced to Synanon's Marshall facility.

Morantz recently won a $300,000 judgment against Synanon for a woman who said last year she had been kidnapped by the organization and abused. He has also represented various clients in child-custody fights with Synanon.

Last Thursday, Synanon atty. Phil Bourdette in Badger, Tulare County, turned over to Los Angeles police two Synanon members suspected of the crime. Also turned over was the suspect vehicle owned by Synanon.

One of the suspects is Lance Kenton, 20, son of bandleader Stan Kenton. Kenton grew up in Synanon's West Marin facility and was in recent years living at Badger.

The second is Joe Musico, 28, a Viet-

nam veteran who entered Synanon over five years ago as a drug addict.

Atty. Bourdette told reporters Synanon will not provide lawyers for the pair and claimed Synanon does not condone unlawful acts.

But Synanon ex-members were quick to contradict Bourdette's claim. One of those who talked to lawmen is Mary Inskip.

Ms. Inskip left Synanon July 8 after 12 years in the organization. She now lives on the West Marin coast; her address is being withheld because she fears retaliation from Synanon.

The ex-member has told authorities she heard Dederich "several times" call for an attack on Morantz over the "Synanon wire."

She said, "This has been general conversation in Synanon for about a year that he is bad and something should be done."

The call for an attack on Morantz was repeated so often "it was like a drum beat," said Ms. Inskip. Dederich would say, "When is one of you cowardly people going to go down there and break his legs?"

Continued on Page 9

Andrea Giacomini dies Sunday at 37

Andrea Giacomini, 37, president of Lagunitas School's board of trustees and wife of Supervisor Gary Giacomini, died Sunday in a local hospital.

The couple lived separately.

Mrs. Giacomini, a San Geronimo resident, had been admitted to the hospital a week earlier for an operation to remove a benign tumor of the brain.

Both the Lagunitas School trustees board and the board of supervisors meetings for this week were cancelled. Supervisor Giacomini, the Republican nominee in the 2nd Senatorial District, halted campaign appearances for now.

Mrs. Giacomini was a native of Eureka. She graduated from San Rafael's Dominican College and received a master's degree in psychology from Lone Mountain College in San Francisco. She served as a teacher and counselor in San Rafael schools, at Sir Francis Drake High School and at the San Geronimo Valley Nursery School.

In March, 1977, Mrs. Giacomini was elected to the Lagunitas school board where her husband had previously served.

She is survived by her husband; two sons, Andrew, 15, a sophomore at Sir Francis Drake, and Antony, 14, a freshman at Sir Francis Drake; her parents, Andrew and Neva Rosaia of Eureka; and a brother, Robert Rosaia of San Francisco.

A Mass of Christian Burial was held at 10 a.m. Wednesday in St. Raphael's Church, San Rafael. Entombment will be in Eureka.

Mrs. Giacomini's family has asked for memorial contributions to go to the Andrea Giacomini Memorial Scholarship Fund at the Lagunitas School District, P.O. Box 266, San Geronimo 94963.

Synanon update

Late Tuesday Joe Musico, one of the suspects in the snake-bite attack on atty. Paul Morantz, was arraigned in Los Angeles.

The district attorney's office there charged Musico with conspiracy to commit murder and conspiracy to commit an assault with a deadly weapon; added to both conspiracy charges was an allegation of "intent to do great bodily harm."

Musico was also charged with assault with a deadly weapon.

Lance Kenton, the second suspect in the case, is scheduled to be arraigned Friday. Last Friday he was released on $25,000 bail posted by his father, bandleader Stan Kenton.

Synanon has announced it will not provide defense for either suspect.

SYNANON GUARD - These pictures from a Synanon newsletter distributed last December show the martial arts training and physical conditioning of Synanon's "National Guard." Noted the caption: "Synanon is developing its own form of a volunteer police department. We call it the Synanon National Guard. Like any other community, we're concerned about the rising crime rate in this country. So we're asking our most responsible adults to learn how to secure our property...If trouble should occur, we're prepared to handle it. We don't need to call the police to handle our problems."

Park buy bill passes

An amended version of the omnibus parks bill passed U.S. Senators last Thursday and breezed through the House of Representatives on Friday.

Unless President Carter vetoes it, which is unlikely, it will add 5,973 acres in West Marin to Golden Gate National Recreation Area and Point Reyes National Seashore.

In the only change affecting West Marin, 3.3 acres near Muir Beach were dropped from the original bill.

The excluded land is owned by Peter Lavalle, the Torres family, and Green Gulch Zen Center.

All other West Marin areas originally proposed by Congressman John Burton are included.

The bill includes conditions on use of the land drafted by Burton.

Among the bill's key features is a strong emphasis on the continuation of agriculture, including a program for leasebacks to present owners, present lessees or future lessees.

The main areas acquired are 1,625 acres on Bolinas Mesa at the Seashore's southern boundary and 3,724 acres between Olema and Samuel Taylor State Park at GGNRA's northern end.

GGNRA has acquired new land for a southern entrance to the beach parking lot.

Front page of the *Light*, October 19, 1978. Used by permission, and with the courtesy of the Marin County libraries.

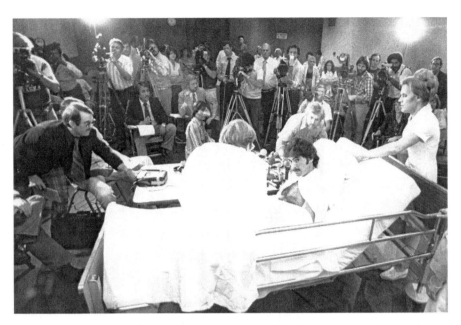

Los Angeles attorney Paul Morantz surrounded by the press in a Los Angeles hospital as he recovers from his 1978 snake bite. Used by permission. United Press International photo provided by Corbis.

Los Angeles police officer Richard Grotsley holds the four-and-a-half-foot snake placed in Morantz's mailbox by members of the Synanon cult. United Press International photo provided by Corbis.

CHAPTER 17

Pulitzer, Reform Thyself

What came from [my study] is a surprising, fascinating, complex, often contradictory portrait of a process now influenced far less by politics and cronyism than its detractors charge—and influenced far more by caprice and sentiment than the general public might believe.

—David Shaw, *Press Watch*, 1984

After the *St. Louis Post-Dispatch* won its fifth Gold Medal in 1952, for its exposé of federal tax system abuses, the storied paper's news operation entered a long Pulitzer Prize dry spell. (Over the next fifty-five years, staffers would win five, but for Editorial Cartooning, Editorial Writing, Criticism, and Commentary, with its latest, in 1989, honoring a freelance photographer's picture.) Still, the *Post-Dispatch* continued to make enormous contributions to the Pulitzer Prizes, through the board chairmanship of the third Joseph Pulitzer.

Joseph Pulitzer Jr., as J.P. III was known, had taken the helm at the paper and at the Pulitzer Advisory Board after the death of his seventy-year-old father in 1955. In both posts, the younger Pulitzer served until his retirement in 1986. (He died in 1993.) Like his father before him, J.P. III had been schooled thoroughly in journalism and Pulitzer family traditions. And on the board, he built a reputation as a fair-minded moderator who rarely tried to dominate a discussion or divert a debate among strong-willed board members.

"There is no record of Joe's having harsh words with anyone in doing Prize Board business," wrote Daniel Pfaff, biographer for both J.P. II and J.P. Jr. John Hohenberg, the Pulitzer Prize administrator for the first ten years of J.P. Jr.'s chairmanship, noted "that he, like his father and grandfather, was an articulate and devoted liberal Democrat of the old school." But while J.P. Jr. often inquired about the political leanings of board members, "I never knew him to make political consideration a condition for a vote on a prize." In fact, the chairman's only shortcoming, in Hohenberg's view, may have been "a distinct form of ancestor worship that caused him to oppose any major change" that could lead the Pulitzer Prizes to deviate from what the first Joseph Pulitzer had intended. Over the years, under both Joseph Pulitzers, the Pulitzer Prize organization quietly and steadfastly rejected expansion into magazines and broadcast journalism, for example, and on the arts side declined to add categories for cinema. (The decision to stick with newspapers and traditional artistic expression certainly facilitated the rise of the film industry's Academy Awards and television's Emmy Awards, along with the National Magazine Awards and other journalism competitions that ranged beyond newspaper work.)

Still, midway through J.P. Jr.'s chairmanship the board did enter into a period of transformation on two fronts that changed the Pulitzer Prizes significantly in the 1970s and early 1980s. He supported both reforms vigorously, and occasionally even took the lead.

The board had made a number of smaller changes in the early decades, of course. It had not taken long for it to choose working journalists for its jury pool, for example, instead of Columbia professors. In the early 1950s, to reduce the domination of the board by the same members year after year, it set maximum service at twelve years. (J.P. Jr., like his father, had been specifically exempted.) The board also stopped describing Pulitzers as honoring "the best" work in a category, calling each winner "a distinguished example" instead. In the case of Gold Medal winners, the citation for "the most disinterested and meritorious public service"—the wording of the benefactor's will—became "a distinguished example of meritorious public service," although on the medal itself the original inscription remains.

Concerns about the Pulitzer Prizes being tightly controlled by a handful of men, though, had remained valid through the 1960s. During his board term from 1940 to 1954, the New York Times's Arthur Krock had been such a power broker, according to David Shaw, the Los Angeles Times media reporter who became a student of the Pulitzer Prizes. Krock met with board friends for dinner the evening before formal voting on the prizes, where the group prepared their choices for consideration by the full group. Too many prizes for one paper was a Krock no-no. Fellow board member John S. Knight told Shaw about Krock's message to him when Knight's paper, the Chicago Daily News, found itself nominated by jurors for prizes in three categories. "Krock just took me out for a little walk and said I might want to be 'more restrained.' I got the message," according to Knight. With his other editors in Chicago, they decided which single prize they preferred.

The reforms that Chairman Pulitzer championed in the 1970s bubbled up from the newspaper business itself, reflecting the growing awareness that all-white, all-male newsrooms were unacceptable, and that diversity in press leadership was something to be sought. By the year J.P. Jr. retired, the board not only contained both women and minority members but also had established a jury system emphasizing ethnic and gender balance.

Just as dramatic was a major alteration in the relationship of the Pulitzer Prizes to Columbia University—a relationship that his grandfather had designed into his plan for the awards before J.P. Jr. was born. And when the time came to revise that relationship, J.P. Jr. took charge of the sensitive negotiations that separated the Columbia Board of Trustees from the prize-awarding process.

At Odds over the Pentagon Papers

Chairman Pulitzer and other board members had begun questioning the role of the trustees during the tumultuous circumstances surrounding the 1972 awarding of the Gold Medal to the *New York Times* for its publication of the Pentagon Papers. Trustees had twice voted down the board's proposed award to the *Times*—objecting that the Pentagon Papers were stolen documents—before Columbia president William McGill talked them out of any decision to veto the prize. In the end, the trustees noted that terms of the Pulitzers allowed the trustees to accept or reject an advisory board recommendation, but not to submit an alternate winner. If the trustees had been in charge of making awards, they noted, "certain of the recipients would not have been chosen." Still, they conceded that the Pulitzer Advisory Board's "judgments are to be accorded great weight by the Trustees," and they eventually voted to accept the recommendations.

There were similar worries about board members potentially being overruled the next year, when the *Washington Post* was selected to win the Gold Medal for its Watergate coverage after having been vilified by the Nixon administration. But on April 30, a week before the trustees met, key White House aides to President Nixon resigned, and the president's press secretary issued a remarkable apology to the *Post* for having accused it of "shabby journalism." With little discussion, the trustees gave all prize recommendations their blessing.

Chairman Pulitzer had fought strenuously for the *Times* to win in 1972, and for the *Post* in 1973. But by 1975 the concerns about trustee political opinions leading to a possible veto of some future prize led Pulitzer to press for a severance of relations with the trustees. With the Columbia body also increasingly wary of the damage that could result from a veto, it backed out of the process, avoiding a legal confrontation that some Pulitzer board members had feared. Instead, Columbia's president would represent the school in the Pulitzer Prize relationship. By 1979, "advisory" was dropped from the board's title, since it was no longer advising anyone on the prizes. It had the final say.

The reforms that Pulitzer championed and supervised *within* the board would have just as powerful an impact on the Prizes, though. Underlying the changes were a combination of issues raised by calmer voices within the group—like that of respected *St. Petersburg Times* editor Eugene Patterson, who wanted to democratize and diversify the system—and by members who did not like the "old boy network" for other reasons.

Years after the 1973 Watergate Gold Medal, the *Washington Post*'s Ben Bradlee still smoldered over having "lost" two prizes that same year. Knowing that the *Post* coverage had been rated third-best by the Public Service jury, he had gone to Columbia prepared to fight for that prize. In the end, he didn't have to; the other board members by then had become Woodward and Bernstein fans. Still, with Bradlee out of the room, the board voted the *Post* one other Pulitzer only (to David Broder, for Commentary). As Bradlee knew, juries had favored *Post* candidates in three categories, yet two of those "front runners" had been voted no prize. Argued Bradlee in his 1995 autobiography, "Votes are subtly, if not openly, traded between advisory board members, and while lobbying is allegedly frowned upon, the crime is lobbying and losing."

Bradlee also was upset that he could not complain to his fellow members. He was "in a shit sandwich, as we graduates of ancient universities like to put it," wrote Bradlee. "[F]or fear of losing the two we had won, I couldn't risk complaining too loud about the two we had lost."

With juries still ranking their favorites, the jurors' opinion was that any other choice by the board represented an overruling of the jury selection. Some on the board—Bradlee among them—shared that view. Other board members thought that jurors had no business indicating their top choices, since the naming of winners was the board's job alone.

While Bradlee was the rare case of a board *member* disgruntled by the Pulitzer operation, journalists had complained about the prizes for decades. David Shaw's study of the Pulitzer Prize process, summarized in his 1984 book *Press Watch,* cited several areas of contention among journalists critical of the Pulitzers. Topping his list was a charge that the Pulitzers were dominated by big eastern establishment newspapers (both the *New York Times* and *Washington Post* were mentioned) and that their gentlemen's agreements colored the prize decisions. Papers in the West, and smaller papers all over the United States, were said to be "systematically and unjustly neglected," while the board also passed over some deserving winners so that it could spread the prizes around. Finally, the critics saw the board as being unlikely ever to reform itself because members were "conservative old men who pick their own successors, a self-perpetuating elite."

In exploring the Watergate-year deliberations, Shaw asked the *New York Times*'s Scotty Reston why the *Post* did not get those three jury-selected Pulitzers in addition to the 1973 Gold Medal. "There was a strong feeling that four was too many . . . that we should spread them around," Reston told Shaw.

Finally, the Finalists

Shaw determined that reforms installed under chairman Pulitzer in the early 1980s significantly improved the Pulitzer selection process. Gene Patterson, a board member from 1973 to 1984, was instrumental in the modernization, which he says may well have diminished "the relaxed atmosphere" of the board in prior years. The revisions moved the board toward diversity of membership and began a movement toward more disclosure about the selection process. At the same time, the board clarified the role of the jurors. They became "nominating jurors," and the board emphasized in its instructions that the panels were not the final decision-makers. That was the board's job.

"There was no particular reformer-in-chief that I remember. We sat around this long table and kicked these things around," says Patterson. "There was just stuff that needed to be done." But within a few years of the Pentagon Papers and Watergate Gold Medals being decided—amid so much controversy—the board had increased its size and geographic representation sharply, and added black members and women members. It shortened board membership even further, to a maximum of nine terms.

For the first time, a system for naming finalists also was approved. There had been movements on the board over the years to do this, and for a time in the 1930s the board had cited some entries as "honorable mentions," in the Public Service category and others. That was short-lived, though, and later attempts by Joseph Pulitzer II and others to set up a formal system for announcing finalists went nowhere.

"There was some ancient feeling that it diminishes the Pulitzer Prizes to say there were people who didn't win. But everybody knew there were. And as editors we stand for the free flow of information," Patterson says. By identifying finalists, the board also acknowledged the honor that went with being in the running for a prize, while giving the jury some credit for its choices. "And the public got a better look at how the Pulitzer works," he notes. The board meetings remained secret, and board members were told not to discuss the decisions afterward. "Like in a jury, you have to go into a room and talk quite frankly about the entries you have before you," he says. "In public, that dries up the spontaneity of the deliberations."

In Shaw's analysis, however, the reforms had not eliminated what he saw as one flaw: sentimentality. He observed that board members especially tended to favor small-town entries over the big newspapers that win year after year.

His prime example was the 1979 Gold Medal for the *Point Reyes Light.* Board members and jurors alike told him that they honored the *Light* "more because it was a small paper whose editors had shown great courage, at considerable financial risk, than because the paper's Synanon stories were necessarily better than the three other finalists in the public service category." All thought the *Light* stories excellent. But Shaw quoted Michael O'Neill, then editor of the *New York Daily News,* and a member of the jury, as saying that "if you took the names of the newspapers off the . . . entries, I would definitely have voted for the *Chicago Tribune* series on the problems of the aging." Shaw also quoted an unnamed board member as saying of the *Light's* Dave and Cathy Mitchell: "The job that couple did was damn good, but the guts they showed, with Synanon just a few miles down the road . . . that's what the Pulitzers are all about, that's what won the award."

"The Folklore Was Wrong"

Recent and current Pulitzer board members uniformly praise today's prize-selection process for its candor and fairness, saying that any vestiges of the past old-boy network are now completely gone.

Gene Roberts, then executive editor of the *Philadelphia Inquirer,* says that when he joined the board in the early 1980s "there were one or two little things that I thought could have been interpreted as efforts to back-scratch. But the attempts were noticeably unsuccessful. In that group, the idea of back-scratching was very repellent."

John Carroll, whose board term ended in 2004, when he was editor of the *Los Angeles Times,* recalls, "One editor once asked me to support his story, and said his paper had come close so many times, and was 'owed one.' He didn't get that one, and I didn't support that story." In general, editors simply viewed lobbying as counterproductive, and were even reluctant to circulate reprints, suspecting that any such promotion might hurt their chances.

"One of the great things when I joined the board was to find that some of the folklore was just absolutely wrong. The model was mutual respect, where you could disagree sharply without being wounded or wounding," says former *Chicago Tribune* editor Jack Fuller, who was president of Tribune Publishing when his nine-year term ended in 2000.

"Integrity oozed out of the process," says Michael Gartner of his nine years on the Pulitzer board, through 1991. The former editor of the *Des Moines Register* and the Ames, Iowa, *Daily Tribune* and president of NBC News recalls that there were few predictable choices during his board stint. "There were never any lay-downs," he says. "You'd go into the meeting thinking, This one's going to be easy. And Jesus, the vote would be five to five to five."

Oregonian editor Sandy Rowe, who left the board in 2004, finds it amusing that people think vote-trading goes on. "In the past I don't know if there were a bunch of white guys in the back room trading votes. I do know that in the nine years I was on the board, that did not happen." Today, "you have these very challenging, engaging discussions of entries back and forth, with sometimes strong disagreements. Then you have somebody call for a vote, and hands are raised, and a majority wins. And there aren't any breaks between discussing and voting. It can't be wink-wink, nod-nod, you vote for mine and I'll vote for yours. A lot of us care very deeply about [the Pulitzer board's] power to confirm what is best about journalism, and in order to do that it does have to be a good process."

Jurors and board members concede that their peers sometimes seem overly cautious about selecting cutting-edge types of stories as winners, tending to favor familiar formats in selecting the Pulitzers. "Journalism is exceedingly conservative about itself as a profession, and when the prize selection process is done by people who are at the top of the profession, it isn't surprising that they are also conservative about the winners they pick," says former *Tribune* editor Fuller. He cites the Feature Writing category as a case in which certain models are accepted and others rejected. "When was the last time you saw something win that was uproariously funny?" he asks. "Winning entries make you want to slit your wrists. They tend to cause excruciating pain."

Another frequent criticism of the Pulitzer system is that it can be "gamed" by editors who know what the Pulitzer board wants. Designing their coverage from conception to layout to fit a certain "Pulitzer mold," it is thought, these editors may be able to build up enough public service to win over the board.

David Shaw's 1984 study of the Pulitzers examined whether certain editors have discovered Pulitzer-winning shortcuts, citing the prize-winning record of Gene Roberts's *Inquirer* in the 1970s and 1980s. A fellow editor and board member at the time, the *Boston Globe's* Thomas Winship, defended the *Inquirer* and the board. "Any story good enough to be considered for a Pulitzer is a good story by any standards," Winship said. "Hell, I've never known a guy who had a better instinct for what will win prizes than Gene Roberts. But his [prize-winning] stories were all good, important, valuable, well-played. . . . What's wrong with that?"

A later *Inquirer* editor, Amanda Bennett, who joined the board in 2002, believes that trying too hard to match coverage with some abstract Pulitzer Prize model hurts a project more than it helps. "Mostly, I find that it creates a brittle, glass-like operation, where you're second-guessing yourself," she says. She recalls one experience in which she did work with someone who was dying to win a Pulitzer. The person, she says, lost sight of the story in the process of researching and writing it. As an editor, says Bennett, "I tell people that we're writing stories that are good enough to win the Pulitzer, but that you're not trying to do that."

The Pulitzers will always be open to criticism. But Ben Bradlee, for one, has mellowed in the decade since his book came out. His *Post* has been a consistent winner, and in 2000 became the only paper with back-to-back Public Service Medals. "I'm totally two-faced about the Pulitzers, and I admit it, because society is impressed by them," says Bradlee, who maintains an office just down the hall from publisher Donald Graham. "Owners love them, too. Katharine Graham loved them, and Don loves them, but he pretends he doesn't."

Part Four

Challenges for a New Era

CHAPTER 18

Everybody's Business

"How shameful it is for the Knight family and its organ, The [Charlotte] Observer, to take the side of OSHA and the opressive bureaucrats against the magnificent Southern textile industry. It is sickening to see the gutless minions of the news media siding with a few crybaby Americans who obviously are looking for a handout from the very hand that fed and clothed their families.

—W. B. Pitts, president, Hermitage Inc., Camden, South Carolina

*B*usiness and technology were on the mind of every reporter and editor in the 1980s, if only because computers were taking over their newsrooms. The machines on their desks started carrying names like IBM or Apple rather than Remington, Royal, or Underwood. The once-incessant clacking of typewriter keys—used in the movie version of *All the President's Men* to suggest machine-gun-like media firepower—did, in fact, cease. The muted tapping that replaced it reminded journalists of the sound of calculators. Overnight, the newsroom turned as quiet as an insurance office.

The lack of clamor was deceptive. Reporters were still inspired to pursue investigations in the spirit of Watergate. The best newspapers remained both vigilant and aggressive, and increasingly they created either formal or informal teams to pursue major projects. Reporters also added computer-assisted reporting to their arsenal. When the *Anchorage Daily News* won its second Gold Medal in 1989, Howard Weaver—by then the managing editor—was using a Macintosh to crunch statistical data that illustrated the plight of native Alaskans. The computer also helped coordinate assignments and deadlines for his far-flung staffers. Compare that to the system used to plot out its 1976 series on the Teamsters. "We drew flow charts with colored pencils to show inter-relationships amongst people," says Weaver.

Public Service Prize—winning stories delved into a range of topics in the decade. Two were religion stories, two looked closely at ethnic groups, and two involved the armed services. Reporters especially dug into what they called the business angle of the stories. But these were not the classic General Motors, Xerox, or Microsoft articles from the financial pages. Rather, newspapers explored the corporation's role in environmental affairs and the military-industrial complex, and even delved into the finances of churches.

The classic government corruption stories of city hall graft or malfeasance in the statehouse faded from the list of winners. But federal agencies and the military came in for plenty of questioning, as did various jurisdictions implicated in damaging the health and welfare of Americans.

In 1985 the Pulitzer board expanded the number of journalism categories to fourteen, essentially creating the award lineup that would take the Pulitzers into the new century. Two divisions described the changing way newspapers were approaching their projects: Explanatory Reporting and Feature Writing. Another area, Specialized Reporting, would be called Beat Reporting in 1991. Editorial Writing and Public Service remained the granddaddies of the Pulitzer journalism awards.

Two Cheers for Charlotte

Knight Ridder's *Charlotte Observer* had a pair of Pulitzer winners in the 1980s. In 1980 the *Observer*'s staff became intrigued with health issues in the giant Carolina textile industry. Factory workers intimately knew the plague of nearly invisible cotton dust that led to an asthmalike condition known as byssinosis, or "brown lung." But government, industry, and even medical professionals seemed to ignore the problem. The idea for the *Observer*'s stories actually originated with the textile workers' union, a source that editor Richard Oppel viewed suspiciously. "In a way this was the wine from poisonous fruit, because the union had an ax to grind," he says. "But I'm a believer that you don't discount information as long as it's verified. A fact is a fact, wherever you get it from."

Over months of investigation, a team of reporters, led by veterans Howard Covington and Marion Ellis, studied the potential dangers of cotton dust. Medical reporter Bob Conn and Robert L. Drogin also participated, along with Washington correspondent Robert Hodierne. Deep into the research, they remained stumped because of the lack of a proved link between the dust and various established ailments. But state government regulations were designed to limit exposure to the dust, and inspections were not being performed as required. That much was clear.

The paper was able to document obvious cases of workers affected by exposure to cotton dust, and the *Observer* used photographs extensively to illustrate their plight. "The pictures showed men who looked like they were ninety years old, but who were forty-five years old," Oppel says. Sometimes these victims had to rely on oxygen tanks. The *Observer*'s eight-part series started on February 3, 1980, and was called "Brown Lung: A Case of Deadly Neglect." It contained twenty-two articles and eight editorials.

The outcry from industry was loud and long. The letter from a textile company president quoted at the beginning of this chapter, and submitted by "gutless minion" Rich Oppel as part of the paper's Pulitzer Prize entry, suggests the level of outrage the series provoked within certain segments of the community. The first story began, "Cotton dust—an invisible product of the most important industry in the Carolinas—is killing people."

After the series, the North Carolina labor commissioner received funding to hire and equip staff members for inspections, and the state industrial commission added deputy commissioners to speed compensation decisions. The governor also ordered changes in the way compensation was granted.

By the end of 1980, $4 million in workers compensation for byssinosis was paid out, more than the total paid in the previous nine-year history of the program. Impressed, the Pulitzer board awarded the *Observer* the 1981 Gold Medal.

The controversy did not subside, however. Medical authorities remained divided about whether byssinosis was a legitimate disease. The Pulitzer Prize archives at Columbia contain a letter from a Duke University epidemiologist who compared the *Observer*'s Pulitzer to the one awarded the same year for "Jimmy's World," a story written by Janet Cooke of the *Washington Post* that later was discovered to be fraudulent. "It was unfortunate that a respectable paper would report in such a biased fashion on a disease whose existence is questioned by many medical authorities," the Duke doctor wrote, adding that "the emotional overload in this series with its unequivocal anti-industry statements did not serve any useful purpose."

While the *Post* had surrendered Cooke's Prize, both the *Observer* and the Pulitzer board stood by the Gold Medal for the Charlotte paper. Today, byssinosis is generally recognized as an industrial health hazard, although government controls—and the migration of the textile industry abroad—has made it much less prevalent in the United States.

1981— *Charlotte Observer:* **For its series on "Brown Lung: A Case of Deadly Neglect."**

When "Enough Isn't Enough"

The *Observer* had been exploring another local business: Jim and Tammy Faye Bakker's PTL television ministry, whose name was an acronym for both Praise The Lord and People That Love. Tipsters were plentiful, but as a private company PTL yielded little by way of a paper trail to be followed. *Observer* stories stretching back to 1976 had raised more questions than they answered. Still, the coverage stirred the anger of the Bakkers and their PTL supporters. Already PTL was claiming, sometimes on the air, that the paper had a "vendetta" against it. As more unconfirmed reports of abuses at PTL streamed in to reporters, however, the *Observer* kept a close eye on the situation. The hard, verifiable evidence of malfeasance that the paper needed did not come its way for years.

In December 1984, the *Observer*'s suspicions about Jim Bakker and PTL intensified when former church secretary Jessica Hahn called reporter Charles E. Shepard to talk about having been sexually assaulted by Bakker four years earlier in a Florida hotel room. Shepard, hired by editor Oppel in 1980, was not that interested in the report of a possible sex offense, which would be very difficult to prove. Rather, he wanted to pursue the possibility that church money was used to hush her up. And he was especially driven to find that out after Hahn called him three weeks later and retracted everything that she had told him. "She threatened to sue [the paper] if anything was printed," Shepard wrote later. Eventually, he learned why. After one of Hahn's representatives had threatened PTL with a lawsuit, the organization had offered her money to keep quiet.

Shepard got information in late 1985 confirming that Hahn was paid off with church funds. "What had seemed merely an episode in the private life of a public figure had become a story about misuse of donors' dollars—the very kind of news the *Observer* had pursued at PTL since the late 1970s," according to Shepard.

The paper, however, set strict standards for sourcing any stories that alleged improper sexual conduct. "The sex lives of public people are not necessarily news unless and until we can establish that it affects their institutions," says Oppel. Any story about PTL would have to show solid evidence of payoffs. And Shepard's information did not qualify, yet. His source for the payoff allegation had demanded confidentiality, and Shepard could not corroborate the information. Shepard's later account of the reporting noted that Oppel insisted on for-the-record confirmation and documentary proof of any payoff before it could be mentioned in an article. "That seemed impossible," wrote Shepard. "PTL had structured the Hahn settlement to avoid a paper trail and seal the lips of those involved."

In January 1986, the *Observer* got a good lead about a separate problem facing PTL. Based on documents obtained through a Freedom of Information Act request, the paper was able to write stories describing a Federal Communications Commission investigation into PTL's over-the-air fund-raising.

Bakker's war with the paper escalated. The televangelist launched a crusade against the *Observer* on his nationally syndicated weekday program with the theme: "Enough Is Enough." According to Shepard, "He sought to intimidate the newspaper and its parent chain, Knight Ridder, with appeals to his supporters to cancel subscriptions, pull ads and deluge his adversary with letters and phone calls. He hired private detectives to investigate the newspaper's publisher, editor and reporters and former coworkers he suspected were aiding the newspaper." Reports of subscription cancellations came to Oppel from as far away as the *San Jose Mercury News.*

By the spring of 1986, Bakker had reason to think his intimidation strategy was working. Even the *Observer's* publisher, Rolfe Neill, thought the paper was being unfair to the Bakkers. "He felt we were picking the institution apart in a slow death," says Oppel. Shepard knew better, but proof remained elusive. Oppel allowed him one more try to get corroboration for the information that Hahn had been paid off to keep quiet. "I went back to the phone," according to Shepard's account. By March 13 he had gotten a copy of a February 1985 check for $115,000 written by PTL's lawyer and an on-the-record confirmation from a Hahn representative. Soon, even publisher Neill had to agree that the reporting had reached critical mass. "He was behind us at that point," says Oppel.

As Shepard prepared his *Observer* story, managing editor Mark Ethridge III got a call from a lawyer for PTL threatening legal action if the paper published the story, and demanding that Bakker and his number-two man, Richard Dortch, be interviewed. The *Observer's* past requests for interviews with Bakker all had been rejected. But now, the story had to be delayed until the interviews could take place. In the meantime, Shepard learned that the church itself had begun an investigation based on the *Observer's* inquiries. Before the paper could run its story on the payoff or the sexual encounter that had precipitated it, Bakker resigned in what the paper called "a pre-emptive strike."

Then Shepard's exclusives started: about a $265,000 payoff to Hahn, with church funds laundered through a building contractor; about Dortch being the one who negotiated the Hahn settlement; and about how Jim and Tammy Bakker had received more than $1.6 million in pay for 1986.

Dortch was fired by a new PTL board. Televangelist Jerry Falwell, who took over as board chairman, complimented the *Observer's* coverage and spoke of PTL's "fiscal sins" of the past. And the 1988 Gold Medal—the paper's second of the decade—was awarded to the *Observer.* The medals were installed in a glass enclosure on a pedestal that visitors pass when they walk through the paper's lobby.

1988—Charlotte Observer: For revealing misuse of funds by the PTL television ministry through persistent coverage conducted in the face of a massive campaign by PTL to discredit the newspaper.

❧

A Sailor Dies, the Navy Lies

The *Detroit News* in 1981, like the *Lufkin News* in Texas five years before, wanted to help the family of a deceased local military man who had died under mysterious circumstances. And the paper accomplished much the same result: its exposure of a cover-up of the true story of the death led to a change in procedures by the military, and the winning of a Public Service Pulitzer Prize for the newspaper.

The paper assigned reporter Sydney P. Freedberg, a second-year *Detroit News* staffer just a few years out of Radcliffe College, to do a piece on the death of Paul Trerice, who had enlisted in the U.S. Navy. The Navy had told Trerice's family that he had died in an unfortunate accident while being disciplined aboard the carrier *USS Ranger* in the Pacific. The rival *Detroit Free Press* did the first story on the incident, but Freedberg and assistant news editor David Ashenfelter saw more to the case. The family did not believe the Navy's story. The two journalists set out to find the truth.

The little Lufkin paper, part of the Cox chain, had been handicapped by its small budget in its attempt to look beyond the basic wire-service obituary that had landed on its news desk. In fact, it had done most of its Pulitzer Prize–winning work by phone, without reporter Ken Herman or editor Joe Murray ever leaving town. The *Detroit News* had fewer constraints.

Freedberg traveled to San Diego to interview witnesses. It was, in fact, one of her first out-of-town assignments for the paper. From those who were with Trerice on the *Ranger*, she and Ashenfelter assembled a picture that showed the sailor had died of heat stroke and a heart attack brought on by the mental and physical torment inflicted while he was being punished for a minor rule infraction. It was not the "accident" that the Navy had described. Then, the reporters went further.

They wanted to determine if the deceptive notification that the Michigan family received was part of a pattern. Freedberg and Ashenfelter eventually found that the military routinely deceived families to protect itself from embarrassment and possible liability. The two reporters worked with editor Janet Mandelstam on sixty stories that analyzed six specific cases. One case involved another *Ranger* crewman whose Oklahoma next-of-kin had been told he fell overboard and drowned during operations. The truth was that he, too, was in detention as punishment, and had gone off the deck while being hazed. "The Navy's initial lies were an effort to shield grieving families from the anguish that the gory details might cause," says Freedberg. "It started out as a humane policy." But the deception had gotten out of hand.

The *Detroit News* was strongly pro-military and Republican, and the Navy and some readers were critical of the reporters' campaign. Eventually, though, resistance from the military petered out, and the service itself conceded that it had "apparently mishandled" each of the six cases examined by the *News*. It ordered reforms in Navy procedures.

While the paper had submitted the work in the Local Investigative Specialized Reporting category, the board moved the entry to Public Service. Two other finalists that year involved industry-related exclusives: the *Providence Journal-Bulletin's* exposure of hazardous working conditions in Rhode Island's jewelry industry and the *Los Angeles Herald-Examiner's* study of exploitation of undocumented workers in that city's garment business.

1982—*Detroit News:* For a series by Sydney P. Freedberg and David Ashenfelter that exposed the U.S. Navy's cover-up of circumstances surrounding the deaths of seamen aboard ship and which led to significant reforms in naval procedures.

On Being Latino in L.A.

In 1984 the *Los Angeles Times* won a Pulitzer for a twenty-seven-part series on the Latino experience in southern California. The Pulitzer board cited the series as "enhancing understanding among the non-Latino majority of a community often perceived as mysterious and even threatening." Seventeen Latino reporters, editors, and photographers—including eleven writers—had been assigned to the project under editors George Ramos and Frank Sotomayor. They interviewed one thousand people and polled nearly fifteen hundred in a survey covering social, cultural, and political issues.

"Most impressive of all," the jurors said, "is the fact that The Times was able to field a task force composed entirely of Latino editors and reporters to provide a unique view of one of America's most important emerging ethnic groups."

By most accounts the series got its start after a number of Latino reporters brought an idea to Bill Thomas, who was promoted from Metro editor to editor in 1971. But Thomas says the actual genesis was more than a year earlier, with what had become known as the "marauder" series. Thomas had the idea for that earlier series after he noted the frequency of burglaries in Santa Barbara and other areas far from Los Angeles, committed by young black men from south Los Angeles. The burglars planned road trips—marauding expeditions—to find their wealthy targets, then returned with their loot. It became a way of life for them.

Thomas suggested an ancient historical connection to explain why this was occurring, and he had reporters put it to the test. "I'd read in the past about the growth of an underclass that became permanent around the time of the Crusades," he says. Then, too, deprived youths had begun criminal marauding all over Europe. The paper rented a house in the Watts area to serve as a base and began collecting information from members of this marauding class—learning how they lived, where they stashed their dope, and where they hid their guns, for example. In interviews, black youths talked freely about their lives of crime. "They were totally candid," says Thomas. They were asked, "Aren't you afraid of going to jail?" And their answer was, "Look around here; is jail any worse than this?"

When the series was completed, according to the editor, "naturally there was an uproar, but nobody challenged our conclusions, or any of its descriptions." One East Coast editor said to Thomas, "Geez, that was a wonderful series, but how in hell did you get away with it?"

Black members of the *Times* staff were distraught, Thomas recalls, and at one meeting with him they made their case. "Bill, this is all true, but did you have to use that word, marauder?" they asked. "You don't know what it's like to have to run into this as a black American—and to have to answer to people who read the series." Says Thomas, "I got to thinking, 'That's true.' I have no idea what it's like as a black person, to have to run into this stuff. And so we did a series on what it's really like to live here as a black person."

The View from the Editor's Desk

The marauder series was never entered for a Pulitzer Prize, although Thomas thinks of it as among the paper's best work during his long tenure. He withheld it from consideration, he says, "because it had already caused enough grief and divisiveness among the black members of my staff. I thought that if I entered it, it would just exacerbate things."

The series on the black experience in Los Angeles was different, though. Thomas and the black staff members were proud of it, seeing the work as a contribution to community understanding. The editor submitted the series for a Pulitzer. "But it didn't go anywhere," he says. "I guess black had been written about so much."

Then the Latino staffers proposed their 1983 series. "They said, 'We did it with blacks, why don't we do it with Latinos?'" according to Thomas. "It was a good scrics," he says, sounding more reserved than about the two earlier ones. As an editor who had observed East Coast Pulitzer board members dominate the prize-giving over the years, though, he suspects that the Latino story may have gotten a better reception because "people in the East had less experience with Latinos; it was new to them."

The thought pattern behind the *Times*'s coverage of ethnic affairs reflected a whole new perspective Thomas gained when he first took over as editor thirteen years earlier. It was a time of somber review for him. "I did a lot of rethinking about a lot of things. You see the world a little differently," he says. "I was thrown into close association with all these heads of businesses, some of whom believed that they were not getting a fair hearing from the paper at a time when activist voices had the ear of reporters." Although Thomas privately was a liberal Democrat, he paid close attention to executives' objections about media biases. Did reporters, for example, really think that "developer is a dirty word?" He began giving more thought to the underpinning of business stories as a result, and out of fairness, he gave *Times* business investigations a higher bar to jump. "Fairness," says Thomas, "became an obsession."

He also reviewed some past editorial decisions—including his own leadership of journalists through the city-government series that won the 1969 Public Service Medal. He wondered, he says, "Did we have enough goods on these guys to do what we did?" Thinking back on it, from the perspective of his new post, it seemed to him that he had used the power of his newspaper too bluntly in trying to keep prosecutors from dragging their feet. "Probably, I had pressured that D.A. so hard that he had to act, because he feared the newspaper," Thomas says now.

Of the two other finalists that the board identified in Public Service in 1984, one involved business: a *Detroit Free Press* series called "Safety in the Slow Lane," exposing auto industry failures in protecting the public from defective cars. The other finalist, the *Fayetteville Times* in Arkansas, looked at weaknesses in the criminal justice system.

1984—*Los Angeles Times:* For an in-depth examination of southern California's growing Latino community by a team of editors and reporters.

A Survivor Seals the Story

The military correspondent for the *Fort Worth Star-Telegram,* Washington-based Mark J. Thompson, was doing his basic "beat reading" when he first came upon a piece in the trade newsletter *Helicopter News.* A problem called mast bumping, it said, had caused some accidents involving Huey troop-carrying and Cobra attack helicopters, then the backbone of Bell Helicopter's business.

Even from the short newsletter story, it was clear that this was a pilot's nightmare. Under certain operating situations the rotor could tilt too far and strike the mast that attaches the blades to the aircraft, causing the mast to snap "and turning the chopper into a coffin for all aboard," as Thompson puts it. But the position of Bell, which built the aircraft in Fort Worth, was clear: the company was blameless. "If this bizarre snafu occurred, it would be either weather, pilot error, or something else that had already gone wrong that had doomed the flight," Thompson was told by Bell representatives. "Their basic line was so long as the pilot was smart, it wouldn't happen."

Having covered aircraft accidents before for the "Startle-Gram," as staffers called the then–Capital Cities publication (it is now owned by McClatchy,) he was familiar with the pilot-error explanation. F-16 fighter planes, also built in Fort Worth, had gone down a number of times, and the reporter had written about how pilots often put themselves in untenable positions in the hot fighter. He thought that the helicopter cases were probably similar, as Bell suggested, but he still began checking out the accident reports.

While the newsletter had mentioned that a single pilot had survived a mast-bumping crash, the pilot wasn't identified. Thompson wanted to talk to him about the Cobra's safety. "I remember spending some period of time tracking him down," says Thompson. Tapping his Pentagon sources for the search, he finally located the pilot at Patuxent River Naval Air Station in Maryland. "I said to myself, Gosh, if he concedes that he did something wrong, that wouldn't be much of a story."

Instead, the interview would become seared in Mark Thompson's memory. Larry Higgins was flying with his copilot, who had been killed instantly when the rotor blade sliced through the cockpit. "He spoke very levelly. It wasn't quite a monotone," according to the reporter. "He knew what he wanted to say. He wanted me to understand that there was nothing goofy that day. They were test pilots, wearing parachutes and ready for any eventuality, they thought."

As Higgins started describing the accident, though, his answers became more halting. "It wasn't until I got to the third or fourth order of questions, where I showed him that I knew what was going on there—and that Bell had said that he must have flown outside the envelope—that he began to get angry," says Thompson. Higgins shot back at him: "You're damn right the helicopter ended up outside the envelope. The rotor isn't supposed to come through the cockpit."

Thompson was stunned. For the story, which would take several months to report completely, "that was, to my mind, really the starting gun." Next came Freedom of Information Act requests, and a raft of accident reports and other documents filled in the scope of the problem.

One other interview, with engineer Tom White at Fort Belvoir in Virginia, had an unpromising start. "Can you tell me about these accidents?" Thompson asked. "No, I can't," White responded. "Well, what if I sent an FOIA?" the reporter followed up. White hesitated. "I've been waiting years for somebody to ask *that,"* he responded. Suddenly, Thompson knew he was about to get a wealth of valuable new documents. "White, it turned out, was an early and ardent advocate of the hub spring, a $5,000 modification that would have corrected the helicopter's problems."

Thompson's five-part series, titled "Deadly Blades," was edited by Roland Lindsey at the *Star-Telegram.* On Sunday, March 25, the first installment was headlined "Design Flaw Mars Bell Military Helicopters." It began:

> WASHINGTON—Nearly 250 U.S. servicemen have been killed since 1967 aboard Bell helicopters that crashed because of a design flaw that remains largely uncorrected even though the Army discovered it in 1973, according to military documents and former Pentagon safety experts.
>
> A top lawyer at Bell Helicopter of Fort Worth acknowledged the seriousness of the matter in 1979 when he urged the company to fix the problem even if it had to spend its own money to do so.
>
> "I consider this matter very serious and, if we do nothing about it, very likely to be the subject of attempts at punitive damages," George Galerstein, Bell's chief legal counsel, told company management in a 1979 internal memo.
>
> Galerstein's prediction has since come true—families of five pilots killed since 1980 in crashes attributed to the design problem have filed suits seeking nearly a quarter of a billion dollars from Bell.

The death toll from the mast-bumping problem might be even higher, the article said: "It could not be determined how many helicopter accidents during the Vietnam War, during which Cobras and Hueys were extensively used, may have been caused by mast bumping." Bell did try to get the military to make changes, but at the military's expense.

Executive editor Jack B. Tinsley's Pulitzer nomination letter noted that "the Army assembled a blue-ribbon panel to investigate the questions raised by the series," finding that the paper's account had been accurate. The Army then took steps to correct the problem.

"The reaction by Bell and its almost 6,000 area employees has been less positive," Tinsley wrote. "While the series was running, Bell sent a letter to Star-

Telegram publisher Phil Meek demanding that the newspaper remove its news racks from Bell property and apologize for the black eye it had given the company." The company asked retail outlets around its plant to refuse to do business with *Star-Telegram* employees, and union representatives launched a drive that resulted in the paper losing about thirteen hundred subscribers. But the story resulted in the 1985 Gold Medal, the *Star-Telegram's* first, and Thompson was named in the citation.

Thompson, who later moved to Knight Ridder Newspapers, and then to *Time* magazine, continued to cover defense-related scandals after the Bell reports. "The military," he says, "is the gift that keeps on giving for reporters."

1985—*Fort Worth Star-Telegram:* For reporting by Mark J. Thompson which revealed that nearly 250 U.S. servicemen had lost their lives as a result of a design problem in helicopters built by Bell Helicopter—a revelation which ultimately led the Army to ground almost six hundred Huey helicopters pending their modification.

⸿

Flying High

An aviation story of another kind led to the 1987 Public Service Prize. *Pittsburgh Press* public health reporter Andrew Schneider had been teamed with Mary Pat Flaherty the previous year on a project exploring the nation's organ transplantation system, which had earned them the 1986 Pulitzer in Specialized Reporting. In early September 1986, Schneider got a tip that set him on a new course, with new teammates.

On a reporting trip in Florida, he received a call from a physician friend with an almost unbelievable tale: A seriously drug-overdosed patient had arrived at Pittsburgh's Mercy Hospital, near death, but then had been whisked out of intensive-care prematurely. Schneider's friend suspected that the individual removing the patient might have been a pusher. Whoever it was, though, had made a peculiar argument to spring the patient: that he had to leave the hospital immediately to get back to work—flying for US Airways.

Confidentiality rules prevented the hospital from notifying the airline or the Federal Aviation Administration about the pilot's drug problem. So this doctor had called his reporter friend instead, hoping somehow to publicize the situation.

Once back in Pittsburgh, Schneider began looking into the pilot's past, including his medical record. "He had track marks every conceivable place he could have them. So this had to go back years," says the reporter, now at the *Baltimore*

Sun. "It raised the question, 'How could he pass his medical exams?'" The FAA requires examinations of pilots every six months.

Schneider's first story, on September 21, examined the USAir pilot's case. Follow-up articles looked at the rules preventing airlines and the FAA from getting reports about impaired pilots and at flaws in the system of physicals. He interviewed the examiner for the overdosed pilot, and was told an unconvincing story. The doctor had not suspected any drug use, he told Schneider.

The reporter found that in many cases pilot physicals were a troubling joke in the aviation business. "The so-called $50 exam meant that you held the 50-dollar bill out, and if you could see it, the doctor took the fifty from you and you passed," he says. Passing cleared the pilot to continue flying. The national press began picking up Schneider's stories.

Later that month the reporter got a call from a federal-government source who had been reading the articles. "He said, 'You have to come meet some friends of mine.'" It sounded urgent, so Schneider flew to Washington, where a group had congregated with the source in the back room of a Japanese restaurant in Georgetown. Schneider did not know them, or what to expect. "They looked as uncomfortable as whores in church. They were just very, very nervous," he says. Then his government friend introduced them—officials from most of the country's largest airlines, each of whom had serious concerns about pilot medical reporting. They could talk to him only off-the-record, but what they said was chilling.

All had numerous pilots at their airlines who were too sick to fly—heart problems were a typical problem, along with drug dependency—and who easily could become incapacitated while flying, which would create a serious hazard to the public. But for various reasons, mostly union agreements, pilots could not be grounded if the FAA said they could fly, the reporter was told.

Schneider told the airline representatives that there was no way he could do an investigation without pilots' names, but assured them that any names provided would be kept in confidence. With their help, Schneider compiled a list of nearly three hundred allegedly impaired pilots.

In spot stories that ran through December 21, Schneider and his reporting teammate on a number of stories, general assignment staffer Matt Brelis, followed leads that presented a picture of a dangerously faulty system. The FAA had been created to protect the flying public, not to make life easy for addicted or medically impaired pilots, but the stories suggested that safety was coming last.

In an arrangement that reflected the power of the pilots' lobby in Washington, the FAA refused to compare names of licensed pilots with easily available registry lists showing motorists with license revocations for substance abuse, for example.

Even when the FAA did learn of criminal abuse-related behavior by pilots, the agency "closed its eyes," according to the *Pittsburgh Press* reports.

The federal air surgeon, Dr. Frank Austin, frequently overruled those few warnings about pilot ailments that made it on the record. That kept impaired pilots flying, as well. In an interview with the *Press,* Austin, a former Navy carrier pilot, defended the pilot's right to fly, and said that in many cases that right had overridden medical information he had been given about individual pilots.

The *Press* also investigated a Catch-22 in the FAA medical regulations. The rules required pilots who *were* found using drugs to be permanently grounded, without any provision for rehabilitation. With their careers at stake, those pilots who sought treatment in good faith were forced to visit clinics secretly, without reporting it. Some of the private clinics were not medically sound.

Schneider had a vital third team member, photographer Vincent Musi. Says Schneider, a number of the *Press*'s stories could only have been prepared with the sourcing and reporting efforts of Musi. The photographer, for example, helped Schneider explore the airport inspection system that allowed pilots with drug problems to bring drugs into the country freely and move them around with them. Musi also succeeded in finding clandestine drug treatment centers across the country and convincing several pilots undergoing treatment to discuss their problems.

The reporters and Musi traveled around the United States for four months, conducting interviews with more than a hundred aviation medical examiners, some of whom told them that because of the way pilot physicals were designed—without even urine or blood tests required—drug or alcohol abuse was almost never detected.

Among the reforms that resulted from the *Press* articles were the removal of Dr. Austin from his post, the installation of provisions for cross-checking pilots and drivers' registry lists, and a tightening of FAA medical-exam requirements.

When it came time for the *Press* to enter the Pulitzer competition, Schneider says he argued that Musi was a photojournalist in the truest sense, and his name should be included in the submission. The head of the paper's photo department, though, called the suggestion silly, and the editorial brass bowed to that opinion.

One Public Service finalist, the *Fort Lauderdale News and Sun-Sentinel,* also had a medical theme, examining serious mishaps in the system of Veterans Hospitals. The other, the *El Paso Herald-Post,* was cited for promoting literacy through community events.

1987—*Pittsburgh Press:* For reporting by Andrew Schneider and Matthew Brelis which revealed the inadequacy of the FAA's medical screening of airline pilots and led to significant reforms.

⸰⸰⸰

"A People in Peril"

A more confident *Anchorage Daily News* staff, grown to eighty people in the years since it had won the 1976 Public Service Prize, took on a daunting social issue as the 1980s ended: explaining and helping to ease the rampant alcoholism and suicide among native Alaskans.

Howard Weaver had become managing editor since his work with Bob Porterfield on the Teamster series. "We were older and smarter," says Weaver of his paper. "And there was that Pulitzer Gold Medal on the wall. That amplifies your voice, which is a wonderful consequence." In addition, the investigative culture that previous owner Kay Fanning had nurtured did not suffer when the paper was purchased by the McClatchy chain. Indeed, investigations became even more important.

Weaver cites several factors that led to the native Alaskan project. His wife, Barbara Hodgin, a specialist for the state department of community and regional affairs, routinely brought home tales of despair and suicide from her travels to remote towns. And one day, *Daily News* staffer Mike Doogan suggested that Weaver read the obituaries from the state's remote parts. There was a pattern there, Doogan said.

Years before, the paper had done a project on native Alaskans. Weaver read it over again. "It was a pretty good series, but it wasn't definitive and it wasn't consequential," he says. As the reporting began, he felt personally challenged to do better. "We had swung at this ball and missed once before, so I was not sure we were going to get it," he says. "But I *was* sure we were going to give it our absolute best effort before we stopped." (Actually, the earlier story had been among the Public Service jury's top picks for 1968, although the *Daily News* did not know that. Only the winner was announced: California's *Riverside Press-Enterprise,* for its own series on native Americans. It had studied Agua Caliente tribe members, whose rich Palm Springs landholdings were the subject of abuse by the legal system.)

The first step in this new effort was to use the Macintosh to create a database from all the press releases that Alaska state troopers had issued about rural deaths in recent years. The reporters analyzed how many were accidental, or alcohol-related, or suicides. While it was a simple idea, no one had ever compiled that data before, says Weaver, who then sent reporter Richard Mauer on a one-month assignment to scout out the situation. Mauer came back and composed a note.

"I can remember the first words of the memo to this day," says Weaver. "'However bad you think this is, it's worse.' This set the stage for a report that would be very ambitious."

There were many challenges. One stemmed from the nature of the perils themselves: alcohol and suicide. "Those are subjects about which people are always in complete denial, whether it's in Manhattan, New York, or Manhattan, Kansas, or in Alaska," Weaver says. "Then we had the additional complication that this was about mainly brown rural people, being written about by a mainly white urban newspaper."

The *Daily News* still thought of itself as a hometown small fry among American newspapers, even with its Gold Medal on the wall. But in the hamlets where it would be reporting, the paper might as well have been the *New York Times* or *Chicago Tribune*. "There would be this sense of a big-city paper—big-city by Alaska terms—ragging on Alaskan Native people," Weaver thought. "You don't have to be a genius to know that's got some pitfalls. Yet we had to get over that because otherwise, our voice would be obscured, and nobody would listen."

Reporter Maurer's observations set the tone for the initial reporting, which eventually would grow into a project for about thirty staffers. "We began to see some patterns: that it was mainly younger people; that there was alcohol involved; there was a lot of violent death, either accidental or suicidal. So we began to get the dimensions of it," Weaver says. Work went on for nine months. "At every stage of the project we were more and more overwhelmed by how important it was. That knowledge increased our desire to do it justice, and so the project expanded on its own significance."

One statistic took on a special, devastating meaning. An Alaskan native boy had about a 250 times greater chance of committing suicide than a similar boy living elsewhere in the United States.

"The Best Snow-Machine Driver in the Village"

The plan was to begin publishing in November, about seven months after the reporting had started. "And then we looked at it and we said, 'We're not done yet,'" recalls Weaver, who took the title of editor during the project, while Pat Dougherty moved to managing editor. As important as the story was, the editors couldn't publish it until they had given it their best effort. In another month the series would collide with Christmas, so the decision was to put it off until late January 1988 to get it the attention it deserved.

The staff set tough rules for itself, including no anonymous sources in the final story. Anonymity was granted in the groundwork phase. "But we knew for the story that wouldn't work. People needed to know this was 'Henry Isaaks from Shaktulak.' And he says this and stands behind it," according to the editor. "The enormous bravery of some of the people who told their stories and shared their experiences was breathtaking."

The reporting itself began to dictate the organization of the series. "We figured out that, for example, there was one village that emerged as the worst case: a village of a few hundred people that had more than a dozen young people kill themselves in a short period of time. We called it Eskimo Armageddon." Reporter Sheila Toomey lived for three weeks in the dysfunctional little town, Alakanuk. In the first of the stories, Toomey wrote:

> In a community of 550, every name on the roll of the dead is someone you know: Louie Edmund, 22; Melvin Tony, 23; Steven Kameroff, 19; Jerry Augline, 21; Karen George, 17; Benjamin Edmund, 21, Timothy Stanislaus, 25; Albert Harry, 29.
>
> "I never went through this before," said Louie's mother, Adeline Edmund, who lost two sons before it was over. "My whole body hurt. . . . I never did get mad at God (before) but I find myself getting mad at Him."
>
> Alakanuk had known many unnatural deaths, yes. Too many. From violence and recklessness, on land and on the river. Most of the victims were drunk when they died.

The stories in the series told of dashed dreams and disappointments. But there was also nobility. In a technique eerily predictive of the "Portraits of Grief" that the *New York Times* would design after the September 11 tragedy, the Anchorage paper prepared full pages of personal notices about native Alaskans who had died in recent years, but whose deaths received no news coverage. "Perhaps they'd just been found in an alley, or they were in a remote village," says Weaver. As would happen in New York in 2001, staffers volunteered to write them, often working overtime to make them special.

"We were worried because we were going back to people and saying, 'Your son Michael died of alcohol poisoning four years ago, and we want to reopen that,'" the editor says. "Instead, they'd say things like, 'I didn't get to tell anybody back then, but he was the best snow-machine driver in the village.'" The paper would call the section In Memoriam. "Authenticity and respect and transparency were the keys. This was real. It happened. What are we going to do about it? It was an extraordinary effort," says Weaver.

Come January 1988, it was ready. Photography played a major part, and the paper spent extra time designing the ten days of the series, with its forty-four stories. "We knew a lot more about both visual storytelling and design than we did in '76," says Weaver. Assistant managing editor Mike Campbell managed the design. Columns of white streamed down the sides of the page, with individual voices framed there.

Before the series ran Weaver did something he had rarely done before. He visited native American leaders around the state, described the story, and warned them: "This is going to be ugly."

Most, however, welcomed his preview. "Everybody knew already that we were working on it. You don't go in and interview people in a village without the chief knowing about it," says the editor. But the early word sent a message that the paper was interested in their reactions. "We really neutralized that white-urban-paper-versus-rural-native-people angle."

Not that the story was embraced universally. In one southeastern village that did not want its despair publicized, people hate the *Anchorage Daily News* to this day, according to Weaver. "But the series had resonance everywhere else, because it was so authentic and real."

The paper's work "focused on misery," as he wrote in his introduction on the first day. "It is not a balanced account, contrasting reports of damage with insights from the rich cultural heritage of Alaska Natives." It did, however, end on a positive note, suggesting that a sobriety movement was gaining support and that native spirituality was being employed in the fight against depression.

The paper shipped thirty thousand reprints out into rural areas, about one copy per nine people outside its normal circulation area. The problem continued to haunt the state. But new suicide prevention programs started and the battle against alcohol abuse strengthened. "It used to be a felony to shoot a moose out of season, but a misdemeanor to sell alcohol to a village that was dry," says Weaver. "The legislature fixed that."

The 1989 Pulitzer Public Service jurors identified several other papers for projects aimed at social or economic problems. Two of them—the *Atlanta Constitution*'s exposure of the "redlining" that lenders used to discriminate against black home-buyers, and the *Philadelphia Inquirer*'s explanation of tax loopholes—won Pulitzers in other categories, for the *Constitution*'s Bill Dedman and the *Inquirer*'s Don Barlett and Jim Steele. In voting the Gold Medal for the *Alaska Daily News,* the board agreed with jurors that the Anchorage series "legitimized discussion of a heretofore ignored serious social problem among a neglected and deprived segment of the states' population."

1989—*Anchorage Daily News:* **For reporting about the high incidence of alcoholism and suicide among native Alaskans in a series that focused attention on their despair and resulted in various reforms.**

Fort Worth Star-Telegram reporter Mark Thompson displays a newspaper announcing the 1985 Gold Medal that the paper won for his work disclosing design problems in Bell military helicopters. *Star-Telegram* staff photo. Used by permission.

Los Angeles Times editor William F. Thomas in a staff photo taken about 1986. Used by permission.

Front page of the *Anchorage Daily News* from January 11, 1988, the first day of its "People in Peril" series. Used by permission.

CHAPTER 19

The Nature of Things

... "The Environment Story" is bigger and more important than ever, and it will only grow more so in years to come. [Journalists] recognize professional challenges in cracking the complexity of environmental issues, overcoming the pitfalls of fragmented reporting, and making important concerns more audience friendly.

—From the Strategic Plan of the Society of
Environmental Journalists, founded 1990

Stories dealing with environmental issues and the natural sciences—or, in two cases, nature's fury—dominated Public Service Prize–winners in the 1990s. Still, the business story was here to stay, and much of the coverage that was honored continued to have a corporate flavor. For one thing, reporters examined more closely the environmental approach that industry and governmental agencies took.

On a smaller scale, newspapers were facing up to a problem with their own *internal* environment: office air pollution. As regulations spread from state to state, publishers gradually banned that ancient crutch of deadline writers and editors everywhere: smoking. Suddenly, newsrooms were not only quiet but also cigarette-, cigar-, and pipe-free—an amazing contrast for anyone who had known the smoky news offices of the 1960s or 1970s. Of course, the same rules applied to every business, not just journalism. But the change particularly shocked reporters, many of whom were convinced that nicotine and caffeine were every bit as important as newsprint and ink to getting the paper out each day. (It will be left, perhaps, to the next generation to witness ink and paper vanish as necessary elements of the daily press.)

Somehow, though, newspapers managed to continue turning out great journalism in the twentieth century's last decade, even if the newsroom tab for coffee skyrocketed.

Blood and Water

The 1990 Pulitzer board picked both the mighty *Philadelphia Inquirer* and North Carolina's tiny *Washington Daily News* as Gold Medal winners, the first time in twenty-three years that more than a single Public Service Prize was awarded. One winning story involved the business of water, the other the business of blood. But both had the simplest of origins. For the family-owned *Washington Daily News,* which claimed its first Pulitzer Prize, it started with the editor puzzling over the small print on his residential water bill. For the *Inquirer,* continuing its long string of Pulitzers under Gene Roberts, the genesis was a reporter's pensive moment during a Red Cross blood drive in the office.

In Washington, North Carolina, Bill Coughlin noted a new statement on his water bill. It said that the city was testing for chemicals in the water system. As editor of the 10,500-circulation *Daily News,* he asked one of the paper's four reporters, Betty Gray, to look into it. Her digging turned up forty-two chemicals in the water, each of which she discussed with state and private toxicologists. One chemical, she was told, was a carcinogen far in excess of the Environmental Protection Agency's safe level. She then obtained memos showing that the state environmental agency knew the city's water was contaminated.

Gray built her knowledge to prepare for an interview with the city manager, which came on the morning of Wednesday, September 13. (An afternoon paper, the *Daily News* had a noon deadline.) She learned that the federal act eliminating unsafe drinking water did not cover communities with populations of less than ten thousand, like the *Daily News*'s city of Washington. Actually, it turned out, there were fifty-six thousand water treatment plants in the United States that were unprotected by the EPA.

After a few minutes with the reporter the city manager interrupted the interview, promising to get back to her in time for her deadline. He then rushed to the newspaper with a legal notice that described the town's water as having "levels of certain chemicals which exceeded EPA recommendations." The notice was too late to run, but it became part of Gray's front-page story for that day. Gray later confirmed that the city's knowledge of carcinogens in the water went back eight years, but that there had been no regulations requiring a mayor, city manager, the state, or the EPA to inform the public.

Next Wednesday, the paper ran a report on a second cancer-causing chemical that was combining with the first to increase hazards so severely that the water plant might have to close. As the coverage continued, the mayor complained that the city was in "turmoil" because of the reports and said that the "citizens are ready to hang us." Though he protested to the paper's owner, the stories kept running—and the situation got worse.

Within ten days, in fact, the state told residents not to drink the water, wash dishes with it, or even shower in it. Soon, the U.S. Marines had set up a water distribution network for the city. "The scene was like conditions in some third world country," the editors of the *Daily News* wrote.

Repercussions started locally but spread nationally. In the next month's election, the mayor and most of the city council were defeated by others who made clean water their issue. Stories of other North Carolina communities with tainted water began appearing, and state and federal regulations were changed to prevent a recurrence of the North Carolina situation. The EPA also moved to extend safe-water assurances to small communities. Publisher Ashley Futrell Jr. took special pride in the small paper's ability to prompt changes in federal standards. But it had been a mixed triumph. "When our town suffers, we suffer as well," Futrell said. "We live here."

1990—*Washington* (North Carolina) *Daily News:* For revealing that the city's water supply was contaminated with carcinogens, a problem that the local government had neither disclosed nor corrected over a period of eight years.

"We Don't Have to Tell You That"

Inquirer business reporter Gilbert M. Gaul was donating blood when he had the idea for what he thought might be a "fun little business story" about what happens to the blood after the Red Cross gets it. "I was lying there as the blood was running out of my arm, and it dawned on me that I didn't know a damn thing about what happened to my blood after they took it," says Gaul, now a *Washington Post* reporter in Philadelphia. He suggested a story to business editor Craig Stock, another loyal blood donor, and he liked the idea. Gaul started a file.

Gaul, a five-year *Inquirer* veteran at the time, had made a name for himself at a small but feisty Pennsylvania journal, the *Pottsville Republican*. There, he had been on a team that uncovered the looting by organized crime of the locally based Blue Coal Company. Gaul and reporter Elliot G. Jaspin won the Local Investigative Specialized Reporting Pulitzer in 1979, and Gaul then won a Nieman Fellowship at Harvard. He found himself in great demand among metropolitan dailies, and chose Gene Roberts's *Inquirer*. "It was everything you could possibly want in terms of journalism," he said of his new surroundings. "If you found something promising, you were encouraged to pursue it. It didn't matter where you were or what desk you were on. It didn't matter if you were 23 years old or 55 years old. You would get the time to see whether there was a great story there."

Gaul had started as a beat reporter covering medical economics for the *Inquirer*'s business desk, and his early stories looked at hospitals, doctors, Medicare, and Medicaid. He also wrote some stories about how nonprofit medical corporations worked, first putting him in touch with the not-for-profit American Red Cross, although he didn't think much about it at the time.

Then came blood-drive day in 1988 at the *Inquirer* offices, and reporting his little story. The first step seemed like it should be an interview with the local Red Cross head. Gaul's interview brought him up short. He had just started through a list of routine questions—How much blood is in the bank? What dollar-value do you place on the blood?—when the director stopped him. "Why are you asking these questions? We don't have to tell you that," he said.

"I was taken aback, and my journalistic antennae went up," Gaul recalls. "I came back saying, 'You know, Craig, this is weird. They don't want to cooperate. They say we don't have a right to know anything. They won't even talk about the basic cost of a unit.' And so I began to poke around. I knew a lot of hospital people, and I asked them if I could talk to the blood banks in their hospitals. The lab people told me, 'this is what we have to pay for a unit of red cells, or for platelets.'" As he pieced together a reporting structure, he says, "I approached the story with my framework in business, which is something I still do today. I put together some spreadsheets—this was pre-Excel—and I began to see there were things that you just couldn't answer from the data that was available."

During his early research the Philadelphia area had an emergency blood appeal, which put Gaul on several new trails. He began to look at the ties between blood shortages and supply management, including widespread trading of blood stocks and the ethics of blood-bank administrators. Basic questions sometimes led to deceptive answers. When Gaul asked a local Red Cross doctor to explain the shortage that led to the appeal, he blamed it "on donors not showing up in sufficient numbers. It happened every year following the Christmas–New Year's holiday. . . . Donors just didn't keep their appointments."

According to Gaul, "The answer didn't sit too well with me. I was ready and willing to give blood. Yet no one from the Red Cross had bothered to call or send me a postcard. When I pressed, the doctor acknowledged he didn't know why donors weren't coming. Management had never fully investigated the issue. It occurred to me that were this any other business, the blood bank would be down in the federal bankruptcy court. Instead, management turned to the media and declared an 'Emergency Appeal' for blood, which cost them nothing."

He built his database to include about a hundred blood banks around the United States. He interviewed administrators, noting which centers bought and which sold. Eventually he was able to track half a million pints of blood around the country, watching them change hands several times.

For additional information he turned to Internal Revenue Service Form 990s, tax returns for nonprofit corporations like the Red Cross. He remembers thinking it was particularly interesting that 61 percent of its business was blood, when Gaul had thought its big business was disaster relief.

As a business beat reporter, he kept working on other things. But soon he was making regional and national calls about this intriguing blood business, and some of his findings were startling. "Red cells are really a commodity and they're sold that way," he says. "And there's this whole secret black market for brokering blood, which on its face was not illegal. But it raised a lot of questions, like what happens to the cost of blood as it moves along, and what happens to the safety of blood as it moves along." While he had not started out thinking about AIDS—still a relatively unexplained phenomenon when he started—it emerged as a huge element as the reporting continued.

Gaul had promised himself that he would only allow on-the-record sources in the story, although he would listen to sources who insisted that they be interviewed confidentially. "Due to the sensitivity of the subject, it absolutely had to be this way," the reporter says.

Eventually, it was time to test the Gene Roberts system that was supposed to free reporters for big projects. "When I needed to be detached, I was detached," Gaul recalls. Not that everything went smoothly, though. At one point, Gaul was unhappy about the initial treatment of his series drafts, which he calculates had been cut in half by an editor. He asked his colleague, investigative reporter Don Barlett, to take a look. Barlett backed Gaul's longer version, and showed the originals and the edited drafts to Roberts. A new editor was assigned, former national editor Lois Wark, who continued on the job through the end of the series.

Well into what would eventually become forty separate Freedom of Information Act requests—for a total of about twenty thousand pages' worth of documents—Gaul produced a March 1989 story on one particularly woeful blood bank, in St. Louis. The five-part series that made up the bulk of the Pulitzer entry ran in September. That series started with a piece on blood brokering, the overarching theme of the story. Subsequent pieces studied such elements as the role of the Food and Drug Administration. "It had been basically co-opted by the blood industry," says Gaul. "Their oversight was just abysmal." He also tackled the AIDS question in the blood distribution system.

"As the reporting had begun, I knew AIDS was getting into the blood supply,"

he says. "I didn't even want to go there, because I was viewing it as purely a financial story." Soon, though, it became clear that AIDS was too important to be
played down, especially with Food and Drug Administration oversight so weak in
the area.

Gaul used a number of editors as sounding boards along the way. He remembers flying the series past editor James Naughton for a comment. The reporter had
been agonizing over a simple way to express the complexity of the transporting of
blood supplies from station to station as it was being sold and resold. Naughton
took one look at the story and said, "Oh, a chain of blood." The image stuck
through the series.

Roberts contributed an organizational eye after Gaul and Wark laid the stories
before him in the order they proposed. "Roberts looked at them and said, 'Why
wouldn't you want your stories to go from the strongest to the weakest?'" according to Gaul, affecting his best North Carolina drawl. The FDA material was strong
enough to carry the second day, they agreed, with the AIDS element moved up to
third. "You get fixed ideas early on," says the reporter. "That's why you need editors."

As a result of the series, new certifications were proposed by a congressional
committee, and more inspectors were authorized, among other reforms—some of
them related to the increasing threat of AIDs to blood supplies. The FDA also
changed its monitoring system for foreign blood. And donors can get more information today about what happens with the blood they donate.

After all he learned, is Gaul still a blood donor? Absolutely, he says. "The point
of this series wasn't to harm blood donations, but to explore an area of medicine
that is at best little understood."

1990—*Philadelphia Inquirer:* **For reporting by Gilbert M. Gaul that disclosed
how the American blood industry operates with little government regulation or
supervision.**

Rape and the Media

The story of Nancy Ziegenmeyer's brutal November 1988 rape—by an assailant
who jumped into her car in a Des Moines parking lot—became the center of national debate in February 1990. That was because the *Des Moines Register,* with
Ziegenmeyer's full support, ran a five-day series that named her as the victim and
detailed all that had happened to her before and after.

Among journalists, the series generated discussion about why newspapers generally do not identify rape victims. More broadly, it focused attention on how underreported the crime of rape is in the first place. "The fundamental issue was, Do we have a crime that is way undercovered, compared to its prevalence in society?" says Geneva Overholser, editor of the *Register* at the time. "And that raises the question of whether it is undercovered *because* it is so faceless."

Overholser had sparked the entire issue with a column she wrote, reflecting on a recent Supreme Court decision supporting a Florida weekly that had published a rape victim's name without her permission, in violation of state law.

Overholser weighed, on one side, the unfair stigma of rape against the journalist's commitment "to come as close as possible to printing the facts as we know them." She asked, "Does not our very delicacy in dealing with rape victims subscribe to the idea that rape is a crime of sex rather than the crime of brutal violence that it really is?" While she supported newspapers in withholding victims' names, Overholser wrote, "I believe that we will not break down the stigma until more and more women take public stands."

The column was read by Ziegenmeyer and her husband, who lived just east of Des Moines, in Grinnell. For three weeks she considered whether to take up what she saw as an invitation from Overholser to identify herself as a rape victim, and to use the newspaper in a good cause.

With the debate about naming rape victims unresolved even now, the series that eventually ran in the *Register* remains a useful journalism tool. Yet the story *behind* the paper's handling of the series, and the credit that was dispensed for it, is almost as intriguing. Indeed, twenty-five years after the Gold Medal was awarded, Jane Schorer, the reporter who wrote the stories, still feels that there was too little acknowledgment for her contribution when the *Register* claimed its Pulitzer.

A Teary Phone Call

Overholser remembers distinctly how close this Pulitzer came to never happening.

"I'm sitting at my desk one lunchtime and my secretary is gone. The phone rings, and I pick it up," she says. "On any other given day I would not have picked up the phone." And had her secretary been there, "she wouldn't have passed it along, probably, because it was this teary woman saying, 'I just want to come in to talk.'"

But with Overholser on the line, the caller continued: "I'm Nancy Ziegenmeyer and I've been raped, and I want you to use my name and use my picture, because your argument is exactly right." Ziegenmeyer wanted readers to understand, too, the harm that the legal system causes victims. Perhaps with one unvarnished case—her own—things could change, she said. Overholser decided to give the story to the feature department for assignment, to run when the assailant's trial ended. Ziegenmeyer's name would be published.

Schorer, a gifted but relatively new reporter who formerly was a secretary on the editorial page, began interviewing Ziegenmeyer on August 2, 1989, the first of more than fifty meetings and telephone conversations the two would have over seven months. From the start, Schorer felt uneasy with how some editors treated her—debating whether "we need to have a real reporter do this," for example. But when she dove in, it was for good, even if there were to be significant interruptions.

An early obstacle was the seemingly interminable dragging out of the rape case itself. For a time it engendered a newsroom debate about whether to hold the story, as was planned. "What if we hold it, and the guy is found innocent?" Schorer's feature editor asked her, seeing the prospect of a good story evaporating. "What if we *run* it, and the guy is found innocent?" Schorer responded. The paper wisely waited.

Schorer had other assignments, even as she stayed close to Ziegenmeyer. For her editors, still waiting for a verdict, "it was pretty much forgotten and on the back burner," she says. But as the months passed, thoughts about the story preoccupied her. "The only way I could do it was make a diary of it," she says. It was unusual, but it seemed to work.

"When I finished the first one or two parts, I took it to Geneva and I asked if she remembered this project," Schorer recalls. "Then I laid it down on her desk."

Alone in her office, Overholser read. "First of all, my jaw dropped because it was so compelling. But second, I thought this is a very nontraditional piece for us," says the editor. It would take special handling in the newsroom.

Overholser went to the small writing room where Schorer was working. "Do you have any idea what you have here?" Overholser asked, leaving the writer speechless for a moment—until Schorer realized that her boss loved the story.

"From that minute on," says Schorer, "Geneva took charge." A top editor at the *Register,* Mike Wegner, was assigned to handle the series. Schorer was impressed with the five-part draft that emerged starting on February 25, 1990.

Part one began:

> She would have to allow extra driving time because of the fog.
>
> A heavy gray veil had enveloped Grinnell overnight, and Nancy Ziegenmeyer—always methodical, always in control—decided to leave home early for her 7:30 a.m. appointment at Grand View College in Des Moines.
>
> It was Nov. 19, 1988, a day Ziegenmeyer had awaited eagerly, because she knew

that whatever happened during those morning hours in Des Moines would determine her future. If she passed the state real-estate licensing exam that Saturday morning, she would begin a new career. If she failed the test, she would continue the child-care service she provided in her home.

At 6 a.m., Ziegenmeyer unlocked the door of her 1988 Pontiac Grand Am and tossed her long denim jacket in the back seat. The weather was mild for mid-November, and her Gloria Vanderbilt denim jumper, and turtleneck sweater and red wool tights would keep her warm enough without a coat.

Arrived Early

The fog lifted as Ziegenmeyer drove west on Interstate Highway 80, and she made good time after all. The digital clock on the dashboard read 7:05 as she pulled into a parking lot near Grand View's Science Building. She had 25 minutes to sit in the car and review her notes before test time.

Suddenly the driver's door opened. She turned to see a man, probably in his late 20s, wearing a navy pin-striped suit. He smelled of alcohol

"Move over," the man ordered, grabbing her neck.

"What Kind of Weird Journalism Is This?"

"When I picked up the paper on the first day, I said, Wow!" recalls Schorer. Together with the story, spread across page one, were two columns headed "How this story came to be," and a reference to another article by Overholser.

Getting to "Wow" had not been easy. "The *Des Moines Register* was a very traditional paper," says Overholser. "It was big on sports, big on agriculture, big on politics, big on agribusiness. It was certainly not a very soft and squishy paper." Schorer had assembled her account from Ziegenmeyer's own story, from her friends, from police officers, from prosecutors, and from the defense attorney. It contained emotional details unusual for a newspaper story of the time. And for some editors at the *Register*, it crossed the line of reporter familiarity with a source.

"The cardinal rule is that a reporter never gets emotionally involved. I got emotionally involved, and I make no bones about it," Schorer says.

But the 1990s were becoming a time of experimenting with new forms, even at the *Register*. And Overholser felt that the paper's approach needed to accommodate the close relationship that Ziegenmeyer and Schorer had formed.

It took two weeks for a final decision on whether to run it, and in what form. Some editors, says Overholser, were uncomfortable not because of the sexual frankness—although it did graphically describe Ziegenmeyer's rape—"but because it was so edgy." The editors asked, "What kind of weird journalism was this?"

she recalls. Telling a story that analyzed what the victim was thinking, some argued, was not serious journalism. But Overholser and other editors persisted. It was, she adds, "a piece of narrative journalism before we really knew the name."

The decision was to stay with the five-part format, and to keep its descriptiveness intact. "If Nancy Ziegenmeyer is coming to me and saying, 'Tell my story,' then we were going to tell it with honesty," says Overholser. She remembers looking over the copy editor's shoulder and noticing that the term "after he had ejaculated" had been changed to "when he had finished." Overholser stopped him. "This is a crime of sex," she told him. "And if she's willing to say 'after he had ejaculated,' then we should say it. 'After he had finished' sounded like he'd had lunch or something."

Another element required careful treatment: the assailant was black and the victim white. That was rare, considering rape statistics, says Overholser. Most attacks are intraracial, and involve people who know each other.

The *Register*'s managing editor, David Westphal, proposed that an editor's note explain some of the unusual features of the series, including "how loath we were to contribute to that stereotype of interracial rape," Overholser says. "I felt then, and I believe now, that the extraordinary opportunity to be able to focus on rape was worth it. You just don't get that opportunity. It's impossible for young women to realize how little rape was written about back then." The editor, now a University of Missouri professor, believes the series' greatest success was putting the crime of rape on the national agenda.

That happened instantly, and with deep controversy. Invitations arrived in Des Moines for national interviews, for Ziegenmeyer and Overholser, mostly, but also for the novice feature writer. "It totally caught us off-guard by getting so much publicity," says Schorer. "At the time it began we had no idea it would be a big story."

Overholser, too, found the attention unsettling. She turned down several appearances, but accepted others. Media attention grew, though, when the William Kennedy Smith case made the national news. Smith, Senator Edward Kennedy's nephew, was accused of rape by an alleged victim who was named by the media. (The case against Smith was dismissed.) In October, the *Register* editor was on the cover of *Working Woman* magazine.

"Geneva was being watched as one of the first female editors of a major newspaper. People were waiting to see what she would accomplish," Schorer says. The writer thought that some acclaim for the *Register* series was misdirected, though. "There was plenty of credit to go around. Nancy deserves all the credit in the world for coming forward, and Geneva deserves all the credit in the world for having the idea in the first place, and for making the finished product so outstanding." But, says Schorer, who now writes for the *Register*'s custom publications under the by-line Jane Schorer Meisner, "it would have been fair for me to have the credit for presenting it the way I did."

The nature of the Gold Medal—going to the *Register* and not to the reporter—rubbed a raw nerve for Schorer, even on the joyous day when the Gold Medal prize was announced. She says she wishes that the work had won for Feature Writing, where the *Register* had nominated it also. In that case, the prize would have been in her name. "Public Service is more noble," she says, "but I would have liked to get the personal recognition."

Overholser understands her irritation. As a reporter, Schorer "absolutely took this story and made a miracle out of it," the editor says. Adds Michael Gartner, who preceded Overholser as *Register* editor, "What made it work was that it was a compelling story. She was really a good writer." Gartner, then the president of NBC News, was also on the Pulitzer Prize Board that year, although he was out of the room for the discussion because of his *Register* connection.

Overholser, too, was out of the room when the Gold Medal was decided, of course. But she did have something to say when she reentered the room and learned that the board was preparing a citation that excluded Schorer's name. "They said the paper was winning, and I said, 'That's great, but you've got to name Jane,'" says Overholser. At her insistence, Schorer's name was inserted.

1991—*Des Moines Register:* For reporting by Jane Schorer that, with the victim's consent, named a woman who had been raped—which prompted widespread reconsideration of the traditional media practice of concealing the identity or rape victims.

Covering the Sierra without a Parachute

Sacramento Bee reporter Tom Knudson once had worked at the *Des Moines Register,* as well, and in 1985 had won a Pulitzer Prize for National Reporting there, for a series on the dangers of farming. "It was a neat place to start out as a young reporter," says Knudson, who credits editors like Geneva Overholser and Mike Gartner for helping him. He later moved to the *New York Times,* but eventually became frustrated with the style of reporting there. "I found myself visiting many places, but not knowing hardly any," he says. "They call it parachute journalism."

Switching to McClatchy's *Bee,* he was chosen to open a Sierra news bureau, based in the town of Truckee. "The idea was to cover this part of the Sierra as a beat, with the forests, the watersheds and what have you," Knudson says. "I jumped at the opportunity and threw a kayak on top of my Jeep and just took a little bit of a road trip. Of course, I fell in love with the geography, as everybody does. But then I began to stop in community after community, talking with people about what are the issues, what are the concerns." Knudson recalls that there was some resistance in the newsroom to his covering the Sierra. It could have been jealousy, or a feeling that the paper was being too lenient with him. Fifteen years and a Pulitzer Prize later, he says, "I guess it's been laid to rest."

When journalists cover the environment, they do well to look past the jurisdictions that governments create. "Water, air, wildlife—all these resources and individual components—they don't pay attention to boundaries," Knudson says. "Everybody was looking at their own backyard, but nobody was looking at the gem that is the Sierra Nevada." Stretching for 450 miles, across dozens of counties, national forests, irrigation districts, and other divisions, he says, "this region has been 'piecemealed' to death." It was that observation that prompted his project on the plight of the Sierra. "The magic of the series," says Knudson, "was that I was able to go out and look at this huge region as a beat, and write about it as a single mountain range."

Knudson brought a fresh set of eyes to the Sierra. He traveled across the range looking for issues that arose over and over again, but in different settings. "If livestock raising is causing problems in one part of the range, and you find that it is in another part of the range as well, you can put two and two together," he notes. Many interviewees didn't know quite what to make of his mountain-range focus. When a reporter is on an important story, "sometimes people know that, and they clam up faster, or they speak up more, than they otherwise might," the reporter says. But to most people he interviewed this time, the Sierra seemed a nonstory.

Knudson knew that it was anything but. "To see that there were all these forces leading to a general state of deterioration struck me as a pretty compelling story."

Air, Forests, Water, Wildlife, Soil, and Mankind

After eight months of investigation and two hundred interviews, the series was ready to run on June 9, with the headline "Majesty and Tragedy: The Sierra in Peril. From Mining to Malls, Onslaught Takes Toll." Part one began:

John Muir said it best.

The Sierra Nevada, the naturalist wrote a century ago, "seems to me above all others the Range of Light, the most divinely beautiful of all the mountain chains I have ever seen."

Remember those words. Savor them like old wine. Share them with young children.

For Muir's words no longer hold true.

Today, California's Sierra Nevada—one of the world's great mountain ranges—is suffering a slow death.

Almost everywhere there are problems: polluted air, dying forests, poisoned rivers, vanishing wildlife, eroding soil and rapid-fire development. Even Muir's holy ground, Yosemite National Park, is hurting: Much of its forest has been damaged by ozone.

Remarkably, the problems have drawn little attention, masked in part by the enormity of the range.

That sixth paragraph served almost as a table of contents for the series. Part two focused on air pollution, part three on forests and wildlife, part four on streams and mining damage, and part five on the plague of growth. The final part also contained a prognosis, and suggestions for how to turn things around.

Because of the project's size and scope, other reporters helped Knudson with basic research. But *Bee* editor Gregory Favre preferred that it be largely a one-man effort. Collecting data had been hard because much of the information was broken down by county or by district, requiring extensive travel among county seats. Computer-assisted reporting was still a few years in the future, the reporter notes.

The editor working over the stories with Knudson was Terry Jackson. The photography ranged from breathtaking to disturbing. It showed the ravages of development. "There was pressure to cut stories," Knudson recalls, "but I don't remember too many knock-down-drag-out disputes with editors."

By creating the feeling that time was running out for corrective measures, Knudson's series got the immediate attention of legislators. A "Sierra summit" was convened to address some of the problems the *Bee* cited. Congress also took an interest. On its own, the U.S. Forest Service, whose policies were treated harshly in the series, conceded that the new perspective was valuable. Said a Forest Service spokesman: "I think there may be some initial hard feelings or concern. There were a lot of vested interests that were obviously challenged. But that's the name of the game. What matters is what happens to the Sierra. This could be a real vector for change."

Other finalists for the Pulitzer Public Service award were the *Washington Post*, for a study of gun violence in its city, and the *Dayton Daily News*, which examined national workplace safety issues—variations of themes that would recur in Public Service competitions ten years later.

While he already had one Pulitzer, Knudson knew that the Gold Medal was special. It was no problem for him that the prize went to the *Bee* rather than to him personally, he says, and that it had no cash reward with it. Investigative journalists know of all sorts of awards that have big money associated with them—like the University of Southern California's Selden Ring Award and its thirty-five thousand dollars in prize money. "But who knows what that award is?" says Knudson. "The gold standard is still the Pulitzers."

1992—*Sacramento Bee:* For "The Sierra in Peril," reporting by Tom Knudson that examined environmental threats and damage to the Sierra Nevada mountain range in California.

⸭

The Big One

There was no question mark on the headline.

On Monday, August 24, 1992, the banner across the top of the *Miami Herald* told readers that Hurricane Andrew would be no ordinary storm:

THE BIG ONE

Hurricane of Our Nightmares
Is Knocking at the Front Door
    Deadly
    Andrew
    Kills 4 in
    Bahamas
        Floridians Flee
        Today's Landfall

Marked "Special Hurricane Edition," the day's paper was a public service in itself. But—far more than the *Herald* staff suspected—it was only setting the scene for what was to come over the rest of the year.

"Hurricane Andrew, the biggest story ever to hit this newsroom, was the one story none of us wanted to see," wrote managing editor Pete Weitzel in the paper's cover letter for its Pulitzer entry in Public Service. "It evoked a responsibility rooted deeply in the finest tradition of newspapers but rarely encountered in 20th Century America: Inform and comfort. A stunned and dislocated population, much of it deprived of shelter, water and electricity, with little or no access to sources of information, needed the news, needed help, needed guidance."

Five years later, that description would apply as well to a second disaster-related Gold Medal awarded to another Knight Ridder paper, the *Grand Forks Herald* in North Dakota.

For the *Miami Herald,* planning to get staffers into the right place made a huge difference, says Weitzel, now retired from the *Herald* and leading the Coalition of Journalists for Open Government. "It's very difficult to get around after a hurricane, so you needed to have some critical people positioned before the storm hit." In a way, it was like preparing for an invasion during wartime. The *Herald* sent some reporters to the Homestead area, where they stayed in a motel the night before the full fury of the storm hit. As it happened, the storm hit in Homestead.

"DESTRUCTION AT DAWN," read the Tuesday paper's banner. To allow for more organized placement of hurricane reports, the paper eliminated the Local section and concentrated Andrew-related news in the first section, an approach it would use for weeks. Some 110,000 copies of the Tuesday paper were distributed free to shelters, hotels, and the few distribution boxes still in operation. The hardest-hit areas got forty thousand free copies for three weeks. "It built an enormous goodwill toward the paper," says Weitzel. The *Herald* published neighborhood-by-neighborhood damage surveys, along with daily updates on the basics: food, water, power and telephones, and street-clearing.

As it provided vital information, the staff learned from its readers, too. "Almost from the first day, we began to realize that some of the traditional stories you begin to file in the wake of a big disaster—a fire or anything like that—didn't really serve the need here. Survey stories of the damage didn't serve concrete needs for people to know, What happened on my block? What happened in my neighborhood?" says Weitzel. "That created a tremendous challenge." The overview reporting, even if it was beautifully handled, lacked the specifics that readers needed. That problem could only be solved by sending the reporters back, with orders, as Weitzel put it, "to get more nitty-gritty."

One surprising twist was what happened when the *Herald* created a phone bank to take incoming calls. "We asked clerks and secretaries to staff the phones to handle an unexpectedly heavy volume of calls from people seeking storm-related information, and also to take notes," he says. In this pre-Internet time, the *Herald* news staff found it was getting fast feedback about the real problems in the community, and where they existed. "My secretary was helping run the phone bank," says Weitzel, "and she said that we were getting all these tremendously poignant calls from people. Can we help them locate a friend, or locate a relative?" The secretary, Bert Alberti, had the idea of putting together a "bulletin board" feature in the newspaper to help them connect. It eventually would take up several full pages each day. The "Readers Helping Readers" section delivered messages from readers for free and told them where help could be found. The response was heavy.

Comparing the 1992 *Herald* feature to the *New York Times's* "Portraits of Grief," which had its genesis in handbills passed around Ground Zero after 9/11, Weitzel says: "The Portraits, those little anecdotes, were one of the most brilliant things

I'd ever seen. And this bulletin board feature had been the same kind of thing for us. It just mushroomed."

The *Herald* itself was working wounded. Three distribution warehouses were destroyed and the roof of its main building sustained heavy damage. Sixty news-room employees had severely damaged homes. "All of us were going through the same experiences of the people we're writing about," says Weitzel. "We really were on the same page. And that's not always the case."

On Sunday, August 30, the paper had the beginnings of a scandal to report. Its headline read:

Shoddy Construction
Left Homes Vulnerable
to Storm, Engineers Say

The next Sunday another headline proclaimed "Older is often better for Dade homes, experts say." *Herald* stories reported that local building codes were either insufficient, or were not being enforced. Also, there were signs that much con-struction was shoddy under any code structure.

The *Herald*'s analysis of why Andrew damaged certain buildings more than oth-ers answered a key question. Readers wanted to know why a community that had prepared so well for a storm could still be so devastated. In a story that same Sun-day headlined "Why Help Took So Long," reporters Jeff Leen and Sydney Freed-berg wrote:

It was as if the emergency disaster planners wrote a super Act I—the evacua-tion—then forgot to script Act II—the recovery.
What went wrong?
A lot.
Mobile hospitals and bulldozers arrived late. Vital phones and radios jammed. Food deliveries and National Guard units got snarled in traffic. Roadblocks turned away volunteers. Police didn't control intersections. City managers plead-ed for help. Nobody activated the Army.
To be sure, thousands of good people labored heroically, monumentally, to es-tablish order from a type of chaos that no one had ever seen before.
But for 100 critical hours after Andrew struck, governments reeled, and no one was in command. No hurricane czar, no Norman Schwarzkopf.

This was the same Sydney Freedberg who had helped win a Public Service award for the *Detroit News* nine years earlier. And Jeff Leen would later become a *Wash-ington Post* investigative reporter and editor, helping it win Gold Medals in 1999 and 2000. Hurricane Andrew "was probably Jeff's statistical baptism," says Weitzel, allowing Leen to develop skills for detecting patterns that teams could use in their investigations.

The paper hammered the building-construction theme. One story noted that the devastating Hurricane Donna in the 1960s had prompted a major storm study that specifically had warned that building codes needed to be properly enforced or storms would continue to cause far more destruction than necessary.

The main headline on Sunday, October 4, read "Unanchored Beams Took Deadly Flight." The story, by Don Finefrock, Leen, and Jacquee Petchel, began:

> Three people who died in Naranja Lakes during Hurricane Andrew were killed after massive concrete beams atop the walls of their homes tore off and turned into lethal 20-foot missiles—flying as far as 150 feet.
>
> The three deaths didn't have to happen, according to engineering and wind experts consulted by The Miami Herald.
>
> Experts say the beams, weighting almost 2,000 pounds, would have held if they had been anchored to the foundation by steel rods costing only a few hundred dollars.
>
> "You've got to be stupid to build like this," says Eugenio Santiago, a structural engineer hired by The Herald to study the homes. "If you know anything about hurricanes you wouldn't have built like this."

The rest of the story explained that stupidity had little to do with the construction. Rather, this "greatest concentration of deaths in a single neighborhood during the hurricane" reflected decisions made in the 1970s by Mob figures who were involved in the Florida construction trades and were suspected of paying off Dade County officials at the time, perhaps to allow shoddy work.

Underlying the stories about building-code and construction problems were long hours of research. Reporter Lisa Getter "went though minutes of every zoning appeals meeting since 1979," says Weitzel. Steve Doig managed the computer research, matching tens of thousands of individual hurricane damage reports against building records. The investigative team was headed by Jim Savage.

The Pulitzer Public Service jury commented on the *Herald*'s "awesome commitment of resources." Specifically, the jury noted the *Herald*'s successes identifying "the economic & political decisions of the past in the form of lax zoning, inspection and building codes that had made them so vulnerable."

Jurors picked a central Florida paper, the *Orlando Sentinel,* as a finalist for work unrelated to the storm. Its nominated series dealt with harassment and intimidation of racial minorities and others by law enforcement. The board gave *Sentinel* reporters Jeff Brazil and Steve Berry the Investigative Prize for that work. The other Public Service finalist was the *Seattle Times,* cited by the jury for "placing its own credibility on the line to expose the personal conduct of a powerful political figure," Senator Brock Adams. In its reporting, the newspaper "pierced the time-honored veil of silence that has surrounded the issue of sexual harassment," the jurors wrote. Adams pulled out of the Senate race as a result of the stories. But the *Herald* storm coverage blew away the board.

1993—*Miami Herald:* For coverage that not only helped readers cope with Hurricane Andrew's devastation but also showed how lax zoning, inspection, and building codes had contributed to the destruction.

Blizzard, Fire, and Flood; What Next: Locusts?

In 1997, April was the cruelest month for the Red River town of Grand Forks, North Dakota. Indeed, a series of plagues bordering on the biblical swept the area. As editor Mike Jacobs and publisher Mike Maidenberg wrote to readers in an April 20 page-one editorial comment:

> Grand Forks has sustained deep wounds, and there will be scars. On Saturday evening, as we write, the river continues its historic rise and fire is tearing at the heart of downtown. Thousands of buildings are immersed. Several of the town's most historic structures are alight. There is no apparent power that can save them. These buildings were part of our past . . . .
>
> We must have wondered, all of us, whether any community anywhere had ever suffered so much, and yet we know that others have. Miraculously, we have been spared loss of life. Marvelously, we have found friendships we didn't know about, as strangers came to offer labor, called to offer shelter, reached out to offer strength. Could it have been so in any other town? Yes, perhaps. But never on such a scale in our hometown. And it is in that spirit, from that indomitable strength, that our hometown will go forward. It is going to be a difficult time. Let us begin this morning.

"We wanted to sound the theme of hope—not to say Woe is me, or Help us, but to look over the horizon and find the opportunity that could come from this disaster," says Maidenberg. It would set the tone for the news coverage, as well. Under extreme deadline pressure, the small staff produced well-crafted news stories that were consistently reassuring and gave readers the information they needed for coping.

From time to time staffers had to reassure themselves. The paper had been driven out of its building, first taking up quarters at the nearby University of North

Dakota campus and later—when the university was flooded—moving to a public elementary school ten miles from town. For seventy-one days the *Herald* put out the paper from the elementary school.

The paper in the past had an almost neighborly relationship with storms, naming the state's blizzards each year, the way the National Weather Service names Atlantic hurricanes. It picked women's and men's names, working up the alphabet one letter at a time. The paper had dubbed this 1997 storm "Hannah." It had no idea how hard-hearted she would be. The same April 20 paper—the first published on presses at its Knight Ridder sister paper, the *St. Paul Pioneer-Press*—carried a lead story by Randy Bradbury under the headline "Downtown Fires Intensify Crisis." It began:

> Water continued to drive residents of Grand Forks and East Grand Forks from their homes Saturday. Too much water, and too little.
>
> In Grand Forks, those who weren't flooded out by the spreading waters of the Red River of the North were put on notice that the city soon would be unable to provide that most essential of services: safe drinking water.

By the second day, the hopeful tone returned. Under the headline "A Heart Destroyed; Officials Take a First Look at the Destroyed Downtown," *Herald* contributor Monte Paulson wrote:

> Clouds of steam rose lazily from the mounds of twisted metal and blackened brick lining Third and Fourth streets on Sunday afternoon as Grand Forks leaders struggled to figure out how their city will rise from the worst disaster it has ever faced.

Jacobs and Maidenberg later shared details of what was going on in their minds:

> We knew we had to keep going, no matter what. Too much depended on us. Even as our own staff members assessed damage to their homes and worked to restore their lives, they did the reporting, editing, photography, and graphics that kept Grand Forks informed.

The two men learned one benefit of being part of a chain. Knight Ridder sent people from other papers, and contributed $1 million from its corporate fund. The storm-hardened *Miami Herald* staffers, particularly, provided ideas to help the Grand Forks paper plan coverage. The bulletin-board approach for reaching victims in print—a technique pioneered during Hurricane Andrew—also was used in Grand Forks. Having Miami staffers around "saved us a lot of trial and error," says Maidenberg.

Jacobs reviewed the 1997 coverage years later:

> I'm a small-town guy. I've always worked in small cities. And I had a fairly well-developed notion of the newspaper's role in a small town. But nothing could have fused those points of view like this crisis did.
>
> I always had thought of the newspaper as the "town nag." Now I describe it as a friend that's in a position to make helpful suggestions.
>
> I think we're a humbler institution after the disaster. We used to be haughty.

Some lessons were less romantic—like how the honeymoon doesn't last, even if a newspaper wins immediate public support for its disaster coverage.

Maidenberg calls it the golden time. "During a time of disaster, you and your readers are in sync. Everybody is really happy to get any scrap of news. But as time goes by, the newspaper has to write more critical kinds of things. It has to be a newspaper. When that happens, the golden time begins to ebb."

It ebbed in a big way during what became known as the Angel Flap, when the *Herald* published a story identifying the donor of $15 million in flood relief. The donor, McDonald's heiress Joan Kroc, had sought anonymity. But the *Herald* editors believed that so many people knew her identity already that it would be wrong to leave its readers out of the "secret." Jacobs felt it was a simple matter: "Never hold the news." A reporter tracked down the registration from the tail of an unmarked private jet that had flown into the area—the so-called N-number—and identified the visiting plane as Kroc's. An article was prepared.

"When people found out we were going to run the story we got frantic calls from the mayors of both Grand Forks and East Grand Forks saying, You can't run that story; she will be offended and we might not get any more assistance from her. I listened to them, and I made the decision that this was news," Maidenberg says. Talk radio hosts turned against the paper, and so did many readers. "People were jarred back to the understanding that newspapers are going to be newspapers," he says. "Still, some people will always stay with you. They'll say, 'I'm angry with this, but I'll never forget what you did after the flood.'"

Jurors and Pulitzer board members liked that the *Herald* remained scrappy as well as eloquent. From the perspective of James Naughton, then the president of the Poynter Institute and a Public Service juror that year, there was "an unspoken yet clear understanding that it would have to take something truly extraordinary to deflect us from picking Grand Forks."

The board did pick it. The Public Service finalists were the *Seattle Times,* for disclosing the ways heavy industry was recycling toxic waste as fertilizer, and the *Los Angeles Times,* for reporter Sonia Nazario's chronicling of the plight of children of drug- and alcohol-addicted parents. The *L.A. Times* photographer for that series, Clarence Williams, won the Feature Photography Prize for his work.

In the wake of 2005's Hurricane Katrina, Mike Jacobs retraced some of his paper's 1997 stories to try to explain "the level of desperation people feel to get home" after being displaced by a storm. "It's a natural human response to return to the nest and start to rebuild," he wrote.

1998— *Grand Forks Herald:* For its sustained and informative coverage, vividly illustrated with photographs, that helped hold its community together in the wake of flooding, a blizzard, and a fire that devastated much of the city, including the newspaper plant itself.

Wrestling with "Boss Hog"

For Raleigh, North Carolina's *News & Observer* in 1995, discovering how heavily pork producers had become concentrated in North Carolina had been the first revelation. It had happened mostly out of the public eye, and so had the pollution that came with it.

"Actually, the story got started when two reporters, Pat Stith and Joby Warrick, worked together on stories about malfeasance connected with the State Fair," says Melanie Sill, who was just back from a Nieman Fellowship at Harvard and had become editor of the Sunday paper, while also running special projects. Eventually, the two reporters uncovered the case of the state veterinarian taking gifts from pork producers.

"Nothing had been reported about this industry," Sill says. "It had been growing quietly in the state, and they're not huge employers." But as reporters looked deeper, "more and more the questions developed."

Soon enough, water-quality issues caught the reporters' notice. "By the time the series got into print, the veterinarian story went by the wayside," according to Sill, now the paper's editor.

The reporters and their editor met once a week and read each others' notes, she says, but three months into the project the focus still was unclear. "We were down in our humble office canteen, and I said, 'What is the story really about?' And Pat said, 'It's about who's in charge here.' The industry was writing its own ticket."

The journalists agreed, and with the basic line of the series finally established, the story came together more easily in the remaining two months of investigation.

The reporters documented evidence that waste pits were leaking into ground water and creeks. One story analyzed how Wendell Murphy, a former state senator and a major hog farmer, had thwarted government regulation. A sidebar was prepared on the most noticeable issue for readers who happened to come close to a hog farm: the odor.

"We thought about doing a scratch-and-sniff to run with the series," says Sill with a laugh, noting that they gave up on that idea quickly.

Metro editor Marion Gregory came up with the Boss Hog rubric that would run with the series. As often happens late in the editing process, the five parts were juggled fairly close to the late-February dates when they were scheduled to run. At first, the story on Murphy was to lead the series. (The headline "Murphy's Laws" seemed to fit.) But as they refined the drafts, the environmental-impact story seemed a better opener. Editor Sill had Warrick root through a stack of discarded story openings to find one that she had recalled loving from an early draft. Opening the first day's story, under the headline "Boss Hog: New Studies Show That Lagoons Are Leaking," the story by Stith and Warrick began:

> Imagine a city as big as New York suddenly grafted onto North Carolina's Coastal Plain. Double it.
>
> Now imagine that this city has no sewage treatment plants. All the wastes from 15 million inhabitants are simply flushed into open pits and sprayed onto fields.
>
> Turn those humans into hogs, and you don't have to imagine at all. It's already here.
>
> A vast city of swine has risen practically overnight in the counties east of Interstate 95. It's a megalopolis of 7 million animals that live in metal confinement barns and produce two to four times as much waste, per hog, as the average human.

The two then examined the critical debate between industry and environmentalists over how much environmental damage results from letting hog manure decompose, then spraying or spreading it on croplands, as was the agricultural method of the time. The *News & Observer* cited studies to show that contaminants were getting into groundwater in unacceptable amounts, both through lagoon leakage and through rainwater that carries ammonia gas that the farms produce.

Sill says that when the Pulitzer entry was being prepared, Stith and Warrick told her she should include her name. "I thought, That's nice, but it's unlikely that we'll win."

After the series, but before the 1996 Pulitzer Prize was announced, McClatchy purchased the paper, giving the chain its fifth Gold Medal. Of the two finalists, one, the *Minneapolis Star Tribune,* would also later become a McClatchy property for a time. (It was put up for sale in 2006.) The Minnesota paper was cited for disclosing how a legal-publishing company had distributed favors to members of the federal judiciary. The other finalist, the *Baltimore Sun,* had reported on activities of the Honduran army in abducting and murdering political suspects in the 1980s, with the knowledge of the CIA. It was a rare case of an international story making the finalist list in Public Service, although such finalists would soon become less rare.

1996—*News & Observer,* Raleigh, North Carolina: For the work of Melanie Sill, Pat Stith, and Joby Warrick on the environmental and health risks of waste disposal systems used in North Carolina's growing hog industry.

"Oceans of Trouble"

The series that won the 1997 Gold Medal for the *Times-Picayune*—its study of the world's fishing industry—certainly tackled global issues. But it did not start that way.

Environmental writer Mark Schleifstein had originally thought about a humbler fishing-and-the-environment feature, aimed at the Gulf Coast alone. In the time-honored tradition of papers everywhere, *Times-Picayune* editors in 1995 had launched a process to encourage story ideas from the staff. Their charge: "If you've got ideas for a story you want to work on for a week or two, tell us what it is," he says. Of course, the reporters knew that the two-week guideline was meaningless. It would be longer if the project turned out to be significant. Scrolling through a list of stories he kept on his computer, Schleifstein came across a fishing-industry proposal he had dropped earlier. When he had checked to see who covered fishing for the paper and might be able to team with him, he was told that the *Times-Picayune* didn't cover fishing any more. Upset, he gave up on the story, which would be too big to do alone. It was to have examined the connection between coastal erosion and poor recent fishing results in the Gulf. Too bad.

But with this new mandate, he brought it up again. Editors liked the idea of a look at the problems of Gulf fisheries. There was still no fishing reporter, but he was put on a team with Washington environmental writer John McQuaid and outdoors writer Bob Marshall, with political editor Tim Morris in charge. The instruction: "First, go find out if there's a story." Says Schleifstein, "The three of us went to our usual sources and we asked the typical questions. We're seeing what's happening all over the United States with fishing going downhill in New England and Alaska and other places." But they were shocked when environmental scientists told them how bad things had gotten in the Gulf—with estimates that all of Louisiana's wetlands would be gone in fifty years, eliminating the habitat for numerous Gulf species. For one thing, runoff from America's heartland was flowing down a Mississippi River that had been permanently channeled, creating a "dead zone" for sea life farther and farther out from the mouth of the great river.

At the same time, the Gulf was being overfished, following the pattern in other troubled fisheries like New England and Alaska. After pursuing the reasons for about five months, though, the team reached a surprising realization: "What was driving overfishing in the Gulf of Mexico was Japan," the leader of the ballooning worldwide fish market. Further, the shrimp industry, so critical to Louisiana, was in trouble, too. It was being flooded by aquaculture, much of it Asian.

Editors were asked to let the team redesign the series as a look at a worldwide crisis, and the team made its case persuasively. "There was an utter connectedness," according to editor Jim Amoss, who approved the expansion. "To do it justice, we had to take a global look at it." Since the story would be much more expensive to report, the *Times-Picayune* went to the Newhouse organization, which approved adding budget.

To decide on who would travel abroad, "they got the guy who had the passport," says Schleifstein only half-jokingly. "That was John, and they sent him to Thailand and Japan." McQuaid also went to New England, while Schleifstein followed the wetland problems in Louisiana and Florida's Everglades, and Marshall studied the sport-fishing angle and ventured to Alaska.

As the work neared completion, extra effort went into graphics under designer George Berke. Photographer Ted Jackson did his own research, developing a theme that often captured the feel of the lone fisherman taking on the world in quiet desperation.

Before taking the stories to Amoss for the final read, managing editor Peter Kovacs worked over the stories that Tim Morris forwarded to him. At the end, the story order was juggled, in part to allow major pieces of the eight-day series to run on Sunday or other days with large display possibilities. Smaller parts of the package were left for the Monday paper with its lighter page counts.

The first day's story, by McQuaid, noted how fishermen must deal with changing environments in pursuit of a catch. "It comes with the job," he wrote. But lately, they have been "helpless before the man-made changes tearing across the Gulf of Mexico, leaving a swath of wrecked lives and ecological havoc in their wake."

> Part of a global sea change in fishing, the forces include disappearing fish and marshlands, a flood of cheap seafood imports and gill net bans. They threaten millions of livelihoods and the Gulf's unique fishing culture.

A second McQuaid story that day highlighted the worldwide scope of the series. Headlined "Are the World's Fisheries Doomed?" it opened with a tale from another gulf, the Gulf of Thailand, where shrimp farming had caused coastal erosion and hurt other fishing industries.

The next day, Schleifstein targeted perils that existed for the oceans themselves. Headlined "The Dead Sea," the story was accompanied by a chart dramatizing how severely fertilizer runoff through the Mississippi deprives the Gulf of oxygen. Stories ran from March 24 to March 31, with the last, headlined "The Big Fix," offering options, none of them easy.

Times-Picayune long-timers often date the paper's coming of age to the 1988 Republican National Convention in New Orleans, when the Newhouse chain decided to use the city's national spotlight to make a mark for the paper. "We spent a year getting ready for a week," says managing editor Peter Kovacs. Adds Amoss of the convention's impact: "It challenged some key people, and it had a residual effect of raising the bar journalistically in the news operation and making us more ambitious."

The 1997 Gold Medal was something of a surprise to Schleifstein because he had sensed the bias that existed, in that particular prize, against global stories. Still, he says, "This really was one of those strange times when the morning we went to press, I looked at John and I said, Can you believe what we've done? We really thought we had a good chance."

Amoss, who joined the Pulitzer board several years later, believes that "Oceans of Trouble" benefited from being seen as a regional, rather than a global story. "There's a natural inclination in the American press to reward strong local journalism, and the Public Service award certainly plays to that," he says. "Were the series just the *Times-Picayune* setting out to write about the world's fisheries, I think it would have been a totally different project, and probably wouldn't have won."

But win it did. The *Philadelphia Inquirer* again was a finalist, this time for a project on the widening gap between America's rich and poor, prepared by its team of Don Barlett and Jim Steele. The *Los Angeles Times* was back, too, for the probe of a murder case that led to revelations of inefficiency and mismanagement in the justice system.

1997—*Times-Picayune*: For its comprehensive series analyzing the conditions that threaten the world's supply of fish.

A dramatic photograph helped Jane Schorer's first story on rape victim Nancy
Ziegenmeyer come alive in the 1990 *Des Moines Register* series.

Des Moines Register editor Geneva Overholser in 1991. *Register* staff photo.

Register reporter Jane Schorer learns that the paper has won the 1991 Pulitzer Gold Medal. *Register* staff photo.

Atop a desk, *Philadelphia Inquirer* reporter Gil Gaul responds to staff acknowledgment when the paper learns it has won the 1990 Pulitzer Prize for Public Service. Photo by *Inquirer* photographer Sharon Wohlmuth. Used by permission.

Sacramento Bee reporter Tom Knudson, whose work won the 1992 Public Service Pulitzer, shares a hug with Deborah Blum, awarded the Beat Reporting Pulitzer the same year. *Bee* photograph by Richard Gilmore.

CHAPTER 20

The *Post* Rings Twice

It is a capital mistake to theorize before one has data. Insensibly one begins to twist facts to suit theories instead of theories to fit facts.

—Sherlock Holmes, quoted on Jeff Leen's office wall

*I*magine attending this story meeting held by *Washington Post* editors and reporters in the fall of 1998: Jeffrey M. Leen notes his investigative team's probe of the high toll of shootings by District of Columbia police, a dark footnote in the city that had become the murder capital of the nation. Taking turns going around the room, *Post* "poverty beat" reporter Katherine Boo is pursuing a story about D.C. homes for the mentally retarded, where she's uncovered horrid conditions. Both sound like winners.

Were they ever.

In 1999 and 2000, for the first time, a newspaper won consecutive Pulitzer Prizes for Public Service—for projects that had overlapped in their newsroom. As a forty-year-old investigative specialist who had just moved to the *Post* from the *Miami Herald* in the prior year, Leen remembers thinking of that meeting, "I've got a good story, but she's got a good story, too. I wonder if all the stories around here are like that." His perspective now that the Gold Medals belong to the *Post*? "You could have a thousand of these meetings and not have that occur."

The two projects actually were very different. The intensive nine-month investigation of police shootings was driven by computer-assisted reporting and involved three main reporters, several editors, and a raft of staffers in supporting roles. Kate Boo's project was essentially a one-woman operation built on a combination of interviews, old-fashioned data mining, and prose that filled her editors with awe. "She writes like a poet, but she's got the skill of an investigative reporter," says Leen, who served as one of her editors during what evolved into two connected series in 1999. "She wrote with a lyrical sensitivity without becoming purple, and without getting in the way of the facts."

Although the two projects might seem a reflection of the same investigative tradition that flowed from Watergate in the 1970s, this newer coverage was in the form of planned projects rather than the day-to-day incremental approach of Bob Woodward and Carl Bernstein's reporting. Woodward, now known more as an author of books on Washington politics than for his role as a *Post* assistant managing editor, knows both those traditions. After Watergate, he became Metro editor—"I was not good at it," he says with a laugh—although he was involved with the creation of the *Post* investigative unit, and led it for more than a decade.

A Job for Teamcop

The 1999 Gold Medal started with a simple statistic.

Jo Craven, a computer-assisted-reporting specialist who was being considered for a job at the *Post*, noted a high number of "Category 81s"—justifiable shootings by city police, charted by the FBI. D.C. officers had killed fifteen citizens in 1995. Said the memo she wrote just before Christmas in 1997: "When measured against the average population for the five-year period, District police racked up 8.7 homicides per 100,000 residents—the highest rate in the country among cities of at least 100,000. It is almost twice the rate of Atlanta, at 4.9, nearly three times the rate of Los Angeles, at 3.4, and more than four times the rate of New York City, which measured 2.1."

The spike the numbers formed over Washington raised eyebrows in the newsroom. "Based on that information, though, you could write about eight paragraphs," says Jeff Leen, who was assigned by investigative editor Rick Atkinson to work with Craven. Leen would decide what to do next with the computer pattern.

Such work was familiar to Leen from his time at the *Herald*, where Hurricane Andrew in 1992 had presented the backdrop for some of his projects, and where—with partner Guy Gugliotta—his stories had first identified the role of Colombia's Medellin and Cali cartels in the U.S. cocaine trade.

For the *Post* police gunplay story, he started with basic updating. "I spent two weeks reading ten years of *Washington Post* clips on shootings and I discovered a number of bad shootings, and a number involving cars," he says. In those cases, the driver often had been struck with a bullet. The introduction of the controversial Glock 9-millimeter sidearm, which tended to fire too easily, seemed to play a role, as well.

Next came a stroll to the police department's public relations office, where

Craven and Leen were told the department did not keep statistics on police shoot-ings. Leen laughs at the wave of embarrassment that came over him as he sat next to the *Post* job applicant. "I'm thinking, boy, I look like an idiot here. She's looking to me thinking, What do we do now? And I'm thinking I can't just walk out of here and say, 'Thank you very much.' So I say, 'You do a press release, right?' Yeah, the P.R. officer replied, there's a stack of them over there. So I say, 'We want that stack.'"

The releases formed one of several streams of information for the *Post*, togeth-er with news clippings on shootings and related lawsuits that had been filed, to help the paper build a list of shootings to explore. "I expected to get five or six, and there were seventy on the final list," Leen says. Those channels led to inter-views with lawyers and other sources. In talking with attorneys, Leen and Craven found yet another data stream: a paper copy of the very police list of shootings that the department had said did not exist. (Not long after the reporting began, the *Post* made a full-time hire of Craven, a former University of Missouri journalism school employee.)

Leen called that police list the crown jewels. It showed every time a police gun had been fired between 1994 and 1997, accounting for 464 incidents involving 576 officers and 2,271 bullets. "That was very useful," Leen says, "because it turned out they literally, in their statistics, did not show as many shootings as we were able to develop from our streams of information."

Leen talks of "Eureka moments" that occur during investigations—usually ear-ly in the data gathering. During Hurricane Andrew, one such moment was the discovery of a pattern showing that "the newer the house, the worse the destruc-tion." The numbers proved that recent building codes, designed to reduce storm-damage levels, were being violated. "When I saw that, I thought, You've got it," he says of the Miami investigation. In the Washington police probe, as Leen and Craven saw the data streams point to the same conclusion—that training lapses and other factors were leading to the high rate of civilian shootings by D.C. po-lice—"I knew we had it, and it would hit like a hydrogen bomb. It would with-stand any criticism."

Leen next exercised the "honest man" approach: finding someone with no ax to grind, who simply knew the situation backwards and forwards. While he won't identify the individual by name, a 2002 book by *Post* editors Leonard Downie Jr. and Robert G. Kaiser, *The News about the News: American Journalism in Peril*, gives the source as former D.C. deputy chief Bob Klotz.

"He just laid it out to me," says Leen of his source: standards were steadily slip-ping and being abused. Initially, the rule was not to shoot unless an officer was threatened by a weapon. That had deteriorated to a possible threat from the ap-parent flash of a weapon, and then just a flash of movement. Leen asked the source about the car-shooting incidents. Officers shoot at cars to stop them, Leen was told, and that is against procedure. The assurances of such a high-ranking expert carried weight with the reporter. "There was a problem with police shootings in the District," his source told him. Leen adds, "If he had said there wasn't, I'm not sure what I would have done."

A Break for Monica

When news broke about Monica Lewinsky's relationship with President Bill Clinton, it stalled the *Post*'s shooting investigation for a time. The paper assigned Leen to join others on the Lewinsky story, while Craven plugged away at the police data gathering. The paper used a Freedom of Information Act request to the District's corporation counsel to obtain a list of five years of cases in which the city had defended thirty-one police shootings. Thirteen were selected for close examination, and Craven pulled them from Superior Court. Next came a March 13 memo in which Craven summarized the cases, hinting at what investigative editor Rick Atkinson called "a clear sense of human drama and shattered lives behind our statistical scaffold." One question in Craven's memo: "Is it acceptable for an officer to step in front of a car, then shoot the driver if he fails to stop?"

By month's end, meetings resumed on the police story, and soon Leen broke free of Lewinsky duty. Marilyn Thompson, who had been away for a time, rejoined Atkinson in investigative editing. Possible approaches for narrowing the story were discussed: concentrate on car shootings—which seemed particularly egregious to Leen—or focus on the peak year of police shootings, 1995. They decided to keep the focus broad and not pick one year or one type of incident.

For the first time, they also discussed a time frame for the series. "This is gigantic," Leen said to Atkinson and Thompson. "How big do you want to make it? Three months? Six months? Nine months? I'll never forget what they said, because it made me so proud to work at the *Washington Post*. Rick and Marilyn said, 'Don't put a limit on it; do what you think needs to be done.'"

That blank check, Leen says, contrasted sharply with his last experiences at Knight Ridder's *Miami Herald*. "It had gotten to the point where I was begging for $500 to buy a copier so I could copy 100,000 documents and save the organization $15,000, which is what it would cost to purchase official copies of the original information." But at the *Post*, he says, a request for one or two more reporters immediately was granted. "I'm thinking I'd died and gone to heaven, because at the *Miami Herald* it was 'Cut back,' or 'Do you need six months? Can't you do it in three?'"

If Bob Woodward calls teaming the creation of a "perfect journalistic brain,"

Jeff Leen chooses the planning of a perfect bank robbery as a metaphor. "You need an inside man, you need a safecracker, and you need a driver," he says. The *Post* team added an investigative specialist with police department knowledge, Sari Horwitz, and a recent *Chicago Tribune* hire, David Jackson. They also gained an office nickname: Teamcop.

An electronic database version of the "crown jewel" shootings printout was created, and three years of data quickly yielded a shocking new statistic: D.C. averaged roughly one car shooting per month by police officers. The number "floored criminologists and law enforcement experts we interviewed," according to a summary of the investigation that Atkinson prepared later. Another court file the *Post* discovered listed more than six hundred suits that alleged excessive force used by D.C. police officers over four years—nearly half of them settled. "This gift horse, however, implied that non-shooting, excessive force was widespread in the District and caused us to broaden our investigation again," according to the Atkinson summary.

How to treat the question of brutality continued to be a sticky issue for what was essentially a story about shootings. From June through August the discussion was over whether the brutality element detracted from the central gunplay line of the story. Less data supported the brutality charges, and team members worried that investigating beatings could stretch the informal deadline they had set. In the end, brutality was retained as a critical part of the project; it illustrated a "continuum of force" principle by which the department operated—and trained its new officers. Shootings grew from that.

Elements of the story were divvied up. Leen took the overall case pattern, the elements of shootings into cars, and problems with the Glock sidearm. Jackson took all other shooting cases. Horwitz took the issue of brutality.

Leen made a presentation for executive editor Len Downie and managing editor Steve Coll. It wasn't easy for Leen. "I was the new guy," he says. "I was nervous and had a pretty dry mouth." But their response was a tonic. "Steve said it was a great project, just go and do it."

Publisher Donald Graham—who once had been a policeman—visited the team about the cop story he was hearing about. "It wasn't one of these pro forma visits," says Leen. "He asked great questions. He was 100 percent behind it. I was just blown away by that." In Leen's experience at the *Herald,* he says, the publisher's only involvement with investigations had been to cut their budgets.

A "Good Shooting"

Sari Horwitz had started as an intern in 1984. "Like so many journalists I came into journalism and was inspired by Watergate, and Bob Woodward, and wanted to be a political journalist and uncover some huge scandal in the country," she says. When offered "the cop shop," she balked, and it took Ben Bradlee to persuade her to take it.

"If you want to write about real life, about love and hate and greed and the human condition, go on the police beat," she remembers being told by the then-executive editor. She did, and she loved it. "I was on the night police beat for a while, which is where I really began to learn how to make sources. It was a significant time in the District, because the murder rate went soaring. And all kinds of things were going on in the city that were really fascinating. One was that Congress decided to give more money to the D.C. police to fight crime, but only if they could get a thousand more officers on the street by a certain deadline."

A related problem—deteriorating training—became a Horwitz specialty. A tipster from the police union suggested that she look at the police academy, where people were being pushed through, "people that are unqualified." Her reporting bore that out, but only because her years of experience allowed her to get her information confirmed. "You have to be on the beat for a couple of years, and do enough stories so that they see you on the crime scene," she says. "You have to be out at the retirement parties and funerals. It's slow going, and sometimes you make them mad and they cut you off."

And things were not always easy getting police stories approved by editors, either, even at the *Post*. One idea for a three-part series on "dangers in the future" posed by this group of deficient trainees was rejected. "It was very frustrating," she says, "and it's a very tricky thing to talk about." But about the same time, Horwitz took a year off and had a baby, leaving the police beat when she returned in the early 1990s. (She had felt "sweet satisfaction," she adds, when two other *Post* reporters pulled together their own police-training story along the lines she had envisioned, using some material she provided. Their work was a finalist for the 1995 Investigative Pulitzer Prize.)

Called in 1998 to join the police-shootings team, Horwitz saw a great opportunity to dig even deeper into old files she had kept at home. "I went back in my basement and found the old notebooks, including one that said, 'This officer is a lawsuit waiting to happen.'" Teamcop would find a place for that example in the series. Horwitz was assigned to develop a story on a "good shooting," one in which all the rules were followed, and the shots fired were clearly necessary. "That turned out to be a very good idea," Horwitz says. "Police work is complicated, and there's a really tough time on the streets, and we needed to tell that story, too."

The good-shooting story also gave her a chance to get back to her first love in journalism: reporting about people. "At first I was frustrated that it was such a dry story. All they had was statistics, and I wanted to get at the human story," she says.

When she found the perfect "shooter" for her case, though, he did not want to co-operate. Officer Keith DeVille had fired on a person who suddenly, shockingly had shot DeVille's partner point-blank in the head. "He had witnessed that, and had to respond," Horwitz says. "And in the gunfight that ensued, he killed the suspect. He was never the same. His marriage fell apart. He ended up drinking. He said no to me three times. No, no, no."

But she managed to change his mind, leading to an emotional interview. "He broke down in tears," Horwitz says. (Something nearly brought the reporter to tears, too: in the middle of their talk, her tape recorder jammed, leaving her to try to restructure her notes later. "I don't think I've used a tape recorder since," she says.) DeVille's story would be one of the highlights of the series.

As the reporting progressed, summaries of sixteen shooting cases were collected and sent to several experts in the use of police force. "Expert" quotes were avoided for publication, for fear of populating the story with "talking heads." But privately, experts confirmed their assessments. Editors continually encouraged the team to spend time with the police, who were about to be grilled in the series. Horwitz and other reporters went on ride-alongs with officers, and shot the Glock at the firing range.

In studying the Glock's problems, Leen had another Eureka moment. Reading through a lawsuit, he found a quote in a deposition describing policeman Frederick Broomfield's accidental shooting by his roommate, Officer Juan "Jay" Martinez Jr. Martinez had been unloading a Glock in his bedroom when Broomfield entered to ask Martinez how he wanted his chicken cooked, and the gun went off. "I looked down and I seen smoke coming from my crotch and then after that, you know, I looked at Jay and I said, 'Damn, Jay.' Then my leg started shaking and I fell." The case provided one of many macabre moments in the series.

Scooped by *City Paper*

Teamcop was clearly developing synergy. "We worked very, very closely for several months, at a rapid clip and under the scrutiny of the paper, the police department and the legal community. Our team worked because we trusted each other with moral questions and reportorial dilemmas alike," wrote Dave Jackson later. "And on those last weekends when there was only Domino's pizza to glue our frayed souls together, we enjoyed each others' company." Horwitz agrees. "I'd come in and say something, and Dave would push me to go further on it," she says.

A six-page e-mail to editor Len Downie and managing editor Steve Coll laid out the plan for a series that was targeted for the week of November 15, and reporters were asked to "defend" the leads they had constructed. In mid-October the two editors received a note on "home-stretch issues"—photos, layout, and the proposal for a six-day package. Drafts of the main stories for the first three days were provided.

Then came a crisis—one all too familiar to reporters and editors working on long-term projects. The team discovered that the rival *City Paper* was preparing a story on what was to be Jackson's third-day lead article. The lawyer who was a Jackson source, it seems, had been talking to both papers. "We're driving a real big battleship, while the *City Paper* is like a speedboat," says Leen. "The story came out, and it was over two hundred inches long, and I have to say they did a pretty good job on it." The *Post* cut back the Jackson story to a long sidebar, and shortened the entire series to five days.

It took a while for the team to bounce back. "I don't know if David Jackson ever did recover," says Leen, "although he ended up doing a great day-three story."

Teamcop went through a final November 9 checklist. Graphics were refined, and everything was in order for Sunday, November 15. Then on Saturday, President Bill Clinton called for an attack against Iraq. Just as suddenly, the attack was cancelled. After a heart-stopping meeting between Atkinson and Coll, the Sunday run date for the police series was reconfirmed.

"Summer into fall was very intense," recalls Horwitz. "There was some question toward the end: Should we have four pieces or five pieces in the series. And some people—especially me, working on the last piece—felt very strongly we needed that last piece. Others thought, How do we keep people reading?"

The way was to write it compellingly. After the overview, the second day covered shootings into cars; the third, problems with police investigations of shootings; the fourth, the Glock and training issues; and the fifth, brutality and the "continuum of force." The first-day story ran under the headline:

D.C. Police Lead
Nation in Shootings
    Lack of Training, Supervision
    Implicated as Key Factors

It began:

The District of Columbia's Metropolitan Police Department has shot and killed more people per resident in the 1990s than any other large American city police force.

Many shootings by Washington police officers were acts of courage and even heroism. But internal police files and court records reveal a pattern of reckless

and indiscriminate gunplay by officers sent into the streets with inadequate training and little oversight, an eight-month Washington Post investigation has found.

Washington's officers fire their weapons at more than double the rate of police in New York, Los Angeles, Chicago or Miami. Deaths and injuries in D.C.
police shooting cases have resulted in nearly $8 million in court settlements and
judgments against the District in the last six months alone.

"We shoot too often, and we shoot too much when we do shoot," said Executive Assistant Chief of Police Terrance W. Gainer, who became the department's
second in command in May.

That story carried all four bylines. A sidebar with a far different feel ran under the
headline "My Partner's Down." It was written by Horwitz:

As he drove across the bridge toward his home in Maryland on a crisp October
afternoon three years ago, it occurred to police officer Keith DeVille that his life
from that day forward would be divided into two halves.

There would be the days before DeVille watched his young partner, Scot S.
Lewis, being shot on the street. And there would be all the days that came after.
Early that morning, after DeVille and Lewis had responded to a call on H Street
in Northeast Washington and then stopped to help someone, a stranger stepped
out of his car and, without warning, fatally shot Lewis point-blank in the back
of the head. What happened next was mostly instinct: DeVille, for the first time
in his police career, drew his weapon and killed a man.

DeVille's actions on Oct. 6, 1995, made him a hero to his 3,550 colleagues in
the Metropolitan Police Department. His shooting of gunman Melvin Darnell
Pate was seen not just as a righteous and courageous act but also as a broader illustration of the dangers all officers face as they patrol neighborhoods in which
every stranger is a potential killer.

Unlike Ben Bradlee, who says he relishes the moment when a big story actually
rolls off the press, Leen often finds publication anticlimactic. "We have this pattern, and when people see it they're not going to believe it," he says. But for the
team, the pattern has been old news for months. Leen's first look at the police database, when he realized that they could not even keep track of their shootings, "is
what sustained me when we took the hit from the David Jackson story being
scooped."

Investigative journalism isn't for everyone, Sari Horwitz cautions. "Lots of reporters don't want to do this. It's tedious. You've got to go through boxes and boxes
to find the needle in the haystack." But for a reporter who is not driven by the
need for a daily deadline, or byline, the rewards are great. "The thing we have is
the luxury of time, which a daily reporter doesn't have," she says.

"I don't think any of us were thinking of a [Pulitzer] Prize, but we were so excited by the story," Horwitz adds. "We were excited when the new police chief said to the mayor, 'We're going to go back and look at all these shootings.' And our thought was, Whoa, this story actually made something happen. I certainly had never been on a story with that kind of impact before."

New training procedures were installed across the thirty-five-hundred-officer police force. Investigative techniques were revised. The changes were strictly monitored. In 1998, thirty-two people had been shot by D.C. policemen, twelve fatally. In 2000, the number killed had fallen to one.

1999—*Washington Post:* **For its series that identified and analyzed patterns of reckless gunplay by city police officers who had little training or supervision.**

⤜⦁⤛

"Invisible Lives, Invisible Deaths"

Not long after the *Post* won its 1999 Gold Medal, Jeff Leen was named an editor on the investigative staff. "I'd been a reporter for twenty years," he says. "I asked myself, Where do I go from the police-shooting series? I thought, If I don't take that editing job, I'm going to get a boss I don't like."

His first assignment as editor was prickly. Marilyn Thompson—who had taken over as chief investigative editor after Rick Atkinson left to write a book—handed Leen a draft of Kate Boo's story on institutions for the mentally retarded and told him he should consider putting a different lead on it.

Leen remembers picturing how his meeting with Boo might go. "I'm going to end up telling her about putting a new lead on this thing she's been working on for a year?" Leen and Boo had lunch. "They think you should change the lead," Leen said. Replied Boo, a 1988 Barnard College Phi Beta Kappa graduate, "Who's they?"

Welcome to the world of editing at the *Post*.

Things would turn out very well for the Boo piece, "Invisible Lives," and for the Boo-Leen editing relationship. But the work on that draft also began a year-long process that eventually led to a second project, delving into the heartbreaking world of D.C. homes for the mentally retarded: "Invisible Deaths." By the end of 2000, the stories would lead to the closure of group homes and would prompt federal and local investigations. City officials would be fired, and several officials would be indicted.

"These stories began in the dark," was the way Len Downie's Pulitzer nomination letter started. And in more ways than one, that was the truth.

Kate Boo had been covering the *Post*'s poverty beat, working late nights on a series on welfare reform. Boo did not drive a car herself, so she sometimes relied on friends for a ride, and one evening her driver-friend had to make a stop at one of the District's homes for the mentally retarded. Boo was shocked by what she saw. "The home had no electricity and it was just swarming with bugs," she says. "And everybody was just sitting around this table, with deformities—physical deformities, mental deformities . . . It was just so different from my perception." Boo, like many Washingtonians, had thought that various reforms over the years had turned such homes into model institutions.

Once the welfare-reform story was reported, she chose mental institutions for her next project. She began to see that her first visit had only revealed shadows of what was really wrong.

Legal reforms clearly had not done much to improve the situation in institutions. "You could burn somebody or rape somebody, whatever, and the institutions would never be penalized because there was this minor bylaw that hadn't been passed," she says. Boo started visiting homes. She interviewed staffers. She met the residents. She was hooked.

Elroy was one of eleven hundred "beneficiaries" of the publicly funded, community-based group homes. Elroy's home, like others in the system, operated under a lucrative contract with entrepreneur Rollie Washington, who lived on a so-called manor farm. Elroy, DeWitt Stith, and others from the home also worked at the farm. They received five dollars a day for cleaning horse stalls and doing other menial labor as part of what Washington called "reality therapy."

Boo followed Elroy's and Stith's lives closely, and she delved into Rollie Washington's business. She established that Elroy had been repeatedly raped in the house, and had become suicidal.

One of her reporting techniques was the impromptu visit. Showing up at Rollie Washington's farm on a Saturday, she managed to get him to sit down and talk. "His general position was the essential point of the story: that I'm every bit as good as the District needed," says Boo. "There it was." Some unscheduled visits to homes led to calls to police, who kept her out. For others, though, she saw what she needed to see.

Boo and her editors set certain standards for the story. It needed to show that past reforms were not working, and also that employees were being abusive. Many reporters aim to concentrate on how taxpayers' money is being squandered, and that makes a good story, she says. "But that's never been the thing for me." Her first goal is to write about people, and what happened to them. "The second part is about profit," she says. "That's the way it should be in my mind."

By concentrating on Elroy, DeWitt, and others, she achieved the personal emphasis she sought, although the financial picture was hardly lost. Her first story was headlined "Who Cares?" It began:

> Elroy lives here. Tiny, half-blind, mentally retarded, 39-year-old Elroy. To find him, go past the counselor flirting on the phone. Past the broken chairs, the roach-dappled kitchen and the housemates whose neglect in this group home has been chronicled for a decade in the files of city agencies. Head upstairs to Elroy's single bed.
> "You're in good hands," reads the Allstate Insurance poster tacked above his mattress—the mattress where the sexual predator would catch him sleeping. Catch him easily. The door between their rooms had fallen from its hinges. Catch him relentlessly—so relentlessly that Elroy tried to commit suicide by running blindly into a busy Southeast Washington street.

"One of the nice things about investigative for me was that there was trust," says Boo. The editors knew she was working hard, and gave her the time she needed.

Still, when it came to convincing editors that a reporter had the facts, the *Post*'s Janet Cooke legacy remained alive at the paper—especially for stories on poverty issues. Cooke's 1980 "Jimmy's World" story, after all, had been a poverty story: the wrenching tale of a supposed eight-year-old heroin addict.

One lesson that the *Post* had learned from that embarrassing episode was that in writing about obscure people, with no voice of their own, standards must be just as high as for profiling public figures.

"Because at the *Post* I worked in the ghetto—and Janet Cooke worked in the ghetto—you just have to presume in poverty reporting that it's going to be challenged, that you must get your ducks in a row. That's not just in this series, it's in all the work I've ever done in the inner city," says Boo. In this case, Boo found sources to back up everything she heard from the retarded individuals. "The burden of proof has to come from elsewhere—from the public record, or admissions from the people who did the wrongdoing themselves. Then it's fair."

In early story development, Boo says, Rick Atkinson helped her shape the project to describe the system rather than one home or one individual case. "The next thing was realizing who was running the homes, and the kind of accountability they had," according to Boo. Working through *Post* lawyers, she filed Freedom of Information Act requests. She followed up on the reports that Elroy had been raped and tried to commit suicide. "The records were saying everything was well and good. It was clear that a false paper trail was being created," she says.

She persisted in trying to get confirmation that Elroy was raped, and finally got it. Yes, the manager of the group homes told her, adding the nuance that the sexual predator who victimized him "was incessant." The manager told her that "whatever this guy's taking . . . is better than Viagra!"

Boo kept detailed documentary backup for the story's claims, both about specific cases and the financial peculiarities of the whole system. "I love documents," she says. "It's a great shy-person's kind of journalism. It's this great intellectual game. What was the relationship of this person, who bought the house for that person. It's a way of seeing the bigger picture."

Boo got along especially well with the paper's attorneys. "The *Post* lawyers are in a class by themselves in terms of caring about justice, as opposed to caring about not getting sued," she says. Plus, working with lawyers reminds reporters of the value of accuracy on details in the story. "With these kinds of stories, one mistake can take out two thousand facts."

Unlike most reporters, Boo is "anti-series," she says. Her Invisible Lives project was intended as one story, she says, but had to run as a two-parter because of the sheer amount of information.

The Letdown—and Another Series

Then came the letdown after the story was in print. "There was a superficial level of outrage," says Boo. "And I got all of that." There were letters to the editor and statements from officials that heads would roll. But Boo felt stymied by the lack of real action. "What really *means* something is if they actually do something about it," she says. "What I care about is if they change the friggin' law."

It was almost as if the first day's headline—Who Cares?—described the reaction to the series as well. "As always when you write about poverty issues, there's a hue and cry, and things go back to normal."

Jeff Leen loved the first series for its lyrical writing and its passion for social justice. With some reporters, passion colors the final product. "She's probably the only person who could pull that off," says Leen. "She is so meticulous and fair-minded and precise, and so intelligent, that it amplifies and raises up her work, and doesn't get in the way of it. She combines these things that most people think are oil and water—incongruous."

All along, Leen had been intrigued by a sidebar that appeared with the first story. It offered just a hint, he thought, of the stark and inhuman end to which Boo's subjects' lives came. "Now," he told her, "you have to do the deaths."

The reporter was not thrilled at the thought. "Nobody wanted to read about it in the first place; nobody's going to want to read about it again," she recalls thinking. So why did she keep at it, aiming for a December run date? "In a way I did it because I didn't know what else to do." In the end, she found that Leen was right. "It took the deaths to make people care," she says.

The project, focusing on what happens after individuals from the homes die, was also broken into two parts.

Boo found official records showing an unrealistically low number of deaths among the institutionalized people—eleven in six years. (Eventually she obtained an admission from the city that the real number was 116.) The lives of some of the deceased simply had been "erased." Further, manipulation of medical records led to some victims of fatal abuse being listed as dying of natural causes.

One example: Frederick E. Brandenburg, who Boo proved had been mistakenly drugged and left to die by a careless attendant. His body was then illegally moved and cremated. When she inquired, Boo was told that an autopsy had been declined by Brandenburg's sisters because they were Jehovah's Witnesses. When she tracked the sisters down, however, she learned that one was Baptist, the other Catholic.

In the end, says Boo, it helped with her reporting on the Brandenburg story that she was a native Washingtonian, familiar with the city. When she received a call from the person who had shredded the records, the caller was reluctant to talk or give a name. "I knew from the phone exchange exactly where he was, and I knew the one bar in that neighborhood, and I said, 'I'll meet you there.'" At the meeting, she was told that employees were rewarded for such shredding. "When I had that, I knew that they couldn't get out of it," she says.

Leen admits to being choked with emotion at times during his editing of Boo's copy. The first story carried the headline "Lives Erased Without a Word." It began:

> The corpse measured 66 inches from blue toes to jutting ears. In a beige house on Tenley Circle, a dentist-entrepreneur lugged this cargo down the stairs into the basement and laid it to rest by the washer.
>
> The body in plaid pajamas was that of a 57-year-old retarded ward of the District of Columbia. On the streets outside the city-funded group home where he had lived and died, kids sometimes called him Retard-O. Inside, he sweetened the hours by printing the name his mother gave him before she gave him up. Frederick Emory Brandenburg. He blanketed old telephone directories with that name, covered the TV Guides the home's staffers tossed aside. He glutted the flyleaves of his large-print Living Bible. The immensity of the effort made his hands shake, but the habit seemed as requisite as breath. In this way Brandenburg, whose thick-tongued words were mysteries to many, impressed the fact of his existence on his world.
>
> In January 1997, that existence was obliterated by his caretakers.

During production week Leen asked managing editor Steve Coll for an extra page. "The project was supposed to be three open pages," but for special graphics and subheadlines that were being planned, four pages were needed. Coll's response: "You got it." Says Leen, "There wasn't even a blink."

Read It and Weep

But making it into print was a whole other story.

On production night, Leen and Boo stayed late in the office, carefully defusing potential problems. There were lots of them. What made the layout tricky was that the subheads and cutlines for the piece were specially designed, with intricate computer coding. Care had to be taken to avoid losing paragraphs when the story "turned" from column to column. As Leen and Boo watched during the evening, type got dropped, and with difficulty was restored. When the situation finally was solved, a cheer went up. Leen took Boo to a Burger King on K Street before each went home. Leen turned in for the night satisfied with "the best story I've ever edited in my career."

The next morning, Boo was staying with her parents, her ritual when a story was finished. "We always do that," she says, "because I say that I'll get to see you one last night before I go to libel jail."

Her father read the story first the next morning. There was a problem, he said. Not libel, but something in the way the story just stopped flowing. Kate read in horror. Missing were several blocks of type, including that hard-earned explanation of how the authorities had lied about Brandenburg being cremated because his next-of-kin were Jehovah's Witnesses. "I read it that Sunday morning and wept," she recalls.

Leen got her first call. "Kate was devastated. She was saying that people said it ruined the project. It doesn't make sense. Talk about a crisis. I didn't know what to say. I told her that at some point this is going to seem like a very small matter," he says. "I didn't even know if that was true."

The post-mortem on the printing glitch—"it would have taken a presidential commission to figure it out," says Leen—showed a typesetting error in the pagination system. A well-meaning technician apparently had seen a small problem during the press run, after Leen and Boo went home. The technician made a "fix," and the delicately balanced layout imploded. No one caught it. "We did have thirty thousand copies that were just perfect," says Leen.

By 2005, Boo had almost forgotten about it—almost. Looking at the two series as a whole, she is proud of the impact it had in the community. Did it occur to her that it might win a Pulitzer? "As a reporter you don't think about that," she says. It is the editors who make the decision to enter your work. "You just wait and see what happens."

She does know what editor to thank most: her mother. "She was my first reader on everything, and a real force," says Boo. "I'm sorry, Jeff, but my best editor is my mom."

2000—*Washington Post:* Notably for the work of Katherine Boo that disclosed wretched neglect and abuse in the city's group homes for the mentally retarded, which forced officials to acknowledge the conditions and begin reforms.

A team of *Washington Post* reporters revealing the high number of police shootings of citizens won the paper's first Pulitzer Prize for Public Service since Watergate. Pictured in the newsroom are (from left) Marilyn Thompson, investigations editor; Ira Chinoy, director of computer-assisted reporting; database researcher Jo Craven and researcher Alice Crites; reporters Sari Horwitz and Jeff Leen; and Rick Atkinson, assistant managing editor/investigative. Photo by *Post* staff, used by permission.

Work by the *Washington Post*'s Katherine Boo led to the first consecutive Pulitzer Gold Medals for a newspaper in 2000. *Post* staff photo.

CHAPTER 21

Covering "De-Portland"

There are services to the public that only a newspaper can perform. . . . Over and over again throughout the year, the paper righted clear-cut wrongs that small-town mayors, petition-writers, colleagues, business people, corporations, school children, federal judges—even members of Congress—were unable to right.

> —*Oregonian* managing editor/enterprise
> Amanda Bennett, January 28, 2001

*T*he *Oregonian* had gone through a dispiriting time in 1992, having seriously botched its coverage of one of Oregon's most influential citizens, Senator Bob Packwood. In November, the *Washington Post* had broken a story on Packwood's history of sexually harassing women, calling attention to the Portland paper's failure to write it first. Things got worse, when the paper's own Capitol Hill reporter turned out to have received inappropriate advances from the senator—and did not report them at the time.

But the Newhouse-owned *Oregonian* began recovering the next year, with the arrival of Sandra Mims Rowe as its first editor recruited from outside. Rowe brought a new vision for the paper—which was among the oldest businesses in the Northwest, having been founded before Oregon became a state in 1859—and a definite sense about whom to hire. Indeed, if there ever was a case of one editor's philosophy laying the groundwork for a Pulitzer Gold Medal, this may have been it.

Her introduction to the *Oregonian* did not come easily. Some staffers worried about being managed by the former editor of the *Virginian-Pilot* in Norfolk, with no ties to the Pacific Northwest. "I was this chick, not just from the East but from the South," she says with a laugh, suspecting that the first staff reaction was probably, "My God, what's going to happen to us?" She had her own doubts, too. "In some ways I felt so alone when I got here," says Rowe. Not only was the area unfamiliar, but nearly the entire *Oregonian* top management changed in the first six months. She had a sense that she "was trying to learn the company by Braille."

Still, publisher Fred Stickel had assured her that she had a free hand to make the journalism as good as it could be. And she loved the challenge of fixing what ailed the paper.

That started with its identity crisis. While the *Oregonian* had bought the *Oregon Journal* and combined the two papers' staffs twelve years earlier, a peculiar sort of caste system still marked staffers. "People would introduce each other to me and say, 'Joe was a *Journal* person,'" she recalls. "At my first staff meeting I found myself standing up and saying, OK, folks, I've got a news flash for you: The merger is over. I don't really care what your beginnings were here."

Quickly she began to surround herself with talented replacement editors who would share her vision of the *Oregonian* as a voice for the Northwest—a voice that would also advance the paper's role on the national press stage. "Regional papers are the backbone of journalism in this country," she says. And her paper had an advantage in its planned transformation, because there were few expectations for the city to produce powerhouse reporting. "We were left alone," she says. "We're isolated out here on the edge of the continent, for gosh sakes. We're not an airline hub, so it's not like the folks from New York are passing through the city." She hired executive editor Peter Bhatia, who had been involved with the *Sacramento Bee*'s 1992 "Sierra in Peril" series. Eventually she also landed Amanda Bennett, a veteran reporter and editor from the *Wall Street Journal,* to be her managing editor/enterprise.

The editors built on the staff's fierce local and regional pride. "All I had to do was help them believe that we could put out a great newspaper in Portland, Oregon, and that the city deserves a great paper," Rowe says. "It was, after all, one of the country's stronger newspaper markets, where the daily still went to 50 percent of all households." If she could reinvigorate the paper and find a story or two capable of making waves from coast to coast, Pulitzer Prizes surely would be a way to create the national image she craved.

"The Girl Who Cries"

As the 1990s ended, such a story came along. It started with a discovery by two reporters about problems infecting Portland's office of the federal Immigration and Naturalization Service. Like many blockbusters, it started small.

Julie Sullivan had recently been recruited by Bhatia, who admired her work at the *Spokane Spokesman-Review.* Covering demographics and the 2000 census for the Portland paper, Sullivan got a tip from a local attorney about a fifteen-year-old Chinese client. The Chinese girl, who had been granted political asylum, had been held for eight months in a county jail because of bureaucratic miscues. At the time, the Elian Gonzalez immigration story was garnering national attention. Immigration was not a beat at the *Oregonian,* but Sullivan knew that anything local that at all resembled Florida's Elian battle could be interesting.

When Sullivan walked into the juvenile jail in December of 1999 she found a scared teenager surrounded by murderers and other hardened criminals. Never naming the girl in her story—but calling her by the phrase the guards used, "the girl who cries"—the reporter pointed out that the youngster was one of five Chinese teens who had been on a freighter that developed mechanical problems. The shock of the story was that authorities were housing rescued youngsters with the overall jail population. This one child clearly had been lost within an inept INS office, without her relatives being notified. Within ten days of the story's appearing, a safe foster home was found for her. Sullivan then went back to her census beat.

Fellow reporter Richard Read took a particular interest in the story. The Cambridge, Massachusetts, native had run a one-person *Oregonian* bureau in Tokyo starting in 1989, before he and his wife had chosen to move back to Portland. (They made the move, he says, because "there was this dynamic new editor in Portland— and Portland's a cool town.") In covering his new international business beat he achieved just the kind of regional-cum-national recognition that Sandy Rowe had sought. In 1999 he won the paper's first Pulitzer Prize in forty-two years, in Explanatory Reporting, for "The French Fry Connection." A remarkable if unlikely-sounding series, it analyzed the Asian economic crisis by tracing a container of fries, made from regionally grown potatoes, to a McDonald's outlet in Singapore.

Read soon started hearing from his own sources about problems at the INS. One exporter of materials for fast-food stores told him in late March that INS errors were upsetting Asian businesspeople. Visitors to Portland "were being either bundled back on the airplane to go home to Asia, or else thrown in the county jail," he was told. Getting at the story was difficult. "It was hard to even get names," he says, "because the companies weren't particularly interested in having this publicity." But he was able to identify enough cases for a story, and the link between his piece and Sullivan's—an apparently dysfunctional INS office in Portland— drew the two reporters together. They puzzled over why INS agents would be motivated to act in a way that was so clearly wrong.

The stories also caught Amanda Bennett's attention, and she began to discuss with Rowe the possibility of a team to look at the INS from a national perspective. The Portland INS district director, David Beebe, seemed part of the problem. Distant and uncommunicative, he invited more controversy with each negative, unanswered story. And soon reporters were hearing about INS failings in other jurisdictions.

Bennett placed the bar high for a decision to take on the INS story as a major national project. First, it had to be established that these were not isolated incidents, but part of a U.S. trend. She knew, too, that so much had been written on INS problems—often by papers in Los Angeles, Texas, or New York, with far better excuses to study immigration issues—that the *Oregonian* would have to do it much better if it was to be heard outside the Northwest.

Sullivan and Read were trying to answer Bennett's initial questions when another INS story broke in August. A Chinese businesswoman, Guo Liming, was stopped at the airport, then strip-searched and jailed for two nights before authorities decided that her problem was a passport that was dog-eared but legitimate. Hearing that the woman was about to fly on to New York after her detention, Read hurriedly found an interpreter and a photographer and rushed to the airport, locating her in the boarding area. In twenty minutes, working through the interpreter, he confirmed the background information he had been given by her lawyer, and heard her describe the pain of the experience.

As the woman was about to slip onto the flight before the doors closed, he recalls, "the last thing she said was, 'I don't want any of this on the record.'" After a panicked discussion, through the interpreter, she finally gave the go-ahead to use her name, and the interview was saved. (When Read asked the interpreter what had changed her mind, he responded that he told her, "This is America. You can't do that.")

The page-one story, headlined "INS jails business traveler," began:

> Immigration inspectors jailed an innocent Chinese businesswoman for two nights after rejecting her passport Saturday, following earlier promises to avoid jailing travelers in all but aggravated cases.
>
> U.S. Immigration and Naturalization Service managers defended their actions Tuesday after letting Guo Liming resume her trip to New York via Portland International Airport. They said they considered the case aggravated because Guo, 36, appeared typical of Chinese sneaking into the United States. They blamed her for not replacing a passport that looked doctored but turned out to be authentic.
>
> Guo said INS inspectors made her strip to her underwear for a search. They interrogated her under oath through an interpreter. Then they handcuffed her for the two-hour drive to jail in The Dalles. "They owe me an apology," she said.
>
> The jailing revived nagging questions concerning INS conduct at the Port-

land airport, where inspectors reject a far higher percentage of foreigners than are turned away from other West Coast airports. Last January, Guo used the same passport to enter the United States without incident in Los Angeles.

"I now understood what this story was about," says Bennett of her reaction to Guo's account. "It was about the INS being capricious, arbitrary, and possibly acting illegally—and doing things to people for which they had no recourse." The project was on, even if Read and Sullivan didn't know it yet.

An interview later that week confirmed that the newspaper was on the right track. In a desperate, bold move to get a story on Beebe, Sullivan went to his office without an appointment. "We were under pressure to do a profile, and he would never even answer his phone," she says. Some politicians had called for his resignation, and she felt readers—and she herself—needed to understand this man. "I told the security guard that I had an appointment with Mr. Beebe. I went to his office and he opened the office door," she says. "There's got to be more to you than this," Sullivan told him as she held out the story about the attacks on him. "It was hard, because I'm a nice person. I just felt I had to get this guy to talk to me," she says. And talk Beebe did.

Under her questioning, the embattled, isolated bureaucrat unburdened himself of the problems of his job. Headlined "Beebe: I Have to Be Who I Am," the story started:

> The morning after the governor, the mayor and members of Congress demanded that he resign, David V. Beebe arrived at his desk, as always, just after 6 a.m.
>
> As critics jammed telephone lines to his supervisors in California and Washington, D.C., Beebe worked alone in the locked, polished stillness of his fourth-floor office. His staff of 135, stationed mostly on the floors around him, were somber. Friends chatting on their lawns near his Beaverton home shared a hushed concern. But the telephone on Beebe's immaculate desk was noticeably quiet.
>
> As district director of the Immigration and Naturalization Service, Beebe is Mr. INS, the point man for immigration law in Oregon. His signature is stamped or signed on almost every significant paper that deals with deporting criminals, arresting illegal workers, approving steps toward citizenship. His name also appears on orders that divide families, incite attorneys and has now mobilized furious business and political critics.
>
> For four months, his handling of INS rejections of Asian travelers at Portland International Airport has drawn a steady stream of senior INS and U.S. State Department officials to Portland, where his methodical, precise response has exasperated even the regional INS public relations director.
>
> "She says I'm a total disaster," Beebe said of his image. "And she's probably

right. It's not like I'm oblivious to that, but I have to be who I am rather than project a veneer of something I'm not."

When reports of Portland's unusually high rates of refusals at PDX drew a chorus of critics in April, Beebe responded exactly as he has in 12 years as district director, with little apology or emotion. He held lengthy public meetings and seminars, explaining in sometimes excruciating detail the alphabet soup of immigration forms and protocol. He telephoned business executives, wrote lengthy explanatory letters and is frankly flabbergasted that so many of the people he's been calling are the very ones calling for his head.

"I thought we were building bridges," he said.

Instead, critics are building a case that Beebe's office is out of sync even with the INS, operating with a draconian mindset that threatens international business and tourist traffic.

Sullivan also got him to talk intimately about his childhood, suggesting an explanation for his unbending management style. She supplemented his words with accounts from friends and family members.

"I came," he said, "from dust." He was born in Minden, Iowa, population 400, the second child of the publisher of the Minden Times, who died of a stroke when Beebe was 1.

His mother remarried and had two more daughters. Shortly after the youngest was born, his mother was infected during a polio epidemic and within three weeks, died. Beebe was an orphan by age 7.

His mother's husband, who never adopted him, struggled to farm 120 acres with four small children. Beebe walked each morning to a one-room school with no running water. But he had to get his work done first: up at 3:45 a.m. to hand milk the cows.

When he was 12, they lost the farm. Beebe went to work alongside his stepfather at a gas station in town. The stepfather, meanwhile, had married a woman with three children. She did not like Beebe, threatening to put him in an orphanage and taking little interest in his well-being.

What saved him were his schoolmates, "my contact with reality," and the planes crossing the Iowa skies. From the time his mother died, he dreamed of flying. He graduated from high school on a Thursday night in 1963 and by Sunday morning was en route to the Air Force.

"None of us knew anything about him until he talked about who he was in the interview," says Sullivan. "He was a frustrated military person who went into the Air Force hoping to fly planes," she says. He had never qualified as a military pilot.

"Julie got all this out of him," Read observes. "He just had this veneer that was very hard to crack." Shortly, Beebe announced that he was going to retire.

Sullivan and Read were set to congratulate themselves on having wrapped up a two-person reporting project that had forced a replacement at the top of the INS office. They had turned up numerous suggestions that problems in Portland—known in some Asian publications as De-Portland because of how many foreigners were turned away—reflected flaws across the giant agency. Still, pushing the investigation nationally did not seem to them like a natural next step for the *Oregonian.*

"I remember walking into Amanda's office and thinking, Wow, that was an incredible run of stories. Now what should we work on?" Read says. "But Amanda just looked at us with that unblinking way she has and said, 'Oh no, this is just the beginning.' I looked at Julie, and Amanda starts talking about this huge story, and going national with it—and, by the way, we have to wrap it up by the end of the year. And Julie and I are looking at each other shell-shocked. And I said, Gee, that's a terrific project, but we're going to need help."

The reporters knew what a year-end target meant. In terms rarely spoken in a newsroom, it often translates into a desire among editors to submit the work for prize consideration. And the biggest prize of all is a Pulitzer. To the request for reinforcements, though, Bennett's response surprised and excited the two reporters. "Usually the editor says, OK, we'll find some people for you," Read notes. "But she just asked, 'If you could pick anyone, who would it be?' I mean, that never happens."

Sullivan and Read asked for two of the paper's top reporters: former Washington correspondent Brent Walth and Kim Christensen, who previously had been on a team that won a 1996 Investigative Reporting Pulitzer at the *Orange County Register.* Both were among Sandy Rowe's hires. They joined the INS team on August 28.

"You can't underestimate how important it was that Rich and Kim were Pulitzer-winners," says Sullivan. "It was a mature group. Kim and Rich were also able to interpret, and in many ways moderate all this energy." (Walth also had been a Pulitzer Explanatory Reporting finalist the prior year, as part of a two-person *Oregonian* team.)

Each team member found a niche that reflected a personal interest, says Read, who chose to concentrate on "petty corruption and the whole culture of the INS." Sullivan built information around how the agency used the prison system, while Walth developed expertise in how the INS dealt with political asylum, and Christensen examined the toll on families. The two newcomers to the team, says Read, "cracked agency secrets, finding documents that revealed abuse, corruption, and bungling."

Amanda Bennett provided the direction for the team reporting and organization, trying to break down a complex collection of story angles. In a way, that fed into one of Rowe's beliefs about the role of a project-minded daily newspaper: that only its brand of intensive investigation can deal with the world's truly difficult problems. "We believe newspapers, for survival, have to embrace complexity. You don't try to reduce it and say this isn't complex, it's really black and white," she says. "What I loved about this story was the degree of difficulty."

Ironically, the job of capturing the situation's complexity involved first arriving at some simple themes to use in reporting. At a September team meeting Brent Walth wrote concepts on a board: "Corruption," "secret prisons," "bungling," "service," "abuse," "waste," "pressure," "economic impact." The idea was to find which ones expressed the massive amount of information each reporter was collecting. Each reporter had access to a group computer file and was able to use the notes of other reporters, while confirming facts.

In early October another Walth-led team meeting broadened the themes, suing a big computer screen, these were entered:

The INS runs a secret, abusive prison system;

The INS has fostered corruption in its ranks;

The INS wrecks families, and

The INS has created an internal culture that has tolerated racism and abuse.

Walth led the team members through their notes, helping the team line up material under the headings "What We Have" and "What We Need" as it moved toward the December finish line. The series was taking shape. Ground rules for the investigation included no second-hand sources and three examples for every point made. Material from interest groups would be shunned. Further, reporters would ask both Democrats and Republicans for opinions on the findings about the INS, and former INS officials would be asked to provide historical perspective.

"We came back to her [Bennett] frequently with our progress reports, but she trusted us and let us manage things," says Read. "A lot of editors think they have to micromanage you daily, or tell you they know better. We could not have accomplished what we did without the unfettered trust she gave us to run things on our own."

"Prosecutorial Editing"

With the INS failing to respond to the team's questions again after Beebe's departure, the reporters lacked the normal procedure for challenging the claims that were about to appear in their stories. In November, Bennett stepped in as devil's advocate. "Amanda started doing what she calls prosecutorial editing, going through every story and ripping it apart," says Read. "She was trying to play the role of the INS." So close to the finish line, it drove some of the reporters crazy.

Read was asked to compare the conduct of the INS to that of other agencies—better or worse. "How am I supposed to figure that out? Am I supposed to do that in the last thirty hours?" he asked Bennett. "Yeah, you are," she replied.

He obliged by interviewing congressional oversight-committee members, federal judges, and former Justice Department officials, and comparing the numbers of internal investigations at various agencies. "That was about the most pressured I've ever felt from an editor," he says. "Bottom line: I had her trust, but this story was not going to run until this story passed the bar."

"There was an adrenaline rush when you passed those bars," adds Sullivan. "I remember bringing her documents like I'd discovered a gold nugget. And she'd be so delighted. She felt enormous pressure, too, but she didn't let on."

Readers seeing the six-part "Liberty's Heavy Hand" package that started on December 10 could not have guessed how rushed the project was at the end. Even the reporters and some editors could hardly believe it. "I was reporting the final installment well into the week the story was running," Read recalls. Kim Christensen called meeting the strict year-end deadline "like making sausage from live animals."

Editor Bhatia acknowledges the chaos in the home stretch. "In hindsight, you look back at it and say, 'Hmm, that probably isn't the best technique ever.' When you've been at it for months and months before publishing, you don't want to be goofing around with it at 10 o'clock at night when the first installment publishes. That's a recipe for something bad to happen. But it was just the reality of how the project worked." Some rigorous editing was necessary to get the first Sunday installment, an overview piece, ready to go to press at 6 a.m. Saturday.

"Somehow, through all this, Kim was the one who sat down and wrote the lead story. To this day I have no idea how he did it," says Read. "We all gave him files of stuff, and we all wanted to hold onto pieces of it for individual bylined stories that would run later on. Without cherry-picking the best stuff, Kim drew together all these themes, and his first draft was pretty much what ran."

Carrying all four bylines, the first story ran under the headline "Unchecked Power of the I.N.S. Shatters American Dream." It began:

> Murder suspects have more rights than many people who encounter the U.S. Immigration and Naturalization Service—and not just the 1.6 million the agency catches trying to sneak across the Mexican border each year.
>
> While its role as protector of the nation's borders shapes the INS' most visible and enduring image, its heavy hand falls on people most Americans will never see.

They are children as young as 8 who are held in a secretive network of prisons and county jails.

They are parents and spouses of U.S. citizens, who are deported or imprisoned without due process of law; the asylum seekers who are greeted not with the promise of haven, but with jail.

They are people for whom the Statue of Liberty stands not as a beacon of hope and welcome, but as a symbol of iron-fisted rejection.

"The INS is like an onion," says U.S. Rep. Janice Schakowsky, D-Ill., whose constituents complain more about the agency than anything else. "The more you peel it away, the more you cry."

The second-day story analyzed the bureaucratic workings of what one person described as "the agency from hell." The next looked at the splintering of families because of immigration law and its application. Later came stories headlined "Overwhelmed I.N.S. Develops Culture of Abuse, Racism" and "Reformers See No Quick or Easy Fix for Troubled I.N.S."

Bennett contrasts the *Oregonian's* work with the approach she took in twenty-three years at the *Wall Street Journal.* "We were turning the telescope around," she says. At the *Journal,* national or global issues prevailed, focusing on local examples to bring it home. In writing about the INS for the *Oregonian* "you start with your local story and see where it takes you. That's what keeps you from being parochial, and it's the best service you can do for your newspaper." Sandy Rowe drove the investigation from above, Bennett says. "She was always asking, 'What can we do that's bigger?'"

During the reporting process, was there a feeling that this story could win a Pulitzer? "Never for a minute did it occur to us," says Bennett. And even after the paper submitted the work for the prize early in 2001, "it actually never crossed my mind that we were going to win. We were absolutely on fire to nail the story, and do the best we could. But when I found out we'd won, I was totally blown away." Bennett had been at Columbia that March as a juror in Beat Reporting, and tried to check informally, without success, on the progress of the entry. "I remember thinking, 'I bet you it made it a long way in the rounds,'" she says. Neither had Sandy Rowe thought about a possible Pulitzer, she says—until she began culling the fifty-story project to bring it down to the required twenty exhibits to enter for Pulitzer Prize consideration. "I looked through them one by one and thought, 'Son of a gun, that's the best we could ever do.' As an editor, I just wanted to cheer. And I thought, I don't know whether this will win, but I promise you this is Pulitzer-caliber work—something I never had said when the series was published."

The *Oregonian* celebrated twice in 2001. Reporter Tom Hallman Jr. also won in Feature Writing, for coverage of a disfigured fourteen-year-old boy who had elected to have life-threatening surgery as a way of improving his appearance. Rowe was on the Pulitzer board at the time, so she did not get to hear the discussions involving the two categories.

The board did not have an easy decision naming a Public Service winner. The Associated Press had been nominated for its coverage of the 2000 presidential election, "particularly during those 36 uncertain days when much of the nation looked to the AP for disciplined, 24-hour reporting on the close votes and recounts," the board wrote. Also, the *Washington Post* was under consideration for its coverage of AIDS in Africa, marking the board's interest in considering more international stories for the Gold Medal.

When Richard Read and Julie Sullivan learned that the INS stories had won the Gold Medal for the *Oregonian,* both reporters recalled their formative years.

Sullivan thought of all the great stories that—unlike the INS series—had *not* been written. Her hometown of Butte, Montana, she says, is the largest continually inhabited Superfund site in America. "To be from a Superfund area, where there is a vat of acid a mile wide on a hill above my mother's house," she says, "you realize that terrible things happen every day right in front of your eyes." When she was acknowledged for her work, Sullivan exclaimed: "This is for Butte!"

"I grew up with the whole Woodward and Bernstein experience," says Read, an Amherst College graduate who remembers as a teenager attending a talk given by Elliot Richardson and Archibald Cox in the mid-1970s. They discussed what was known as the Saturday Night Massacre, during which Attorney General Richardson refused President Nixon's order to fire Cox as special prosecutor, after which Richardson himself resigned. It was then that Read had decided on journalism as a career.

"I thought, 'Here are Woodward and Bernstein getting in there and finding out things and changing the country. What better job could there be than that?'"

2001—*Oregonian:* For its detailed and unflinching examination of systematic problems within the U.S. Immigration and Naturalization Service, including harsh treatment of foreign nationals and other widespread abuses, which prompted various reforms.

Oregonian staffers (from left) Kim Christensen, Julie Sullivan, Rich Read, and Brent Walth tease managing editor Amanda Bennett after learning of the paper's 2001 Pulitzer. *Oregonian* photo by Fredrick D. Joe.

The *Oregonian*'s editor, Sandra Mims Rowe, celebrates with executive editor Peter Bhatia. *Oregonian* staff photo.

AFTERWORD

Back to the Future

The research into this near century of Pulitzer Prize Gold Medals began in mid 2002. The *New York Times* had been awarded the Gold Medal for having helped its city and its country cope with the September 11 terrorist attacks. The *Boston Globe* was deep into exposing two nationwide evils—priests preying on young parishioners, and the cover-up by Catholic Church leaders—and would be honored for it in 2003. Two great years for the Public Service Pulitzers.

Entering 2007, though, the last stages of writing *Pulitzer's Gold* at times felt like a race against the unraveling of the very American newspaper business that had produced all this great journalism. Certainly, the 2006 prizes won by the *Times-Picayune* in New Orleans and the *Sun Herald* in Gulfport, Mississippi, for their Hurricane Katrina coverage focused attention on the difference that the daily press can make in a time of community crisis. But elsewhere, a shocking Carnegie Corporation statistic kept popping up: that the average age of readers had soared to fifty-three. Younger generations were looking elsewhere—or nowhere—for their news, and papers across the nation searched for ways to win them over. Meanwhile, as daily readership and revenues both continued to slide, several storied franchises went on the block. Most had trouble selling.

Selection of the venerable *Wall Street Journal* for its first-ever Public Service Pulitzer, announced on April 16, 2007, provided some respite from those worries —for two weeks, at least. The prize recognized a team effort centered in the Boston bureau of the two-million-circulation business paper. Its coverage analyzed how some corporations improperly "backdated" the stock-option incentives awarded to executives, giving them richer pay packages than they merited. By the time of the announcement of the prizes, federal investigations had targeted 140 companies, and more than seventy executives had lost their jobs.

The Public Service honor added to a powerful Pulitzer-winning tradition at the 118-year-old *Journal.* The paper also won the 2007 International Reporting Prize for its analysis of global complications arising from a surging Chinese economy. The two awards gave the paper a total of thirty-three Pulitzers in all—twenty-five of them won since 1980. Through those decades, the Pulitzer board's selections had been tracing the emergence of a dominant force in American journalism.

By April 30, though, the *Journal* was making headlines for another reason. Rupert Murdoch's News Corporation had offered to acquire the paper and its parent, Dow Jones and Company, for $5 billion. The bid, reflecting a hefty premium over the company's stock-market value, was directed squarely at the Bancroft family, descendants of Clarence Barron, the turn-of-the-century Boston journalist and then-owner of Dow Jones. The family members held majority voting control of the stock, and no sale could be approved without them.

Even at $5 billion, Dow Jones and its *Journal* crown jewel were cheap compared to media enterprises less tied to print, like Bloomberg, a relatively new entry to the media scene, or Reuters and Thomson Publishing. The latter two companies, in fact, announced their own merger plan at around the same time, worth $17.2 billion. News Corporation itself had a stock market capitalization of around $70 billion. In addition to the *New York Post* and other papers in the United States and abroad, Murdoch's empire included the Fox movie and television businesses and global satellite television interests. Still, in the eyes of many, his personal penchant for meddling with editorial policy—and his sensationalist proclivities—threatened to undermine the integrity of one of America's great press institutions. Talk circulated at midyear about other potential buyers, though none was eager to pay Murdoch's price.

No matter who owns the *Journal* in the future, though, the story behind its coverage of stock-option backdating will serve to illustrate the best work of a news operation that long has cherished entrepreneurial reporting and national teamwork, tying it together with an extraordinary New York–based editing mechanism.

Extra, Extra

In late 2005, Boston investigative team leader Mark Maremont was the first *Wall Street Journal* staffer to take note of reports about the strange games being played by companies in setting the options "strike price"—the price at which executives are entitled to buy their shares when the terms of their grants allow it. In most cases, the strike price is the quoted value of the stock on the day the company's board of directors approves the options. Such a design provides a fair corporate baseline to use in rating the performance of individual executives over time. All within a week, reporter Maremont was tipped to some peculiar legal disclosures being made by a handful of companies in Securities and Exchange Commission filings, and also to the existence of academic research focusing on unusual stock-option timing issues.

At first, he had trouble understanding the filings. There almost certainly was hanky-panky in the corporate accounting for stock options at some companies, but Maremont wasn't sure exactly what was being masked by the bookkeeping. As for the academic research, the tipster had pointed the reporter to a study by University of Iowa professor Eric Lie, who thought that low strike-price patterns might reflect companies using hindsight to identify historical lows, and then to set their strike prices after the fact. Maremont found other academic research, including an eight-year-old study by David Yermack at New York University's Stern School of Business, suggesting that companies may have manipulated strike prices by controlling the release of news to depress the quote on the day in question.

As October 2005 ended, the picture got clearer. "One of the companies I'd been looking at fired its top three executives and said they'd been doing funny things with stock-option dating," Maremont recalls. An article that he prepared with two other reporters appeared on November 3 on page seven, mainly discussing the problems at Mountain View, California, software maker Mercury Interactive Corporation. It was a typical *Journal* collaboration between reporters from its news bureaus. While two other staffers had closer contact with the company involved, Maremont brought to the story his recent familiarity with the backdating issue. A week later, he wrote his own article. It began: "Federal regulators and academics, scrutinizing a broad pattern of well-timed stock-option grants, are exploring the extent to which companies improperly backdated grants to provide insiders an extra pay windfall." Maremont again focused on Mercury, which admitted in SEC filings to backdating and acknowledged that it had been improper. Noting the academic research at Iowa and New York University, his article mentioned several other companies that had disclosed that they were being investigated by the SEC. The story ran on page one as an "extra," a term the *Journal* uses for a major news article each day that is elevated to run on the first page. (The *Journal's* front page is dominated most days by three feature stories that are its signature attractions: two "leaders," its main magazine-style features, and the "A-head," so named because of the shape of the hood that appears above the italic headline type. Headlines of leaders often are topped with snappy, boldface "flash lines.") The decision to include the backdating story on the front page was made at the previous day's New York national news meeting, where the final call belonged to managing editor Paul Steiger.

With Maremont's story airing the academic work on backdating for the first time in the general press, the reporter expected others in the media to pick up on the phenomenon. He was wrong.

"I'm not sure why exactly," says Maremont, "but the story didn't really gain any traction." Indeed, he can't remember competitors publishing a single word about the backdating. Why didn't other papers follow the *Journal*? Competitive pride may have played a part. Even among editors at the archrival *New York Times,* he speculates, there may have been a hands-off attitude: "Somebody else had gotten it, and they weren't going to pay any attention." Journalists also might have thought the problem was limited to some obscure technology companies. Finally, it was possible that—even after following the blatant criminality of the Enron Corporation six years earlier—reporters found it hard to believe that corporate executives would secretly game the system to increase the haul for themselves and their compatriots.

As the competition ignored the story, Maremont and the *Journal* were only getting started. New York–based James Bandler, a reporter on Maremont's investigative team, joined him in studying the subject, as did fellow Boston staffer Charles Forelle. At twenty-five years old, Forelle was not long out of Yale, where he had been a math student. (Eventually, Boston reporter Steve Stecklow would become the fourth team member.) In addition to further developing the academic research, the team learned as much as it could about the SEC investigations that were under way. The reporters' main goal was to identify companies that issued options with low strike prices year after year, to see if the trend was broad enough to suggest a wider page-one feature story.

While Professor Lie provided the reporters with data showing patterns of historically low strike prices at certain corporations, that by itself wasn't very compelling. The *Journal* needed solid evidence of companies misdating their options. "We figured it was unlikely that you'd call these companies up and they'd say, 'Yup, we did it—you caught us,'" says the team leader. "And it would take enormous effort to find a mole."

Charles Forelle had an idea. Talking with Maremont in the hallway one day, the young math graduate suggested that the paper do its own probability analysis to determine the odds of these historically low stock prices being accidentally chosen. Maremont liked the approach, and asked Bandler and Forelle to work together on a formula that used data from daily electronic stock-trading charts, applying it to companies suspected of strike-price manipulation. Since the algorithm being used was the *Journal*'s own, the team members knew that extreme care had to be taken in their research. "Essentially, what we were doing was accusing these companies of improper or even illegal behavior on the basis of stock charts and our own mathematical analysis," Maremont notes. "There were no Deep Throats here"—and no governmental or corporate leakers whose accounts could backstop them if they were wrong. The reporters were on their own.

They spent nearly four months trying to figure out which companies had the most egregious patterns of low strike prices between 1995 and 2002, and thus might qualify for a place on page one of the *Journal.* They then called directors on the compensation committees of those companies to see if anyone remembered how the grants were made. Meanwhile, Forelle continued to refine the methodology, consulting with an assistant professor of statistics at Yale.

"The Perfect Payday"

The first front-page feature story to result, on Saturday, March 18, 2006, was "The Perfect Payday"—the headline that Joe Barrett, of the *Journal*'s page-one editing staff, contributed. (Page-one flash lines typically emerge from brainstorming sessions among the page editors.) Wrote Forelle in a sidebar that ran with the main article:

> To quantify how unusual a particular pattern of grants is, the *Journal* calculated how much each company's stock rose in the 20 trading days following each grant date. The analysis then ranked that appreciation against the stock performance in the 20 days following all other trading days of the year. It ranked all 252 or so trading days in a given year according to how much the stock rose or fell following them.

In the *Journal*'s centralized national editing system, designed by legendary editor Bernard Kilgore in the 1940s, bureau chiefs or team leaders were responsible for proposing front-page projects to the editing staff in New York, and then for delivering the articles. When submitted, the stories went into a backlog of page-one candidates to be processed for publication. Managing editor Steiger and his deputies—for the backdating stories the key deputy was Pulitzer-winner Daniel Hertzberg—had overall authority for when and how the stories would be presented. The basic editing of feature articles after they flowed in to New York, however, was in the hands of a special page-one staff headed by Michael Miller. Veteran editor Dan Kelly was assigned to work with the backdating story, and successive feature articles on that theme.

The decision to run "Perfect Payday" on a weekend fit with the paper's deliberate goal of beefing up the Saturday edition, only a few months old at the time.
But the placement at first gave Maremont pause, because Saturday *Journals* had
become a showcase for softer features and lifestyle coverage, not major investigations like this one. Still, there was an upside: more space for graphics and display.

As the story—which carried the byline of Forelle and Bandler, with a contributing line for George Anders—worked toward the top of the New York backlog, its seemingly glacial progress tested the nerves of Maremont's team. The *Journal* had asked the companies cited in the article to respond, but now they had time
to go further than merely issuing a comment. One of them, Affiliated Computer
Services Incorporated, announced that it had begun internally investigating possible stock-option improprieties. The *Journal,* its feature story still not ready, published a deliberately small news article on the announcement, buried in the back
of the paper. "We wanted to get it on the record," says Maremont, "but we didn't
want to call a lot of attention to it."

Affiliated Computer was the lead example on March 18. Ironically, the comments of its chief executive, Jeffrey Rich, provided nearly as much punch as the
Journal's stunning statistical calculation—that the chances of a company randomly picking Affiliated's historically low strike prices over seven years was
"around one in 300 billion." For comparison, the article added: "The odds of winning the multistate Powerball lottery with a $1 ticket are one in 146 million." Rich,
however, attributed the repeated choice of favorable option-grant dates to "blind
luck." Indeed, he said, backdating would have been absolutely wrong. Maremont
smiles at the blind-luck comment provided to Bandler, who "was very happy when
he finally got hold of that guy and got that great quote out of him."

The article finally put backdating on the national journalistic map, even if the
Journal retained a huge head start. Staying out front, Maremont's investigative
team wrote more feature articles, and news stories frequently were positioned as
page-one extras. Managing editor Steiger, says Maremont, "was very much in favor of keeping up the drumbeat of coverage." Later stories showed how companies backdated options as a way of cutting executives' taxes, and demonstrated that
the stock market's post–9/11 plunge had provided corporate backdaters with cover for their schemes.

Maremont and editor Dan Kelly agreed that not much needed to be written
about backdating's legal status. Whether criminal or not, the activity would clearly be seen as deceptive by readers, the two men believed. And the value of any stock
that was not fairly earned should have belonged to all the shareholders. The *Journal* focused more on explaining how companies originally had intended stock-option mechanisms to provide a more equitable, performance-based incentive sys-

tem, and how backdating distorted that design. (Later, when the federal government pursued cases of backdating-related securities fraud, tax fraud, and other offenses—many against companies that had been cited in *Journal* stories—officials detailed the lawbreaking involved. In its case against Mercury Interactive, for example, the SEC alleged that former senior officers "perpetrated a fraudulent and deceptive scheme from 1997 to 2005 to award themselves and other employees undisclosed, secret compensation by backdating stock option grants, failing to record hundreds of millions of dollars of compensation expense, and falsifying documents to further the scheme." The government was litigating cases against four former Mercury executives. But the $28 million corporate penalty that Mercury paid, according to SEC chairman Christopher Cox, "should send a clear signal that fraudulent stock option backdating and other financial fraud will be severely punished.")

The *Journal,* which has had excellent success building a paid online readership, did something special for those readers. It created an elaborate Portable Document Format (PDF) chart that linked the cases of stock-option backdating at various companies. As the number of backdating cases expanded, along with the information available about the backdating, so did the *Journal*'s chart. While the online PDF chart was made part of its Pulitzer entry through the Web site, however, jurors and Pulitzer board members paid more attention to the actual stories.

The *Journal*'s creation of a database of company backdaters is reminiscent of investigative techniques employed in past Gold Medal–winning work, like the cataloging of suspicious priests by the *Boston Globe* Spotlight Team, the *Anchorage Daily News* research into deaths of native Alaskans, or the files about government payoffs that Bob Greene compiled for *Newsday,* to name only a few. There was one feature of the backdating coverage by the *Wall Street Journal*—the commentary on its editorial pages—that may be unique, however. At most papers, columnists roundly support the investigative campaigns of reporters, and often have their work included with the Pulitzer Public Service submission. But on the laissez-faire *Journal* editorial pages, columnist Holman W. Jenkins Jr. kept up his *own* drumbeat: ridiculing the news articles as a witch hunt, and characterizing the practice of backdating as "innocuous and even sensible."

At first, Jenkins's columns infuriated Maremont, although the reporter "eventually found it almost comical." A logical extension of one argument seemed to be that executives should be free to ignore an accounting rule if they disagreed with it. "That strikes me as a recipe for chaos," says Maremont, "and something that the editorial page should have repudiated, not welcomed." Reflecting on the split, though, he soon saw Jenkins's columns as "a net positive, because being attacked by the paper's far-right editorial page was seen in most of the media world as a

badge of honor, and a sign that the scandal had really hit a nerve in the plutocrat-
ic class."

Jenkins's criticisms were the exception, and most *Journal* reporters and editors
took pride in the groundbreaking coverage. In the spring, the Dow Jones board of
directors asked Maremont to make a presentation and discuss the stock-option
scandals. When one board member asked how many companies Maremont
thought eventually might be tarred with the backdating brush, the reporter estimated thirty or forty. "Of course, I was wildly underestimating the scale of the
scandal at that point," he says now. (Asked whether Dow Jones itself was ever suspected of such abuses, he laughs. "As a recipient of Dow Jones stock options, I can
assure you there was never any backdating," says Maremont. Indeed, "they kept
granting them at a high point.")

After being selected as a finalist by the Pulitzer Public Service jury, the *Journal*'s
entry was forwarded to the full Pulitzer board, which happened to be chaired by
Journal managing editor Steiger, then in his final year both on the board and as
the newspaper's managing editor. That made the Gold Medal—voted on while
Steiger was out of the room—especially precious. "I believe one of our highest callings as a news organization is to unearth the ills of business so that society can fix
them," he said in a memo to the staff. "The exposure of the pernicious disease of
options backdating was a particularly dramatic example of just that."

Readers may have noticed a thread connecting recent ownership questions at
the *Wall Street Journal* to events during the early days of Joseph Pulitzer's prizes. It
was Clarence Barron, after all, who helped the old *Boston Post* unmask Charles
Ponzi's scheme—work that resulted in the third Gold Medal ever awarded, in 1921.
Barron had used his wife's money to purchase Dow Jones and its *Journal* in 1902—
the very same year that Pulitzer, perhaps while sitting in the Tower of Silence on
his Bar Harbor retreat in Maine, dreamed up the idea of national journalism
awards.

Control of the *Journal* had then passed down to members of the Bancroft family, who in 2007 were charged with deciding who would guide the future of the
reigning Pulitzer Gold Medal winner.

APPENDIX

The Gold Medal in History

$\mathscr{T}$his listing includes all journalism Pulitzer Prizes awarded from 1917 through 2007. Each year's entry is led by the actual Public Service citation prepared by the Pulitzer Prize Board before its announcement. Some citations are terse and some quite florid. They often reflect in a few words the board's feelings about the winner. Others say almost nothing. The actual prize listings generally reflect the wording as listed on the www.Pulitzer.org Web site.

Pulitzer's Gold views the development of American journalism through the lens provided by the Pulitzer Public Service body of work. The book concentrates on selected cases so that readers can follow themes in coverage—and in the board's selection process—through the twentieth century and into the twenty-first. The sampling also attempts to shed light on the evolution of the Public Service Prize itself, first as the Pulitzer Prize Board struggled to give it an identity, and later as the nature of newspaper public service broadened to reflect new kinds of journalism.

Choosing which winners to abbreviate in this appendix was often extremely difficult. Many examples deserve entire books of their own. The author is also sadly aware that many fascinating "stories behind the stories" involved with the Pulitzer Prizes for Public Service remain untold.

The following descriptions reflect reviews of entries and supporting material in Columbia University's Pulitzer Prize archives, and comments from the jurors that the Pulitzer Prize office provided. These summaries employ *Editor & Publisher*'s annual discussion of prize-winners, along with other observations as noted.

1917
   Public Service: No Award
   Reporting: Herbert Bayard Swope, *New York World*
   Editorial Writing: *New York Tribune*

1918

Public Service: *New York Times,* for its public service in publishing in full so many official reports, documents, and speeches by European statesmen relating to the progress and conduct of the war.
Reporting: Harold A. Littledale, *New York Evening Post*
Editorial Writing: *Louisville Courier Journal*

1919

Public Service: *Milwaukee Journal,* for its strong and courageous campaign for Americanism in a constituency where foreign elements made such a policy hazardous from a business point of view.
Reporting: No Award
Editorial Writing: No Award

1920

Public Service: No Award
Reporting: John J. Leary Jr., *New York World*
Editorial Writing: Harvey E. Newbranch, *Evening World Herald,* Omaha

1921

Public Service: *Boston Post,* for its exposure of the operations of Charles Ponzi by a series of articles which finally led to his arrest.
Reporting: Louis Siebold, *New York World*
Editorial Writing: No Award

1922

Public Service—*New York World,* for articles exposing the operations of the Ku Klux Klan, published during September and October, 1921.
Reporting: Kirke L. Simpson, Associated Press
Editorial Writing: Frank M. O'Brien, *New York Herald*
Editorial Cartooning: Rollin Kirby, *New York World*

1923

Memphis Commercial Appeal: As a southern paper, the *Commercial Appeal* took special risks launching a campaign against the Ku Klux Klan in the early 1920s. Cartoonist James Alley produced several cartoons that ridiculed Klan members, including one from December 1922 that pictured a Klan member in full regalia reading a book titled *Law Enforcement.* For the first time there was real competition for the Public Service Prize. Jurors forwarded five nominees to the board, with the others—the *Baltimore Sun, Boston Post, Brooklyn Standard Union,* and Boston's *Christian Science Monitor*—covering topics from local election abuses to Prohibition to an arms-limitation conference.

Public Service: *Memphis Commercial Appeal,* for its courageous attitude in the publication of cartoons and the handling of news in reference to the operations of the Ku Klux Klan.
Reporting: Alva Johnson, *New York Times*
Editorial Writing: William Allen White, *Emporia* (Kansas) *Gazette*
Editorial Cartooning: No Award

1924
Public Service: *New York World,* for its work in connection with the exposure of the Florida peonage evil.
Reporting: Magner White, *San Diego Sun*
Editorial Writing: *Boston Herald*
Editorial Cartooning: Jay Norwood Darling, *Des Moines Register & Tribune*

1925
Public Service: No Award
Reporting: James W. Mulroy, Alvin H. Goldstein, *Chicago Daily News*
Editorial Writing: *Charleston* (S.C.) *News & Courier*
Editorial Cartooning: Rollin Kirby, *New York World*

1926
Columbus (Ga.) *Enquirer Sun:* The Pulitzer board picked the *Enquirer Sun* from seventeen Public Service entries. The Columbus paper's submission was mainly a series of opinion pieces written by editor Julian LaRose Harris. Opposition to the Ku Klux Klan was prominent among the articles, but other topics were covered, too. One column opposed those who stood against teaching evolution. (The Scopes Trial in Tennessee had captivated the nation in the summer of 1925, pitting Clarence Darrow against William Jennings Bryan.) Said one column, headlined "Is It Great to Be a Georgian?":

> Is it great to be a citizen of a state which is the proud parent of a cowardly hooded order founded and fostered by men who have been proved liars, drunkards, blackmailers, and murderers? Is it great to be a citizen of a state whose governor is a member of and subservient to that vicious masked gang, and whose officials are either members or in sympathy with it? . . . Is it great to be a Georgian? Let each one answer as he will, but the reply of the Enquirer Sun is no.

Public Service: *Columbus Enquirer Sun,* for the service which it rendered in its brave and energetic fight against the Ku Klux Klan; against the enactment of a law barring the teaching of evolution; against dishonest and incompetent public officials; and for justice to the Negro and against lynching.
Reporting: William Burke Miller, *Louisville Courier-Journal*

Editorial Writing: Edward M. Kingsbury, *New York Times*
Editorial Cartooning: D. R. Fitzpatrick, *St. Louis Post-Dispatch*

1927

Public Service: *Canton* (Ohio) *Daily News,* for its brave, patriotic, and effective fight for
the ending of a vicious state of affairs brought about by collusion between city authorities and the criminal element, a fight which had a tragic result in the assassination of the editor of the paper, Mr. Don R. Mellett.
Reporting: John T. Rogers, *St. Louis Post-Dispatch*
Editorial Writing: F. Lauriston Bullard, *Boston Herald*
Editorial Cartooning: Nelson Harding, *Brooklyn Daily Eagle*

1928

Indianapolis Times: The anti-corruption work of the *Indianapolis Times* had a Ku Klux Klan
connection. The paper exposed illegal activities involving the governor and a former
state treasurer, and also ties the two had to a former Grand Dragon of the Klan and
"political dictator of the state." Both the governor and the former treasurer were indicted. The board vote overruled the Columbia faculty jury, which had recommended the *Minneapolis Tribune* for a campaign to improve farming methods.

—————

Public Service: *Indianapolis Times,* for its work in exposing political corruption to In-
diana, prosecuting the guilty, and bringing about a more wholesome state of affairs
in civil government.
Reporting: No Award
Editorial Writing: Grover Cleveland Hall, *Montgomery* (Ala.) *Advertiser*
Editorial Cartooning: Nelson Harding, *Brooklyn Daily Eagle*

1929

New York World: The lead series in the wide-ranging *New York Evening World* entry was
written by reporter William O. Trapp and exposed ambulance-chasing lawyers,
while another urged legislation against the fencing of stolen property. The board selected the *Evening World*'s submission from an eclectic group of twenty-one entries,
from Wenatchee, Washington, to Sanford, Florida. Selection of the *Evening World*
was bitterly protested by the Philadelphia *Sunday Transcript,* which claimed that "the
whole enterprise upon which the award was made to the *New York World* was originated by the *Sunday Transcript.*" The Philadelphia paper "certainly will not compete in any contest so long as it is under Columbia University and the City of New
York," the paper said. Two years later, though, the *Transcript* was back with another Public Service entry.

—————

Public Service: *New York Evening World,* for its effective campaign to correct evils in the
administration of justice, including the fight to curb "ambulance chasers," support
of the "fence" bill, and measures to simplify procedure, prevent perjury, and elimi-

nate politics from municipal courts; a campaign which has been instrumental in se-
curing remedial action.
Reporting: Paul Y. Anderson, *St. Louis Post-Dispatch*
Correspondence: Paul Scott Maurer, *Chicago Daily News*
Editorial Writing: Louis Isaac Jaffe, *Norfolk Virginian-Pilot*
Editorial Cartooning: Rollin Kirby, *New York World*

1930

Public Service: No Award
Reporting: Russell D. Owen, *New York Times*
Editorial Writing: Leland Stowe, *New York Herald Tribune*
Editorial Cartooning: Charles R. Macauley, *Brooklyn Daily Eagle*

1931

Atlanta Constitution: Solicitor General John A. Boykin of the Atlanta Judicial Circuit
wrote to support the *Atlanta Constitution:* "For many months there had been veiled
allusions and undercover rumors of wholesale graft in the city government of Atlanta, but not until the *Constitution* courageously called for a sweeping investigation
was my office able to obtain evidence upon which I could lay the situation before
the grand jury." The paper's own nomination letter was written by *Constitution* director of news and Pulitzer board member Julian LaRose Harris, who had moved
from Georgia's *Columbus Enquirer Sun.* The board picked the *Constitution* over the
jury's first choice, the *Louisville Times,* which worked to save the Cumberland Falls
in a state park.

—⟨∞⟩—

Public Service: *Atlanta Constitution,* for a successful municipal graft exposure and con-
sequent convictions.
Reporting: A. B. MacDonald, *Kansas City Star*
Correspondence: H. R. Knickerbocker, *Philadelphia Public Ledger & New York Evening
Post*
Editorial Writing: Charles S. Ryckman, *Fremont* (Neb.) *Tribune*
Editorial Cartooning: Edmund Duffy, *Baltimore Sun*

1932

Indianapolis News: The packet of *Indianapolis News* articles and editorials that was submitted described an eighteen-month effort to rein in city government spending under the pressures of the Great Depression. The state legislature passed laws denying
jurisdictions the right to boost their expenses, and the paper said its effort would
produce estimated savings of $12 million in a state budget of $156 million. One other Public Service nomination was forwarded by jurors to the board. The entry, for a
study of the Depression by Charles G. Ross of the *St. Louis Post-Dispatch,* was moved
to the Correspondence category, where it won.

—⟨∞⟩—

Public Service: *Indianapolis News,* for its successful campaign to eliminate waste in city management and to reduce the tax levy.

Reporting: W. C. Richards, D. D. Martin, J. S. Pooler, F. D. Webb, and J. N. W. Sloan, *Detroit Free Press*

Correspondence: Charles G. Ross, *St. Louis Post-Dispatch*

Correspondence: Walter Duranty, *New York Times*

Editorial Writing: No Award

Editorial Cartooning: John T. McCutcheon, *Chicago Tribune*

1933

New York World-Telegram: The Scripps-Howard–owned *New York World-Telegram* won for an entry that covered a selection of issues, some of them Depression-related. The centerpiece was a campaign calling attention to federal mismanagement of World War I veterans' bonuses. Disabled veterans often were treated unfavorably compared to some who had seen no battlefield duty. Legislation was proposed to change veterans' compensation and boost dependent pay for families of killed soldiers. Jurors said: "When others were pussyfooting, The *World-Telegram,* in the open, assailed evil where it found it. We believe it has followed in the footsteps of the editor whose benefaction established the prize for public service."

Public Service: *New York World-Telegram,* for its series of articles on veterans' relief, on the real estate bond evil, the campaign urging voters in the late New York City municipal election to "write in" the name of Joseph V. McKee, and the articles exposing the lottery schemes of various fraternal organizations.

Reporting: Francis A. Jamieson, Associated Press

Correspondence: Edgar Ansel Mowrer, *Chicago Daily News*

Editorial Writing: *Kansas City Star*

Editorial Cartooning: H. M. Talburt, *Washington Daily News*

1934

Public Service: *Medford* (Ore.) *Mail Tribune,* for its campaign against unscrupulous politicians in Jackson County, Oregon.

Reporting: Royce Brier, *San Francisco Chronicle*

Correspondence: Frederick T. Birchall, *New York Times*

Editorial Writing: E. P. Chase, *Atlantic* (Iowa) *News-Telegraph*

Editorial Cartooning: Edmund Duffy, *Baltimore Sun*

1935

Sacramento (Calif.) *Bee:* The Pulitzer board passed over five jury nominations to select the *Bee,* which was on the Reporting jury's list. The winning work was associate editor Arthur B. Waugh's investigation of the qualifications of two of President Franklin Roosevelt's federal judge nominees in Nevada. Waugh showed that Judge Frank H. Norcross, named to the circuit court of appeals, and William Woodburn, named to replace Norcross on the federal district bench, were associates of crime

boss George Wingfield, who had masterminded the closure of a chain of banks in
Nevada and was implicated in looting several companies. The appointments were
dropped, and Nevadans overthrew the Wingfield machine in the fall elections.

Public Service: *Sacramento Bee,* for its campaign against political machine influence in
the appointment of two federal judges in Nevada.
Reporting: William H. Taylor, *New York Herald Tribune*
Correspondence: Arthur Krock, *New York Times*
Editorial Writing: No Award
Editorial Cartooning: Ross A. Lewis, *Milwaukee Journal*

1936
Cedar Rapids (Iowa) *Gazette:* Publisher Verne Marshall used Iowa's *Cedar Rapids Gazette*
to report on bootleggers, illegal slot machine operators, crooked state authorities,
and Democratic Party campaign fund contributors who were involved in payoffs to
public officials. The *Gazette's* stories started a six-month grand jury inquiry into
gambling and liquor violations, much of it across the state in Sioux City. Marshall
and the *Gazette* defended themselves against several libel suits during the reporting.
In leading a campaign against Iowa graft, according to a May 9, 1936, account in *Editor & Publisher,* he "testified before grand juries, dug up evidence, interviewed possible witnesses, [and] wrote news stories of sweeping charges of graft in the state and
stinging page one articles." *E&P* noted that the Iowa Supreme Court quashed thirty-
one indictments stemming from the reporting, and suggested that "one of the major reasons for disqualification of the indictments was payment of $700 by the *Ga-
zette*" to a special prosecutor in the case.

Public Service: *Cedar Rapids Gazette,* for its crusade against corruption and misgov-
ernment in the State of Iowa.
Reporting: Lauren D. Lyman, *New York Times*
Correspondence: Wilfred C. Barber, *Chicago Tribune*
Editorial Writing: Felix Morley, *Washington Post;* George B. Parker, Scripps-Howard
Editorial Cartooning: No Award

1937
Public Service: *St. Louis Post-Dispatch,* for its exposure of wholesale fraudulent voter
registration in St. Louis. By a coordinated news, editorial, and cartoon campaign
this newspaper succeeded in invalidating upwards of forty thousand fraudulent bal-
lots in November and brought about the appointment of a new election board.
Reporting: John J. O'Neill, William L. Laurence, Howard W. Blakeslee, Gobind Be-
hari Lal, David Dietz; *New York Herald Tribune, New York Times,* Associated Press,
Universal Service, Scripps-Howard
Correspondence: Arthur Krock, *New York Times*
Editorial Writing: William Wesley Waymack, *Des Moines Register and Tribune*
Editorial Cartooning: Vaughn Shoemaker, *Chicago Daily News*

1938

Public Service: *Bismarck* (N.D.) *Tribune,* for its news reports and editorials entitled, "Self Help in the Dust Bowl."

Reporting: Raymond Sprigle, *Pittsburgh Post-Gazette*

Correspondence: Arthur Krock, *New York Times*

Editorial Writing: William Wesley Waymack, *Register and Tribune,* Des Moines

Editorial Cartooning: Vaughn Shoemaker, *Chicago Daily News*

1939

Miami Daily News: The *Miami Daily News* successfully fought for a landmark recall of the city commissioners, who had tried to double their own salaries and botched a harbor development project. Meanwhile, commissioners paid off attorneys, created funds to remunerate campaign workers, and solicited a $250,000 bribe from a utility company president—until the president took out a newspaper ad announcing: "I Won't Pay a Bribe." At one point the paper started a front-page series called "Speaking of Termites," attacking the city commission majority for "boring from within." The newspaper helped the recall campaign collect twenty thousand signatures in a city with only thirty-six thousand registered voters. Newspapers submitted thirty-one nominations from twenty states for the Public Service award.

———

Public Service: *Miami Daily News,* for its campaign for the recall of the Miami City Commission.

Reporting: Thomas Lunsford Stokes, Scripps-Howard Newspaper Alliance

Correspondence: Louis P. Lochner, Associated Press

Editorial Writing: Ronald G. Callvert, *Oregonian,* Portland

Editorial Cartooning: Charles G. Werner, *Daily Oklahoman*

1940

Waterbury (Conn.) *Republican & American:* The *Republican & American* had spent ten years investigating the mayor and city controller under publisher William J. Pape and editor E. Robert Stevenson. Exposing wrongdoing had taken that long because officials had severely limited access to city records. The city government also had fought back using devious means. At one point, the paper reported finding a Dictaphone hidden in the fireplace of Pape's office—to record his conversations—and documented that the city had underwritten the spying with monthly payments to an investigator. The paper found indications of voting-list padding and illicit financial dealings. Eventually, Mayor H. Frank Hayes and city controller Daniel J. Leary were sentenced to the maximum prison terms of ten to fifteen years.

———

Public Service: *Waterbury Republican & American,* for its campaign exposing municipal graft.

Reporting: S. Burton Heath, *New York World-Telegram*

Correspondence: Otto D. Tolischus, *New York Times*

Editorial Writing: Bart Howard, *St. Louis Post-Dispatch*
Editorial Cartooning: Edmund Duffy, *Baltimore Sun*

1941

Public Service: *St. Louis Post-Dispatch,* for its successful campaign against the city smoke
   nuisance.
Reporting: Westbrook Pegler, *New York World-Telegram*
Correspondence: All American war correspondents
Editorial Writing: Reuben Maury, *New York Daily News*
Editorial Cartooning: Jacob Burck, *Chicago Times*
Photography: Arnold Hardy, amateur

1942

Los Angeles Times: Publisher Harry Chandler's *Los Angeles Times,* long known for its anti-
   union stands, California boosterism, and a sensationalist streak, fought with the Los
   Angeles County Bar Association over the right of the press to comment on court
   proceedings. Acting on a bar association petition, a judge had issued contempt citations declaring that publishing the editorials had interfered with the dispensation
   of justice. The *Times* could have paid a small fine and simply stopped such commentary. But it chose to fight. The bar association was upheld by higher courts
   until the case got to the U.S. Supreme Court, which ruled for the *Times.* Justices
   said there must be "clear and present danger" to the administration of justice before
   contempt citations are issued and the press is restrained. It was, in a way, a strange
   time for a First Amendment victory. "For the time being, the issue was set aside because American newspapers as a whole had accepted a voluntary program of self-
   censorship during World War II out of concern for national security," wrote Pulitzer
   Prize historian John Hohenberg.

Public Service: *Los Angeles Times,* for its successful campaign which resulted in the
   clarification and confirmation for all American newspapers of the right of free press
   as guaranteed under the Constitution.
Reporting: Stanton Delaplane, *San Francisco Chronicle*
Correspondence: Carlos P. Romulo, *Philippines Herald*
Telegraphic Reporting (National): Louis Stark, *New York Times*
Telegraphic Reporting (International): Laurence Edmund Allen, Associated Press
Editorial Writing: Geoffrey Parsons, *New York Herald Tribune*
Editorial Cartooning: Herbert Lawrence Block (Herblock), NEA Service
Photography: Milton Brooks, *Detroit News*

1943

Omaha World Herald: The *World Herald*'s campaign to collect scrap metal for the war
   effort had a significant impact, producing 103 pounds of scrap metal per person in
   its circulation area over three weeks in the summer of 1942. It also sparked a national

scrap drive involving newspaper publishers from coast to coast. That effort, called the Nebraska Plan, produced enough scrap to ensure full operation of U.S. steel mills for war production during the winter of 1942.

—∞∞∞—

Public Service: *Omaha World-Herald,* for its initiative and originality in planning a statewide campaign for the collection of scrap metal for the war effort. The Nebraska plan was adopted on a national scale by the daily newspapers, resulting in a united effort which succeeded in supplying our war industries with necessary scrap material.
Reporting: George Weller, *Chicago Daily News*
Correspondence: Hanson W. Baldwin, *New York Times*
Telegraphic Reporting (National): No Award
Telegraphic Reporting (International): Ira Wolfert, North American Newspaper Alliance
Editorial Writing, Forrest W. Seymour, *Des Moines Register and Tribune*
Editorial Cartooning: Jay Norwood Darling, *Des Moines Register and Tribune*
Photography: Frank Noel, Associated Press

1944

Public Service: *New York Times,* for its survey of the teaching of American History.
Reporting: Paul Schoenstein and Associates, *New York Journal-American*
Correspondence: Ernest Taylor Pyle, Scripps-Howard Newspaper Alliance
Telegraphic Reporting (National): Dewey L. Fleming, *Baltimore Sun*
Telegraphic Reporting (International): Daniel De Luce, Associated Press
Editorial Writing: Henry J. Haskell, *Kansas City Star*
Editorial Cartooning: Clifford K. Berryman, *Washington Evening Star*
Photography: Earle L. Bunker, *Omaha World-Herald*
Photography: Frank Filan, Associated Press

1945

Public Service: *Detroit Free Press,* for its investigation of legislative graft and corruption at Lansing, Michigan.
Reporting: Jack S. McDowell, *San Francisco Call-Bulletin*
Correspondence: Harold V. (Hal) Boyle, Associated Press
Telegraphic Reporting (National): James B. Reston, *New York Times*
Telegraphic Reporting (International): Mark S. Watson, *Baltimore Sun*
Editorial Writing: George W. Potter, *Providence Journal-Bulletin*
Editorial Cartooning: Sergeant Bill Mauldin, United Feature Syndicate
Photography: Joe Rosenthal, Associated Press

1946

Scranton (Pa.) *Times: Scranton Times* assistant city editor George H. Martin, who discovered irregularities while he was doing routine federal courts rounds, learned that a seventy-three-year-old federal judge, Albert W. Johnson, was taking bribes in the courthouse. Crime-fighting Tennessee congressman Estes Kefauver said the judge was "selling justice" and called his case "the most corrupt situation that could possibly exist in any federal court." The judge resigned and was denied his pension, and finally was indicted for conspiracy to defraud the United States and obstructing justice.

—∞∞—

Public Service: *Scranton Times,* for its fifteen-year investigation of judicial practices in the U.S. District Court for the middle district of Pennsylvania, resulting in removal of the district judge and indictment of many others.
Reporting: William Leonard Laurence, *New York Times*
Correspondence: Arnaldo Cortesi, *New York Times*
Telegraphic Reporting (National): Edward A. Harris, *St. Louis Post-Dispatch*
Telegraphic Reporting (International): Homer William Bigart, *New York Herald Tribune*
Editorial Writing: Hodding Carter, *Delta Democrat-Times,* Greenville, Miss.
Editorial Cartooning: Bruce Alexander Russell, *Los Angeles Times*
Photography: No Award

1947

Baltimore Sun: Baltimore Sun reporter Howard M. Norton wrote a series of eighteen articles on problems with Maryland's unemployment compensation system. Assigned to study the system, he explored lax controls governing payouts and excessive costs of plan administration. Part of the reason for the high cost was that racketeers and cheats were taking advantage of loopholes. The Maryland General Assembly proposed changes in the law, and a number of people abusing the system were convicted or pleaded guilty to charges. Norton became the first individual to be named in the citation accompanying the Public Service Prize. After that, naming one or more reporters became an option for the Pulitzer board. Between 1947 and 2006 it named reporters eleven times, although the approach is becoming more common. Individuals were named seven times between 1990 and 2007.

—∞∞—

Public Service: *Baltimore Sun,* for its series of articles by Howard M. Norton dealing with the administration of unemployment compensation in Maryland, resulting in convictions and pleas of guilty in criminal court of ninety-three persons.
Reporting: Frederick Woltman, *New York World-Telegram*
Correspondence: Brooks Atkinson, *New York Times*
Telegraphic Reporting (National): Edward T. Folliard, *Washington Post*
Telegraphic Reporting (International): Eddy Gillmore, Associated Press
Editorial Writing: William H. Grimes, *Wall Street Journal*
Editorial Cartooning: Vaughn Shoemaker, *Chicago Daily News*
Photography: Arnold Hardy, amateur

1948

Public Service: *St. Louis Post-Dispatch,* for the coverage of the Centralia, Illinois, mine disaster and the follow-up which resulted in impressive reforms in mine safety laws and regulations.

Reporting: George E. Goodwin, *Atlanta Journal*
National Reporting: Nat S. Finney, *Minneapolis Tribune*
National Reporting: Bert Andrews, *New York Herald Tribune*
Editorial Writing: Virginius Dabney, *Richmond Times-Dispatch*
Editorial Cartooning: Reuben L. Goldberg, *New York Sun*
Photography: Frank Cushing, *Boston Traveler*

1949

Nebraska State Journal: A civic project by the Lincoln-based *Nebraska State Journal* created an "All-Star Primary" as a new element in the presidential election campaign. The brainchild of editor Raymond A. McConnell Jr., the presidential preference primary filled a void in the presidential nominating system and prompted a review of a primary election approach that had been created during the Andrew Jackson administration. The new primary, managed by a bipartisan committee, allowed names to be entered on the ballot without the permission of the individuals proposed by the committee.

Public Service: *Nebraska State Journal,* for the campaign establishing the "Nebraska All-Star Primary which spotlighted, though a bipartisan committee, issues early in the presidential campaign."
Local Reporting: Malcolm Johnson, *New York Sun*
National Reporting: C. P. Trussel, *New York Times*
International Reporting: Price Day, *Baltimore Sun*
Editorial Writing: Herbert Elliston, *Washington Post*
Editorial Writing: John H. Crider, *Boston Herald*
Editorial Cartooning: Lute Pease, *Newark Evening News*
Photography: Nathaniel Fein, *New York Herald-Tribune*

1950

Public Service: *St. Louis Post-Dispatch* and *Chicago Daily News,* for the work of George Thiem and Roy J. Harris, respectively, in exposing the presence of thirty-seven Illinois newspapermen on the Illinois state payroll.
Local Reporting: Meyer Berger, *New York Times*
National Reporting: Edwin O. Guthman, *Seattle Times*
International Reporting: Edmund Stevens, *Christian Science Monitor*
Editorial Writing: Carl M. Saunders, *Jackson* (Mich.) *Citizen Patriot*
Editorial Cartooning: James T. Berryman, *Washington Evening Star*
Photography: Bill Crouch, *Oakland* (Calif.) *Tribune*

1951

Miami Herald and *Brooklyn Eagle:* The *Miami Herald* and *Brooklyn Eagle,* independently, had fought organized crime for years. The *Herald*'s stories concluded a seven-year campaign that resulted in the removal of both the Dade County and Broward County sheriffs and broke a national gambling syndicate in Miami Beach that used wire communications illegally. *Eagle* reporter Ed Reid exposed Brooklyn rackets and their connections to police. The paper sparked an investigation by the district attorney that led to numerous indictments.

———∞———

Public Service: *Miami Herald* and *Brooklyn Eagle,* for their crime reporting during the year.

Local Reporting: Edward S. Montgomery, *San Francisco Examiner*

National Reporting: No Award

International Reporting: Keyes Beech and Fred Sparks, *Chicago Daily News;* Homer Bigart and Marguerite Higgins, *New York Herald Tribune;* Relman Morin and Don Whitehead, Associated Press

Editorial Writing: William Harry Fitzpatrick, *New Orleans States-Item*

Editorial Cartooning: Reg (Reginald W.) Manning, *Arizona Republic*

Photography: Max Desfor, Associated Press

1952

Public Service: *St. Louis Post-Dispatch,* for its investigation and disclosures of widespread corruption in the Internal Revenue Bureau and other departments of the government.

Local Reporting: George De Carvalho, *San Francisco Chronicle*

National Reporting: Anthony Leviero, *New York Times*

International Reporting: John M. Hightower, Associated Press

Editorial Writing: Louis LaCoss, *St. Louis Globe-Democrat*

Editorial Cartooning: Fred L. Packer, *New York Mirror*

Photography: John Robinson, Don Ultang, *Des Moines Register and Tribune*

1953

Public Service: *Whiteville News Reporter* and *Tabor City Tribune* (N.C.), for their successful campaign against the Ku Klux Klan, waged on their own doorstep at the risk of economic loss and personal danger, culminating in the conviction of over one hundred Klansmen and an end to terrorism in their communities.

Local Reporting, Edition Time: Editorial staff of *Providence Journal and Evening Bulletin*

Local Reporting, No Edition Time: Edward J. Mowery, *New York World-Telegram & Sun*

National Reporting: Don Whitehead, Associated Press

International Reporting: Austin Wehrwein, *Milwaukee Journal*

Editorial Writing: Vermont Connecticut Royster, *Wall Street Journal*

Editorial Cartooning: Edward D. Kuekes, *Cleveland Plain Dealer*

Photography: William M. Gallagher, *Flint* (Mich.) *Journal*

1954

Public Service: *Newsday,* Garden City, New York, for its exposé of New York's racetrack scandals and labor racketeering, which led to the extortion indictment, guilty plea, and imprisonment of William C. DeKoning Sr., New York labor racketeer.

Local Reporting, Edition Time: *Vicksburg* (Miss.) *Sunday Post-Herald*
Local Reporting, No Edition Time: Alvin Scott McCoy, *Kansas City Star*
National Reporting: Richard Wilson, *Des Moines Register and Tribune*
International Reporting: Jim G. Lucas, Scripps-Howard Newspapers
Editorial Writing: Don Murray, *Boston Herald*
Editorial Cartooning: Herbert L. Block (Herblock), *Washington Post & Times-Herald*
Photography: Mrs. Walter M. Schau, amateur

1955

Columbus (Ga.) *Ledger* and *Sunday Ledger-Enquirer:* The *Ledger* and *Sunday Ledger-Enquirer* investigated vice-ridden Phenix City, Alabama, across the Chattahoochee River. The work gained national attention when Alabama's crusading attorney general nominee, Albert L. Patterson, was gunned down in a parking lot in June 1954. Reporters, too, had been attacked by thugs. The investigation was largely done by Carlton Johnson, who had been detached from duties as city editor to take over the Phenix City staff, along with assistant city editor Thomas J. Sellers Jr. and county courthouse reporter Ray Jenkins. Eighty-seven racketeers and corrupt politicians had been imprisoned, indicted, or become fugitives from justice by the time of the award submission. Said the nomination letter: "Phenix City is now truly what its solicitor, under indictment at this time for the murder of Albert L. Patterson, once called it: 'The cleanest little city in America.'"

———

Public Service: *Columbus Ledger* and *Sunday Ledger-Enquirer,* for its complete news coverage and fearless editorial attack on widespread corruption in neighboring Phenix City, Alabama, which was effective in destroying a corrupt and racket-ridden city government. The newspaper exhibited an early awareness of the evils of lax law enforcement before the situation in Phenix City erupted into murder. It covered the whole unfolding story of the final prosecution of the wrongdoers with skill, perception, force, and courage.
Local Reporting, Edition Time: Caro Brown, *Alice* (Texas) *Daily Echo*
Local Reporting, No Edition Time: Roland Kenneth Towery, *Cuero* (Texas) *Record*
National Reporting: Anthony Lewis, *Washington Daily News*
International Reporting: Harrison E. Salisbury, *New York Times*
Editorial Writing: Royce Howes, *Detroit Free Press*
Editorial Cartooning: Daniel R. Fitzpatrick, *St. Louis Post-Dispatch*
Photography: John L. Gaunt Jr., *Los Angeles Times*

1956

Watsonville (Calif.) *Register-Pajaronian:* The seven-thousand-circulation *Register-Pajaronian,* south of San Francisco, became suspicious of the city's new district attorney. During the paper's investigation, a reporter and photographer assigned by editor Roy Pinkerton discovered the D.A. visiting a gambler in a midnight meeting. When noticed by a thug in the gambler's employ, the two journalists were held at gunpoint, and the camera was destroyed. As disclosures poured out, community support developed. The California attorney general began an investigation, and the D.A. resigned just as he was about to be tried for malicious misconduct.

—∞∞∞—

Public Service: *Watsonville Register-Pajaronian,* for courageous exposure of corruption in public office, which led to the resignation of a district attorney and the conviction of one of his associates.

Local Reporting, Edition Time: Lee Hills, *Detroit Free Press*

Local Reporting, No Edition Time: Arthur Daley, *New York Times*

National Reporting: Charles L. Bartlett, *Chattanooga Times*

International Reporting: William Randolph Hearst Jr., J. Kingsbury-Smith, Frank Conniff, International News Service

Editorial Writing: Lauren K. Soth, *Register and Tribune,* Des Moines

Editorial Cartooning: Robert York, *Louisville Times*

Photography: Staff of *New York Daily News*

1957

Chicago Daily News: The *Chicago Daily News*—and George Thiem, who had helped the paper win a Gold Medal in 1950—targeted state auditor Orville L. Hodge based on a tip from a reader who said the respected millionaire businessman was involved in illegal activities. Hodge had been mentioned as a possible Republican candidate for governor. But twenty-one reporters and other staffers, with Thiem in charge, dug into Hodge's affairs and unearthed a $2.5 million fraud that eventually sent him and assistant Edward Epping to prison, along with the bank president who had facilitated their crimes. During the pressure-filled investigation, the paper said that two city editors had suffered heart attacks while directing coverage.

—∞∞∞—

Public Service: *Chicago Daily News,* for determined and courageous public service in exposing a $2.5 million fraud centering in the office of the state auditor of Illinois, resulting in the indictment and conviction of the state auditor and others. This led to the reorganization of state procedures to prevent a recurrence of the fraud.

Local Reporting, Edition Time: *Salt Lake Tribune*

Local Reporting, No Edition Time: Wallace Turner, William Lambert, *Oregonian*

National Reporting: James Reston, *New York Times*

International Reporting: Russell Jones, United Press

Editorial Writing: Buford Boone, *Tuscaloosa News*

Editorial Cartooning: Tom Little, *Nashville Tennessean*

Photography: Harry A. Trask, *Boston Traveler*

1958

Public Service: *Arkansas Gazette* of Little Rock, for demonstrating the highest qualities of civic leadership, journalistic responsibility, and moral courage in the face of great public tension during the school integration crisis of 1957. The newspaper's fearless and completely objective news coverage, plus its reasoned and moderate policy, did much to restore calmness and order to an overwrought community, reflecting great credit on its editors and its management.

Local Reporting, Edition Time: *Fargo* (N.D.) *Forum*
Local Reporting, No Edition Time: George Beveridge, *Evening Star,* Washington
National Reporting: Clark Mollenhoff, *Des Moines Register and Tribune*
National Reporting: Relman Morin, Associated Press
International Reporting: *New York Times*
Editorial Writing: Harry S. Ashmore, *Arkansas Gazette*
Editorial Cartooning: Bruce M. Shanks, *Buffalo* (N.Y.) *Evening News*
Photography: William C. Beall, *Washington* (D.C.) *Daily News*

1959

Utica (N.Y.) *Observer-Dispatch* and *Utica Daily Press:* The Gannett-owned *Observer-Dispatch* and *Daily Press* fought a campaign against corruption, gambling, and vice, upsetting powerful forces in the community. Many local leaders did not want Utica's image tarnished by association with crime. The common council tried to levy a 5 percent tax on newspaper advertising to send a message to the editors. But the papers—published separately at the time, but since combined—did not give up and ran more than eighty editorials attacking law enforcement lapses and suggesting that taxpayers were being defrauded. They used the Gannett News Service resources, including Albany bureau chief Jack Germond. *Daily Press* city editor Tony Vella and city hall reporter William Lohden were involved in the coverage, a job that was made harder because city officials had declared a news blackout against the two papers. Sweeping reforms were approved, and a number of crime figures were indicted and jailed.

Public Service: *Utica Observer-Dispatch* and *Utica Daily Press,* for their successful campaign against corruption, gambling, and vice in their home city and the achievement of sweeping civic reforms in the face of political pressure and threats of violence. By their stalwart leadership of the forces of good government, these newspapers upheld the best tradition of a free press.

Local Reporting, Edition Time: Mary Lou Werner, *Evening Star,* Washington
Local Reporting, No Edition Time: John Harold Brislin, *Scranton Tribune & Scrantonian*
National Reporting: Howard Van Smith, *Miami News*
International Reporting: Joseph Martin, Philip Santora, *New York Daily News*
Editorial Writing: Ralph McGill, *Atlanta Constitution*
Editorial Cartooning: William H. "Bill" Mauldin, *St. Louis Post-Dispatch*
Photography: William Seaman, *Minneapolis Star*

1960

Los Angeles Times: Los Angeles Times editor Nick Williams and city editor Taylor Trumbo put reporter Gene Sherman on the track of Mexican narcotics smugglers after they noticed a pattern in several drug seizures. Sherman wrote an eight-part series on Mexican narcotics smuggling after a seven-month investigation that took him through Tijuana, Tecate, Nogales, and Juarez to Mexicali and El Paso. He estimated that 75 percent of southern California's heroin and 99 percent of its marijuana had been imported from Mexico. State and federal inquiries sprang from the investigation, and the United States and Mexico began discussing measures for increasing enforcement to reduce drug trafficking.

───

Public Service: *Los Angeles Times,* for its thorough, sustained, and well-conceived attack on narcotics traffic and the enterprising reporting of Gene Sherman, which led to the opening of negotiations between the United States and Mexico to halt the flow of illegal drugs into southern California and other border states.
Local Reporting, Edition Time: Jack Nelson, *Atlanta Constitution*
Local Reporting, No Edition Time: Miriam Ottenberg, *Evening Star,* Washington
National Reporting: Vance Trimble, Scripps-Howard Newspaper Alliance
International Reporting: A. M. Rosenthal, *New York Times*
Editorial Writing: Lenoir Chambers, *Norfolk Virginian-Pilot*
Editorial Cartooning: No Award
Photography: Andrew Lopez, United Press

1961

Amarillo (Texas) *Globe-Times:* A phone tip to *Globe-Times* editor Thomas H. Thompson led to a meeting in a bar where he was told he could have "information that would blow the top off the court house" if the tipster could be protected. The source, private detective Armand James Chandonnet, revealed that he had worked for county judge Roy Joe Stevens and knew of bribe-taking and other wrongdoing by the judge. The string of stories in the paper—some by John Masterman and Don Boyett, working under city editor Paul Timmons—led to various legal proceedings against Stevens. He was acquitted, but was disbarred and left the state. State legislation was enacted to close loopholes that Judge Stevens had used to go free at trial.

───

Public Service: *Amarillo Globe-Times,* for exposing a breakdown in local law enforcement with resultant punitive action that swept lax officials from their posts and brought about the election of a reform slate. The newspaper thus exerted its civic leadership in the finest tradition of journalism.
Local Reporting, Edition Time: Sanche De Gramont, *New York Herald Tribune*
Local Reporting, No Edition Time: Edgar May, *Buffalo Evening News*
National Reporting: Edward R. Cony, *Wall Street Journal*
International Reporting: Lynn Heinzerling, Associated Press
Editorial Writing: William J. Dorvillier, *San Juan* (Puerto Rico) *Star*
Editorial Cartooning: Carey Orr, *Chicago Tribune*
Photography: Yasushi Nagao, *Mainichi,* Tokyo

1962

Panama City (Fla.) *News & Herald:* The *News & Herald*, with its six-person news operation, ran a three-year campaign against illegal gambling and moonshining operations supported by political corruption. The paper's campaign—under executive editor and editorial writer Edwin B. Callaway and managing editor Bob Brown—relied on the reporting work of W. U. (Duke) Newcome. When the state did not take action on the paper's reports, editors went to newly elected Governor Farris Bryant. Together, they hatched a plan for digging out the entrenched crime. State investigators and *News & Herald* reporters combined their efforts on a long-term basis, with the paper agreeing to withhold publication until results were in. Eventually, a former sheriff and police chief, among others, were indicted.

Public Service: *Panama City News & Herald*, for its three-year campaign against entrenched power and corruption, with resultant reforms in Panama City and Bay County.
Local Reporting, Edition Time: Robert D. Mullins, *Deseret News*, Salt Lake City
Local Reporting, No Edition Time: George Bliss, *Chicago Tribune*
National Reporting: Nathan G. Caldwell, Gene S. Graham, *Nashville Tennessean*
International Reporting: Walter Lippmann, New York Herald Tribune Syndicate
Editorial Writing: Thomas M. Storke, *Santa Barbara* (Calif.) *News-Press*
Editorial Cartooning: Edmund S. Valtman, *Hartford Times*
Photography: Paul Vathis, Associated Press

1963

Public Service: *Chicago Daily News*, for calling public attention to the issue of providing birth control services in the public health programs in its area.
Local Reporting, Edition Time: Sylvan Fox, Anthony Shannon, William Longgood, *New York World-Telegram and Sun*
Local Reporting, No Edition Time: Oscar Griffin Jr., *Pecos* (Texas) *Independent and Enterprise*
National Reporting: Anthony Lewis, *New York Times*
International Reporting: Hal Hendrix, *Miami News*
Editorial Writing: Ira B. Harkey Jr., *Pascagoula* (Miss.) *Chronicle*
Editorial Cartooning: Frank Miller, *Des Moines Register*
Photography: Hector Rondon, *La Republica*, Caracas, Venezuela

1964

Public Service: *St. Petersburg Times*, for its aggressive investigation of the Florida Turnpike Authority which disclosed widespread illegal acts and resulted in a major reorganization of the state's road construction program.
Local Reporting, Edition Time: Norman C. Miller Jr., *Wall Street Journal*
Local Reporting, No Edition Time: James V. Magee, Albert V. Gaudiosi; Frederick Meyer, photographer, *Philadelphia Bulletin*
National Reporting: Merriman Smith, United Press International

International Reporting: Malcolm W. Browne, Associated Press; David Halberstam, *New York Times*
Editorial Writing: Hazel Brannon Smith, *Lexington* (Miss.) *Advertiser*
Editorial Cartooning: Paul Conrad, *Denver Post*
Photography: Robert H. Jackson, *Dallas Times Herald*

1965

Hutchinson (Kans.) *News:* The *Hutchinson News* took the side of voters who had been disenfranchised by politicians through faulty district apportionment in the state legislature. When the *News,* under editor John McCormally, began its campaign for reapportionment, Kansas did not use a strict population basis for determining votes. That left many people poorly represented, and locked politicians in for reelection. The same was true in many other states. The Supreme Court's landmark 1962 *Baker vs. Carr* ruling had mandated fair, population-based reapportionment in setting districts. By then, however, the *Hutchinson News* already had proposed how Kansas could achieve that end. The paper had brought suit in the state courts, with board chairman John P. Harris, publisher Peter Macdonald, and McCormally leading the drive. It also made the case on its editorial pages. The Kansas courts ruled in the newspaper's favor in 1964 and changed the basis of the state senate apportionment. In one editorial, McCormally criticized those opposing representative apportionment:

> What are they afraid of—those who now frantically are crying states rights, imploring the Founding Fathers and castigating the court? Why, the people, that's what they're afraid of. Ever since the first kings started toppling and the first revolutionary thoughts began to find their way into print, they've been afraid that if the people ever really got control of their own governments, all hell would break loose.

Public Service: *Hutchinson News,* for its courageous and constructive campaign, culminating in 1964, to bring about more equitable reapportionment of the Kansas Legislature, despite powerful opposition in its own community.
Local General or Spot News Reporting: Melvin H. Ruder, *Hungry Horse News,* Columbia Falls, Montana
Local Investigative Specialized Reporting: Gene Goltz, *Houston Post*
National Reporting: Louis M. Kohlmeier, *Wall Street Journal*
International Reporting: J. A. Livingston, *Philadelphia Bulletin*
Editorial Writing: John R. Harrison, *Gainesville* (Fla.) *Sun*
Editorial Cartooning: No Award
Photography: Horst Faas, Associated Press

1966

Boston Globe: The *Boston Globe,* under editor Thomas Winship, successfully campaigned to prevent Judge Francis X. Morrissey's confirmation as a federal district judge. Mor-

rissey had been a political worker for Joseph P. Kennedy, and had been sponsored first
by President John Kennedy and then by his brother, Edward M. "Ted" Kennedy, the
Massachusetts Democratic senator. The *Globe*'s reporting was the work of a team
spearheaded by political editor Robert L. Healey. It examined Judge Morrissey's legal
qualifications and found them wanting, and eventually it questioned his veracity. The
Globe thought the appointment "another example of politically inspired actions
which had attained for Massachusetts a reputation of operating without a civic con-
science in public matters." But then reporters turned up apparent discrepancies in his
testimony to a congressional subcommittee. In one, they showed that Morrissey had
not attended Boston College Law School, as he claimed. When the *Globe*'s reporting
drew national attention, opposition in the Senate grew, and Morrissey eventually requested that President Lyndon Johnson withdraw his name.

Public Service: *Boston Globe,* for its campaign to prevent confirmation of Francis X.
    Morrissey as a federal district judge in Massachusetts.
Local General or Spot News Reporting: Staff of *Los Angeles Times*
Local Investigative Specialized Reporting: John Anthony Frasca, *Tampa* (Fla.) *Tribune*
National Reporting: Haynes Johnson, *Washington Evening Star*
International Reporting: Peter Arnett, Associated Press
Editorial Writing: Robert Lasch, *St. Louis Post-Dispatch*
Editorial Cartooning: Don Wright, *Miami News*
Photography: Kyoichi Sawada, United Press International

1967

Milwaukee Journal and *Louisville Courier-Journal:* The *Louisville Courier-Journal* and
    the *Milwaukee Journal* won for unrelated environmental campaigns in their states.
    The *Courier-Journal* had launched a drive to preserve Kentucky's natural beauty with
    a special 1964 section, "Kentucky's Ravaged Land." It followed up that work in 1965
    and 1966. In 1966, the state assembly reacted and passed a tough strip-mining con-
    trol law. The *Milwaukee Journal*'s Public Service Prize—its first since 1919, when it
    campaigned against World War I "Germanism" in Wisconsin—was aimed at water
    pollution. A three-part series in its Picture Journal section used color photographs
    to show the effects of polluted water. The Wisconsin legislature cited the series when
    it passed a $300 million water pollution control law.

Public Service: *Milwaukee Journal,* for its successful campaign to stiffen the law against
    water pollution in Wisconsin, a notable advance in the national effort for the con-
    servation of natural resources.
Public Service: *Louisville Courier-Journal,* for its successful campaign to control the
    Kentucky strip-mining industry, a notable advance in the national effort for the con-
    servation of natural resources.
Local General or Spot News Reporting: Robert V. Cox, *Chambersburg* (Pa.) *Public
    Opinion*
Local Investigative Specialized Reporting: Gene Miller, *Miami Herald*

National Reporting: Vance Trimble, Scripps-Howard Newspaper Alliance
International Reporting: A. M. Rosenthal, *New York Times*
Editorial Writing: Lenoir Chambers, *Norfolk Virginian-Pilot*
Editorial Cartooning: No Award
Photography: Andrew Lopez, United Press International

1968

Riverside (Calif.) *Press-Enterprise:* Reporter George Ringwald of the *Press-Enterprise* focused on cases of apparent judicial and legal abuse involving the large Palm Springs–area landholdings of about a hundred members of the Agua Caliente tribe of native Americans. The tribal members were represented by court-appointed guardians and conservators who were responsible to the Department of Interior's Bureau of Indian Affairs. Ringwald learned that some judges were being paid as executors of estate wills for tribal members. Meanwhile, fellow judges rubber-stamped the lucrative arrangements. Eventually, the Department of the Interior and the state judicial qualifications commission both investigated. In selecting the *Press-Enterprise,* the Pulitzer board passed over two entries with ethnic themes that jurors ranked higher: *Washington Post* coverage of race relations, and a series on problems of Alaska's native Americans in the *Anchorage Daily News*. In 1989, the Alaskan paper revisited the topic of "A People in Peril," and won the Gold Medal.

Public Service: *Riverside Press-Enterprise,* for its exposé of corruption in the courts in connection with the handling of the property and estates of an Indian tribe in California, and its successful efforts to punish the culprits.
Local General or Spot News Reporting: Staff of *Detroit Free Press*
Local Investigative Specialized Reporting: J. Anthony Lukas, *New York Times*
National Reporting: Nathan K. "Nick" Kotz, *Des Moines Register* and *Minneapolis Tribune*
International Reporting: Howard James, *Christian Science Monitor*
Editorial Writing: John S. Knight, Knight Newspapers
Editorial Cartooning: Eugene Gray Payne, *Charlotte Observer*
Photography: Toshio Sakai, United Press International

1969

Public Service: *Los Angeles Times,* for its exposé of wrongdoing within the Los Angeles City Government Commissions, resulting in resignations or criminal convictions of certain members, as well as widespread reforms.
Local General or Spot News Reporting: John Fetterman, *Louisville Times and Courier-Journal*
Local Investigative Specialized Reporting: Albert L. Delugach, Denny Walsh, *St. Louis Globe-Democrat*
National Reporting: Robert Cahn, *Christian Science Monitor*
International Reporting: William Tuohy, *Los Angeles Times*
Editorial Writing: Paul Greenberg, *Pine Bluff* (Ark.) *Commercial*

Editorial Cartooning: John Fischetti, *Chicago Daily News*
Spot News Photography: Edward T. Adams
Feature Photography: Moneta Sleet Jr., *Ebony* magazine

1970

Public Service: *Newsday,* for its three-year investigation and exposure of secret land deals in eastern Long Island, which led to a series of criminal convictions, discharges, and resignations among public and political officeholders in the area.
Local General or Spot News Reporting: Thomas Fitzpatrick, *Chicago Sun-Times*
Local Investigative Specialized Reporting: Harold Eugene Martin, *Montgomery Advertiser and Alabama Journal*
National Reporting: William J. Eaton, *Chicago Daily News*
International Reporting: Seymour M. Hersh, *Dispatch News Service*
Commentary: Marquis W. Childs, *St. Louis Post-Dispatch*
Criticism: Ada Louise Huxtable, *New York Times*
Editorial Writing: Philip L. Geyelin, *Washington Post*
Editorial Cartooning: Thomas F. Darcy, *Newsday*
Spot News Photography: Steve Starr, Associated Press
Feature Photography: Dallas Kinney, *Palm Beach Post*

1971

Winston-Salem (N.C.) *Journal and Sentinel:* The *Winston-Salem Journal and Sentinel* covered the plans for a strip-mining enterprise after a reader tipped the paper that a New York company, Gibbsite Corp., was buying up mineral leases in North Carolina's remote Surry County. Reporter Arlene Edwards found that thousands of acres of mineral leases had been optioned to the company. It planned to strip-mine for alumina, which is processed into aluminum. Public opposition grew and the paper added reporters Joe Goodman, Jesse Poindexter, Raleigh correspondent Joe Doster, and state editor Jack Trawick to the project. At midyear Gibbsite said it was letting its options expire. Editor and publisher Wallace Carroll, formerly of the *New York Times,* was a Pulitzer board member the year the *Journal and Sentinel* won. One little-discussed element of Gold Medal–winning is the staff exodus. Joe Goodman noted that "when the prizes started showing up in '71, hell, your whole staff is out there looking for jobs. I sure as hell was. So come, say, '72, everybody's gone." Some went to Gene Roberts's *Philadelphia Inquirer,* which had an eye for Pulitzer winners. It also had John Carroll as an *Inquirer* editor. Carroll, later the *Los Angeles Times* editor, was Wallace Carroll's son. (John Carroll notes that his father kept battling for the environment after retiring in 1974, leading editors in a successful campaign against Duke Power Co.'s damming of the New River. When his parents died, John Carroll says, their ashes were spread on the river's still-pristine waters.)

———

Public Service: *Winston-Salem Journal and Sentinel,* for coverage of environmental problems, as exemplified by a successful campaign to block strip-mining operations that would have caused irreparable damage to the hill country of northwest North Carolina.

Local General or Spot News Reporting: Staff of *Akron Beacon Journal*
Local Investigative Specialized Reporting: William Jones, *Chicago Tribune*
National Reporting: Lucinda Franks and Thomas Powers, United Press International
International Reporting: Jimmie Lee Hoagland, *Washington Post*
Commentary: William A. Caldwell, *Record,* Hackensack, N.J.
Criticism: Harold C. Schonberg, *New York Times*
Editorial Writing: Horace G. Davis Jr., *Gainesville* (Fla.) *Sun*
Editorial Cartooning: Paul Conrad, *Los Angeles Times*
Spot News Photography: John Paul Filo, *Valley Daily News, Daily Dispatch,* Tarentum
and New Kensington, Pa.
Feature Photography: Jack Dykinga, *Chicago Sun-Times*

1972
Public Service: *New York Times,* for the publication of the Pentagon Papers.
Local General or Spot News Reporting: Richard Cooper, John Machacek, *Rochester
Times-Union*
Local Investigative Specialized Reporting: Timothy Leland, Gerard M. O'Neill, Stephen A. Kurkjian, Ann Desantis, *Boston Globe*
National Reporting: Jack Anderson, syndicated columnist
International Reporting: Peter R. Kann, *Wall Street Journal*
Commentary: Mike Royko, *Chicago Daily News*
Criticism: Frank Peters Jr., *St. Louis Post-Dispatch*
Editorial Writing: John Strohmeyer, *Bethlehem Globe-Times*
Editorial Cartooning: Jeffrey K. MacNelly, *Richmond News-Leader*
Spot News Photography: Horst Faas, Michel Laurent, Associated Press
Feature Photography: Dave Kennerly, United Press International

1973
Public Service: *Washington Post,* for its investigation of the Watergate case.
Local General or Spot News Reporting: *Chicago Tribune*
Local Investigative Specialized Reporting: Sun Newspapers, Omaha
National Reporting: Robert Boyd, Clark Hoyt, Knight Newspapers
International Reporting: Max Frankel, *New York Times*
Commentary: David S. Broder, *Washington Post*
Criticism: Ronald Powers, *Chicago Sun-Times*
Editorial Writing: Roger B. Linscott, *Berkshire Eagle,* Pittsfield, Mass.
Editorial Cartooning: No Award
Spot News Photography: Huynh Cong Ut, Associated Press
Feature Photography: Brian Lanker, *Topeka Capital-Journal*

1974
Public Service: *Newsday,* for its definitive report on the illicit narcotic traffic in the United States and abroad, entitled "The Heroin Trail."
Local General or Spot News Reporting: Arthur M. Petacque, Hugh F. Hough, *Chicago Sun-Times*

Local Investigative Specialized Reporting: William Sherman, *New York Daily News*
National Reporting: Jack White, *Providence Journal and Evening Bulletin*
International Reporting: Hedrick Smith, *New York Times*
Commentary: Edwin A. Roberts Jr., *National Observer*
Criticism: Emily Genauer, *Newsday* Syndicate
Editorial Writing: F. Gilman Spencer, *Trentonian*
Editorial Cartooning: Paul Szep, *Boston Globe*
Spot News Photography: Anthony K. Roberts
Feature Photography: Slava Veder, Associated Press

1975

Boston Globe: As many northern cities faced high-pressure decisions about how to im-
plement court-ordered integration, the *Boston Globe* took an approach to news coverage that alienated everybody. It reported the story from all sides. Angry white parents were stoning buses that carried black children to segregated south Boston
schools. Senator Edward Kennedy, trying to calm the situation, was pelted with
tomatoes and eggs at a rally, where someone yelled, "You're a disgrace to the Irish."
The *Globe,* too, tried to calm things—leading some blacks to see it as too accepting
of racism—but it was unquestionably thorough. Editor Thomas Winship and executive editor Jack Driscoll deployed sixty reporters, and in direct charge of this dispassionate coverage was the assistant managing editor for local news, Robert H.
Phelps, a former chief of the paper's Spotlight Team. The fairer the *Globe* was, the
nastier the repercussions. Groups of parents who favored all-white schools broke
windows at the paper's offices. Rifle shots were fired and bomb threats received. The
Globe installed steel shutters. Wrote Pulitzer Prize administrator John Hohenberg in
a discussion of its winning work: "Do not look for elegant writing in the *Globe*'s re-
portage. What went into the paper, day after day and week after week, was the guts
of the best kind of newspaper journalism in this land—an unemotional, impartial,
immensely detailed and thoroughly honest and accurate report of what was going
on in the schools, the streets, the entire community."

Public Service: *Boston Globe,* for its massive and balanced coverage of the Boston school
desegregation crisis.
Local General or Spot News Reporting: Staff of *Xenia* (Ohio) *Daily Gazette*
Local Investigative Specialized Reporting: *Indianapolis Star*
National Reporting: Donald L. Barlett, James B. Steele, *Philadelphia Inquirer*
International Reporting: William Mullen, reporter; Ovie Carter, photographer, *Chica-
go Tribune*
Commentary: Mary McGrory, *Washington Star*
Criticism: Roger Ebert, *Chicago Sun-Times*
Editorial Writing: John Daniell Maurice, *Charleston* (W. Va.) *Daily Mail*
Editorial Cartooning: Garry Trudeau, Universal Press Syndicate
Spot News Photography: Gerald H. Gay, *Seattle Times*
Feature Photography: Matthew Lewis, *Washington Post*

1976

Public Service: *Anchorage Daily News,* for its disclosures of the impact and influence of the Teamsters Union on Alaska's economy and politics.
Local General or Spot News Reporting: Gene Miller, *Miami Herald*
Local Investigative Specialized Reporting: Staff of *Chicago Tribune*
National Reporting: James Risser, *Des Moines Register*
International Reporting: Sydney H. Schanberg, *New York Times*
Commentary: Walter Wellesley (Red) Smith, *New York Times*
Criticism: Alan M. Kriegsman, *Washington Post*
Editorial Writing: Philip P. Kerby, *Los Angeles Times*
Editorial Cartooning: Tony Auth, *Philadelphia Inquirer*
Spot News Photography: Stanley Forman, *Boston Herald American*
Feature Photography: Staff of *Louisville Courier-Journal and Times*

1977

Public Service: *Lufkin* (Texas) *News,* for an obituary of a local man who died in Marine training camp, which grew into an investigation of that death and a fundamental reform in the recruiting and training practices of the U.S. Marine Corps.
Local General or Spot News Reporting: Margo Huston, *Milwaukee Journal*
Local Investigative Specialized Reporting: Acel Moore, Wendell Rawls Jr., *Philadelphia Inquirer*
National Reporting: Walter Mears, Associated Press
International Reporting: No Award
Commentary: George F. Will, Washington Post Writers Group
Criticism: William McPherson, *Washington Post*
Editorial Writing: Warren L. Lerude, Foster Church, Norman F. Cardoza, *Reno Evening Gazette* and *Nevada State Journal*
Editorial Cartooning: Paul Szep, *Boston Globe*
Spot News Photography: Stanley Forman, *Boston Herald American*
Spot News Photography: Neal Ulevich, Associated Press
Feature Photography: Robin Hood, *Chattanooga News-Free Press*

1978

Public Service: *Philadelphia Inquirer,* for a series of articles showing abuses of power by the police in its home city.
Local General or Spot News Reporting: Richard Whitt, *Louisville Courier-Journal*
Local Investigative Specialized Reporting: Anthony R. Dolan, *Stamford Advocate*
National Reporting: Gaylord D. Shaw, *Los Angeles Times*
International Reporting: Henry Kamm, *New York Times*
Commentary: William Safire, *New York Times*
Criticism: Walter Kerr, *New York Times*
Editorial Writing: Meg Greenfield, *Washington Post*
Editorial Cartooning: Jeffrey K. MacNelly, *Richmond News Leader*
Spot News Photography: John H. Blair, United Press International
Feature Photography: J. Ross Baughman, Associated Press

1979

Public Service: *Point Reyes* (Calif.) *Light,* for its investigation of Synanon.

Local General or Spot News Reporting: *San Diego Evening Tribune*

Local Investigative Specialized Reporting: Gilbert M. Gaul, Elliot G. Jaspin, *Pottsville* (Pa.) *Republican*

National Reporting: James Risser, *Des Moines Register*

International Reporting: Richard Ben Cramer, *Philadelphia Inquirer*

Feature Writing: Jon D. Franklin, *Baltimore Evening Sun*

Commentary: Russell Baker, *New York Times*

Criticism: Paul Gapp, *Chicago Tribune*

Editorial Writing: Edwin M. Yoder Jr., *Washington Star*

Editorial Cartooning: Herbert L. Block, *Washington Post*

Spot News Photography: Thomas J. Kelly III of *Pottstown* (Pa.) *Mercury*

Feature Photography: *Boston Herald American*

1980

Gannett News Service: Three Gannett News Service journalists—Tallahassee bureau chief John M. Hanchette, state editor William F. Schmick, and GNS national staffer Carlton A. Sherwood—examined financial mismanagement within the Pauline Fathers, an order of the Roman Catholic Church. All three had Catholic backgrounds, and Sherwood once had been a news editor of the *Catholic Star-Herald* in Camden, New Jersey. The investigation involved more than two hundred thousand miles of travel to Italy, Poland, Hungary, and England, as well as to seventeen U.S. states. The result was an eighteen-day series showing that officials had squandered millions of dollars of loans and charitable donations at the order, once known as the Order of St. Paul the First Hermit. As many as twenty-five hundred elderly Catholics were victims, having invested in bonds sold by the Pauline Fathers, ostensibly to build a devotional shrine in Kittanning, Pennsylvania. Angry responses came from the Paulines, but a papal investigation confirmed many of the claims in the series, and those who invested in the bonds were repaid in full. It was the first instance of a Public Service Prize going to a news service, and occurred also in the first year that the Pulitzer board announced finalists. It named four in Public Service: the *Miami Herald,* twice, for work on medical malpractice and on police brutality; the *Philadelphia Inquirer* for a series on toxic waste, and the *St. Petersburg Times* for its investigation of the Church of Scientology. The board awarded two *Times* reporters, Bette Swenson Orsini and Charles Stafford, the National Reporting Prize for the Scientology stories.

⸺∞⸺

Public Service: Gannett News Service, for its series on financial contributions to the Pauline Fathers.

Local General or Spot New Reporting: Staff of *Philadelphia Inquirer*

Local Investigative Specialized Reporting: Stephen A. Kurkjian, Alexander B. Hawes Jr., Nils Bruzelius, Joan Vennochi, Robert M. Porterfield, *Boston Globe*

National Reporting: Bette Swenson Orsini, Charles Stafford, *St. Petersburg Times*

International Reporting: Joel Brinkley, Jay Mather, *Louisville Courier-Journal*
Feature Writing: Madeleine Blais, *Miami Herald*
Commentary: Ellen H. Goodman, *Boston Globe*
Criticism: William A. Henry III, *Boston Globe*
Editorial Writing: Robert L. Bartley, *Wall Street Journal*
Editorial Cartooning: Don Wright, *Miami Herald*
Spot News Photography: United Press International
Feature Photography: Edwin H. Hagler, *Dallas Times Herald*

1981

Public Service: *Charlotte Observer,* for its series on "Brown Lung: A Case of Deadly Neglect."
Local General or Spot New Reporting: Staff of *Longview* (Wash.) *Daily News*
Local Investigative Specialized Reporting: Clark Hallas, Robert B. Lowe, *Arizona Daily Star*
National Reporting: John M. Crewdson, *New York Times*
International Reporting: Shirley Christian, *Miami Herald*
Feature Writing: Teresa Carpenter, *Village Voice*
Commentary: Dave Anderson, *New York Times*
Criticism: Jonathan Yardley, *Washington Star*
Editorial Writing: No Award
Editorial Cartooning: Mike Peters, *Dayton Daily News*
Spot News Photography: Larry C. Price, *Fort Worth Star-Telegram*
Feature Photography: Taro M. Yamasaki, *Detroit Free Press*

1982

Public Service: *Detroit News,* for a series by Sydney P. Freedberg and David Ashenfelter which exposed the U.S. Navy's cover-up of circumstances surrounding the deaths of seamen aboard ship and which led to significant reforms in naval procedures.
Local General or Spot New Reporting: *Kansas City Star, Kansas City Times*
Local Investigative Specialized Reporting: Paul Henderson, *Seattle Times*
National Reporting: Rick Atkinson, *Kansas City Times*
International Reporting: John Darnton, *New York Times*
Feature Writing: Saul Pett, Associated Press
Commentary: Art Buchwald, Los Angeles Times Syndicate
Criticism: Martin Bernheimer, *Los Angeles Times*
Editorial Writing: Jack Rosenthal, *New York Times*
Editorial Cartooning: Ben Sargent, *Austin American-Statesman*
Spot News Photography: Ron Edmonds, Associated Press
Feature Photography: John H. White, *Chicago Sun-Times*

1983

Jackson (Miss.) *Clarion-Ledger:* The *Jackson Clarion-Ledger* explored why Mississippi's public schools "didn't make the grade," and editorials proposed solutions that fit with what reform-minded Governor William Winter was doing. Reporter Nancy Weaver's project was first put on hold during an ownership change that made Gannett its owner. New executive editor Charles Overby took charge and assigned more than half a dozen other staffers to work with Weaver on what turned out to be a six-month investigation. Overby managed both the news and editorial components. It had been twenty-nine years since the state legislature's last major improvement in the education system, and not even compulsory education was required. Mississippi's management of desegregation also had hurt school financing, and led to white children withdrawing from public schools. Weaver worked with reporters Fred Anklam Jr. and Cliff Tryens, among others, to produce a twenty-four-day series titled "Mississippi Schools, Hard Lessons." Lee Cearnal was project editor, and editorials were written by editorial director Dave Hardin, who helped analyze reform options. Results included new taxes passed by the voters to support schools, a mandatory attendance law, and the first state-supported kindergartens.

Public Service: *Jackson Clarion-Ledger,* for its successful campaign supporting Governor Winter in his legislative battle for reform of Mississippi's public education system.

Local General or Spot News Reporting: Editorial staff of *Fort Wayne News-Sentinel*

Local Investigative Specialized Reporting: Loretta Tofani, *Washington Post*

National Reporting: *Boston Globe*

International Reporting: Thomas L. Friedman, *New York Times;* Loren Jenkins, *Washington Post*

Feature Writing: Nan Robertson, *New York Times*

Commentary: Claude Sitton, *News & Observer,* Raleigh, N.C.

Criticism: Manuela Hoelterhoff, *Wall Street Journal*

Editorial Writing: Editorial board of *Miami Herald*

Editorial Cartooning: Richard Locher, *Chicago Tribune*

Spot News Photography: Bill Foley, Associated Press

Feature Photography: James B. Dickman, *Dallas Times Herald*

1984

Public Service: *Los Angeles Times,* for an in-depth examination of southern California's growing Latino community by a team of editors and reporters.

Local General or Spot New Reporting: *Newsday*

Local Investigative Specialized Reporting: Kenneth Cooper, Joan Fitz Gerald, Jonathan Kaufman, Norman Lockman, Gary McMillan, Kirk Scharfenberg, David Wessel, *Boston Globe*

National Reporting: John Noble Wilford, *New York Times*

International Reporting: Karen Elliott House, *Wall Street Journal*

Feature Writing: Peter Mark Rinearson, *Seattle Times*

Commentary: Vermont Royster, *Wall Street Journal*

Criticism: Paul Goldberger, *New York Times*

Editorial Writing: Albert Scardino, *Georgia Gazette,* Savannah

Editorial Cartooning: Paul Conrad, *Los Angeles Times*
Spot News Photography: Stan Grossfeld, *Boston Globe*
Feature Photography: Anthony Suau, *Denver Post*

1985

Public Service, *Fort Worth Star-Telegram,* for reporting by Mark J. Thompson which revealed that nearly 250 U.S. servicemen had lost their lives as a result of a design problem in helicopters built by Bell Helicopter—a revelation which ultimately led the Army to ground almost 600 Huey helicopters pending their modification.
General News Reporting: Thomas Turcol, *Virginian-Pilot and Ledger-Star,* Norfolk, Virginia
Investigative Reporting: William K. Marimow, *Philadelphia Inquirer*
Investigative Reporting: Lucy Morgan, Jack Reed, *St. Petersburg Times*
Explanatory Journalism: Jon Franklin, *Baltimore Evening Sun*
National Reporting: Thomas J. Knudson, *Des Moines Register*
International Reporting: Josh Friedman, Dennis Bell, Ozier Muhammad (photographer), *Newsday*
Feature Writing: Alice Steinbach, *Baltimore Sun*
Commentary: Murray Kempton, *Newsday*
Criticism: Howard Rosenberg, *Los Angeles Times*
Editorial Writing: Richard Aregood, *Philadelphia Daily News*
Editorial Cartooning: Jeff MacNelly, *Chicago Tribune*
Spot News Photography: *Register,* Santa Ana, Calif.
Feature Photography: Larry C. Price, *Philadelphia Inquirer*

1986

Denver Post: The *Denver Post*'s project stemmed from reporter Diana Griego's skepticism about government statistics on missing children—statistics that helped create the widespread belief that thousands of American children were kidnapped and murdered each year by strangers. With reporter Louis Kilzer, she worked under deputy Metro editor Charles R. Buxton Jr. to produce a series called "The Truth about Missing Kids." Later, Kilzer and reporter Norman Udevitz found a Denver fund-raising firm that solicited money on behalf of a missing children's organization, but turned over little of the proceeds to charity. Eventually, the agency was shut down by authorities. A polling firm hired by the *Post* suggested that public perceptions in Denver exaggerated the threat to children, which accompanying *Post* projects illustrated. "Our reporting exposed a myth and told the truth about one of America's most emotionally charged issues," *Post* editor David Hall said after the prize was announced.

Public Service: *Denver Post,* for its in-depth study of "missing children," which revealed that most are involved in custody disputes or are runaways, and which helped mitigate national fears stirred by exaggerated statistics.
General News Reporting: Edna Buchanan, *Miami Herald*

Investigative Reporting: Jeffrey A. Marx, Michael M. York, *Lexington* (Ky.) *Herald Leader*

Explanatory Journalism: Staff of *New York Times*

Specialized Reporting: Andrew Schneider, Mary Pat Flaherty, *Pittsburgh Press*

National Reporting: Craig Flournoy, George Rodrigue, *Dallas Morning News*

International Reporting: Lewis M. Simons, Pete Carey, Katherine Ellison, *San Jose Mercury News*

Feature Writing: John Camp, *St. Paul Pioneer Press and Dispatch*

Commentary: Jimmy Breslin, *New York Daily News*

Criticism: Donal Henahan, *New York Times*

Editorial Writing: Jack Fuller, *Chicago Tribune*

Editorial Cartooning: Jules Feiffer, *Village Voice*

Spot News Photography: Carol Guzy, Michel duCille, *Miami Herald*

Feature Photography: Tom Gralish, *Philadelphia Inquirer*

1987

Public Service: *Pittsburgh Press,* for reporting by Andrew Schneider and Matthew Brelis which revealed the inadequacy of the Federal Aviation Administration's medical screening of airline pilots and led to significant reforms.

General News Reporting: Staff of *Akron Beacon Journal*

Investigative Reporting: John Woestendiek, *Philadelphia Inquirer*

Investigative Reporting: Daniel R. Biddle, H. G. Bissinger, Fredric N. Tulsky, *Philadelphia Inquirer*

Explanatory Journalism: Jeff Lyon, Peter Gorner, *Chicago Tribune*

Specialized Reporting: Alex S. Jones, *New York Times*

National Reporting: Staff of *Miami Herald*

National Reporting: Staff of *New York Times*

International Reporting: Michael Parks, *Los Angeles Times*

Feature Writing: Steve Twomey, *Philadelphia Inquirer*

Commentary: Charles Krauthammer, Washington Post Writers Group

Criticism: Richard Eder, *Los Angeles Times*

Editorial Writing: Jonathan Freedman, *Tribune,* San Diego

Editorial Cartooning: Berke Breathed, Washington Post Writers Group

Spot News Photography: Kim Komenich, *San Francisco Examiner*

Feature Photography: David Peterson, *Des Moines Register*

1988

Public Service: *Charlotte Observer,* for revealing misuse of funds by the PTL television ministry through persistent coverage conducted in the face of a massive campaign by PTL to discredit the newspaper.

General News Reporting: Staff of *Lawrence* (Mass.) *Eagle-Tribune*

Local General News Reporting: Staff of *Alabama Journal of Montgomery*

Investigative Reporting: Dean Baquet, William Gaines, Ann Marie Lipinski, *Chicago Tribune*

Explanatory Journalism: Daniel Hertzberg, James B. Stewart, *Wall Street Journal*
Specialized Reporting: Walt Bogdanich, *Wall Street Journal*
International Reporting: Thomas L. Friedman, *New York Times*
Feature Writing: Jacqui Banaszynski, *St. Paul Pioneer Press Dispatch*
Commentary: Dave Barry, *Miami Herald*
Criticism: Tom Shales, *Washington Post*
Editorial Writing: Jane Healy, *Orlando Sentinel*
Editorial Cartooning: Doug Marlette, *Atlanta Constitution, Charlotte Observer*
Spot News Photography: Scott Shaw, *Odessa* (Texas) *American*
Feature Photography: Michel duCille, *Miami Herald*

1989

Public Service: *Anchorage Daily News,* for reporting about the high incidence of alco-
holism and suicide among native Alaskans in a series that focused attention on their
despair and resulted in various reforms.
General News Reporting: Staff of *Louisville Courier-Journal*
Specialized Reporting: Edward Humes, *Orange County Register*
Investigative Reporting: Bill Dedman, *Atlanta Journal and Constitution*
Explanatory Journalism: David Hanners; William Snyder, photographer; Karen Bles-
sen, artist, *Dallas Morning News*
National Reporting: Donald L. Barlett and James B. Steele, *Philadelphia Inquirer*
International Reporting: Bill Keller, *New York Times*
International Reporting: Glenn Frankel, *Washington Post*
Feature Writing: David Zucchino, *Philadelphia Inquirer*
Commentary: Clarence Page, *Chicago Tribune*
Criticism: Michael Skube, *News and Observer,* Raleigh, N.C.
Editorial Writing: Lois Wille, *Chicago Tribune*
Editorial Cartooning: Jack Higgins, *Chicago Sun-Times*
Spot News Photography: Ron Olshwanger, freelance
Feature Photography: Manny Crisostomo, *Detroit Free Press*

1990

Public Service: *Washington* (N.C.) *Daily News,* for revealing that the city's water supply
was contaminated with carcinogens, a problem that the local government had nei-
ther disclosed nor corrected over a period of eight years.
Public Service: *Philadelphia Inquirer,* for reporting by Gilbert M. Gaul that disclosed
how the American blood industry operates with little government regulation or su-
pervision.
General News Reporting: Staff of *San Jose Mercury News*
Investigative Reporting: Lou Kilzer, Chris Ison, *Star Tribune,* Minneapolis
Explanatory Journalism: David A. Vise, Steve Coll, *Washington Post*
Specialized Reporting: Tamar Stieber, *Albuquerque Journal*
National Reporting: Ross Anderson, Bill Dietrich, Mary Ann Gwinn, Eric Nalder,
Seattle Times

International Reporting: Nicholas D. Kristof, Sheryl Wu Dunn, *New York Times*
Feature Writing: Dave Curtin, *Colorado Springs Gazette Telegraph*
Commentary: Jim Murray, *Los Angeles Times*
Criticism: Allan Temko, *San Francisco Chronicle*
Editorial Writing: Thomas J. Hylton, *Pottstown* (Pa.) *Mercury*
Editorial Cartooning: Tom Toles, *Buffalo News*
Spot News Photography: Photo Staff of *Tribune,* Oakland, California
Feature Photography: David C. Turnley, *Detroit Free Press*

1991

Public Service: *Des Moines Register,* for reporting by Jane Schorer that, with the victim's consent, named a woman who had been raped—which prompted widespread reconsideration of the traditional media practice of concealing the identity of rape victims.
Spot News Reporting: Staff of *Miami Herald*
Investigative Reporting: Joseph T. Hallinan, Susan M. Headden, *Indianapolis Star*
Explanatory Journalism: Susan C. Faludi, *Wall Street Journal*
Beat Reporting: Natalie Angier, *New York Times*
National Reporting: Marjie Lundstrom, Rochelle Sharpe, *Gannett News Service*
International Reporting: Serge Schmemann, *New York Times*
Feature Writing: Sheryl James, *St. Petersburg Times*
Commentary: Jim Hoagland, *Washington Post*
Criticism: David Shaw, *Los Angeles Times*
Editorial Writing: Ron Casey, Harold Jackson, Joey Kennedy, *Birmingham News*
Editorial Cartooning: Jim Borgman, *Cincinnati Enquirer*
Spot News Photography: Greg Marinovich, Associated Press
Feature Photography: William Snyder, *Dallas Morning News*

1992

Public Service: *Sacramento Bee,* for "The Sierra in Peril," reporting by Tom Knudson that examined environmental threats and damage to the Sierra Nevada mountain range in California.
Spot News Reporting: Staff of *New York Newsday*
Investigative Reporting: Lorraine Adams, Dan Malone, *Dallas Morning News*
Explanatory Journalism: Robert S. Capers, Eric Lipton, *Hartford Courant*
Beat Reporting: Deborah Blum, *Sacramento Bee*
National Reporting: Jeff Taylor, Mike McGraw, *Kansas City Star*
International Reporting: Patrick J. Sloyan, *Newsday*
Feature Writing: Howell Raines, *New York Times*
Commentary: Anna Quindlen, *New York Times*
Criticism: No Award
Editorial Writing: Maria Henson, *Lexington* (Ky.) *Herald-Leader*
Editorial Cartooning: Signe Wilkinson, *Philadelphia Daily News*

Spot News Photography: Staff of Associated Press
Feature Photography: John Kaplan, Block Newspapers, Toledo

1993

Public Service: *Miami Herald,* for coverage that not only helped readers cope with Hurricane Andrew's devastation but also showed how lax zoning, inspection, and building codes had contributed to the destruction.
Spot News Reporting: Staff of *Los Angeles Times*
Investigative Reporting: Jeff Brazil, Steve Berry, *Orlando Sentinel*
Explanatory Journalism: Mike Toner, *Atlanta Journal-Constitution*
Beat Reporting: Paul Ingrassia, Joseph B. White, *Wall Street Journal*
National Reporting: David Maraniss, *Washington Post*
International Reporting: Roy Gutman, *Newsday*
International Reporting: John F. Burns, *New York Times*
Feature Writing: George Lardner Jr., *Washington Post*
Commentary: Liz Balmaseda, *Miami Herald*
Criticism: Michael Dirda, *Washington Post*
Editorial Writing: No Award
Editorial Cartooning: Stephen R. Benson, *Arizona Republic*
Spot News Photography: Ken Geiger, William Snyder, *Dallas Morning News*
Feature Photography: Staff of Associated Press

1994

Akron Beacon Journal: The *Akron Beacon Journal* launched a year-long study of racial attitudes under the heading "A Question of Color." Through it, the paper looked at how housing, education, economic opportunity, and crime were affected by race. Said managing editor Glenn Guzzo, "All these are intractable problems and what we found is that you can't talk about solving these problems unless you also address the issue of race." The paper produced twelve separate series, one a month for the entire year, examining different elements of race in the community. The 1992 Los Angeles riots prompted the series, Guzzo said, after "we recognized that the supposed progress in race relations we have made in the last decade maybe hadn't come as far as we'd believed." The *Beacon Journal* committed twenty-nine staffers to the project for the year. The community responded, with twenty-two thousand individuals and scores of organizations offering to help improve race relations.

Public Service: *Akron Beacon Journal,* for its broad examination of local racial attitudes and its subsequent effort to promote improved communication in the community.
Spot News Reporting: Staff of *New York Times*
Investigative Reporting: Staff of *Providence Journal-Bulletin*
Explanatory Journalism: Ronald Kotulak, *Chicago Tribune*
Beat Reporting: Eric Freedman, Jim Mitzelfeld, *Detroit News*
National Reporting: Eileen Welsome, *Albuquerque Tribune*

International Reporting: *Dallas Morning News*
Feature Writing: Isabel Wilkerson, *New York Times*
Commentary: William Raspberry, *Washington Post*
Criticism: Lloyd Schwartz, *Boston Phoenix*
Editorial Writing: R. Bruce Dold, *Chicago Tribune*
Editorial Cartooning: Michael P. Ramirez, *Commercial Appeal,* Memphis
Spot News Photography: Paul Watson, *Toronto Star*
Feature Photography: Kevin Carter, freelance

1995

Virgin Islands Daily News: Investigating widespread crime in the territory, *Virgin Islands
   Daily News* reporter Melvin Claxton identified numerous issues: the ease of criminals getting guns, law-enforcement corruption and incompetence, inept criminal
   prosecutions, light sentencing by judges, and a flawed probation system. A six-
   month investigation, timed so a series would run in December, drew on a statistical
   analysis showing that of twenty-five thousand violent crimes reported over four
   years ending in 1993, only fourteen hundred cases had gone to court. Fewer than
   10 percent of reported crimes were even investigated; mistakes by police or prosecutors were rife. The ten-day series exposed money misspent on the prison system,
   along with woeful crime prevention measures. "The territory spends more than
   any state—$55,000 a year—to house and feed a juvenile inmate. That is more than
   10 times the amount experts say it costs to run preventive programs that would
   keep them straight," wrote Claxton, an Antigua native. Executive editor Penny
   Feuerzeig wrote in her Pulitzer nomination letter that the paper dug beneath the
   "facile explanations" of high crime: poverty, education, and too few jobs. The extent of criminal infiltration in the territory's criminal justice system was revealed
   on the tenth day of Claxton's series when, as Feuerzeig put it, "the unthinkable
   happened." The paper "discovered that the outgoing governor had quietly par-
   doned seven convicts and commuted the sentences of five murderers"—including
   one who had been involved in multiple murders on a golf course. Before being par-
   doned, he had received a sentence of eight life terms without possibility of parole.
   Feuerzeig wrote:

> When we reported the pardons, the people of the territory literally revolt-
> ed. They marched and protested in the streets, wrote volumes of letters to
> the editor and demanded federal intervention.
>   They all said the same thing: If *The Daily News* had not done the series,
> they would not have understood that this was another case of how the Vir-
> gin Island authorities—even at the governor's level—treated crime lightly
> and allowed it to go unchecked.

Public Service: *Virgin Islands Daily News,* St. Thomas, for its disclosure of the links between the region's rampant crime rate and corruption in the local criminal justice system. The reporting, largely the work of Melvin Claxton, initiated political reforms.
Spot News Reporting: Staff of *Los Angeles Times*

Investigative Reporting: Brian Donovan, Stephanie Saul, *Newsday*
Explanatory Journalism: Leon Dash; Lucian Perkins, photographer, *Washington Post*
Beat Reporting: David Shribman, *Boston Globe*
National Reporting: Tony Horwitz, *Wall Street Journal*
International Reporting: Mark Fritz, Associated Press
Feature Writing: Ron Suskind, *Wall Street Journal*
Commentary: Jim Dwyer, *Newsday*
Criticism: Margo Jefferson, *New York Times*
Editorial Writing: Jeffrey Good, *St. Petersburg Times*
Editorial Cartooning: Mike Luckovich, *Atlanta Constitution*
Spot News Photography: Carol Guzy, *Washington Post*
Feature Photography: Staff of Associated Press

1996

Public Service: *News & Observer,* Raleigh, N.C., for the work of Melanie Sill, Pat Stith, and Joby Warrick on the environmental and health risks of waste disposal systems used in North Carolina's growing hog industry.
Spot News Reporting: Robert D. McFadden, *New York Times*
Investigative Reporting: Staff of *Orange County Register*
Explanatory Journalism: Laurie Garrett, *Newsday*
Beat Reporting: Bob Keeler, *Newsday*
National Reporting: Alix M. Freedman, *Wall Street Journal*
International Reporting: David Rohde, *Christian Science Monitor*
Feature Writing: Rick Bragg, *New York Times*
Commentary: E. R. Shipp, *New York Daily News*
Criticism: Robert Campbell, *Boston Globe*
Editorial Writing: Robert B. Semple Jr., *New York Times*
Editorial Cartooning: Jim Morin, *Miami Herald*
Spot News Photography: Charles Porter IV, freelance
Feature Photography: Stephanie Welsh, freelance

1997

Public Service: *Times-Picayune* of New Orleans, for its comprehensive series analyzing the conditions that threaten the world's supply of fish.
Spot News Reporting: Staff of *Newsday*
Investigative Reporting: Eric Nalder, Deborah Nelson, Alex Tizon, *Seattle Times*
Explanatory Journalism: Michael Vitez; April Saul, Ron Cortes, photographers, *Philadelphia Inquirer*
Beat Reporting: Byron Acohido, *Seattle Times*
National Reporting: Staff of *Wall Street Journal*
International Reporting: John F. Burns, *New York Times*
Feature Writing: Lisa Pollak, *Baltimore Sun*
Commentary: Eileen McNamara, *Boston Globe*
Criticism: Tim Page, *Washington Post*
Editorial Writing: Michael Gartner, *Daily Tribune,* Ames, Iowa

Editorial Cartooning: Walt Handelsman, *Times-Picayune,* New Orleans
Spot News Photography: Annie Wells, *Press Democrat,* Santa Rosa, Calif.
Feature Photography: Alexander Zemlianichenko, Associated Press

1998

Public Service: *Grand Forks* (N.D.) *Herald,* for its sustained and informative coverage,
vividly illustrated with photographs, that helped hold its community together in the
wake of flooding, a blizzard, and a fire that devastated much of the city, including
the newspaper plant itself.
Breaking News Reporting: Staff of *Los Angeles Times*
Investigative Reporting: Gary Cohn, Will Englund, *Baltimore Sun*
Explanatory Journalism: Paul Salopek, *Chicago Tribune*
Beat Reporting: Linda Greenhouse, *New York Times*
National Reporting: Russell Carollo, Jeff Nesmith, *Dayton Daily News*
International Reporting: Staff of *New York Times*
Feature Writing: Thomas French, *St. Petersburg Times*
Commentary: Mike McAlary, *New York Daily News*
Criticism: Michiko Kakutani, *New York Times*
Editorial Writing: Bernard L. Stein, *Riverdale* (N.Y.) *Press*
Editorial Cartooning: Stephen P. Breen, *Asbury Park* (N.J.) *Press*
Spot News Photography: Martha Rial, *Pittsburgh Post-Gazette*
Feature Photography: Clarence Williams, *Los Angeles Times*

1999

Public Service: *Washington Post,* for its series that identified and analyzed patterns of
reckless gunplay by city police officers who had little training or supervision.
Breaking News Reporting: Staff of *Hartford Courant*
Investigative Reporting: Staff of *Miami Herald*
Explanatory Journalism: Richard Read, *Oregonian*
Beat Reporting: Chuck Phillips, Michael A. Hiltzik, *Los Angeles Times*
National Reporting: Staff of *New York Times,* and notably Jeff Gerth
International Reporting: Staff of *Wall Street Journal*
Feature Writing: Angelo B. Henderson, *Wall Street Journal*
Commentary: Maureen Dowd, *New York Times*
Criticism: Blair Kamin, *Chicago Tribune*
Editorial Writing: Editorial board of *New York Daily News*
Editorial Cartooning: David Horsey, *Seattle Post-Intelligencer*
Spot News Photography: Staff of Associated Press
Feature Photography: Staff of Associated Press

2000

Public Service: *Washington Post,* notably for the work of Katherine Boo that disclosed
wretched neglect and abuse in the city's group homes for the mentally retarded,
which forced officials to acknowledge the conditions and begin reforms.

Breaking News Reporting: Staff of *Denver Post*

Investigative Reporting: Sang-Hun Choe, Charles J. Hanley, Martha Mendoza, Associated Press

Explanatory Journalism: Eric Newhouse, *Great Falls* (Mont.) *Tribune*

Beat Reporting: George Dohrmann, *St. Paul Pioneer Press*

National Reporting: Staff of *Wall Street Journal*

International Reporting: Mark Schoofs, *Village Voice*

Feature Writing: J. R. Moehringer, *Los Angeles Times*

Commentary: Paul A. Gigot, *Wall Street Journal*

Criticism: Henry Allen, *Washington Post*

Editorial Writing: John C. Bersia, *Orlando Sentinel*

Editorial Cartooning: Joel Pett, *Lexington* (Ky.) *Herald-Leader*

Breaking News Photography: Photo staff of *Rocky Mountain News,* Denver

Feature Photography: Carol Guzy, Michael Williamson, Lucian Perkins, *Washington Post*

2001

Public Service: *Oregonian,* Portland, for its detailed and unflinching examination of systematic problems within the U.S. Immigration and Naturalization Service, including harsh treatment of foreign nationals and other widespread abuses, which prompted various reforms.

Breaking News: Staff of *Miami Herald*

Investigative: David Willman, *Los Angeles Times*

Explanatory: Staff of *Chicago Tribune*

Beat: David Cay Johnson, *New York Times*

National: Staff of *New York Times*

International: Ian Johnson, *Wall Street Journal*

International: Paul Salopek, *Chicago Tribune*

Feature Writing: Tom Hallman Jr., *Oregonian*

Commentary: Dorothy Rabinowitz, *Wall Street Journal*

Criticism: Gail Caldwell, *Boston Globe*

Editorial Writing: David Moats, *Rutland* (Vt.) *Herald*

Breaking News Photography: Alan Diaz, Associated Press

Feature Photography: Matt Rainey, *Star-Ledger,* Newark

2002

Public Service: *New York Times,* for "A Nation Challenged," a special section published regularly after the September 11 terrorist attacks on America, which coherently and comprehensively covered the tragic events, profiled the victims, and tracked the developing story, locally and globally.

Breaking News: Staff of *Wall Street Journal*

Investigative: Sari Horwitz, Scott Higham and Sarah Cohen, *Washington Post*

Explanatory: Staff of *New York Times*

Beat: Gretchen Morgenson, *New York Times*

National: Staff of *Washington Post*
International: Barry Bearak, *New York Times*
Feature Writing: Barry Siegel, *Los Angeles Times*
Commentary: Thomas Friedman, *New York Times*
Criticism: Justin Davidson, *Newsday*
Editorial Writing: Alex Raksin and Bob Sipchen, *Los Angeles Times*
Editorial Cartooning: Clay Bennett, *Christian Science Monitor*
Breaking News Photography: Staff of *New York Times*
Feature Photography: Staff of *New York Times*

2003

Public Service: *Boston Globe,* for its courageous, comprehensive coverage of sexual abuse
by priests, an effort that pierced secrecy, stirred local, national, and international re-
action, and produced changes in the Roman Catholic Church.
Breaking News: Staff of *Eagle-Tribune,* Lawrence, Mass.
Investigative: Clifford J. Levy, *New York Times*
Explanatory: Staff of *Wall Street Journal*
Beat: Diana K. Sugg, *Baltimore Sun*
National: Alan Miller and Kevin Sachs, *Los Angeles Times*
International: Kevin Sullivan and Mary Jordan, *Washington Post*
Feature Writing: Sonia Nazario, *Los Angeles Times*
Commentary: Colbert I. King, *Washington Post*
Criticism: Stephen Hunter, *Washington Post*
Editorial Writing: Cornelia Grumman, *Chicago Tribune*
Editorial Cartooning: David Horsey, *Seattle Post-Intelligencer*
Breaking News Photography: Staff of *Rocky Mountain News*
Feature Photography: Don Barletti, *Los Angeles Times*

2004

Public Service: *New York Times,* for the work of David Barstow and Lowell Bergman
that relentlessly examined death and injury among American workers and exposed
employers who break basic safety rules.
Breaking News: Staff of *Los Angeles Times*
Investigative: Michael D. Sallah, Mitch Weiss and Joe Mahr, *The Blade,* Toledo
Explanatory: Kevin Helliker and Thomas M. Burton, *Wall Street Journal*
Beat: Daniel Golden, *Wall Street Journal*
National: Staff of *Los Angeles Times*
International: Anthony Shadid, *Washington Post*
Feature Writing: No Award
Commentary: Leonard Pitts Jr., *Miami Herald*
Criticism: Dan Neil, *Los Angeles Times*
Editorial Writing: William R. Stall, *Los Angeles Times*
Editorial Cartooning: Matt Davies, *Seattle Post-Intelligencer*

Breaking News Photography: David Leeson, Cheryl Diaz Meyer, *Dallas Morning News*
Feature Photography: Carolyn Cole, *Los Angeles Times*

2005

Public Service: *Los Angeles Times,* for its courageous, exhaustively researched series exposing deadly medical problems and racial injustice at a major public hospital.
Breaking News: Staff of *Star-Ledger,* Newark, N.J.
Investigative: Nigel Jaquiss, *Willamette Week,* Portland, Ore.
Explanatory: Gareth Cook, *Boston Globe*
Beat: Amy Dockser Marcus, *Wall Street Journal*
National: Walt Bogdanich, *New York Times*
International: Kim Murphy, *Los Angeles Times;* Dele Olojede, *Newsday*
Feature Writing: Julia Keller, *Chicago Tribune*
Commentary: Connie Schultz, *Plain Dealer,* Cleveland
Criticism: Joe Morgenstern, *Wall Street Journal*
Editorial Writing: Tom Philp, *Sacramento Bee*
Editorial Cartooning: Nick Anderson, *Louisville Courier-Journal*
Breaking News Photography: Associated Press staff
Feature Photography: Deanne Fitzmaurice, *San Francisco Chronicle*

2006

Public Service: *Sun Herald,* Biloxi-Gulfport, Miss., for its valorous and comprehensive coverage of Hurricane Katrina, providing a lifeline for devastated readers, in print and online, during their time of greatest need.
Public Service: *Times-Picayune,* New Orleans, for its heroic, multifaceted coverage of Hurricane Katrina and its aftermath, making exceptional use of the newspaper's resources to serve an inundated city even after evacuation of the newspaper plant.
Breaking News: Staff of *Times-Picayune*
Investigative: Susan Schmidt, James V. Grimaldi, R. Jeffrey Smith, *Washington Post*
Explanatory: David Finkel, *Washington Post*
Beat: Dana Priest, *Washington Post*
National: James Risen and Eric Lichtblau, *New York Times*
National: Staffs of *San Diego Union-Tribune, Copley News Service*
International: Joseph Kahn, Jim Yardley, *New York Times*
Feature Writing: Jim Sheeler, *Rocky Mountain News,* Denver
Commentary: Nicholas D. Kristof, *New York Times*
Criticism: Robin Givhan, *Washington Post*
Editorial Writing: Rick Attig and Doug Bates, *Oregonian*
Editorial Cartooning: Mike Luckovich, *Atlanta Journal-Constitution*
Breaking News Photography: Staff of *Dallas Morning News*
Feature Photography: Todd Heisler, *Rocky Mountain News*

2007

Public Service: *Wall Street Journal,* for its creative and comprehensive probe into back-dated stock options for business executives that triggered investigations, the ouster of top officials, and widespread change in corporate America.

Breaking News: Staff of *Oregonian,* Portland

Investigative Reporting: Brett Blackledge, *Birmingham* (Ala.) *News*

Explanatory: Kenneth R. Weiss, Usha Lee McFarling, Rick Loomis, *Los Angeles Times*

Local Reporting: Debbie Cenziper, *Miami Herald*

National: Charlie Savage, *Boston Globe*

International: Staff of *Wall Street Journal*

Feature Writing: Andrea Elliott, *New York Times*

Commentary: Cynthia Tucker, *Atlanta Journal-Constitution*

Criticism: Jonathan Gold, *LA Weekly*

Editorial Writing: Arthur Browne, Beverly Weintraub, Heidi Evans, *New York Daily News*

Editorial Cartooning: Walt Handelsman, *Newsday*

Breaking News Photography: Oded Balilty, Associated Press

Feature Photography: Renee C. Byer, *Sacramento Bee*

NOTES ON SOURCES

*I*n building cases from a sampling of Pulitzer Prize winners over ninety years, *Pulitzer's Gold* attempts to trace the development of one important facet of American journalism in a new way. I also wanted to acknowledge reporters, editors, and others who may have gotten little personal attention at the time because the Gold Medal is a newspaper honor, not an award for individuals.

As the research evolved, I became fascinated as well with the Pulitzer Prize selection process, long steeped in secrecy. The Pulitzer organization graciously made jury reports and other documents available for this research. Further, current and former board members were willing to be interviewed about the inner workings of the Pulitzers. And for earlier periods, the private papers of Joseph Pulitzer II opened an intriguing window into the operation. J.P. II, a board member from 1920 until his death in 1955 and chairman starting in 1940, loved to write notes to fellow board members about the decision-making. Likewise, he often communicated with his editors at the *St. Louis Post-Dispatch* as they prepared to compete for Pulitzer Prizes.

Because this book covers some newspaper work that is very fresh, and some that has been all but lost in dusty newspaper morgues and library archives, my research took a variety of forms. Reviewing the winning entries and supporting material kept in the Pulitzer archives at Columbia University was a starting point. But for most cases— including all ten winners from 1999 to 2007—I conducted in-person interviews in their newsrooms. Other interviews were by telephone, with follow-up e-mails.

Published information about the journalism that won Gold Medals over the years is surprisingly thin. Fortunately, journalists who were involved in a number of the prizes, dating back to the 1960s and earlier, were willing to share their own experiences to help expand the record. (My first in-person interviews were with people involved in the work that won the 1937 Public Service Prize for the *Post-Dispatch*.)

The most valuable library resource for research on the Pulitzer Prizes is the Columbia archive. Columbia has administered the prizes since they began, and keeps original entries and other material in the Rare Manuscripts area of Butler Library, just across the quadrangle from the Journalism Building. The Pulitzer Prize microfilm file is at Columbia's Lehman Library. The www.pulitzer.org Web site is a convenient resource for checking prize-winners going back to 1917. For work from 1995 to the present, the site offers links to digitized versions of the articles that prize-winning newspapers submitted with their entries. A list of each year's winners and finalists is easily retrieved by clicking on the Pulitzer timeline across the top of the Web page. As of 2007, however, the organization had not created links to winners for years prior to 1995.

In the fall of 2005, I became a denizen of Butler's Rare Manuscripts section, some days from the time it opened until it closed. For those interested in American journalism history, leafing through entries there is an epic adventure. As a newspaper junky, I found holding the actual submissions, just as the editors had prepared them for the Pulitzer judging, to be a true contact high. It is hard not to feel a sense of history in examining the blue-bound 1973 *Washington Post* entry with its Watergate clippings from June 18 through the end of 1972, and introduced by managing editor Howard Simons's impassioned attempt to persuade Pulitzer jurors of the importance of the coverage.

Among the volumes written about the Pulitzer Prizes, John Hohenberg's are the most authoritative. The late administrator of the Pulitzers shared his considerable knowledge of how the board worked, and told wonderful stories about the process. However, only a relative handful of Public Service story descriptions appear in his books.

One other record that is helpful, as much for its continuity as for the brief descriptions, is the archive of stories about the Pulitzer awards in *Editor & Publisher*, a newspaper trade publication that was already going strong when the Pulitzers began.

At individual newspapers, articles about a Pulitzer project may appear in the reference library, sometimes in the form of an anniversary-year review of the prize. Many newspapers have commissioned corporate histories that devote special sections to any Pulitzer-winning. Academics or journalism students—at schools in the newspaper's locale, especially—on occasion have written papers on award-winning work. Rarely, however, do these analyses describe in much detail the work that went into the coverage.

Jury reports provided by the Pulitzer organization are uneven, but often give insights about why certain recommendations were made to the board. And, of course, they identify the contenders each year. Officially, finalists for the Public Service award and other Pulitzer Prizes were not disclosed until 1980, so it will come as news to some journalists from the 1970s and earlier that their work even made the finals.

Chapter Notes

INTRODUCTION: FILLING A BLACK HOLE

2. Bill Blundell, who travels from paper to paper . . . "a black hole that exists": William E. Blundell, letter to the Alicia Patterson Foundation, September 25, 2003.

4. In April 2006, from his post at Harvard's Jane Shorenstein Center: John Carroll delivered "Last Call at the ASNE Saloon," at the convention in Seattle on April 26, 2006.

Part One. Gold for a New Century

CHAPTER 1. THE STORM BEFORE THE CALM

7. "a real part": Michael Gartner, telephone interview by author, April 3, 2006.

7–8. Building on the prize-winning work: "Washing Away" appeared in the *Times-Picayune* June 23 to 27.

8. The newspaper had designed its building . . . "Standing in our building's lobby": Jim Amoss, "The Story of Our Lives," *Quill*, April 2006, 27.

8. "On Monday morning": Butch Ward, "From Biloxi and New Orleans: The Stories behind the Pulitzers," Poynter.org, April 17, 2006, http://www.Poynter.org.

8. From what Amoss could see and hear: "I thought this is great . . . ." Mark Fitzgerald, "Jim Amoss, *E&P*'s 2006 Editor of the Year," *Editor & Publisher,* February 1, 2006, http://editorandpublisher.com.

9. At 9:30 on Monday night . . . "When we started the meeting": Ward, "From Biloxi and New Orleans."

9. "Don't worry about spinning it": Fitzgerald, "Jim Amoss, *E&P*'s 2006 Editor."

9–10. For five years, executive editor Stan Tiner: See CJR Daily, Liz Cox Barrett, interview with Stan Tiner, December 2, 2005.

10. "Stan rallied the troops": Stan Hawkins, telephone interview by author, July 7, 2006.

10. On Saturday, Tiner's theme: Stan Tiner, interview by author, *Sun Herald* offices, March 30, 2006.

11. As detailed in the will: John Hohenberg, *The Pulitzer Prizes,* 18–20.

11. Today there are fourteen journalism categories: Basic information on the Pulitzer Prizes, current and past, is found at http://www.Pulitzer.org.

12. Over the years there has been considerable friction: One good account is in David Shaw, *Press Watch,* 178–214.

12. While much has changed: One discussion of French's medals is in Michael Richman's monograph, "The Medals of Daniel Chester French," in *The Medal in America,* edited by Alan M. Stahl, September 1987.

12. "That's Big Casino": Ben Bradlee Sr., interview by author, *Post* offices, October 13, 2005.

12. For any paper, winning a Gold Medal . . . "the strongest reverberating recognition": Jim Amoss, interview by author, *Times-Picayune* offices, May 30, 2006.

13. Many other Gold Medals . . . "boring": Bob Woodward, interview by author, Washington, D.C., October 12, 2005.

14. In terms of subject matter: The breakdown is somewhat subjective, depending on how one defines "government wrongdoing" or the other categories. But my count shows thirty-six falling under that heading, with twenty-three registering as dealing with human rights or social ills, and eleven dealing with environmental issues.

14. The Pulitzer bar is high . . . "You shouldn't automatically win": Gartner, interview.

14. The sky was cloudless . . . rising one inch every seven minutes: Amoss, "The Story of Our Lives," 28.

15. It was time to evacuate . . . "We had planned for the wind": Ibid.

15. Loaded in the back of a flotilla: Ibid.

15–16. Veteran reporter Mark Schleifstein: Mark Schleifstein, interview by author, May 29, 2006.

17. *As the fog of warlike conditions:* The story—and all stories in winning entries since 1995—can be accessed year by year at http://www.Pulitzer.org.

17. Michael Perlstein, a criminal justice reporter: Michael Perlstein, interview by author, May 30, 2006.

17. Amoss now writes off the worst . . . "You see it again": Amoss, interview.

17. Managing editor Peter Kovacs quickly: Peter Kovacs, interview by author, May 30, 2006.

18. In addition to the storm's human toll . . . killed more than 1,800 people: "Tropical Cyclone Report," National Hurricane Center, December 20, 2005, updated August 10, 2006.

18–19. Amoss himself is a low-key . . . "Any good newspaper": Amoss, interview.

19. It was Weaver's third time as a juror: Janet Weaver, telephone interview by author, April 21, 2006.

20. At that point, the job got much tougher: Eugene Roberts, telephone interview by author, August 2, 2006.

21. Columbia's Pulitzer organization: For a fuller discussion of the Pulitzer rumor mill, see Harris, "Prizes and Rumors of Prizes," Poynter.org, April 1, 2005, http://Poynter .org. . . . "The Sun Herald likes to emphasize . . . .," Katharine Q. Seelye, "As Katrina Recedes, Newspapers Still Float," *New York Times,* April 10, 2006, C1.

22. And then there was the underdog factor: Copy of the letter provided by Tiner.

23. "Bryan's a large guy": Tiner, interview.

24. But in yet another surprise: See Harris, "Shared Glory for Pulitzer's Top Prize," Poynter.org, April 17, 2006.

CHAPTER 2. THE MOST PRIZED PULITZER

30. *I think I am safe in saying:* Letter from Joseph Pulitzer II to Stanley Frank of the *Saturday Evening Post,* February 10, 1947. Joseph Pulitzer II papers, Library of Congress.

30. Taken together though . . . "first rough draft": This longer description of the quote, cited by editors and correspondents at the time of Philip Graham's death, August 3, 1963, is at http://Bartleby.com. However, according to *Morrow's International Dictionary of Quotations* (1982), Graham apparently used the "first rough draft of history" line also to describe his hopes for *Newsweek* when the Washington Post Company purchased that magazine. The connection of news and history has been made by others, including Mark Twain, in volume one of the autobiography published years after his death in 1910. Wrote Twain: "News is history in its first and best form . . . history is the pale and tranquil reflection of it."

31–32. The cult of self-congratulation . . . "as a standard of excellence": Ben Bradlee, *A Good Life: Newspapering and Other Adventures,* 365–66.

32. Ask winners about the value . . . "We don't write": Quoted in e-mail from Catherine J. Mathis, *New York Times,* January 30, 2006.

32. More recently, however . . . "The Pulitzer Prize is": Ben Bradlee Sr., interview by author, October 13, 2005.

32. The McClatchy Company prides itself . . . "the Pulitzer Prize, particularly": Gary Pruitt, interview by author, McClatchy office, November 15, 2005.

32. The wide acceptance of this standard: Original in the Joseph Pulitzer papers, August 1902, Columbia University Rare Manuscripts area, Butler Library. Also cited in Hohenberg, *The Pulitzer Prizes,* 10.

33. Joseph Pulitzer's career had started brilliantly: W. A. Swanberg, *Pulitzer: The Life of the Greatest Figure in American Journalism and One of the Most Extraordinary Men in Our History,* 44.

33. One such Pulitzer promotion made the *World* the leader: Ibid., 104–5.

33–34. Then came a darker period . . . It was a nasty, no-holds-barred conflict: Ibid., 136.

34. *Our Republic and its press:* Quoted in Seymour Topping, "Joseph Pulitzer and the Pulitzer Prizes," http://www.Pulitzer.org.

35. *[I]f this is to be a government of the people:* Swanberg, *Pulitzer,* 374.

35. A near recluse: Hohenberg, *The Pulitzer Prizes,* 9–11.

35. Some historians have suggested that Pulitzer and Nobel indeed shared: The Alfred

Nobel story is often told. One reference is http://www.Britannica.com, which calls this explanation for Nobel's action the "most plausible assumption" that may be made about the reason for Nobel's creation of the Nobel Prizes.

35–36. Columbia had been Pulitzer's first choice: A full account of Pulitzer's establishment of the prizes is in Hohenberg, *The Pulitzer Prizes*, 9–27.

38. In 1985, *Los Angeles Times* media critic: David Shaw, *Press Watch*, 191. David Shaw, who died in 2005, was an early supporter of *Pulitzer's Gold*. He covered the Pulitzer Prizes for the *Times* more closely than any other journalist. His stories on the Pulitzers are summarized in chapter 7 of *Press Watch*.

38. Jurors today infuse: Columbia purchased the Liberty Window—installed in the old World Building to memorialize Joseph Pulitzer's campaign to build the Statue of Liberty's platform—from New York City for one dollar. It is dedicated to Herbert Bayard Swope, who helped arrange the deal. The city had condemned the World Building to improve access to the Brooklyn Bridge. See the footnote in Hohenberg, *The Pulitzer Diaries*, 313.

38. Although Howard Weaver first served: Howard Weaver, interview by author, McClatchy office, November 15, 2005.

38–39. The journalist-jurors often are moved: Gilbert Gaul, interview by author, *Philadelphia Inquirer* office, November 2, 2005, and Walter Robinson, *Boston Globe* office, January 12, 2006.

39. These days, team-based journalism projects: *Washington Post* team members, interview by author, *Post* office, October 12, 2005.

39. The lack of a formal fact-checking: One very personal discussion of the Janet Cooke case is in chapter 17 of Bradlee, *A Good Life*.

39. But former board member Geneva Overholser: Pulitzer Prize board members say . . . . Geneva Overholser, interview by author, Washington, D.C., December 1, 2005.

39–40. In 2007, the nineteen-member board: Board member biographies are on http://www.Pulitzer.org.

40. When the winners are announced: For a fuller description of Pulitzer Prize day, see Harris, "The Eye of the Pulitzer Storm," April 6, 2005, http://www.Poynter.org. For a description of Pulitzer Day for the losers, see Harris, "The Pulitzers That Got Away," April 6, 2004.

CHAPTER 3. SPOTLIGHT ON THE CHURCH

43. *Newspapers exist so that investigative journalism can take place:* Michael Rezendes, interview by author, *Globe* office, November 3, 2005.

43. The Florida-born Baron . . . "balanced and gripping on-the-scene coverage": Quotes from the citations that accompany Pulitzer Prizes, like this one from the 2001 Breaking News Reporting award to the *Miami Herald*, are accessible at http://www.Pulitzer.org.

44. The *Globe* had been flown down: The first series of interviews with Martin Baron and his *Boston Globe* staff members began at its offices on Monday, April 7, 2003, the day its Pulitzer Prize was announced.

44. While the Geoghan stories were not particularly prominent: The McNamara stories appeared in the *Globe* on July 22 and July 29, 2002, B-1.

45. That day, a call went out: E-mail exchange between Jonathan Albano and author, January 17, 2006.

46. It also crossed Robinson's mind . . . "the assignment from hell": Walter V. Robinson, "Shining the Globe's Spotlight on the Catholic Church," *Nieman Reports,* Spring 2003, 56.

46. Spotlight itself was one of the oldest: A three-page history of the Spotlight Team was prepared for Robinson and the author by Timothy Leland, the team's founder, on March 5, 2006. A discussion of *Newsday's* influence is also in Robert F. Keeler, *Newsday: A Candid History of the Respectable Tabloid,* 431–32.

47. Looking for complementary skills: Robinson, interview.

47. Rezendes remembers that on the afternoon: Rezendes, interview.

50. Carroll had trained in CAR: Matt Carroll, interview by author, Hanover, Massachusetts, November 2, 2005.

51. The team did not publish any stories based on its database: Sacha Pfeiffer, interview by author, *Globe* office, October 11, 2005.

53. The image of what constituted a Spotlight story . . . "the lure of never having to write a lead": Robinson, "Shining the Globe's Spotlight," 56.

53. As the team labored on, religion writer Paulson: Michael Paulson, interview by author, *Globe* office, November 7, 2005.

54. Was there any danger that the existence: Martin Baron, e-mail exchange with author, January 22, 2006.

56. "The whole paper was mobilized": Baron, interview.

CHAPTER 4. A NEWSROOM CHALLENGED

57. *I have seen reporters crying:* New York Times, *Portraits 9/11/01,* Foreword, vii.

57. The barber was Haitian: Gerald Boyd, telephone interview by author, February 2, 2006.

59–60. With staffers the caliber of the *Times's*: David Barstow, interview by author, New York, September 9, 2005.

60. Christine Kay, too, would never forget: Christine Kay, interview by author, *Times* office, November 29, 2005.

63. Who had come up with the "Portraits" name?: Jonathan Landman, e-mail exchange with author, March 27, 2006.

64. On the first Monday after 9/11: Allan M. Siegal, e-mail exchange with author, March 14, 2006.

65. Subscribers from around the country: New York Times, *Portraits 9/11/01,* Janny Scott, Introduction, ix.

66. Most were moved: "These lives . . . ." Ibid., Howell Raines, Foreword, vii.

67. David Barstow was on the team: The lengthy report on Jayson Blair's record at the *Times* ran on May 11, 2003, headlined "Reporter Who Left the Times Left Long Trail of Deception." The Times archive on the case is found at http://www.nytimes.com/ref/business/media/blair-archive.html.

67. "Blair gamed that situation": Boyd, interview.

67. While the Gold Medal was among the record seven: An account of the occasions is in "Newsroom Celebrates 'Days of Legend,'" from the Times Company newsletter "Ahead of the Times," vol. 10, no. 2, April 2002.

CHAPTER 5. EPIPHANY IN BOSTON

72. *In fact, the investigative staff of the Boston Globe:* From 2003 nomination letter for Pulitzer Prize submitted by *Globe* editor Martin Baron, quoting from an Andrew Greeley review of the 2002 *Globe* book *Betrayal.*

73. Bradlee was encouraged about the interviews: Ben Bradlee Jr., interview by author, Boston, September 19, 2005.

79. As the new editor who was ultimately responsible: Baron, interview.

79. Robinson later hinted: For more on the *Globe's* newsroom Pulitzer announcement, see Harris, "A Prized Moment for the Globe, and the Pulitzers," http://www.Poynter.org, April 7, 2003.

79–80. *Globe* investigative specialist Steven Kurkjian: Steve Kurkjian, interview by author, *Globe* office, November 3, 2005.

82. Pfeiffer and other Spotlight reporters . . . And Patrick McSorley: McSorley died in February 2004.

83. As personal as the issue of priest abuse was: Thomas Farragher, interview by author, Hingham, Mass., November 2, 2005.

85. But much was known: Cover letter from Martin Baron to judges of the Pulitzer Prize, undated, 2003.

85. When Public Service jury chair Bill Ketter met: Ketter, interview.

85. For the Pulitzer board members who convened: Sandra Mims Rowe, interview by author, *Oregonian* office, Portland, November 16, 2005.

85–86. That opinion extended far beyond the board: "In some ways . . ." Elizabeth Mehren, Nieman Reports, Spring 2003, 55.

86. Baron had also learned: Howell Raines "was annoyed . . ." Baron, e-mail.

87. From Bob Woodward: Woodward, interview.

CHAPTER 6. FROM *TIMES* TO *TIMES*

90. *It's not enough to be good at what you do:* John Carroll, telephone interview by author, April 16, 2006. Quoted in "For the Post, Four's a Crowd—But Not a Record," http://www.Poynter.org, April 17, 2006.

90. *Journal* executive editor Joel Rawson: Joel Rawson, interview by author, *Providence Journal* offices, April 5, 2004. For a fuller description, see Harris, "The Pulitzers That Got Away," http://www.Poynter.org, April 6, 2004.

90–91. In March, the Pulitzer Public Service jury . . . "their time in the sunlight": Deborah Howell, telephone interview by author, March 29, 2005.

91. David Barstow of the *New York Times:* Barstow, interview.

91. What happened was this: Robinson, interview. He served on the Investigative Reporting jury. *San Francisco Chronicle* Robert J. Rosenthal, a Public Service juror, was interviewed by author for "The Pulitzers That Got Away."

91–92. Most board members had already read . . . "Thanks to the indefatigable": Pulitzer Prize Investigative jury report, 2004, from the Pulitzer Prize files, Columbia University.

97. Even as editor John Carroll: The section describing the *Los Angeles Times* King/Drew project reflects interviews conducted by the author primarily on May 25, 2005. Interviews were at *Times* offices with John Carroll, Julie Marquis, Mitchell Landsberg, Tracy Weber, Charles Ornstein, and Steve Hymon.

104. A year later, though, John Carroll was gone: John Carroll, telephone interview.

Part Two: Coming of Age

CHAPTER 7. FIRST GOLD

109. *The medal is most artistic . . . : New York Times* files, copy provided to author.

109. With the Pulitzer Prizes today . . . And even the Pulitzer Advisory Board members: Hohenberg, *The Pulitzer Prizes,* 28.

109. Not that the jurors had given: Ibid., 31.

111. Joseph Pulitzer himself had been sharply at odds: Meyer Berger, *The Story of the New York Times,* 153. Also cited in Swanberg, *Pulitzer,* 300.

111. Ochs had worked wonders . . . "You may not know": Ibid.

111. With good reason . . . "There may have been somewhere": Ibid., 160.

111–12. Those readers had plenty . . . "The years were to prove": Ibid., 161.

112. There were lapses: Ibid., 202–5.

112. AUSTRIA BREAKS WITH SERVIA: The *Times* used that spelling of what it now calls Serbia.

113. *The editors of the* Times *believed:* Elmer Davis, *History of the New York Times, 1851–1921,* 365.

114. It was also Van Anda who "went feverish": Berger, 253–54.

114. Columbia president Butler commissioned sculptor Daniel Chester French: Michael Richman, *The Medal in America,* 150–53.

116. The jurors, again Columbia professors: Pulitzer Prize jury reports, 1919.

116. According to a 1982 history: Robert W. Wells, *The Milwaukee Journal: An Informal Chronicle of Its First 100 Years,* 116.

CHAPTER 8. REPORTING ON THE ROARING

121. *The Jazz Age had a wild youth:* "Echoes of the Jazz Age, 1931," from *The Crack-Up,* edited by Edmund Wilson. New York: New Directions, 1945, 21.

121. Together, Ralph Pulitzer and his idealistic younger brother: This emerges from the collected letters of Joseph Pulitzer II, featuring regular communications with other board members before their meetings.

122. The board started to take its job seriously: Hohenberg, *The Pulitzer Prizes,* 33.

122–23. For once, the board had a real choice: Ibid, 41–42; jury report, 1921.

123. The remark was something of a slight to Boston: selling more copies even than the *New York World.* Mitchell Zuckoff, *Ponzi's Scheme,* 43.

124. Edwin Grozier, after working for a time: Ibid., 36–37.

125. In 1919, Ponzi examined . . . "in a flash of insight": Ibid., 95.

125. It was a moment reminiscent . . . "But those critical details would wait": Ibid., 96.

125–126. For fifty cents he registered: Ibid., 107.

126. Just for fun, he put out feelers: Ibid., 120.

126. He also was digging himself deeper: Ibid., 134.

126–27. Enter the newspapers . . . "We haven't figure out": Ibid., 138–9. Also, "pounding home runs for the New York Yankees": Ibid., 128–29.

127. It was July 4 before the *Boston Post:* From *Post* 1921 Pulitzer entry. Also, Zuckoff, *Ponzi's Scheme,* 160.

127. Richard Grozier was incredulous: Zuckoff, *Ponzi's Scheme,* 183.

128. QUESTIONS THE MOTIVE: From Pulitzer 1921 entry; Barron material from Zuckoff, *Ponzi's Scheme,* 184.

128. The public reaction . . . "Pigs being led": Zuckoff, *Ponzi's Scheme,* 187.

129. But the charming Ponzi: Ibid., 209–10. Finally, to shouts of "Ponzi for mayor!": 221. Example of a *Traveler* sports story comparing Ponzi to Ruth, 219.

129. *The first steps taken against Ponzi:* "Bursting Golden Bubble Wins Gold Medal," *Editor & Publisher,* June 4, 1921, 5.

130. Why had McMasters: Zuckoff, *Ponzi's Scheme,* 229.

130. On August 8, Ponzi was comfortable: Ibid., 255–56.

130–31. Being Ponzi, the trader still made efforts: "Then you are going to get the presses ripped out of your building." Ibid., 272.

131. Ever chatty . . . "You did a fine job on me": Ibid., 299. "My business was simple": 313.

131. In *Editor & Publisher's* June 4 recap: "Bursting Golden Bubble," 5.

131–32. The winner of the very first . . . he was best known: Hohenberg, *The Pulitzer Prizes,* 39–40.

132. "What I try to do in my paper": Ibid., 91.

132. Even finding a job title: Alfred Allan Lewis, *Man of the World,* 80.

132. One Joseph Pulitzer aphorism: E. J. Kahn, Jr., *The World of Swope,* 233.

133. Swope himself tracked down: Ibid., 240–42; Lewis, *Man of the World,* 92–94.

133. The sources tapped . . . had "blabbed": Kahn, *The World of Swope,* 241.

133. SECRETS OF THE KU KLUX KLAN: From 1922 Pulitzer entry. Some of the series is reprinted in Snyder and Morris, eds., *A Treasury of Great Reporting.*

134. For the *World,* it was a phenomenal circulation booster: Lewis, *Man of the World,* 94.

134–35. The Klan series was also the unanimous choice: Pulitzer jury report, April 18, 1922.

135. One of Swope's many credos: Kahn, *The World of Swope,* 243; also, 1924 Pulitzer entry.

136. *"Now, then, where shall we begin:* Lewis, *Man of the World,* 152.

136–37. Mellett, one of seven sons: Helen Bloom, New York University, *News Workshop,* January 1965. . . . promotional stunts, like hiring the "Marvel Man" . . . John Bartlow Martin, "Murder of a Journalist," *Harper's,* September 1946, 274.

137. *It is the opinion:* From 1927 Pulitzer entry.

137–38. *Canton's clean-up of vice conditions:* Ibid.

138. *Mr. Mellett not so long ago blessed:* Bloom, NYU *News Workshop,* 2. Also in Hohenberg, *The Pulitzer Prize Story,* 47–48, with reply to Janson.

138. Wrote Cox in a tribute: Ibid., 48.

139–40. When the *New York Evening World* won: Joseph Pulitzer II's collected papers show that he kept close track of the numbers of awards the *World* papers and the *Post-Dispatch* won each year.

140. The board members—and especially . . . "If we cannot manage to get more entries": J.P. II letter to Butler dated April 13, 1928, in J.P. II papers.

140. In November 1929 . . . "indifference and apathy encountered": Letter from executive secretary Robert A. Parker to the Pulitzer Advisory Board, November 14, 1929. In J.P. II's papers.

140. The Pulitzer brothers quietly agreed: Telegram from J.P. to Ralph dated August 6, 1929, one of several in the J.P. II papers with this subject.

CHAPTER 9. FROM DEPRESSION TO WARTIME

146. *[In the 'Thirties] the Pulitzer Prizes in journalism became an intrinsic part:* Hohenberg, *The Pulitzer Prizes,* 84.

147. After honoring three cases . . . considering twenty-three nominations: Pulitzer jury notes, 1934. The case is summarized in Hohenberg, *The Pulitzer Prize Story,* 50–55.

148. *Do the people of Jackson County:* Dated March 17, 1933. From Pulitzer Prize archives, 1934. Also republished in Hohenberg, *The Pulitzer Prize Story,* 51–52.

148. Banks eventually was sentenced . . . "the show is over": Seven-page Ruhl letter, "Public Service Award," undated, in Pulitzer Prize archive.

148. Why was the Pulitzer Board left: Pulitzer jury report, March 6, 1934.

149. *What are its implications?:* Lester Markel, letter to Advisory Board, March 8, 1934.

149–50. *At the meeting I first stated:* Letter from Ralph Pulitzer in J.P. II papers.

150. Yet in many ways: Jury report, 1934.

151. Public Service jurors called it a tie: Jury report, April 1938.

151. It was the work of publisher and editor George D. Mann: From 1938 Pulitzer entry.

153. The *Tribune,* now owned by Lee Enterprises: Dave Bundy, e-mail exchange with author, February 22, 2006.

153. While its war coverage again was superb . . . Iphegene Ochs Sulzberger: From the *Times*'s cover letter with the entry.

154. There had been plenty of controversy: An April 8, 1943, *Times* article noted the *Harvard Crimson* comments.

154. The *Free Press* had been reporting regularly: From 1945 Pulitzer entry and jury report, March 1945.

155. *I am much impressed:* J.P. II Papers, letter to Arthur Krock, March 29, 1945.

155. Krock wrote back: Ibid., Krock letter to J.P. on March 31, 1945.

155–56. Pulitzer pondered the proposal: Ibid., J.P. II note to Ben Reese, April 2, 1945.

CHAPTER 10. A HANDFUL OF GOLD

158. *I know that my retirement:* As published daily on the *St. Louis Post-Dispatch* editorial page.

158. How would one go about: This chapter reflects work for the James C. Millstone Memorial Lecture delivered by the author to the Missouri Historical Society and the *Post-Dispatch* staff, September 9, 2002, and published by the Saint Louis University School of Law. It was also summarized in *Quill,* May 2003.

159. For one thing, the paper's: *Story of the St. Louis Post-Dispatch,* 5, 10.

159. O. K. Bovard personified the newsroom "field general": Discussed in Daniel Pfaff, *Joseph Pulitzer II and the Post-Dispatch,* 154–67.

160. J.P. II has sometimes been pictured: Ibid., 37–39. More detail in Pfaff, James Yeatman Lecture, "Pulitzer Journalism and Public Service," St. Louis, November 10, 2006.

161. Such stimulation . . . "yellow memos": Pfaff, *Joseph Pulitzer II,* 227–28. Also, Louis Starr, "Oral History of Ben Reese."

161. *[T]his is probably a stupid thing:* Starr, "Oral History of Joseph Pulitzer II."

161. William E. Blundell, a retired *Wall Street Journal* reporter: Blundell, telephone conversations with author, August 2002.

161–62. Editors and reporters identified . . . "I'm afraid I'm not as religious": Starr, "Oral History of J.P. II."

162. *There was one thing about the Post-Dispatch:* Starr, "Oral History of Reese."

162. Much later, after the *Post-Dispatch* had won: Ibid.

162. What Selwyn Pepper remembers: Selwyn Pepper, interview by author, St. Louis, June 29, 2002; also from 1937 Pulitzer entry.

164–65. Another staffer put on canvassing duty: Wayne Leeman, interview by author, Webster Groves, Mo., June 29, 2002.

164. *Memo for O.K.B:* J.P. II papers.

164. Of the twenty-one entries: 1941 Public Service jury report.

164. When Bovard left the *Post-Dispatch:* Pfaff, *Joseph Pulitzer II,* 212–13.

165. Pulitzer himself inspired: *Post-Dispatch* 1941 Pulitzer entry.

167. *Although I do not believe there is one chance in a million:* J.P. II memorandum to Reese, J.P. II papers.

168. *. . . [H]e said there'd been an explosion:* Pepper, interview.

168. By late in the day, the tableau: Stories taken from *Post-Dispatch* 1948 Pulitzer entry.

169–70. *The Post-Dispatch having so often had to damn:* Pfaff, *Joseph Pulitzer II,* 225–26.

171. In August 1948, Ben Reese assigned: *Post-Dispatch* 1950 Pulitzer entry.

171. "About the end of March": "Chicago, St. Louis Dailies Win Pulitzer Gold Medals," *Editor & Publisher,* May 6, 1950, 7.

172. While it was perhaps a rare reporting arrangement: *Editor & Publisher,* August 27, 1949, 24.

173. *At best, this looks like crass indifference: Post-Dispatch* 1950 Pulitzer entry.

173. Theodore C. Link returned: "Theodore C. Link Dies; Investigative Reporter," *Post-Dispatch,* February 14, 1974.

174. In October 1953: William R. Mathews letter to Virgil Pinkley, editor and publisher, *The Mirror,* Los Angeles, October 2, 1953. J.P. II papers.

CHAPTER II. A NEW STEW OF ISSUES

186. *Somehow, sometime, every Arkansan:* 1958 Pulitzer entry of the *Arkansas Gazette.* Also quoted in Hohenberg, *The Pulitzer Prize Story,* 101.

187. In 1953, the *Whiteville News Reporter:* Ray Erwin, "2 Weeklies Win Pulitzer Prizes For Anti-KKK War," *Editor & Publisher,* May 9, 1953, 9.

187. The fears in the community: Cole called the North Carolina Klan "as dead as a door nail." Associated Press account, May 5, 1943.

188. Being taken as a serious publisher: "Alicia's Toy." Discussed in Robert Keeler, *Newsday: A Candid History of the Respectable Tabloid,* 46–50.

188. While individual names . . . Dudar may be the first: Ibid., 196–98. Since individual reporters were rarely discussed in connection with the Public Service Prize, there is no good way to document this. Material on Bob Greene, 199–203.

189. The state investigation turned: Ray Erwin, "3 Pulitzer Prizes Awarded For Exclusive Exposes," *Editor & Publisher,* May 9, 1954, 13. Also discussed by Keeler.

189. *Newsday's* victory over the labor boss: Fred Cook quoted in Keeler, 208. "Soggy suburban" was a term of criticism used by Westbrook Pegler, and cited by Bob Greene, telephone interview by author, March 3, 2006.

189. In a statement: Ray Erwin, "3 Pulitzer Prizes Awarded," 13.

187–90. Editor Harry S. Ashmore and the *Gazette:* Ray Erwin, "3 Pulitzer Prizes Awarded for the Little Rock Story, *Editor & Publisher,* May 10, 1958, 11. Also, 1958 Pulitzer entry.

190. "Little Rock was actually a progressive city": Eugene Roberts, interview by author, Baltimore, November 30, 2005.

190–91. *Little Rock arose yesterday:* 1958 Pulitzer entry of *Arkansas Gazette,* also quoted in Hohenberg, *The Pulitzer Prize Story,* 102.

191. *This is a tragic day in the history:* Ibid., 104.

191. As for the Pulitzer Public Service Prize: From 1958 jury report.

191. Some *Gazette* readers: "Arkansas' Past Entwined with Newspaper's Vivid Story," on http://www.arkansasonline.com, Web site, *Arkansas Gazette Democrat,* 2006.

192. Like many newly hired women reporters: Lois Wille, telephone interview by author, April 3, 2006. Also, *Chicago Daily News* 1957 Pulitzer entry, and Erwin, "Pulitzer Prizes Awarded for Crusades, Enterprise," *Editor & Publisher,* May 11, 1963, 12.

194–95. In the "time capsules": Cortland Anderson, "Gold Medal Stories Save Florida Taxpayers Millions," 13, and Ray Erwin, "St. Petersburg Times Wins Public Service 'Pulitzer,'" *Editor & Publisher,* May 9, 1964.

195. Like many investigations that lead to Gold Medals: William F. Thomas, interview by author, Sherman Oaks, Calif., May 28, 2005. Other accounts of coverage in "Pulitzer medal for public service is awarded to Los Angeles Times," *Editor & Publisher,* May 10, 1969, 9, and Richard Dougherty, "Times Honored with Two Pulitzer Prizes," *Los Angeles Times,* May 6, 1969, 1.

196. *Times* editor Nick Williams wrote: *L.A. Times*'s 1969 Pulitzer entry.

Part Three. The Golden Seventies

CHAPTER 12. SECRET REPORTING, SECRET PAPERS

205. *The balance of political power in America:* James Reston, quoted in Hohenberg, *The Pulitzer Prizes,* 293.

206. Still, Watergate certainly played: "This didn't last very long . . ." Anthony Marro, "Watergate & The Press," talk delivered at the University of Texas, Austin, March 23, 2005. Transcript provided to author by Marro.

207. *As Sulzberger checked over:* Harrison E. Salisbury, *Without Fear or Favor,* 230.

207. So Butterfield was uneasy: Fox Butterfield, telephone interview by author, March 11, 2006.

208. It was no secret . . . "we never found out": Ben Bradlee, *A Good Life,* 310. Nat Hentoff wrote: Salisbury, *Without Fear or Favor,* 166–67.

208–9. Sheehan's source: Ibid., 47–93. Salisbury's account takes the reader through Daniel Ellsberg's process in making Sheehan the outlet for the Pentagon Papers.

209. On April 20, at 3 p.m.: Ibid., 118–24.

209–10. *Frankel then put the key question to his colleagues:* Ibid., 122.

210. They discussed the closest apparent precedents: Ibid., 127–33, reviews the William Bayard Hale interview with Kaiser Wilhelm. The Bay of Pigs precedent is discussed in pp. 148–64.

211. Through May, Sheehan, and the Pentagon Papers team: Ibid., 165.

211. On June 10, the publisher reviewed . . . "improbable collaborators": Ibid., 202.

211. Editors made last-minute presentations to Sulzberger: Ibid., 204–5.

211. "I've decided you can use the documents: Ibid., 205; "In retrospect, the decision": Floyd Abrams, *Speaking Freely: Trials of the First Amendment,* 12.

211. The first day's thirteen-paragraph introduction . . . "Usually we lead": Butterfield, interview.

212. Vietnam Archive: Pentagon Study Traces: From 1972 Pulitzer entry.

212. An exception was the *Washington Post* . . . "*The New York Times* has begun publication": E-mail to the author from John Lynch, Vanderbilt University Television News Archive, Nashville, Tennessee, April 17, 2006.

212. The Nixon administration, too, had seemed to ignore: Detailed speculation about Nixon administration reaction is in Salisbury, *Without Fear or Favor,* 231–47.

212. One account of President Nixon's Monday communications . . . "show you're a

weakling": Abrams, *Speaking Freely,* 12. Abrams cites a number of books describing the Nixon administration reaction to the Pentagon Papers, including David Rudenstine's *The Day the Presses Stopped,* Richard Reeves's *President Nixon: Alone in the White House,* and John Prados and Margaret Pratt Parker's *Inside the Pentagon Papers,* citing transcripts of telephone conversations between Nixon and aides.

212–13. On Monday evening, a message came: Salisbury, *Without Fear or Favor,* 240–47.

213. With the Tuesday paper being readied: Ibid., 243–44.

213. On the day of the third installment, the *Times* lawyers lost: Abrams, *Speaking Freely,* 17–18.

213. Meanwhile, the *Washington Post* had managed . . . "the ethos of the paper changed": Bradlee, *A Good Life,* 313–17.

213–14. *Times* reporters at the New York Hilton: Butterfield, interview.

214. *The security of the Nation is not at the ramparts alone:* Abrams, *Speaking Freely,* 30–31.

214–15. *Prior restraints fall on speech:* Ibid., 37.

215. *[T]he press was protected:* Ibid., 44–45.

215. *. . . that if it had said, "The Times Agrees":* Hohenberg, *The Pulitzer Prize Story II, 1959–1980,* 155.

215. After such a victory . . . "It is fortuitous": Public Service jury report, March 10, 1972. Also, Hohenberg, *The Pulitzer Prizes,* 308.

216. But the board was divided . . . "anything hand-delivered": Daniel Pfaff, *No Ordinary Joe: A Life of Joseph Pulitzer III,* 288. Pfaff cites a January 24, 1972, note from Bradlee in the papers of J.P. III.

216. At that point the board decided: Hohenberg, *The Pulitzer Prize Story II,* 157.

217. For many of those papers, too: Bradlee, *A Good Life,* 323.

CHAPTER 13. ALL THE EDITOR'S MEN

222. *People don't win Pulitzer Prizes by being for:* President Nixon at the National Association of Broadcasters. Hohenberg, *The Pulitzer Prize Diaries,* 273.

222. Bob Woodward had not seen the movie: Interview, Woodward.

223. The case is so familiar . . . "The fact is that Nixon was ousted": Anthony Marro, transcript of March 23, 2005, seminar, University of Texas.

223. Woodward himself concedes . . . "The truth of the matter": Interview, Woodward.

224. The blue-bound Pulitzer Prize entry folders: Rare Manuscripts room, Butler Library, Columbia University. All original Pulitzer Prize entries and supporting material reside in this archive.

224. The *Post's* bid for a prize was a tough sell: The best accounts are Hohenberg's, in *The Pulitzer Prize Story II, 1959–1980,* 208–37; *The Pulitzer Prizes,* 313–18, and *The Pulitzer Diaries,* 265–72.

224. *It began as pure opera bouffe:* Simons's letter was dated January 29, 1973.

225. "No three letters in the English language": Bradlee, *A Good Life,* 325. The accounts of the *Post's* Watergate coverage here are largely from Carl Bernstein and Bob Woodward, *All the President's Men,* and Bradlee, 324–84, supplemented by the author's interviews with Woodward and Bradlee.

226. "They got the story assigned to them": Bradlee, interview.

226. "Both are bright": Katharine Graham, *Personal History,* 461.

228. It is well known now . . . "especially strange of [Mitchell] to call me Katie": Ibid., 405.

229. To get the demanding Bradlee to sign off . . . "It grew out of paranoia": Woodward, interview.

229. Among perhaps two hundred Watergate stories . . . "You worked all day": Marro, interview. His evaluation of the key stories was covered in the March 2005 University of Texas seminar.

229–30. "There'd be a little story on B-38": Woodward, interview.

230–31. The best-known of Woodward and Bernstein's mistakes: The reporters' account is in *All the President's Men,* 170–98.

231. It would eventually come out . . . "You shouldn't make any mistakes": Woodward, interview.

231. *Mercifully for us:* Bradlee, *A Good Life,* 341. For his discussion of the reporting error, in which "our Watergate machine blew a fuse," see 337–43.

231. Along with the package of news stories: From the *Post* 1973 Pulitzer Prize entry.

231–32. In notes submitted to the Pulitzer Board: Jury report of March 8, 1973, Pulitzer Prize office.

232. Beyond that, some jurors felt . . . "Watergate is only a pimple": Hohenberg, *The Pulitzer Prize Story II,* 223.

232. *It was in this charged atmosphere:* Hohenberg, *The Pulitzer Prizes,* 315.

232. Bradlee was prepared to resign: Bradlee, interview. A discussion that falls just short of that declaration is in *A Good Life,* 367–68.

232. "It was one of his all-time understatements": Woodward, interview.

232–33. The board never gave any explanation . . . "It would seem to me": Seymour Topping, telephone interview by author, March 11, 2006.

233. Gene Roberts, executive editor of the *Philadelphia Inquirer:* "It was maybe the single greatest . . . " Roberts, November 30, 2005, interview.

233. Other board veterans . . . "It's not as if": Jack Fuller, telephone interview by author, March 23, 2006.

233. *The main thing is that the Post:* Graham, *Personal History,* 404.

234. Marro noted that the Washington press corps . . . "There were a lot of reporters at the *Post*": Marro, transcript, March 23, 2005.

234. The coverage created some mixed blessings: Marro, interview.

234–35. Criticisms aside: Marro, March 23, 2005, transcript.

235. Just after President Nixon resigned: Woodward, interview.

CHAPTER 14. TWO TYPES OF TEAMING

238. *That's a good paper:* Marro, telephone interview.

238. Truth be told, it was a seriously flawed *Newsday:* Robert F. Keeler, *Newsday: A Candid History of the Respectable Tabloid.* Case discussed, 192–209; "combined with his private ambition": 194; "triggering event": 196.

239. The vintage 1954 *Newsday* . . . "Seizing her newspaper's greatest moment of glory": Ibid., 210.

239. After she invested heavily: Ibid., 311–15.

239. Bob Greene was a born snoop: Ibid., 199–203.

240. At *Newsday,* he was far: "He was the barnyard dog . . . " Robert Greene, telephone interview by author, March 3, 2006.

240–41. Then in 1967, Hathway retired: "could never get any movement . . ." Keeler, *Newsday: A Candid History,* 419.

241. Instead, he devoted time . . . "You get something really good": Greene, interview.

241–42. Shanahan, now assistant foreign editor: Geraldine Shanahan, interview by author, *New York Times* newsroom, November 29, 2005.

242. "I knew very little about the team": Marro, interview.

242–43. Greene sometimes used reporters as foils . . . "Greene wrote": Shanahan, interview.

243. If he had 80 percent of what he needed . . . "three from Column A": Keeler, *Newsday: A Candid History,* 430.

243. *There are many different versions of this story:* Marro, transcript of *Newsday* talk, September 26, 2002, *Newsday* anniversary party, provided by Marro.

244. The third time was a golden charm: Pulitzer jury report, 1970. Unbeknownst to the paper . . . Jury report, 1969.

244. How strange, then: Keeler, *Newsday: A Candid History,* 474–75.

244–45. Greene says that Fellman: "Wait a second . . ." Greene, telephone interview. Story also told in Keeler, Newsday: *A Candid History,* 431.

245. Greene himself sees the assignment: Greene, interview.

246. Marro, who had been in the Washington bureau . . . "I can't pretend": Marro, interview.

246. As might be expected . . . "the *Newsday* invasion of Europe": Keeler, 511; "Let's get the black guy": Marro, interview.

246. At one point, when Attwood asked: Greene, interview.

246–47. One story from abroad . . . "He was walking majestically": Marro, interview.

247. But thanks to the time spent . . . "The results of such a far-reaching series . . . *Newsday* Pulitzer entry, 1974.

247. Some at the paper felt . . . "It was a good story . . ." Marro, interview.

247. Bob Greene went on to hold a succession of jobs: Keeler, 548–49. The Arizona Project brought many top reporters together on the same story under the auspices of the new Investigative Reporters and Editors, or IRE.

248. When Greene was not at the helm: Marro, interview.

248. Having led two teams . . . "when their grandchildren go to look it up": Greene, interview.

248. The *Philadelphia Inquirer* was a grand experiment . . . "the best journalist living and breathing": Salisbury quoted in *Columbia Journalism Review,* May/June 2003.

248–49. Roberts had moved north: Roberts, interview.

249. Steve Lovelady . . . "It was a terrible paper": Steve Lovelady, interview by author, New York, November 29, 2005.

249. Bill Marimow still recalls: William Marimow, telephone interview by author, March 13, 2006.

250. The police brutality story . . . "most of the best journalism is bottom up": Roberts, interview.

251. Marimow had moved to city hall: Marimow, interview.

251. *It can be said:* The *Inquirer* series ran April 24–27.

252. Carroll says he had a secret weapon: Carroll, interview.

252. *It's a fight every day: Inquirer,* April 24, 1977.

253. How were things on the Philadelphia police beat: "I took a lot of grief . . ." Robert (Bo) Terry, telephone interview by author, March 14, 2006.

CHAPTER 15. DAVIDS AND GOLIATHS

258. *Kay Fanning knew that a newspaper is a public trust:* Howard Weaver, eulogy for Fanning, Summer 2000, transcript from Weaver.

258–59. Bob Woodward proposes: Woodward, interview.

259. Howard Weaver was twenty-five: Weaver, interview. Section based largely on his account, along with the 1976 *Anchorage Daily News* Pulitzer Prize entry.

263. *Teamsters Union Local 959 is fashioning: Anchorage Daily News,* December 20, 1975.

264. *A ringing telephone:* Text provided to author by Weaver.

265. Editor Joe Murray was in a grumpy mood: Joe Murray, telephone interview by author, March 3, 2006. The section is based on the accounts of Murray and Ken Herman, with material from the *Lufkin News's* 1977 Pulitzer entry. A 2001 report by Dr. Wanda Mouton, Department of Communication, Stephen F. Austin State University, Nacogdoches, Texas, contains additional detail and interviews. It is titled "A Case Study Analysis and Quarter-Century Perspective of a Story That Won the Pulitzer Prize."

266. Herman remembers vividly: Ken Herman, telephone interview by author, March 7, 2006.

266. *Lynn (Bubba) McClure, 20, joined the Marines: Lufkin News,* March 16, 1976.

268. *The use of fake names has opened up the possibility: Lufkin News,* April 4, 1976.

CHAPTER 16. MIGHTIER THAN THE SNAKE

274. *God, I thought, wouldn't it be amazing to win?: The Light on Synanon,* 280. The 1980 book by Dave Mitchell, Cathy Mitchell, and Richard Ofshe offers a fascinating firsthand account.

274. "Today is the first day": While it may surprise that this is a New Age quotation, and not much older, *Morrow's International Dictionary of Contemporary Quotations* (1982) is among the references crediting Dederich as its originator, circa 1969.

274–75. Mitchell had visited: "fairly evenly divided . . . " Mitchell, Mitchell, and Ofshe, 4; "above all it is big . . . " 22.

275. In retrospect, Mitchell calls . . . "Potemkin Village tour": Dave Mitchell, interview by author, Point Reyes Station, California, November 18, 2005.

279. Attorney Paul Morantz . . . "Dave and I are similar personalities": Paul Morantz, telephone interview by author, October 25, 2005.

279. *Each case of violence by Synanon members is treated as unrelated: Light,* September 28, from Pulitzer entry.

280. One day, as Mitchell was reporting . . . "I don't want to alarm you": Mitchell, Mitchell, and Ofshe, 181.

280. On Wednesday, October 11, Mitchell had driven: Ibid., 191–203.

282. It would be the paper's lead . . . "When I wrote the story": Dave Mitchell, interview.

283. The moves were wise . . . "Dave is more macho": Cathy Mitchell, telephone interview by author, December 20, 2005.

283. Dave Mitchell had one scare: Dave Mitchell, interview.

284. The new owner immediately . . . "This is the place where the new literary movement": Robert Plotkin, interview by author, *Point Reyes Light* office, November 19, 2005.

CHAPTER 17. PULITZER, REFORM THYSELF

288. *What came from [my study] is a surprising, fascinating, complex, often contradictory portrait:* David Shaw, *Press Watch,* 185.

288. Joseph Pulitzer Jr., as he was known: The biographies of both J.P. II and J.P. Jr. by Daniel W. Pfaff give detail on their relationship. Additional insight is in Pfaff's November 2006 Yeatman Lecture in St. Louis.

288. "There is no record": Pfaff, *No Ordinary Joe,* 290; "that he, like his father": Hohenberg, *The Pulitzer Diaries,* 22. Discussions of several attempts to expand the reach of the Pulitzer Prize are found in the private papers of J.P. II.

289. Concerns about the Pulitzer Prizes: Shaw's discussion of the Prizes in chapter 7 of *Press Watch,* 178–214, was based on a *Los Angeles Times* series on the Pulitzers.

290. Chairman Pulitzer and other board members had begun questioning: Hohenberg, *The Pulitzer Prize Story II,* 151–58.

291. There were similar worries: Ibid., 222–28.

291. Years after the 1973 Watergate Gold Medal . . . "Votes are subtly, if not openly, traded": Bradlee, *A Good Life,* 366.

291. Bradley also was upset: Ibid., 367–68.

292. "There was no particular reformer-in-chief": Eugene Patterson, telephone interview by author, April 19, 2006.

292. For the first time, a system for naming finalists . . . "honorable mentions": These are available for review year-by-year in the Rare Manuscript area of the Pulitzer archives at Columbia's Butler Library.

293. His prime example was the 1979 Gold Medal: Shaw, *Press Watch,* 195–96.

293. Gene Roberts, then executive editor: Roberts, interview.

293. John Carroll, whose board term ended in 2004: "Once an editor asked me . . ." Carroll, interview.

293. "One of the great things when I joined the board": Jack Fuller, telephone interview by author, March 23, 2006.

293–94. "Integrity oozed": Gartner, telephone interview.

294. *Oregonian* editor Sandy Rowe . . . "In the past, I don't know": Rowe, interview by author, *Oregonian* office in Portland, November 16, 2005.

294. David Shaw's 1984 study . . . "Any story good enough": *Press Watch,* 211.

294. A later *Inquirer* editor, Amanda Bennett . . . "Mostly, I find that it creates a brittle, glasslike operation": Bennett, interview by author, *Inquirer* office, October 13, 2005.

295. The Pulitzers will always . . . "I'm totally two-faced . . . ." Bradlee, interview.

Part Four. Challenges for a New Era

CHAPTER 18. EVERYBODY'S BUSINESS

299. *How shameful it is for the Knight family: Charlotte Observer* 1981 Pulitzer Prize entry, quoted in cover letter by Richard A. Oppel.

299. The lack of clamor . . . "We drew flow charts": Howard Weaver, interview.

300. Knight Ridder's *Charlotte Observer:* This section is based largely on the *Observer* 1981 Pulitzer entry. Also, Richard A. Oppel, telephone interview by author, April 3, 2006.

301. The controversy did not subside . . . "It was unfortunate that a respectable paper": The author of the April 17, 1981, letter was identified as Siegfried Heydon, professor of community and family medicine at Duke University.

302. In December 1984, the *Observer's* suspicions . . . "She threatened to sue": Charles Shepard, in Kendall J. Wills, *The Pulitzer Prizes 1987*, 21–24. Wills put together four books for Simon and Schuster from 1988 to 1991, each a compendium of Pulitzer journalism for the prior year.

302. The paper, however, set strict standards: Oppel, telephone interview.

304. The *Detroit News* in 1981: Sydney P. Freedberg, telephone interview by author, March 29, 2006. Story references also come from the *Detroit News* 1981 Pulitzer entry.

305. In 1984 the *Los Angeles Times* won: Descriptions of the series are from the paper's 1984 Pulitzer entry and a page one *Times* account by David Shaw, "Times Wins 2 Pulitzers: Public Service, Conrad," April 17, 1984; "enhancing understanding": quoted as a board comment.

305. "Most impressive of all": Pulitzer jury report, 1984.

305–6. By most accounts the series got its start: William Thomas, interview.

307. Of the two other 1984 finalists: Pulitzer jury report, 1984.

307–8. The military correspondent for the *Fort Worth Star-Telegram:* Mark J. Thompson, telephone interview by author, March 27, 2006. Other material from the 1985 *Star-Telegram* Pulitzer entry.

310. An aviation story of another kind: Andrew Schneider, telephone interview by author, April 2, 2006. Story material from 1986 *Pittsburgh Press* Pulitzer entry was also used, along with another account, in Wills, *The Pulitzer Prizes 1987*, by Brelis and Schneider, 22–25.

312. One Public Service finalist, the *Fort Lauderdale News:* Pulitzer jury report, 1986.

313. Howard Weaver had become managing editor . . . "We were older and smarter": Weaver, interview. Also, a Weaver account is in Wills, *The Pulitzer Prizes 1989*, 2–5.

315. *In a community of 550: Anchorage Daily News* Special Reprint, January 1988.

316. The 1989 Pulitzer Public Service jurors identified: Pulitzer jury report, 1989.

CHAPTER 19. THE NATURE OF THINGS

319. . . . *"The Environment Story" is bigger and more important than ever:* From the Organizing Principles, the Society of Environmental Journalists, http:// www.sej.org.

320. The 1990 Pulitzer Board picked both: One account of the Pulitzer Board's decision is discussed in J. Douglas Bates, *The Pulitzer Prize*, which concentrates on the process in 1990, especially 209–11.

320. In Washington, North Carolina: Wills, *The Pulitzer Prizes 1990*, 2–6.

321. *Inquirer* business reporter Gilbert M. Gaul . . . "I was lying there as the blood was running out of my arm": Gaul, interview by author, *Inquirer* office, October 13, 2005. Also, see Wills, *The Pulitzer Prizes 1990*, 31–33.

324–25. Among journalists, the series generated . . . "The fundamental issue was": Overholser, interview. This account balances the views of editor Overholser and reporter Jane Schorer Meisner. References to articles are from the *Register's* 1991 Pulitzer entry.

326. Jane Schorer, a gifted but relatively new reporter . . . "we need to have a real reporter": Jane Schorer Meisner, telephone interview by author, April 3, 2006.

326–27. *She would have to allow extra driving time: Des Moines Register,* February 25, 1990, from Pulitzer archives.

329. Overholser understands her irritation . . . "What made it work": Gartner, interview.

329. *Sacramento Bee* reporter Tom Knudson, interview by author, Truckee, Calif., November 16, 2005.

331. Finalists in Public Service: Pulitzer jury report, 1992.

332. THE BIG ONE: Miami Herald, p. 1, from 1992 Pulitzer entry.

332–33. For the *Miami Herald*... "It's very difficult to get around": Pete Weitzel, telephone interview by author, April 4, 2006.

335. The Pulitzer Public Service jury commented: 1993 jury report.

336. *Grand Forks has sustained deep wounds:* April 4, 1997, *Herald,* part of the paper's 1998 Pulitzer entry.

336. "We wanted to sound the theme of hope": Mike Maidenberg, telephone interview by author, April 11, 2006.

338. It ebbed in a big way... "Never hold the news": Mike Jacobs, "Four Lessons of Newspapering... Come Hell and High Water," http://www.Poynter.org, June 18, 2003, from American Society of Newspaper Editors speech.

338. Jurors and Pulitzer Board members... an unspoken yet clear understanding": James Naughton, e-mail exchange with author, April 4, 2006.

339. In the wake of 2005's Hurricane Katrina: Butch Ward, "Journalism in Recovering Communities: Lessons from Grand Forks," http://www.Poynter.org, August 31, 2005.

339. "Actually, the story got started": Melanie Sill, telephone interview by author, April 4, 2006. Also, see "80th Annual Pulitzer Prizes," *Editor & Publisher,* April 13, 1996.

340. *Imagine a city as big as New York: News & Observer,* from Pulitzer entry, 1996. Series ran in February 1995. See http://www.Pulitzer.org.

340–41. After the series, but before the Pulitzer Prize: Jury report, 1996.

341. Environmental writer Mark Schleifstein... "If you've got ideas for a story": Schleifstein, telephone interview by author, April 6, 2006. Also, *Times-Picayune* Pulitzer entry, 1997.

343. *Times-Picayune* long-timers... "We spent a year": Kovacs, interview; Adds Amoss: Amoss, interview. The *Times-Picayune* series, and other Pulitzer winners since 1995, can be reviewed at http://www.Pulitzer.org.

CHAPTER 20. THE *POST* RINGS TWICE

346. *It is a capital mistake:* From Sir Arthur Conan Doyle's *A Scandal in Bohemia, The Complete Sherlock Holmes, Adventures of Sherlock Holmes,* vol. 1, p. 5, Doubleday, Doran and Company, Inc., Garden City, N.Y., 1930.

346–47. In 1999 and 2000, for the first time... "You could have a thousand": Jeffrey M. Leen, interview by author, *Post* office, October 12, 2005.

347. Although the two projects... "I was not good at it": Woodward, interview.

347. Jo Craven, a computer-assisted-reporting specialist... "When measured against the average population": Memo titled "Deadly Force: The Making of the Post's Police Project," December 1999, lead writer Rick Atkinson. Memo provided to author by Leen.

349. When the news broke about Monica... "a clear sense of human drama": Ibid.

350–52. Sari Horwitz had started: Sari Horwitz, interview by author, *Post* offices, October 12, 2005.

352. Teamcop was clearly... "We worked very, very closely": Dave Jackson comments quoted in December 1999 Atkinson memo.

353. D.C. Police Lead Nation in Shootings: *Post,* November 15, 1998. See http://www.Pulitzer.org.

355. Not long after the *Post* won: Leen, interview.

355. "These stories began in the dark": *Post* Pulitzer entry, 2000.

355–61. Kate Boo had been covering: Boo, interview by author, Washington, D.C., October 12, 2005.

357. *Elroy lives here: Post,* March 14, 1999.

359. *The corpse measured 66 inches: Post,* December 5, 1999.

CHAPTER 21. COVERING "DE-PORTLAND"

363. *There are services to the public only a newspaper:* The letter is part of the *Oregonian* 2001 Pulitzer nomination.

363–64. Her introduction to the *Oregonian:* Rowe, interview.

365. When Sullivan walked into the juvenile jail: Julie Sullivan and Richard Read, joint interview by author, November 16, 2006.

366–67. *Immigration inspectors jailed an innocent: Oregonian,* August 23, 2000.

367–68. *The morning after the governor: Oregonian,* August 27, 2000.

370. Ironically, the job of capturing: Brent Walth's team meeting is also discussed in Richard Read, "The Oregonian Investigates Mistreatment of Foreigners," *Nieman Reports,* Winter 2002, 27–29.

371. Readers seeing the six-part package: "like making sausage from live animals." Christensen quoted by Read, interview.

371. Editor Bhatia acknowledges: Bhatia, interview by author, November 16, 2006.

371–72. *Murder suspects have more rights: Oregonian,* December 10, 2000.

372. Bennett contrasts the *Oregonian's* work: Bennett, interview. See also Bennett and Jack Hart, "How We Got Those Stories," *Columbia Journalism Review,* September/October 2001.

373. The board did not have an easy decision: Finalists are listed under 2001 Prizes on http://www.Pulitzer.org.

AFTERWORD: BACK TO THE FUTURE

376–82. In late 2005: Mark Maremont, interview by author, April 30, 2007.

380–81. Maremont and editor Dan Kelly agreed: Kelly, telephone interview by author, May 4, 2007.

381. The *Journal's* creation . . . "Innocuous and even sensible": *Wall Street Journal,* June 21, 2006.

382. After being selected . . . "I believe one of our highest callings": *Wall Street Journal,* April 17, 2007, A2.

APPENDIX: THE GOLD MEDAL IN HISTORY

384. As a southern paper, the *Memphis Commercial Appeal:* A study of James P. Alley's cartooning was being prepared in 2006 by Berkley Hudson, University of Missouri, under the title "Hambone and the Ku Klux Klan in 1922." Alley's six-day-a-week syndicated cartoon, "Hambone's Meditation," featured "Uncle-Remus-style" philosophy from a character speaking in African American dialect and with a sense of humor. Alley, a self-taught illustrator, grew up in Benton, a town southwest of Little Rock. Writes Hudson, "Alley is virtually absent in media history scholarship."

385. The Pulitzer Board picked Georgia's *Columbus Enquirer Sun:* This case is also discussed in Hohenberg, the *Pulitzer Prize Story,* 69–70.

386. The lead series in the wide-ranging . . . "the whole enterprise": *Sunday Transcript* letter, dated September 18, 1929, is in files of J.P. II.

387. The packet of *Indianapolis News* articles: Joseph Pulitzer II, while eager to reduce the sense that Pulitzer-owned papers had an edge in prize-winning, badly wanted *Post-Dispatch* staffer Charles G. Ross's article on the Great Depression, "The Country's Plight," to win for Public Service in 1932. "I am loath to appear before the Advisory Board as an advocate of the *Post-Dispatch* for I have deliberately avoided entering *Post-Dispatch* material in the competitions for the past several years," he wrote on April 3, 1932, to Columbia Dean Carl Ackerman. "However, now that the article has been entered and has been awarded the Reporter's Prize, I feel that in fairness to this newspaper, to its staff, and to the underlying purpose of the Pulitzer Prizes, I must do so, unless I can find someone else to do this." The board left the selections as they had approved them.

390–91. Publisher Harry Chandler's *Los Angeles Times:* The 1942 case is discussed in Hohenberg, *The Pulitzer Prize Story*, 313–16.

393. A civic project by the Lincoln-based *Nebraska State Journal:* Discussed in "'All-Star Primary' Wins Pulitzer Medal,'" *Editor & Publisher*, May 7, 1949, 7.

394. The *Miami Herald* and *Brooklyn Eagle:* See *Editor & Publisher*, May 12, 1951, 7.

395. The *Columbus Ledger* and *Sunday Ledger-Enquirer* investigated crime-ridden Phenix City, Alabama: See *Editor & Publisher*, May 7, 1955, 13.

396. The seven-thousand-circulation *Watsonville Register-Pajaronian . . .* Noted in Hohenberg, *The Pulitzer Prize Story*, 45.

396. The *Chicago Daily News*—and George Thiem: Ibid., 66–68. Also see Ray Erwin, "Pulitzer Gold Medal Given For Exposure of Fund Fraud," *Editor & Publisher*, May 11, 1957.

397. The Gannett-owned *Utica Observer-Dispatch* and *Utica Daily Press:* See Ray Erwin, "Utica Papers Win Pulitzer Medal for Crime Exposure," *Editor & Publisher*, May 12, 1958.

398. *Los Angeles Times* editor Nick Williams: Gene Sherman, "Prize-Winning Series Background Described," *Los Angeles Times*, May 3, 1960. Also, Ray Erwin, "Exposes of Civic Sins Win 5 Pulitzer Prizes," *Editor & Publisher*, May 7, 1960, 15.

398. A phone tip to *Amarillo Globe-Times* editor Thomas H. Thompson: Thomas H. Thompson, "First Failure, Then Sweeping Victory in Gold Medal Exposé," *Editor & Publisher*, May 6, 1961, 59.

399. *Panama City News & Herald*, with its six-person: See "Ex-Detective Led Expose That Won Pulitzer Prize," and Ray Erwin, "Crusades Versus Corruption & Collusion Win Pulitzers," *Editor & Publisher*, May 12, 1962, 11–12. Also, Pulitzer entry cover letter from Edwin B. Callaway, executive editor, January 30, 1962.

400. The *Hutchinson News* took the side: See Ray Erwin, "Hutchinson News Wins Public Service 'Pulitzer,'" *Editor & Publisher*, May 8, 1965, 12.

401. The *Boston Globe*, under editor Thomas Winship: See "Boston Globe Wins the Pulitzer Prize," *Boston Globe*, May 3, 1966, 1. Also, Ray Erwin, "Boston Globe Wins Pulitzer Gold Medal," *Editor & Publisher*, May 7, 1966.

401. The *Louisville Courier-Journal* and *Milwaukee Journal* won: See Ray Erwin, "Louisville and Milwaukee Win Pulitzer Gold Medals," *Editor & Publisher*, May 6, 1967, 11.

402. Reporter George Ringwald of California's *Riverside Press-Enterprise:* Newton H. Fulbright, "Crusade for Indians Wins Pulitzer Medal," *Editor & Publisher*, May 11, 1968, 11 . . . In selecting the *Press-Enterprise,* the Pulitzer Board . . . Pulitzer 1968 jury report.

403–4. The *Winston-Salem Journal and Sentinel* covered the plans for a strip-mining: See Frank V. Tursi's *The Winston-Salem Journal: Magnolia Trees and Pulitzer Prizes*, 191–95,

John F. Blair and the Winston-Salem Journal, Winston-Salem, North Carolina, 1996. Also, "Pulitzers again applaud crusade for environment," *Editor & Publisher,* May 8, 1971, 10.

405. As many northern cities faced high-pressure decisions: See "Globe wins Pulitzer Gold Medal for Hub school busing coverage," *Boston Globe,* May 5, 1975. "Do not look for elegant writing": Hohenberg, *The Pulitzer Prize Story II,* 287; stories excerpted 286–91.

407. Three Gannett News Service journalists: See Lenora Williamson, "Pulitzer for public service won by Gannett News," *Editor & Publisher,* April 19, 1980, 11.

409. The *Jackson Clarion-Ledger* explored why: See Lenora Williamson, "Jackson Clarion-Ledger tops Pulitzers," *Editor & Publisher,* April 23, 1983, 16.

410. The *Denver Post*'s project stemmed from reporter Diana Griego's skepticism: See Lenora Williamson, *Editor & Publisher,* April 26, 1986, 16.

414. The *Akron Beacon Journal* launched a year-long study of racial attitudes: See Tony Case, *Editor & Publisher,* April 16, 1994, 9–10.

415. Investigating widespread crime in the territory: See Case and Dorothy Giobbe, *Editor & Publisher,* April 22, 1995, 17–18. Also, "After the Pulitzers," http://editorandpublisher .com, November 4, 1995, and Ryan Frank, "Three Tips for Project Reporting," on a talk by Claxton at 2002 National Writers Workshop, Portland, Ore. http://www.Poynterextra .org/nww/portland2002/claxton;frank.htm.

BIBLIOGRAPHY

Abrams, Floyd. *Speaking Freely: Trials of the First Amendment.* New York: Viking, 2005.

Aucoin, James L. *The Evolution of American Investigative Journalism.* Columbia: University of Missouri Press, 2006.

Bates, J. Douglas. *The Pulitzer Prize: The Inside Story of America's Most Prestigious Award.* New York: Birch Lane Press, 1991.

Bent, Silas. *Newspaper Crusaders: Neglected Story.* Westport, Conn.: Greenwood Press, 1970.

Berger, Meyer. *The Story of the New York Times.* New York: Simon and Schuster, 1951.

Bernstein, Carl, and Bob Woodward. *All the President's Men.* New York: Simon and Schuster, 1974.

Boston Globe. *Betrayal: The Crisis in the Catholic Church.* (By the Investigative Staff.) Boston: Little, Brown and Company, 2002.

Bradlee, Ben. *A Good Life. Newspapering and Other Adventures.* New York: Touchstone, 1995.

France, David. *Our Fathers: The Secret Life of the Catholic Church in an Age of Scandal.* New York: Broadway Books, 2004.

Davis, Elmer. *History of the New York Times, 1851–1921.* New York: Classic Books, 1922.

Downie, Leonard Jr., and Robert G. Kaiser. *The News about the News: American Journalism in Peril.* New York: Alfred A. Knopf, 2002.

Hohenberg, John. *The Pulitzer Diaries: Inside America's Greatest Prize.* Syracuse, N.Y.: Syracuse University Press, 1997.

———. *The Pulitzer Prizes: A History of the Awards in Books, Drama, Music, and Journalism Based on the Private Files Over Six Decades.* New York: Columbia University Press, 1974.

———, editor and commentator. *The Pulitzer Prize Story.* New York: Columbia University Press, 1959.

———, editor and commentator. *The Pulitzer Prize Story II: 1959–1980.* New York: Columbia University Press, 1980.

Kahn, E. J., Jr. *The World of Swope: A Biography of Herbert Bayard Swope.* New York: Simon and Schuster, Inc., 1965.

Keeler, Robert F. *Newsday, A Candid History of the Respectable Tabloid.* New York: Arbor House/Morro, 1990.

Lewis, Alfred Allan. *Man of the World: Herbert Bayard Swope: A Charmed Life of Pulitzer Prizes, Poker and Politics.* Indianapolis: Bobbs-Merrill Company, Inc., 1978.

Lewis, Anthony. *Written Into History: Pulitzer Prize Reporting of the Twentieth Century from the New York Times.* New York: Times Books, 2002.

Merritt, Davis. *Knightfall: Knight Ridder and How the Erosion of Newspaper Journalism Is Putting Democracy at Risk.* New York: Amacom, 2005.

Mindich, David T. Z. *Tuned Out: Why Americans under 40 Don't Follow the News.* Oxford: Oxford University Press, 2004.

Mitchell, Dave, Cathy Mitchell, and Richard Ofshe. *The Light on Synanon: How a Country Weekly Exposed a Corporate Cult—and Won the Pulitzer Prize.* New York: Seaview Books, 1980.

Mnookin, Seth. *Hard News: The Scandals at the New York Times and the Future of American Media.* New York: Random House, 2004.

New York Times. *Portraits 9/11/01.* New York: Times Books/Henry Holt and Co., 2002.

Pfaff, Daniel W. *Joseph Pulitzer II and the Post-Dispatch.* University Park: Pennsylvania State University Press, 1991.

———. *No Ordinary Joe: A Life of Joseph Pulitzer III.* Columbia: University of Missouri Press, 2005.

Plante, Thomas G., ed. *Sin against the Innocents: Sexual Abuse by Priests and the Role of the Catholic Church.* Westport, Conn.: Praeger, 2004.

Roberts, Gene, and Hank Klibanoff. *The Race Beat: The Press, the Civil Rights Struggle, and the Awakening of a Nation.* New York: Alfred A. Knopf, 2006.

Rothmyer, Karen. *Winning Pulitzers: The Stories behind Some of the Best News Coverage of Our Time.* New York: Columbia University Press, 1991.

St. Louis Post-Dispatch. *The Story of the St. Louis Post-Dispatch.* Revised and supplemented by Richard G. Baumhoff. 6th ed. St. Louis: Pulitzer Publishing Co., 1954.

Salisbury, Harrison E. *Without Fear or Favor: An Uncompromising Look at the New York Times.* New York: Ballantine Books, 1980.

Serrin, Judith, and William Serrin, eds. *Muckraking! The Journalism That Changed America.* New York: New Press, 2002.

Shaw, David. *Press Watch: A Provocative Look at How Newspapers Report the News.* New York: Macmillan Publishing Co., 1984.

Shepard, Alicia C. *Woodward and Bernstein: Life in the Shadow of Watergate.* New York: John Wiley and Sons, Inc., 2007.

Snyder, Louis L., and Richard B. Morris, eds. *A Treasury of Great Reporting.* New York: Simon and Schuster, 1949.

Stephens, Mitchell. *A History of News: From the Drum to the Satellite.* New York: Viking Penguin, 1988.

Streitmatter, Rodger. *Mightier than the Sword: How the News Media Have Shaped History.* Boulder, Colo.: Westview Press, 1997.

Swanberg, W. A. *Pulitzer: The Life of the Greatest Figure in American Journalism and One of the Most Extraordinary Men in Our History.* New York: Charles Scribner's Sons, 1967.

Tursi, Frank V. *The Winston-Salem Journal: Magnolia Trees and Pulitzer Prizes.* Winston-Salem, N.C.: John F. Blair and Winston-Salem Journal, 1996.

Wells, Robert W. *The Milwaukee Journal: An Informal Chronicle of Its First 100 Years.* Milwaukee: Milwaukee Journal, 1982.

Wendt, Lloyd. *The* Wall Street Journal: *The Story of Dow Jones and the Nation's Business Newspaper.* Chicago: Rand McNally and Co., 1982.

Williams, Paul N. *Investigative Reporting and Editing.* Englewood Cliffs, N.J.: Prentice Hall, Inc., 1978.

Wills, Kendall J. *The Pulitzer Prizes, 1987, 1988, 1989, 1990.* New York: Simon & Schuster, 1987–1990.

Zuckoff, Mitchell. *Ponzi's Scheme: The True Story of a Financial Legend.* New York: Random House, 2005.

ARTICLES, PERIODICALS, AND WEB SITES

American Journalism Review. Published bimonthly by the University of Maryland. Online at http://AJR.org, College Park, Md.

Bloom, Helen. *News Workshop.* New York University Department of Journalism newsletter, January 1965.

Columbia Journalism Review. Published bimonthly; affiliated with Columbia University Graduate School of Journalism. Online at http://www.CJR.org, New York.

Editor & Publisher. Published monthly. Magazine dates to 1884 as *The Journalist,* and as *E&P* since 1901. Online at http://EditorandPublisher.com, New York.

Fitzgerald, Mark. "Jim Amoss, E&P's 2006 Editor of the Year." *Editor & Publisher,* February 1, 2006, http://EditorandPublisher.com.

Harris, Roy J., Jr. "A Prize Moment for the Globe, and the Pulitzers," April 7, 2003. "The Pulitzers That Got Away," April 6, 2004. "Prizes and Rumors of Prizes," April 6, 2005. "Shared Glory for Pulitzer's Top Prize," April 17, 2006. http://www.Poynter.org.

———. *The Gold Medal Crusade Years.* St. Louis: Saint Louis University Law School, 2002.

———. "An Era of Crusaders." *Quill,* May 2003. Society of Professional Journalists.

IRE Journal. Published bimonthly since 1978 by Investigative Reporters and Editors, Inc. Online at http://www.IRE.org, Columbia, Mo.

Jacobs, Mike. "Four Lessons of Newspapering . . . Come Hell and High Water." http://www.Poynter.org, June 18, 2003.

Martin, John Bartlow. "Murder of a Journalist." *Harper's,* September 1946, 271–82.

Mehren, Elizabeth, Walter V. Robinson, and Steve Kurkjian. "Journalist's Trade: Investigating Scandal in the Catholic Church." *Nieman Reports,* Spring 2003, 52–61.

Nieman Reports. A quarterly published by the Nieman Foundation for Journalism at Harvard University. Online at http://www.Nieman.Harvard.edu, Cambridge, Mass.

Poynteronline. The Web site of the Poynter Institute, a school for journalists and teachers. http://www.Poynter.org, St. Petersburg, Fla.

Read, Richard. "The Oregonian Investigates Mistreatment of Foreigners." *Nieman Reports,* Winter 2002, 27–29.

New York Times Co. "Ahead of the Times" newsletter, vol. 10, no. 2, April 2002.

Quill. Published ten times per year by the Society of Professional Journalist. Online at http://www.SPJ.org, Indianapolis.

Richman, Michael. "The Medals of Daniel Chester French." In Alan M. Stahl, ed., *The Medal in America* (Coinage of the Americas Conference at The American Numismatic Society, New York, September 26–27, 1987).

Ward, Butch. "From Biloxi and New Orleans: The Stories behind the Pulitzers." http://
    www.Poynter.org, April 17, 2006.
————. "Journalism in Recovering Communities: Lessons from Grand Forks." http://
    www.Poynter.org, August 31, 2005.

UNPUBLISHED MATERIAL

Carroll, John. "Last Call at the ASNE Saloon." Speech delivered at American Society of
    Newspaper Editors convention, Seattle, April 26, 2006.
Cohen, Murray. "The Crusade against Election Fraud by the *Post-Dispatch* and *Star-Times*
    of St. Louis in 1936." Master's thesis, University of Missouri–Columbia, 1953.
Columbia University. The Pulitzer Prizes. Jury reports from 1917, maintained in the Jour-
    nalism Building, Pulitzer Prize office, New York.
————. Pulitzer Prize archive of entries and supporting documentation. Microfilm,
    Lehman Library.
————. Rare Manuscripts, Butler Library.
Dessauer, Philip Edward. "A Contemporary Study of the 1938–1940 Campaign for Smoke
    Control by the *St. Louis Post-Dispatch.*" Master's thesis, University of Missouri–
    Columbia, 1940.
French, Daniel Chester. Family Papers. Library of Congress, Washington, D.C. Reel 20,
    222–37.
Hudson, Berkley. "Hambone and the Ku Klux Klan in 1922: James P. Alley's Cartoons of
    a Southern White Conservative Mentality and the Pulitzer Prize." Excerpted from notes
    by Hudson, University of Missouri–Columbia, 2006.
Marro, Anthony. "Watergate and the Press." University of Texas–Austin, March 23, 2005.
Mouton, Wanda. "A Case Study Analysis and Quarter-Century Perspective of a Story That
    Won the Pulitzer Prize." Department of Communication, Stephen F. Austin State Uni-
    versity, Nacogdoches, Texas, 2001.
Nappier, Teresa A. "Ben Reese: Managing the *St. Louis Post-Dispatch.*" Master's thesis, Uni-
    versity of Missouri– Columbia, August 1993.
New York Times Co. Communications from the Times files, including letter exchanges be-
    tween Arthur S. Ochs and Nicholas Murray Butler. June-July 1920.
Pulitzer, Joseph II. Collected Papers. Library of Congress, Containers 167–69.
Starr, Louis W. "Reminiscences of Ben Reese." Oral History Research Office, Columbia
    University, New York, 1957.
————. Joseph Pulitzer II Oral History. From interviews conducted October 7, 1954. Co-
    lumbia University, New York, 1957.

INDEX

Page numbers in italics refer to photographs.